ROUTLEDGE LIBRARY EDITIONS:
THE LABOUR MOVEMENT

Volume 27

THE POLITICAL DIMENSION OF LABOR-MANAGEMENT RELATIONS

THE POLITICAL DIMENSION OF LABOR-MANAGEMENT RELATIONS

National Trends and State Level Developments in Massachusetts (Volume 1)

PHILLIP SAUNDERS

LONDON AND NEW YORK

First published in 1986 by Garland Publishing, Inc.

This edition first published in 2019
by Routledge
2 Park Square, Milton Park, Abingdon, Oxon OX14 4RN

and by Routledge
711 Third Avenue, New York, NY 10017

Routledge is an imprint of the Taylor & Francis Group, an informa business

British Library Cataloguing in Publication Data
A catalogue record for this book is available from the British Library

ISBN: 978-1-138-32435-0 (Set)
ISBN: 978-0-429-43443-3 (Set) (ebk)
ISBN: 978-1-138-35237-7 (Volume 27) (hbk)
ISBN: 978-1-138-35241-4 (Volume 27) (pbk)
ISBN: 978-0-429-43478-5 (Volume 27) (ebk)

Publisher's Note
The publisher has gone to great lengths to ensure the quality of this reprint but points out that some imperfections in the original copies may be apparent.

Disclaimer
The publisher has made every effort to trace copyright holders and would welcome correspondence from those they have been unable to trace.

POLITICAL DIMENSION OF LABOR-MANAGEMENT RELATIONS ★ National Trends and State Level Developments in Massachusetts

Volume I

Phillip Saunders

Garland Publishing, Inc.
New York & London ★ 1986

Library of Congress Cataloging-in-Publication Data

Saunders, Phillip.
The political dimension of labor-management relations.

(American business history)
Thesis (Ph.D.)—Massachusetts Institute of Technology, 1964.
Bibliography: p.
1. Industrial relations—Massachusetts—History—20th century. 2. Labor laws and legislation—Massachusetts—History—20th century. 3. Industrial relations—United States—History. I. Title. II. Series.
HD8083.M4S28 1986 331'.09744 86-15026
ISBN 0-8240-8369-5 (set)

All volumes in this series are printed on acid-free, 250-year-life paper:

Printed in the United States of America

TABLE OF CONTENTS

PREFACE

The data presented and analyzed in this thesis were collected during the period from late 1959 through the summer of 1962. During this time comprehensive and detailed information on labor and management legislative and election activities at both the national level and in the state of Massachusetts became available through the year 1960, and more fragmentary information was available up to and including the summer of 1962. An unavoidable delay in the final drafting and editing of the manusctipt has meant that some information is now available beyond that gathered in the formal data collection stages of this thesis preparation. Since this subsequent information does not alter the main conclusions of this thesis in any substantial way, there has been no attempt to systematically update any of the data presented beyond that available in 1962, but some additions have been made where they seem appropriate. It is hoped that future research may use additional data to elaborate or modify the conclusions of this thesis in a manner that will keep them viable in the dynamic environment of the years ahead.

In presenting the material in this thesis, the bracketed citations of published works refer to a numbered list of references at the end of each chapter by the number of the work cited, with page references where appropriate. Explanatory footnotes are placed at the bottom of each page where they are relevant.

The writer wishes to express his sincere thanks and appreciation to Professor Charles A. Myers for his patience and guidance while serving as the advisor for this thesis.

Special acknowledgement also goes to the writer's wife, Nancy, whose inspiration and untiring assistance have made this manuscript possible.

LIST OF TABLES

Table		Page

CHAPTER I

INTRODUCTION

Speaking in 1955, George Meany, soon to become the first president of the merged AFL-CIO labor federation, stated "The scene of the battle is no longer the company plant or the picket line. It has moved into the legislative halls of Congress and the state legislatures." [5,p.9]

Some three years later, Archie D. Gray, a senior vice president of the Gulf Oil Corporation, stated:

> If we are to survive, labor's political power must now be opposed by a matching force, and there is no place in the United States where such a force can be generated except among the corporations that make up American business. [6,p.41]

And in the following year, John Marsh, an insightful foreign observer, commented on the trend of American labor and management to get "further into the field of political action", and stated "the processes of industrial and social change are likely to be so volatile that political involvement on both sides of industry would seem to be irrevocable." [4,p.119]

Reading such comments, and accepting them at face value, one would be tempted to conclude that the political dimension of labor-management relations might be expanding. That is, during the late 1950's many people seemed to be arguing that many of the traditional issues of labor-management relations were becoming more and more involved with the political process and the institutions of government in a society that, for the past twenty years at least, had relied primarily on the private institutions of collective bargaining to resolve the inevitable differences that arise between workers and managers in an industrial society.

A casual reading of our nation's history indicates that we have always had both a private and a public or political dimension to our labor-management problems. Furthermore, the relative importance of each of these dimensions has tended to shift and change over time. When this thesis was originally conceived in late 1959, the writer was intrigued by the questions "Is the political dimension of labor management relations in the United States expanding?", "If so, what might be some of the implications of this movement?", and finally, "Is there any evidence that any of these implications are materializing at this time?"

Beginning with these questions, the writer made an extensive survey of the published literature to get a feel for the development of labor-management political struggles and their influence on government or public policy. One impression which seemed to stand out from this survey, was the fact that most previous writings in the general area of the political dimension of labor-management relations tended to emphasize only organized labor's political activities. This literature also seemed to be concerned primarily with Presidential politics and with the national labor federations and their official pronouncements, with a strong focus on whether there would, could, or should be a labor party in the United States.

In this light, it was felt that a study emphasizing both labor's and management's political activities might be useful, and an attempt was made to go beyond official pronouncements and gather data on what was and is actually being done to influence public policy by organized labor and management groups. Since there was a relative dearth of reliable evidence at the national level, it was also decided to push the analysis further by examining in some detail the labor-management political struggles within a particular state.

In terms of the state selected for study, sheer geographical propinquity indicated that the state of Massachusetts was the most appropriate--particularly since this state would still be a good choice on other grounds as it contains many elements characteristic of the developments on the national scene, and it also contains enough unique features to make it worth studying in itself.

In essence the burden of this thesis is largely historical in character, and the central problem of history is the study and interpretation of change. There are essentially two kinds of contributions that a historical study can make to the clearer understanding of human behavior. One is descriptive. The second and more valuable contribution, however, involves not only identifying and describing temporal sequences; it also involves explaining them. The [illegible]k of interpretation is crucial. In the words of the Social Science Research Council, "historians, whether they wish it or not, furnish the materials to guide or at least to justify policies, opinions and predictions." [7,p.86]

As a modest attempt at these ambitious goals, this thesis will attempt to briefly trace the evolution of public policy in the United States in the broad area of labor-management relations. Then the attempts of organized labor and management groups to influence public policy through the political process will be examined at the national level in an attempt to answer some of the key questions mentioned above and posed more formally later in this chapter. Finally, an attempt will be made to further examine these tentative answers by a more detailed examination of labor and management political struggles in Massachusetts.

Before pushing on, however, a few basic assumptions and the tentative avenues of investigation initially considered in this thesis should be stated more explicitly. The basic assumptions concerning the nature of labor-management relations and the nature of the political process are drawn largely from two sources: (1) an article by Clark Kerr and Abraham Siegel, "The Structuring of the Labor Force in Industrial Society: New Dimensions and New Questions" [1]; and (2) David B. Truman's book, The Governmental Process [8].

It appears that every industrializing society generates workers and employers (or managers). Thus, labor-management relations can be viewed in terms of a contest between workers and their organizations and employers and their organizations for the authority to establish the rules needed to "structure" the labor force in our industrial society.[1] This

---

1 "By 'structuring of the labor force,' we mean rather the whole 'web of rule' which developes to relate workers to their jobs, to each other, to other elements in society--the employer, the state and so forth." [2,p.121]

struggle can be viewed as having two dimensions: (1) a private dimension; and (2) a political or public dimension. The boundary line can be arbitrarily drawn in such a way that we may say that we enter the political dimension of labor-management relations when either party makes any recourse to any of the institutions of government as an aid in the rule making process or when the government itself intervenes in the rule making process. Within each dimension, each party may seek to create a "monistic" system and try to establish unilateral rule-making authority. In general terms, however, a primarily "dualistic" system has developed in the private dimension of American labor-management relations; and a "pluralistic" system has developed in the political or public dimension.[1] This pluralistic political system is a result of the fact that on many issues no single interest group in the United States has a sufficient majority to completely control the governmental mechanism of the "state." As a result, alliances of differing degrees of formality are formed among various interest groups in an attempt to get the power of the state or the government in support of their position on certain issues. In this way, public political action can be viewed as either a supplement to or a substitute for private economic action in labor-management relations.

This conception of the political process is taken largely from Truman who has stated:

---

[1] There is of course no clear line of demarcation between the private and the public dimension of any particular labor-management problem. While some qualifications may thus be necessary in particular cases, we need not dwell on this problem at this time.

> The total pattern of government over a period of time thus presents a protean complex of criss-crossing relationships that change in strength and direction with alterations in the power and standing of interests, organized and unorganized. [8,p.508]

A complete model of this conception of the political process becomes even more complex, since the element of multiple or overlapping membership in interest groups and the element of unorganized interests or potential interest groups must also be considered. Truman has emphasized:

> . . . It is only as the effects of overlapping memberships and the functions of unorganized interests and potential groups are included in the equation that it is accurate to speak of governmental activity as the product or resultant of interest group activity. [8,p.505]

The fundamental role of government as a regulator of economic and class interest has been explicitly pointed out in this country at least since James Madison's Federalist Paper Number X. The way and the extent to which government has performed this role, however, have not always been uniform or even consistent in the area of labor management relations. This in turn has resulted in various attempts by labor and management to alter the performance of government in its role of mediator between labor and management interest. Indeed, as pointed out earlier, many persons now believe that the political dimension of labor-management relations has been expanding recently. If so, does this have any implications for the basic structure of our country's industrial relations system?

To some, an expanded political dimension of labor-management relations may mean revived hope or fear, as the case may be, of the possibility of a labor party in this country. If not a labor party, increased political activity on the part of American unions has been seen by some writers as one means of restoring more vitality, participation, and internal democracy to the American labor movement. Others have seen it as an attempt by labor bosses to extend and consolidate their dominance over union membership.

In terms of the structure of present labor and management organizations, the possibility of an expanded political dimension of labor-management relations has some interesting implications. Presently, strong national unions, organized along industry or product-market lines, constitute the centers of power within the American labor movement. Local, state, and national federations of unions organized on a geographic basis play a relatively minor role. Yet the political process of this country operates on the geographical basis of ward, precinct, legislative district, and state-wide organization. Even the President and Vice President of the United States, the only truly nationwide offices in this country, are placed in office by an electoral college that allocates so many electoral votes to each state. Would an expanding political dimension of labor-management relations result in a relative shift of power toward geographical federations within the labor movement as organized labor tried to become more effective in geographical districts which cut across the economic lines that lie at the heart of the private collective bargaining process? The same question might be asked of management organization. Would an expanding political dimension of labor-management relations result in individual corporations turning more political functions over to geographically oriented employer associations?

One might also speculate as to the appropriateness of the political process as a forum for resolving labor-management differences. Legislation and public policy by its very nature tends to be general and inclusive in its application, and therefore does not lend itself well to subtle adjustments or accommodation to special situations or particular circumstances. Even more basically, one feature of the private collective bargaining process is the necessity for agreement and the compulsion to compromise on some of the basic issues of labor-management relations. One party may strongly desire a certain course of action, but the necessity to reach agreement and sign a contract or a "truce" for a certain period of time compels each side to evaluate its desires in terms of the penalties and costs of not reaching an agreement. And in the private collective bargaining dimension of labor-management relations, the penalties of not agreeing can be very real and immediate. In the political process, however, one could argue that the compulsion to agree or work out a "liveable" arrangement on particular issues is not so strong. If one party seeks a particular law or ruling and fails to get it, it can always try again; and, in most cases, there is no acute penalty in the interim. The polemics of political debate can encourage both sides to adopt adamant and polarized positions, take an all-or-nothing -at-all approach, and hope for the best. If nothing is accomplished the tendency is to shore up the extremes even further and keep trying. Soon dominance rather than agreement becomes the goal, and increasing hostility is thus injected into the "climate" of labor-management relations.

If there is any substance to such a hypothesis, does it help to explain the recent "hardening of attitudes" witnessed by many observers of the current labor-management scene?

Beginning with speculations such as these, this thesis will attempt to determine if the political dimension of labor-management relations is expanding at the present time. And, if so, if there is any evidence that any of the possible implications mentioned above are materializing, i.e., does contemporary labor political activity seem destined to lead to a labor party? Does it seem to have any influence on internal union democracy? Do geographical labor or management organizations appear to be increasing in influence relative to the traditional center of power within labor and management organizations? Can the recent "hardening of attitudes" noticed in the collective bargaining process be explained at least in part by the increased political participation of labor and management groups in the polarized atmosphere of the political process?

Part I of this thesis will attempt to answer these questions in terms of the published data which are available on the national political scene. Aside from books and journal articles, primary reliance will be placed on the data published annually by Congressional Quarterly *Almanac* and a more detailed investigation of political spending activities made by the Senate Privileges and Elections Subcommittee in 1956, the results of which were summarized and analyzed in Alexander Heard's book, The Cost of Democracy. [3]

Parts II and III of the thesis will then attempt to examine these answers in terms of the development of the political dimension of labor-management relations in the state of Massachusetts. Part II serves as an introduction to the contemporary political scene in the Bay State and traces the development of labor legislation in Massachusetts up to the end of World II. Part III then examines the postwar period in greater detail. Since there are almost no published sources on labor-management political activities in the Bay State, the latter parts of the thesis are based on primary sources, such as newspaper clippings, convention proceedings, legislative bulletins, and personal interviews.

REFERENCES - CHAPTER I

1. Clark Kerr and Abraham Siegel, "The Structuring of the Labor Force in Industrial Society: New Dimensions and New Questions," Industrial and Labor Relations Review, January, 1955, Vol. 8, pp. 151-168

2. ———— . "Reply" [To a communication by Milton Derber], Industrial and Labor Relations Review, October, 1955, Vol. 9, pp. 118-121.

3. Alexander Heard, The Cost of Democracy (Chapel Hill: University of North Carolina, 1960).

4. John Marsh, "Some Impressions of Industrial America," Industrial Welfare, May-June, 1959, Vol. XLI, pp. 119 ff.

5. New York Times, November 5, 1955.

6. Horace E. Sheldon, "Businessmen Must Get Into Politics," Harvard Business Review, March-April, 1959, Vol. 37, pp. 37-47.

7. The Social Sciences in Historical Study (New York: Social Science Research Council, 1954).

8. David B. Truman, The Governmental Process (New York: Knopf, 1955).

PART I

GOVERNMENT, ORGANIZED LABOR, AND MANAGEMENT IN THE UNITED STATES: TRADITIONAL PATTERNS AND CHANGING TENDENCIES IN THE PUBLIC POLICY ASPECTS OF THE INDUSTRIAL RULE MAKING PROCESS

CHAPTER II

GOVERNMENT AND PUBLIC POLICY IN THE INDUSTRIAL RULE MAKING PROCESS

Although the United States is one nation, the laws and regulations governing its citizens come from several sources. Our government is based upon a written constitution; and, in formal terms, it is a federal system with national, state, county, and city dimensions. In addition to these areal divisions, creating public policy and enacting legislation, judging its validity and applicability, and executing and administering the policy are also formally viewed as separate functions to be performed by the separate legislative, judicial, and executive branches of government respectively. The actual creation of public policy in American labor-management relations, however, has rarely been the exclusive function of any one level or any one branch of our pluralistic system of government.

In terms of significant impact, we have seen a relative shift from judicial to legislative primacy in labor-management relations, and within the legislative area we have seen a shift from the state level to the national level of government. Furthermore, while there has been and will probably continue to be "law making" by both courts and the executive, this type of policy creation is usually limited to emergency situations and/or situations in which adequate legislative guidance does not exist. Since legislation tends to lag behind and, indeed, is based on experience, however, much of the "pioneering" policy at the frontiers of action may still have to rely on these forms of policy creation. And, of course, no law is any better than its interpretation and administration.

Under our Constitution, the national government is one of delegated powers. It may exercise only those powers specifically given or implied in the Constitution, and practically all of our federal labor legislation has been based upon either the power to regulate interstate and foreign commerce or the federal power to tax. And, historically, it has been the opinion of the judiciary which determined whether these provisions were flexible enough to permit specific acts of federal legislation.

State labor controls spring from a power that is not mentioned in the Constitution. The states are assumed to have a police power which is not attributed to the federal government. The police power is a rather broad and indefinite authorization given to the states to use the power of their sovereignty in order to promote the "general welfare". The bulk of present state labor legislation looks for authorization to the police power. Commons and Andrews have stated:

> It is the police power, for the most part, that affords, in the case of the state governments, that elastic justification by which the state abridges or enlarges liberty or property

> without compensation, in order to achieve newly recognized public purpose through a newly recognized class of persons or things. [3,p.515]

Although the states, acting under the police power, have traditionally been freer to act than the federal government, certain constitutional provisions, particularly the Fifth and Fourteenth Amendments have tended to limit the scope of labor legislation at both the federal and state level.

As the result of a "narrow" interpretation of the Constitution, the judicial branch of the government had almost exclusive jurisdiction in the area of labor-management relations until 1932. The only exceptions at the national level were: isolated instances of executive initiative; legislation regarding government employees; and railway labor legislation, which was justified by the interstate nature of the railroad industry. Thus, with the exception of the Railway Labor Act of 1926 and some earlier railway labor legislation, it was not until the Norris-La Guardia (Anti-Injunction) Act of 1932, that Congress stepped into the field of labor-management relations on a truly national scale. Under a broadened interpretation of the interstate commerce clause, the Jones and Laughlin case in 1937 upheld the constitutionality of the Wagner (National Labor Relations) Act of 1935 and established the national legislature as our chief formulator of federal labor policy. Congress has subsequently exercised this role in enacting the Taft-Hartley (Labor-Management Relations) Act in 1947; and, most recently, the Landrun-Griffin (Labor Management Reporting and Disclosure) Act of 1959. In addition to this legislation regulating the activities of workers and employers in their delaings with each other, the federal government has also attempted to provide some basic measures of security for working people, and set certain minimum working conditions directly by law, which apply to employees who work for employers producing goods that move in interstate commerce or who work for employers holding government contracts. Throughout both the earlier period of judicial dominance and the more recent period of legislative dominance in policy formation, the executive branch of the federal government has played a relatively minor, but not insignificant, role.

A very brief review of the role of government in American labor-management relations may be helpful at this point, but the reader is referred to one of the standard text on labor law for a more detailed description of the main points developed below.[1]

The Period of Judicial Dominance, Prior to 1932

The history of governmental regulation prior to the 1930's was dominated by the judiciary. The courts exercised their dominance in three main ways: the application of common law; the issuance of injunctions in equity proceedings; and the use of judicial review to pass on the validity and applicability of statutes, most of which were state statutes, with the federal anti-trust laws being a notable

---

1 In the area of public policy in labor-management relations, Gregory [6] is one of the best sources. In the area of "protective" labor legislation such as child labor, hours of work, industrial accidents and workmen's compensation, and minimum wage legislation, two good sources are Miller [7] and, more recently the U.S. Department of Labor [9].

exception. As a general rule it might be stated that the main issue in labor-management relations during this period concerned the right of workers to organize into trade unions and employ certain tactics in furthering their collective aims. Few state legislatures dealt with this problem, however, since most state legislation during this period was "protective" in nature, and dealt directly with working conditions regardless of the nature of the existing relationship between the employer and his employees.

This period was marked by a highly restrictive judicial concept of the process of unionization, and of the permissible means of accomplishing that process. Although the early American courts embraced the English common law notion that the unions were criminal conspiracies, they had virtually discarded it by the middle of the nineteenth century.[1] The civil conspiracy doctrine continued, however, and as administered through narrow "ends" and "means" tests it was decidedly restrictive of labor's efforts at concerted action. In determining the legality of union tactics and objectives, the court still relied on common law. Because of its assumption that human

---

1 Perhaps the two most notable cases in this connection are the famous Philadelphia Cordwainers case in 1806, and the equally famous case of Commonwealth v Hunt in 1842. In the cordwainers case (Commonwealth v Pullis) the court held that a combination of workmen to raise wages constituted a criminal conspiracy; and, in effect, ruled that unions were illegal *per se*. Some 36 years later, however, Massachusetts Chief Justice Lemuel Shaw ruled that the legality of a concerted action on the part of employees depended on the purpose or objectives sought, and also on the means used, not the mere fact of combination. This decision is believed to have greatly weakened the criminal conspiracy doctrine that conspiracy and concerted action were synonymous, and it marked the beginning of the civil conspiracy doctrine that the legality of concerted action depends on the legality of its purpose and/or the means for accomplishing it.

relationships are relationships between equal individuals, and because of its emphasis on property rights, common law applied to labor disputes inevitably resulted in severe restrictions on unions.

Against this background of early judicial restraints, the period from around 1890 to 1932 was characterized by the inception and growth of modern labor unions as well as the last ditch struggle through litigation in our courts to keep them from expanding. In this connection, the Supreme Court ruled in the famous Danbury Hatters case (Lowe v Lawlor, 1908) that the Sherman Antitrust Act of 1890 applied to labor unions and held that secondary boycotts affecting the flow of goods in interstate commerce constituted an illegal restraint of trade and commerce under the Act. After further litigation, it was also ruled that suits for damages under the Act might be brought against individual union members.

Starting in the nineties, the use of injunctions also became common in labor disputes. The right to do business came to be considered a property right which both state and federal courts could protect from the aggressive tactics of organized workers. The labor injunction was particularly effective in defeating efforts at unionization when coupled with judicial recognition of the yellow dog contract, which required the employee, as a condition of employment, to agree not to join a labor organization. The continued application of the Sherman Antitrust Act to labor union boycott activities, even after the Clayton Act of 1914, further frustrated labor's attempts to improve what they felt to be their self interest in their struggles with employers.

This period also saw the emergence of many of the problems of our modern industrial economy. Protective social and labor legislation attempting to meet these problems, however, came slowly. Much of the early legislation came from the state legislatures; and it was not received in a friendly fashion by the courts, which were not quick to recognize and adapt to the social changes accompanying industrialization. The spirit of an individualistic economy was deeply ingrained in the thinking of our judges, who remained devoted chiefly to insuring the integrity of private property and the complete freedom of its use. The traditional emphasis laid on the importance of property and its incidents seemed to overshadow assertions of purely personal rights dissociated from property, and freedom of contract was vigorously maintained on the increasingly debatable assumption of equality between employer and employee. Nevertheless, in some instances, such as child labor legislation and workmen's compensation legislation at the state level, court rulings and attitudes did not long retard the development of protective legislation. In others, such as child labor legislation at the federal level and all types of minimum wage laws, the disapprovals held until the judicial revolution of the 1930's.

In addition to purely "protective" measures such as child labor laws, maximum working hours, workmen's compensation and industrial accident legislation, and minimum wage laws, there was also a limited amount of legislation prior to the 1930's dealing with the operation of the labor market as well as some rather insignificant legislation regulating labor-management relations as such. Most of the former legislation dealt with public employment agencies, and much of the latter dealt with the right of workers to organize and use certain tactics in dealing with their employers.

Ohio established the first public employment office in the nation by legislative enactment in 1890, but a genuine federal system of public employment offices did not develop until the mobilization efforts of World War I. Following the war, the system was sharply curtailed.

Between 1892 and 1921 various state legislatures passed laws limiting the issuance on injunctions in labor disputes, but most of these early state laws were either declared unconstitutional or interpreted into meaninglessness by the courts. Such judicial action tended to make statutory regulation of unions superfluous, but between 1870 and 1925, various state legislatures adopted measures prohibiting specific types of conduct by union members. Most of this legislation provided criminal penalties where the courts already afforded injunctive relief and civil penalties on the basis of common law.

There is one interesting anomaly with regard to the right of employees to organize during the period before 1930, however, and the Lloyd-LaFollette Act of 1912 is all the more anomalous in that it involves federal legislation in this period of judicial dominance and primacy of state legislation. Brown and Myers note that "This act protected the right of postal employees to organize into unions, subject to the condition that the unions not be affiliated with outside organizations imposing an obligation to strike against the government."[1,p.4]

And they quote Kurt Braun as saying "In the absence of legislation guaranteeing freedom of association of government employees outside the postal service, the Lloyd-LaFollette Act has been widely regarded as containing the principles guiding general public policy in this respect, at least in the federal public service." [1, pp. 4-5]

Laws that put the states in the business of trying to settle labor disputes also stem from this early period. They began in Maryland in 1878 and spread rapidly. By 1900, twenty-five states had laws or constitutional provisions on the subject, and provisions for such action continued to spread, but they had little effect on the conduct of labor-management relations prior to the 1930's.

Even during these years of judicial dominance, however, the seeds of change were being planted. On the Supreme Court itself they were vigorously nurtured in many dissenting opinions of Justice Brandeis, whose dissents later often became the opinion of the majority. In Justice Brandeis' view, law was essentially an instrument of social policy; and the following quotation indicates that he regarded the legislatures, not the courts, as the more effective instrument for judging changing social and economic needs.

> All rights are derived from the purposes of the society in which they exist; above all rights rises duty to the community. The conditions developed in industry may be such that those engaged in it cannot continue their struggle without danger to the community. But it is not for judges to determine whether such conditions exist, nor is it their function to set the limits of permissible contest and to declare the duties which the new situation demands. This is the function of the legislature which, while limiting individual and group rights of aggressions and defense, may substitute processes of justice for the more primitive method of trial by combat. [7, p. 133]

The Modern Emergence of the Legislature, Since 1932

The year 1930 witnessed the beginnings of a trend which was to see Justice Brandeis' aspirations achieved. A revolution in the Supreme Court's interpretation of the federal government's interstate commerce power eventually resulted in the emergence of the Congress of the United States as the nation's chief formulator of public policy in labor-management relations. The shift from judicial to legislative primacy was also accompanied by a significant change in the substance of our national labor policy. The economic, social, and judicial revolution of the 1930's saw the Congress attempt to remedy the generations-old union complaints against what they regarded as the one-sided position of the governmental agencies of justice. It was during this period that the right of workers to organize and bargain collectively was established and guaranteed as a principle of public policy. Restraints on various forms of union activity were also relaxed considerably during this period, but several restraints still exist and many have been receiving increasing attention in recent years.

A glimpse of things to come could be seen as early in 1930, when the case of Texas and New Orleans Railroad v Brotherhood of Railroad Clerks upheld the constitutionality of the previously mentioned Railway Labor Act of 1926. This act was premised on the notion that stable labor relations could be based upon collective agreements between employers and unions representing their employees. At that time, this was a big step; and the Texas and N.O.R. decision also came admidst the confusion and despair following the stock market collapse of 1929. Nevertheless, the problems of the acceptability and the workability of the Railway Labor Act were greatly simplified by the fact that it applied only to a single cohesive industry and by the fact that it was "agreed to" legislation between the railroad employers and the railroad unions, both of whom were dissatisfied with the operation of earlier railway legislation.

Congressional Regulation of Labor-Management Relations

Before Congress attempted to expand the Railway Labor Act's principle of governmentally sanctioned collective bargaining to all industry in interstate commerce through section 7 (a) of the National Industrial Recovery Act in 1933, it first attempted to make the government "neutral" in labor disputes by removing some of the previously imposed judicial restraints against unions by enacting the Norris-LaGuardia Act of 1932. This Act was designed primarily to overcome the restrictive judicial attitudes toward organized labor discussed in the previous section. The injunction itself was not outlawed; but this statute, which was passed in the waning days of the Hoover administration, severely restricted its use. By clearly spelling out a broad definition of a "labor dispute", by a specific listing of activities not to be enjoined, and by carefully outlining the type of proof necessary before a federal court could issue a permanent restraining order, the major judicial restrictions on self-help by unions including the strike, picketing, and the boycott, were drastically reduced. The constitutionality of the Norris-LaGuardia act was upheld six years after its passage in the case of Lauf v Shinner. (1938).

In addition to its influence on federal court equity practice, the Act also outlawed the yellow dog contract; and, while it was primarily a procedural act, it was later used as a substansive justification for removing organized labor from under the coverage of the Sherman Anti-Trust Act.

For a brief period following the passage of the Norris-LaGuardia Act labor was free to pursue its activities relatively unhampered by previously imposed governmental restraints; and in the railroad industry union organizations and collective bargaining were actually protected by legislative enactment. Section 7 (a) of the National Industrial Recovery Act of 1933 attempted to expand this protection to all industries in interstate commerce, but the Schechter decision in 1934 invalidated this statute. Its labor provisions, however, were elaborated and expanded in the National Labor Relations Act of 1935. The principle terms of the Wagner Act, as it is commonly known, were as follows: employees were given the right to organize into trade unions, to bargain collectively through representatives of their own choosing, and to engage in other concerted activities for the purpose of mutual protection. In order to assure them the exercise of this basic right, employers were prohibited from carrying out certain anti-union practices designated as "unfair labor practices". The Act also provided that, where doubt existed as to the majority status of a union, the matter could be determined by a secret ballot of the workers involved or by some other suitable method.

Administration of the Act was entrusted to a National Labor Relations Board, which was made responsible for prosecuting unfair labor practices by employers and deciding disputes over union representation. In cases of violation of the Act, the Board was empowered to issue cease and desist orders which if not complied with were enforceable in the Circut Courts of the United States.

The Wagner Act was one of the most bitterly disputed of all the New Deal measures. The law was subject to much criticism from the very first, and many proposed amendments were introduced in every session of Congress. The fact that the law contained no specifications of duties or responsibilities for unions and no rights for employers was widely criticized. It was attacked especially on the grounds that it denied to employers the freedom of speech. Objections were raised to the fact that the N.L.R.B. acted as both prosecutor and judge, and many critics felt the Board was biased in its application of the law.

After the Jones and Laughlin case (1937) established the constitutionality of the law, the Wagner Act not only brought the federal government into labor-management relations on an unprecedented scale, but its provisions also facilitated a tremendous increase in the size and power of organized labor in the United States. Labor union membership climbed from something less than three million workers in 1933 to approximately fourteen million members by 1945. The split in the labor movement between the craft unions in the American Federation of Labor and the industrial unions which later federated into the Congress of Industrial Organizations, however, produced unforeseen difficulties for the N.L.R.B. By 1939 the leaders of the AFL were convinced that the Board's decisions showed favoritism to their CIO opponents, and they soon ranked among the most bitter critics of the administration of the Act.

There was also evidence that public opinion, particularly in small town and rural areas, was becoming increasingly disenchanted with certain union objectives and tactics as employed by an expanding and bickering labor movement at this time. Congress held hearings on the operation of the law in 1939, but it failed to act on any of the amendments designed to meet the objections of the increasing number of critics. As will be seen later, however, state labor legislation at this time gave clear indications that legislative framework less favorable to labor than the existing national policy would eventually gain more support. This became apparent at the national level in July 1943, when Congress, under the threat of a nation-wide coal strike, passed the Smith-Connally Act over President Roosevelt's veto. A temporary wartime measure, this law reflected the changing public attitude toward "Big Labor". It required unions to observe a 30-day cooling off period after taking a strike vote, and authorized the federal government to take over and operate any essential industry threatened by a labor stoppage. The law also forbade union political contributions in national election campaigns, and threatened union leaders with prosecution for criminal conspiracy under certain circumstances. In practice, the Smith-Connally Act had little effect on either the prevention or the solution of labor-management disputes, but its passage indicated a growing disposition to alter the Wagner Act so as to curb labor's power. This was done with the passage of the Taft-Hartley Act in 1947.

The Taft-Hartley Act, which was passed over President Truman's veto, retained the essential provisions of the Wagner Act, but greatly expanded its scope and appeared to be based on a different underlying philosophy of labor management relations. In essence the basic philosophy behind the Wagner Act had assumed that, once unions were permitted to organize on an equal basis with employers, collective bargaining would solve all the major problems of industrial relations without further government intervention. Taft-Hartley, however, was essentially based on a different premise. It assumed that, in order to protect the interest of all parties concerned, government regulation must extend to the procedures and content of collective bargaining. Workers were guaranteed the right to refuse to participate in collective bargaining as well as the right to organize, and the government assumed the responsibility of protecting the employer, the individual worker, and the public from certain practices of labor unions.

The act expanded the N.L.R.B. from 3 to 5 members, and the position of General Counsel of the Board was created to separate the judicial and prosecution functions of the Board. It listed certain unfair labor practices on the part of unions to parallel the list of unfair employer practices, which was carried over intact from the Wagner Act.

The Act also substantially modified public policy on union security. It outlawed the closed shop, and originally provided that a union shop could not be established unless a majority of workers had voted in favor of such a clause in a secret ballot conducted by the N.L.R.B. (This latter provision was eventually repealed when experience overwhelmingly demonstrated that workers consistently voted for the union shop by large majorities.) Section 14 (b) of the Act also reversed the traditional doctrine of federal preemption, by providing that state law would take precedence over federal law if, in union security matters, states wanted to pass laws restricting union security further than the limited union shop sanctioned by Taft-Hartley. Under these provisions 19 states have passed so called "right-to-work laws" outlawing all types of union security provisions in labor-management agreements.[1]

The Act also required union officers to file non-Communist affidavits, and other reports before they could use the facilities of the N.L.R.B., and it spelled out specific limitations on the determination of "appropriate bargaining units". Supervisory personnel were denied protection under the law, and plant guards were not allowed representation by unions directly affiliated with other rank and file employees. Professional employees and craftsmen were also permitted to vote out of bargaining units which represented other production employees.

---

[1] In addition to the 19 states with right-to-work laws of general application, Louisiana, also has a right-to-work law, but its application is limited to agricultural laborers and employees engaged in the processing of certain agricultural products. See [9, pp. 244-247].

Finally, Taft-Hartley permitted the President to secure an injunction for a maximum period of 80 days to prevent a "national emergency" dispute if he felt that a particular strike would imperil the national health or safety. The law also abolished the Department of Labor's Conciliation Service, and transferred its functions to a new independent Federal Mediation and Conciliation Service designed to help settle labor-management disputes. This Act remained intact as our national labor policy for 12 controversial years until the Labor-Management Reporting and Disclosure Act was signed into law September 14, 1959.

Pressure to amend or repeal the Taft-Hartley Act began building almost from the time of its passage. With the exception of two comparatively minor amendments in 1951, however, and despite numerous attempts to revise the law, no general revision of the act every passed either house of Congress before 1958.[1]

The political alignment in Congress was the chief inhibiting factor in this stalemate. Amendments favored by organized labor received most of their support from Northern Democrats, and amendments favored by employers were largely backed by Republicans and Southern Democrats. Neither faction, however, commanded a clear majority in both Houses. Over a decade of deadlock on labor legislation resulted.

During this period of stalemate, however, the basis for future labor legislation was being laid in a series of Congressional

---

[1] In 1958 the so-called Kennedy-Ives Labor Reform Bill passed the Senate, but was not enacted. One year later, in 1959, the more comprehensive Landrum-Griffin Act passed both houses of Congress, and was signed by President Eisenhower.

investigations beginning in 1953 and culminating in the 1957-58 investigations of the Senate's Select Committee on Improper Activities in the Labor or Management Field, better known as the McClellan Committee. These investigations uncovered labor-management abuses ranging from outright embezzlement of union funds by corrupt union officers, who often maintained their position through dictatorial abuse of union trusteeship and election provisions, to all sorts of labor-management collusion against the interests of the employees. Cases were uncovered of unions using the threat of picketing and boycotts to extort money from employers, and employers using "labor relations consultant firms" (so called management "middlemen") to do such dirty work as bribing union officials, carrying out anti-union propaganda, and performing labor spy work. Attention was also focussed on the "no man's land" which arose between federal and state law when a labor dispute occured in an establishment of small size. If the N.L.R.B. felt the effect of a labor dispute on interstate commerce was too small, it often refused to consider these cases. Since several federal court decisions prohibited state agencies from adjudicating these disputes under the preemption doctrine, however, the parties were left free to slug it out between themselves with no recourse to legal sanctions whatsoever.

The McClellan Committee's revelations stirred public opinion to demand remedial action, and early in 1958 Congress began action on two labor reform bills. One dealt almost exclusively with pension and welfare funds, and one dealt almost exclusively with pension and welfare funds, and one dealt more generally with union-management corruption. Floor fights developed on both bills largely over the issue of whether or not Taft-Hartley amendments, dealing with the rules of collective bargaining, should be tacked on to basic reform legislation primarily concerned with the conduct of internal union affairs. The Senate eventually passed both bills, but only the welfare fund bill passed the House and was signed into law by the President as the Welfare and Pension Plans Disclosure Act of 1958.

In 1959, however, the Labor-Management Reporting and Disclosure Act, better known as the Landrum-Griffin Act, emerged after one of the bitterest fights in Congressional history. The Act has seven main sections and most of the administrative responsibility for its provisions rest with the Secretary of Labor. The first section of the Act contains a "Bill of Rights" for members of labor organizations. These provisions attempt to safeguard member's rights to participate in union meetings and to help formulate union policy. Union members whose rights are violated by their officers are permitted to bring suit in a federal district court and receive such relief, including injunctions, as might be appropriate.

The second section deals with various detailed reports required by labor organizations, officers and employees of labor organizations, employers, and labor relations consultants. All reports, from labor and management sources alike, are open to public inspection, and any person filing a false report is subject to a fine of $10,000 and a year's imprisonment.

The third section, dealing with union trusteeships, requires that the unions exercising trusteeship must file reports semiannually on such trusteeship, and the law established certain controls over the trustee union. Section four, dealing with union elections, stipulates that unions must choose their officers through regular secret ballot elections, and persons convicted of certain crimes were excluded from union office for as much as five years after their conviction or imprisonment. Under section five of the Act, union officers or employees handling union funds must be bonded, and controls are established for their conduct. Among other things, the miscellaneous provisions of section six, tightened the Taft-Hartley prohibition on employer bribes to labor leaders, and extortionate picketing was declared subject to a fine of $10,000 and twenty years imprisonment.

Lastly, through a series of controversial amendments, the new law attempted to tighten the Taft-Hartley Act's prohibitions on secondary boycotts and recognition picketing, although some parts of the construction industry and some parts of the clothing industry were given special treatment with regard to the ban on "hot cargo" clauses. Economic strikers are now allowed to vote in N.L.R.B. elections, and certain provisions are made to certify unions in the Construction industry without conducting a representation election. The Act also stipulates that certain unfair labor practice complaints must receive precedence by the N.L.R.B., and it authorizes the states to intervene in cases where the Board declines to act.

While the Landrum-Griffin Act is still a new piece of legislation, it is clear that much of its effect will depend upon the Secretary of Labor in enforcing and publicizing the reports required of labor and management. It is equally clear that, in establishing detailed control over the internal affairs of labor unions, Congress has embarked on a newer and broader role in labor-management relations.

In this section on the Congressional regulation of labor-management relations we have seen the position of the federal government pass from an earlier hostility towards union objectives to official neutrality to positive support of union organization, and finally to detailed federal regulation of union-management relations and a close supervision of the internal affairs of labor organizations. The revolution in the Supreme Court's reinterpretation of the federal government's interstate commerce power, which made this shift possible through successive legislative enactments, also enabled Congress to enact legislation establishing national minimum working standards for all employees engaged in the production of goods which enter into interstate commerce. The right to legislate for government employees and those who worked for employers holding government contracts was also exercised during this period. We will now turn to a closer examination of this Congressional ascendency in the area of protective labor and social legislation.

Congressional Ascendency in Protective Labor Legislation

As previously noted, most early protective legislation was the result of state action. By the onset of the Great Depression the right of states to legislate in the areas of child labor, industrial accidents, and hours of work had been established, but minimum wages for women and children were still in a state of confusion, and no attempts had been made to legislate for men in this area. Aside from the right to legislate, actual state legislation was spotty and provisions and enforcement procedures varied widely. Outside the railroad industry and government employees, Congressional attempts to legislate in the areas approved for state action had been thwarted by adverse court decisions. Attempts to deal with the problem of unemployment were limited to some rather ineffective state employment agencies and a weakening federal employment service in the Department of Labor.

During the Great Depression, the increase of unemployment to nearly one-third of the labor force led the federal government to make several attempts to cut hours and to spread the available work among more persons. The first such attempt came with the enactment of the National Industrial Recovery Act in 1933. This Act, which was based on the interstate commerce power, was a broad and inclusive attempt at economic recovery which dealt with wages, hours, child labor, pricing policies, relief, and public works. The means of putting these measures into effect was through codes of fair competition, which were called for in the Act.

Prior to the NIRA, and following its invalidation by the Schechter decision in 1934, other attempts were also made to deal with these problems before the Fair Labor Standards Act of 1938 marked the culmination of Congressional attempts to control wages, hours, and child labor. Thus, the Davis-Bacon Act of 1931 required that contractors on all government construction projects exceeding $5,000 (amended in 1936 to $2,000) pay the prevailing wage for any work done on the project. A similar law, which was much broader in coverage and also included provisions on hours of work and child labor was passed shortly after the demise of the NIRA. Thus, the Public Contracts Act of 1936, commonly known as the Walsh-Healy Act, required that employees working on government contracts exceeding $10,000 be paid not less than the prevailing wages for the industry, as determined by the Secretary of Labor. Like the NIRA, this law did not specify a maximum number of hours that could be worked, but it established a basic work day and work week beyond which overtime was to be paid. With certain exceptions, the Walsh-Healy Act also prohibited the employment of males under 16 and females under 18 years of age. This Act was examined and validated by the Supreme Court in 1940 in the case of Perkins v Lukens Steel.

Meanwhile, with regard to the problem of increasing unemployment, the Wager-Peyser Act was passed and signed into law by President Roosevelt in 1933. This Act established federal standards for public employment offices, and 75% of the federal funds appropriated under the act were to be made available to the states if they agreed to abide by the federal standards and match the federal grant. All the states and Alaska and Hawaii, became affiliated by 1937, and in

1939 the employment service was moved from the Department of Labor to the Social Security Board where it could work in closer cooperation with the unemployment compensation system established by the federal Social Security Act of 1935.

Probably more than any other measure, the Social Security Act was truly a child of the Great Depression. The people and the Courts of the United States were convinced by this catastrophe that, older philosophies of rugged individualism aside, in the complex and interdependent industrial economy of our contemporary society there are many forces and factors over which the individual has no control. Therefore, acting on the basis of its power to tax, Congress passed the Social Security Act of 1935. The act consists of 10 distinct programs all having the principal aim of providing a minimum basic security for most of the people in the United States.[1] The four direct assistance programs and the four health and welfare programs are not as well known as the old age and unemployment programs, which have traditionally been regarded as protective labor legislation.

---

[1] The ten programs can be grouped in the three following categories, of which the two social insurance programs are the most important:

(1) Social Insurance:
  (a) Old-age and survivors insurance
  (b) Unemployment insurance
(2) Public Aid to the Needy:
  (a) Old-age assistance
  (b) Aid to the needy blind
  (c) Aid to dependent children
  (d) Aid to the permanently and totally disabled
(3) Health and Welfare Services
  (a) Child welfare services
  (b) Services for crippled children
  (c) Maternal and child-health services
  (d) Public health services

Despite the fact that the Social Security Act is a Federal law, the Federal Government operates only one of the programs—old-age and survivors insurance. The other main social insurance program—unemployment insurance—is administered by the states due to the fact that the Social Security Act used the federal tax power to create an "atmosphere" that "encouraged" the several states to enact legislation providing for a system of unemployment compensation.[1]

The constitutionality of the Social Security Act was upheld by the U. S. Supreme Court on May 24, 1937, in three cases. The Steward Machine Co. case concerned the validity of the Federal Unemployment Tax. The Helvering case dealt with the legality of the Old Age Benefits tax, and in the Carmichael case, the Court passed upon the constitutionality of the Unemployment Insurance Law of the state of Alabama. As with labor relations, Congress did not extend old age and survivors insurance or unemployment insurance to railroad employees under the Social Security Act. They enacted special legislation for that group.

---

[1] The Act provided for an excise tax on the payrolls of all American business employing 8 or more employees (4 or more since 1956). If a state enacted an acceptable unemployment compensation law, the Social Security Act provided further that the employers of that state might credit the amount paid into the state fund against the Federal tax as long as the credit did not exceed 2.7% of the 3.0% Federal Tax. Also, the Act provided that the Federal government would pay the cost of administering approved state unemployment compensation systems, the funds to come from the .3% of the payroll tax retained by the Federal government. For these reasons, as well as the desirability of such legislation, all of the states soon passed unemployment compensation acts. (In 1961 a new rate of 3.1% became effective with .4% now being retained at the Federal level.)

While the Social Security Act of 1935 was adopted by Congress partly to insure workers against the ravages of unemployment and to assure them of a financially independent old age, the Fair Labor Standards Act of 1938 marked the successful culmination of the Federal government's attempt to directly influence wages, hours, and child labor. Previous attempts to legislate in these areas had failed because of Supreme Court rulings, but some provisions had been placed in the public contracts acts. Following the Jones and Laughlin decision sanctioning a much broader interpretation of the commerce clause, however, Congress again sought to use its power under this clause to directly regulate working conditions in the Fair Labor Standards Act.

The provisions of the Act and its initial methods of administration were both declared constitutional in 1941 by the two important decisions of U. S. v. Darby Lumber Co. and Opp Cotton Mills v. Flemming. As subsequently amended, the Act now makes illegal wages below $1.25 an hour in "covered" employment, but this provision does not become applicable until September 1965 for those employees newly covered by the 1961 amendment. The law also compels payment of time-and-one-half for all hours worked in excess of 40 in one week. With certain exceptions, the FLSA also prohibits the employment of children under 16 years of age, and it sets up control of industrial homework by provisions under which the administrator of the law can forbid homework all together.

It should be remembered, however, that many workers are employed in establishments which do not market their goods across state lines and in restaurants, hotels, laundries, and other places of business which supply services only in a given locality. To cover these cases to which the federal law does not apply, there remains a vast bulk of protective labor legislation at the State level. Although the states originally pioneered in this area, much of the existing state protective legislation is now inadequate and out of date compared to present federal standards. Indeed, following the enactment of the Wagner Act in 1935, the primary emphasis in state labor legislation shifted to issues concerning labor-management relations in intra state commerce.

Before turning to an examination of state legislation, however, it should be noted that while the Norris-LaGuardia Act, the Wagner Act, the Taft-Hartley Act, and the Landrum-Griffin Act are the major federal laws affecting labor-management relations, there are other federal laws which affect union activity. There are also several convict labor laws of a "protective" nature supplementing the Social Security Act, the Fair Labor Standards Act, and the public contract laws. Thus, the Hobbs Anti-Racketeering Act of 1934 was a federal attempt to restrict the activities of labor organizations. It prohibited the use of violence, force, coersion or intimidation in interstate commerce and was directed against labor racketeers. Some of the provisions of the Landrum-Griffin act have supplanted the Hobbs Act in this area. The Byrne's Anti-Strikebreaker Law of 1936 made it a felony to transport in interstate commerce persons who are hired to interfere with peaceful picketing in a labor dispute. The Lea (Anti-Petrillo) Act of 1946 placed a ban on "featherbedding" in radio broadcasting. The Act makes it unlawful to compel radio broadcasters to hire more employees than they need on the job, to pay more than once for services performed, or to pay for services which are not to be performed.

Congress passed a law prohibiting the contracting out of the labor of U. S. prisoners as early as 1877; but a more comprehensive convict-labor code, known as the Hawes-Cooper Act, was enacted in 1929. This act, however, was merely permissive in nature. It provided that, after January 1, 1934, any state could regulate or forbid the sale within its borders of convict-made goods shipped from another state. Further limitations were placed upon the shipment and sale of prison made goods by the passage of the Ashurst-Summers Act in 1935. This Act supplements the Hawes-Cooper Act, and provides for the proper labeling of goods manufactured by penal institutions. With certain exceptions, the Ashurst-Summers Act was amended in 1940 to completely prohibit the transportation of prison made goods in interstate commerce. Prohibitions on convict labor were also included in the NIRA in 1933 and the Walsh-Healey Act in 1936.

Changing Tendencies in State Labor Legislation

Since existing laws vary tremendously in both scope and content, a comprehensive treatment of state labor legislation is a practical impossibility for the purposes of this dissertation. This section will merely attempt to emphasize post-1930 developments in the broadest outline.

Prior to the Congressional enactment of the Norris-LaGuardia Act, several states had passed anti-injunction legislation comparable to the labor sections of the Clayton Act. These laws, however, met the same emasculation at the hands of the courts as did their mother provisions; and in 1921 the Supreme Court's decision in the case of Truax v. Corrigan went even further and declared a 1913 Arizona anti-injunction act unconstitutional. Renewed efforts by the states to pass anti-injunction legislation after 1932, however, were more favorably received; and at the present time half the states have laws restricting the issuance of labor injunctions, and 31 specifically prohibit yellow dog contracts.

Just as many "baby Norris-LaGuardia Acts" appeared in the states following federal legislation, so did five states pass "baby Wagner Acts" in 1937 following the judicial substantiation of the national act. These acts (Utah, Wisconsin, Massachusetts, New York, Pennsylvania) attempted to established in the area of intrastate commerce what the national act had done in the area of interstate commerce. That is, union membership and collective bargaining were encouraged, employer interference was prohibited, and no restrictions were placed on union activities; but a small indication of things to come could be found in the Massachusetts' provision which outlawed the sit-down strike.

The rapidly increasing numercial strength of unions, accompanied by the sit-down strikes in the auto industry and elsewhere, and intra labor jurisdictional fights following the AFL-CIO split soon led to a reaction at the state level. The year 1939 marked the beginnings of a trend more restrictive of union activities. The Wisconsin and Pennsylvania acts were amended to include a section of unfair labor practices for employees as well as for employers, and the Minnesota and Michigan acts of 1939 went beyond mere attempts to facilitate union organization and collective bargaining to establish restrictive rules of conduct in collective bargaining.

The three-year period from 1940 through 1942 was preoccupied with the conversion to a war economy, and little state labor legislation was enacted. In 1943, however, a rather full measure of restrictive state legislation was enacted paralleling and going beyond the wartime Smith-Connally Act at the national level. Kansas and Colorado passed comprehensive labor legislation which included extensive regulation of the internal affairs of unions, and several other states passed more limited and more restrictive laws. This latter legislation differed from the labor relations acts in that they were aimed at one or a few union practices, placed no restrictions on employers, and did not attempt to establish a comprehensive labor relations policy. Many of the provisions of these state laws anticipated by several years the provisions of the federal Taft-Hartley Act. At the present time 12 states have comprehensive labor relations acts, 17 states have specific laws for the settlement of labor disputes in public utilities, and 5 states now regulate union welfare funds. As mentioned previously, 19 states now have "right to work" laws generally outlawing all forms of union-security under section 14b of the Taft-Hartley Act. Most of the right to work laws, however, as is the case with most of the other strongly restrictive measures, are confined to the less industrialized states with few union members to start with.

With regard to labor-management relations legislation, then, the pattern was one of the states following the federal government's lead in encouraging unrestrained collective bargaining, and the federal government then following the states in imposing increasing restrictions on the rules of conduct in the collective bargaining arena. Just the reverse is true with regard to protective labor legislation. The states pioneered in the area of child labor, hours of work, minimum wages, and workmen's compensation. Workmen's compensation has remained exclusively a state concern, but once the federal government became interested in the other protective measures and effectively followed their example through the Fair Labor Standards Act of 1938, further state action in these areas has dwindled sharply. This has resulted in the somewhat paradoxical situation that after the Supreme Court enunciated principles under which nearly all protective labor legislation became constitutional far fewer of these laws were enacted than when their constitutionality was in doubt. At present all the states have some form of child labor legislation, but the minimum ages and the types of employment covered vary widely. Forty-three states now have maximum hours legislation for women in various occupations, but some allow as many as 60 hours per week. The hours of male employees are covered by these provisions in only 13 states, although the FLSA coverage extends to both sexes. Provisions for minimum wage orders now exists in 33 states, but only 15 cover male employees. All the states but North Carolina have prevailing wage laws, and industrial homework is regulated in 20 states. All states now have Workmen's Compensation and Unemployment Compensation benefit systems, but again the provisions of these laws vary widely.

One of the most recent developments in the field of labor law, broadly conceived, is the attempt to prevent discrimination in employment through so-called Fair Employment Practice Acts. Some twenty-one states now have such legislation. Twenty prohibit discrimination by reason of race, color, religion, or national origin. Nine of these states also prohibit discrimination by reason of age, and Louisana prohibits only discrimination by age. Some cities, including 8 in states without FEP laws also have their own anti-discrimination laws. The power of the filibuster exercised by the southern states in the United States Senate, however has placed a large stumbling block in the way of efforts to enact a federal Fair Employment Practices Act. The federal government, however, has taken some action in this area. During World War II and after, Executive Orders have been used to provide that all contracts signed by the United States government contain provisions obligating contractors not to discriminate on the basis or race, creed, color, or national origin.

Modern Modification in Judicial Opinion

By upholding the Railway Labor Act, the Norris-LaGuardia Act, the Wagner Act, the Social Security Act, and the Fair Labor Standards Act, the Supreme Court removed the judiciary from the labor relations picture to a large extent. With regard to labor-management relations, our most important legislation is now administered by quasi-judicial administrative boards. While these boards base their decisions on statute law and not on common law, their decisions are enforced by court orders and can be reviewed by the federal courts. In this role the judiciary has retained some of its previous influence, and it has also exerted its influence in the older areas of defining permissible union conduct and regulating union activity under the antitrust laws—although its modern decisions in these areas differ sharply from the pre-1930 pattern.

For example, the Norris-LaGuardia Act was given added significance by the Court in the early 1940's when it was integrated and construed together with the Sherman and Clayton Acts to remove most labor activities from the control of the antitrust laws in the cases of Apex v. Leader and U.S. v. Hutcheson. In these cases the Court held that the acts made non-enjoinable by the Norris-LaGuardia Act were legal as a matter of substansive law, and could not be challenged under the antitrust laws. Many of the specific boycott activities formerly prohibited under the antitrust laws have since been regulated by the Taft-Hartley and Landrum-Griffin Acts, however, and the Allen Bradley case in 1945 held that labor unions can still be prosecuted under the Sherman Act if a union acts in collusion with an employer to rig the market.

One other area of labor-management relations that has seen considerable judicial activity since the 1930's is the area of peaceful picketing. The leading decision on picketing prior to 1930 came in the 1921 case of American Steel Foundaries v. Tri City Central Trades Council. No statute was involved in this case. It concerned non-violent picketing by outsiders, by a few actual strikers, and by former employees who had been laid off but were hopeful of resuming their employment. The opinion outlined a limited kind of peaceful picketing in which only the strikers and laid off employees might indulge.

In 1937, however, the case of Senn v. Tile Layers Union upheld a Wisconsin anti injunction statute which did not permit injunctions to be issued against peaceful picketing, even if the picketing was by "strangers" not directly employed by the person picketed. In 1940, the Court then went way beyond this position; and the Thornhill case held that peaceful picketing was a form of speech and entitled to the protection of the fourteenth amendment. Therefore, since peaceful picketing now involved Constitutional rights, states were theoretically forbidden from passing any laws which limited this activity. This extreme position came at a time when we have seen that many state legislatures were reacting to alleged abuses accompanying the upsurge of union membership under the Wagner Act. Therefore the Court soon found itself in the position of trying to modify its position without overruling the Thornhill doctrine. A whole series of confusing decisions resulted, and the Taft-Hartley Act specifically restricted several activities involving stranger picketing which had previously been sanctioned by the Court. Then in 1949, the Giboney case held that peaceful picketing could be enjoined when the object sought by the pickets violated a written state anti monopoly law. Thus, it appeared that states could escape the Thornhill doctrine if they outlawed the purpose of peaceful picketing but did not outlaw peaceful picketing per se. The Hanke decision in 1950 went even further, since in this case the peaceful picketing enjoined did not violate a written law but merely ran counter to a judicially declared public policy in favor of self-employment free from restraint. Finally, in 1957, the case of Teamster's Union v. Vogt simply allowed the state of Wisconsin to enjoin stranger picketing as such, and for all practical purposes the courts have now turned the right to restrict peaceful picketing back to the state legislatures.

Given the post-1930 tendencies in the area of labor-management relations just described, however, one should still not make the mistake of understating the continuing role of the courts in this area of public policy. Brown and Myers, for example have reminded us:

> ...state common law still has a role to play in the area of labor relations. Many things still rest with the states, and many states have little or no legislation in this area. The 1959 amendments to the Taft-Hartley Act, ceding to the states cases in which the National Labor Relations Board declines to take jurisdiction, lend added significance to this point. 1, p.2

The Continuing Role of The Executive

Edward S. Corwin has stated that the federal executive power is "the power of government that is the most spontaneously responsive to emergency conditions." [4, p.1] This being the case, presidential influence on labor-management relations has been most pronounced during industrial disputes and during times of war. The president's normal appointive powers with regard to the increasing administrative machinery in the area of labor relations, and his ability to influence legislation, however, also give him other important sources of influence on public policy.

Presidential Intervention in Industrial Disputes and Special Executive Committees and Conference Groups

The federal executive first participated in labor management relations as a "keeper of the peace" when local and state authorities were judged unable or unwilling to control the outbreak of industrial conflict in the Railway Strike of 1877. There is a long record of subsequent presidential intervention in especially difficult situations. In the case of the Pullman Strike of 1894, President Cleveland followed up an injunction with the use of federal troops, over the objection of the Governor of Illinois. President McKinley sent troops into the Coeur d'Alene metal mines in Idaho. President Theodore Roosevelt felt impelled to assert the government's interest in the 1902 anthracite strike and was instrumental in bringing about a settlement.

President Wilson was called on to intervene in more labor disputes than any of his predecessors, and the mines and the railroads were the chief objects of his attention. In the West Virginia mine disputes of 1921 attempts were made by the National Guard and the State Police to supress disturbances. When disorder increased, President Harding sent in federal troops to restore peace. President Harding also found himself involved in efforts to settle the railway shopmen's strike in 1922. During the threatened bituminous coal strike in 1924 Secretary of Commerce Herbert Hoover sought to get the parties together with the approval of President Coolidge. Several times Franklin D. Roosevelt practically insisted that the parties to a dispute submit it to arbitration; and like his predecessors he was particularly preoccupied with railroad and coal mine disputes. The last pre-Taft-Hartley experience with presidential intervention in labor disputes was President Truman's abortive effort in the railway strike of 1946.

Since the establishment of the Department of Labor as a separate cabinet post in 1913, the services of professional conciliators have also been made available in the case of significant labor disputes. Congress has established special machinery to assist in reconciling disputes on the nation's railroads and airlines, and the Taft-Hartley Act removed the Conciliation Service from the Department of Labor and created a separate Federal Mediation and Conciliation Service in 1947. The president's emergency dispute powers were also formalized in this Act, however, and it emphasized the continuing potential of executive influence in labor disputes. The 1959 steel strike saw executive intervention above and beyond that provided by law when

Secretary of Labor Mitchell and Vice President Nixon entered the dispute with President Eisenhower's permission.

The continuing impasse over work rules on the nation's railroads, however, appears to have broken new ground in the area of dispute settlement in this much beleagured industry. Even the extraordinary influence of the executive, including President Eisenhower's special tri-partite Presidential Railroad Commission in 1960 and the continuing mediation efforts of President Kennedy's Secretaries of Labor, and a later Presidential Board failed to reconcile the differences between the parties, and in 1963, for the first time in peacetime history, Congress was forced to impose compulsory arbitration in a labor-management dispute.

Although some may argue that there is some historical and practical justification for special Congressional action in railroad affairs, there has been considerable dissatisfaction with the emergency dispute provisions of the Taft-Hartley Act as well as those of the Railway Labor Act. And this may be the next broad area of Congressional legislation in labor-management relations despite the fact that President Johnson seemed to have been successful in re-exerting some of the traditional executive influence in this area once Congress had removed the thorny work rules question from the recent railroad negotiations.

In addition to intervention in labor disputes, executive action in labor-management relations has also resulted in the appointment of special committees or Conference groups. Theodore

Roosevelt's Anthracite Coal Commission of 1902 was perhaps the most notable of several early governmental investigations of labor-management relations. Both President Wilson and President Truman called conferences of labor and management representatives shortly after the conclusion of both World Wars in the futile hope that a plan for postwar industrial peace could be worked out. President Eisenhower's special tri-partite Presidential Railroad Commission in 1960 has already been mentioned, and President Kennedy convened an even broader tri-partite, 21-member President's Advisory Committee on Labor-Management Policy which has been retained under President Johnson following Kennedy's tragic assassination.

Executive Orders and Wartime Emergencies

At the federal level, executive action of a quasi-legislative character has occurred through the issuance of executive orders. The presidential executive order has become a government tool of increasing importance in implementing economic controls. It was broadened in scope as executive power was increased during the First World War to permit the creation of the first War Labor Board and other emergency agencies. The codes of fair competition provided for in the National Industrial Recovery Act were put into effect by executive orders, and some of the most far reaching and controversial economic controls ever imposed in the nation's history came through the "law-making" of the chief executive during World War II. Although many World War II measures were of a temporary emergency nature, some action born of emergency usually carries over to become a normal part of our economic system. The strenghthening of union membership during both World Wars is a case in point.

The two agencies created by executive orders which had the greatest influence on labor matters during World War II were the War Labor Board, which replaced the National Defense Mediation Board, and the War Manpower Commission. Although the second War Labor Board was originally created to settle labor disputes for which existing government procedures for adjustment were inadequate or ineffective, it eventually became involved in passing on the majority of all wage increases and deciding union security questions. The War Manpower Commission was also given broad powers; and, in addition to supervising a nation-wide system of employment exchanges, it eventually was given control over many management hiring decisions. The problem of allocating manpower between the civilian and military establishments of the nation, of determining which employers could hire workers, and of specifying what classes of workers were essential to the war effort and which were not, became a part of this agency's functions.

Administrative Appointments and Legislative Influence

Actions of a quasi-judicial nature eminating from the executive branch of government are represented by the rulings of the National Mediation Board and the National Labor Relations Board under our two major federal labor laws. The actions of the Department of Labor in administering the Fair Labor Standards Act, the public contracts acts, and the Landrum-Griffin Act also affect public policy in labor-management matters. By his appointments to these key administrative posts, a president can sometimes have a significant impact in public policy on labor-management relations. Judicial appointments offer a less frequent opportunity to influence public policy, but Franklin Roosevelt's threat to "pack" the Supreme Court and the subsequent modification of Court doctrine indicates that executive influence can be a very flexible thing. Finally, the President's role in suggesting and supporting particular legislative measures provides another avenue of influence. President Eisenhower's nationwide address to the people just prior to the passage of the Landrum-Griffin Act in the most recent example of how this avenue can be traveled to affect public policy on labor-management relations.

Actions by State and Local Executives

At the state and local level the influence of the executive is somewhat similar to that of the president on the national scale, although most states do not have labor relation acts or labor boards to administer them.

Governors frequently intervene in labor disputes within the states, and for labor disturbances on a smaller scale, local government officials frequently bring the weight of their office to bear in an attempt to force settlement. Local executives can also exert influence by their treatment of municipal workers, the wages paid, their attitude toward organization, and the consultation or use of labor and management officials in public programs. Also, for both local and state officials, the manner in which the police are used in labor disputes is an important means of exerting control in labor-management relations.

Some Concluding Observations and Further Comments

This chapter has shown that the present legal framework of labor-management relations is indeed complex. The government touches the industrial rule making process in many ways and with different degrees of effectiveness. Nevertheless, there are some conclusions which can be drawn from this rather lenghty presentation.

First, as our economy has become more industrialized and more complex, there has been an expansion in the role of government in the industrial rule making process--both with regard to labor-management relations legislation and with regard to protective labor legislation.

Second, this expansion has been uneven in its development over time, and the substansive content of the policy has also been modified considerably.

Third, the means of effectuating government controls have shifted within branches of government and between levels of government, but the present legal framework is still highly diversified with regard to both procedure and substance.

While the first statement is too obvious to require elaboration, we might briefly discuss the last two conclusions in reverse order.

We have seen that there have been various means of exercising governmental influence in labor-management relations at both the federal and state levels. The relative significance of legislative enactments and federal regulations have increased since 1930, however, and these developments are largely the result of a change in judicial philosophy and interpretation during the upheval of the Great Depression. Not only did the Supreme Court create a larger role for the U.S. Congress by expanding its interpretation of the commerce power, but it also permitted the enactment of legislation which apparently reflected a growing national concern for personal rights aside from those rights arising from the ownership of property. An older concept of freedom in terms of legal property rights was modified and enriched with a newer conception of freedom which also included considerations of economic opportunity and economic welfare in an industrial society.

Despite the increasing importance of federal legislation, however, considerable diversity remains. The courts and the executive continue to exert influence in those areas where legislative guidelines are either absent or ambigious. There are differences between state and federal legislative requirements, and there are geographical differences at the state level among the various states. Even at the federal level there are inter-industry differences in public policy. Not only does the policy applied the railways differ in some respects from that applied to other industries engaged in interstate commerce, but the Landrum-Griffin Act even goes so far as to single out particular industries in the non-railway category for special treatment with regard to some of its provisions.

Going even further into the substance of present labor policy, it is also apparent that some issues of labor-management relations are much more closely regulated than others. Thus, while union security is rather closely regulated; there has been no overt attempt (barring the exceptions of war time emergencies) to regulate the wages determined through collective bargaining.[1] The internal affairs of unions particularly with regard to financial matters, are now more closely regulated than those of management organizations, and so on.

Despite these variations, however, we can say that, over time, the substance of our public policy has changed to permit the direct governmental establishment of minimum working conditions; and, with regard to union organization and collective bargaining, we can say that the trend has been from a policy of hostility, to tolerance, to encouragement, to detailed regulations.

This, however, has not been a gradual development. Aside from the abnormal increase in governmental influence during the wartime emergencies, two periods stand out as being especially significant for increasing direct government regulation of working conditions and promoting unionism and collective bargaining. Subsequent restrictive modifications of collective bargaining policy at the national level have also been produced in two sharp spurts.

Following some previously ineffectual attempts to enact

---

[1] The wage-price "guidelines" enunciated by the President's Council of Economic Advisors in 1961, do not appear to be a real exception to this statement, but they do indicate increasing public attention to some of the results of private collective bargaining agreements.

effective or judicially approvable labor legislation at the state level in the late 1880's, the years 1911 to 1915 stand out in the history of American Labor legislation. These years marked the culmination of the "Progressive Era" in American politics. During this time America was being transformed from an agrarian nation into an urban industrial society. This was a period of great public unrest. It was also a period of sensitivity and awareness, and the liberal forces in the nation hammered away at economic and social reforms on a scale surpassed only by the New Deal "revolution" of the 1930's. Although the attempts of the Clayton Act to curtail the use of the labor injunction and remove labor from the anti trust laws later proved abortive, many states enacted workmen's compensation laws for the first time, and vigorous new attempts in the areas of child labor, hours of work, and minimum wages for women and children were launched. With the exception of minimum wage legislation, these statues had received judicial acceptance by the outbreak of the First World War.

Then, after the wartime emergency and the "return to normalcy" during the 1920's, the years 1932 to 1938 witnessed the greatest single outburst of labor legislation this nation has ever seen. Amid the turmoil and unrest surrounding the Great Depression, the Federal Government moved into the field of protective labor legislation. Old restraints on union activity were first removed then collective bargaining was strongly encouraged, and several states followed the federal example and passed "baby" Norris LaGuardia Acts and "baby" Wagner Acts before a general reaction began to set in around 1939.

Since that time most state-labor relations legislation has been increasingly restrictive of union activities, including "right-to-work" laws outlawing union security provisions in 19 states.

Following the frenzied activities of the late 30's, there have been no really new developments in social or protective legislation since that time. Although the federal statutes have been amended from time to time, many states seem to have largely neglected this area of legislation except for the fact that, under the stimulus of the tax-offset provisions of the Social Security Act, all of the states have enacted some form of unemployment compensation, and in 1948 Mississippi became the last state in the union to adopt a system of workmen's compensation for industrial accidents. In the area of labor-management relations legislation, however, the Taft-Hartley Act made seemingly permanent and significant changes in our national labor policy some 12 years after the enactment of the Wagner Act. Another 12-year interval separated the Taft-Hartley Act from the most recent modification of our public policy through the Landrum-Griffin Act of 1959.

It is more than coincidence that 12-year intervals have separated the three modern landmarks in federal labor legislation. Few areas of legislation are so highly charged with emotional and political overtones, and regardless of the party in power, the balance in Congress has been so close on labor issues over the past two decades that action on major legislation has come about only when public interest in a new law has reached a high pitch. Thus the 1935 Wagner Act was surrounded by the catastrophe of the Great Depression. We were striving to achieve the hopes of a "New Deal", business prestige was at a low ebb and was further undermined by Congressional investigations like those of the La Follete Committee, which revealed vicious anti-union activity by American employers. The passage of the Taft-Hartley Act also occured amidst an unusual combination of circumstances. By 1947 the American people were in the grip of a profound post-war disillusionment. Relations with our wartime allies were deteriorating, we were experiencing a relatively acute inflation, the Republican party was resurging after 15 years of New Deal domination, and the 1946 strike wave had aroused growing concern over the enhanced power and prestige of organized labor. Likewise, the labor reform bill of 1959 was enacted amidst the moral outrage of the American public which accompanied the shocking revelations of the McClellan Committee.

Given this observation that periodic and fairly sustained outburst of public sentiment appear to be necessary to get labor legislation through a closely balanced Congress, however, how do we explain the <u>specific</u> proposals which have been enacted? How is public opinion given form and direction in contemporary American politics? Cantwell has observed:

> It is characteristic of public opinion that it cannot generate a proposal or series of proposals serving to satisfy its needs. Public opinion can indicate very powerfully the general area of its needs, but it remains for an individual or group of individuals to come forward with specific proposals towards which opinion can display approval or disapproval. [2, pp. 933-35]

This thesis will assume that interest groups, pressure groups, or lobbies, as they are variously called, perform this "crystalizing" or "leadership" function which channels active public opinion in such a way as to get support for specific proposals in the area of their general concern. These terms will be used interchangeably, and to make this assumption as clear as possible, it can be assumed in the abstract that individuals hold feelings or opinions on various issues. These opinions are formed as the result of a combination of logical, emotional, and environmental conditionings. These opinions or feelings become politically significant, however, only if they are held with sufficient strength that the people are willing to actively express them and act on them. Public opinion on any issue is assumed to be the opinions of that "public" which has reached the "active" stage. Given a sufficient degree of active opinion on any issue, it is assumed that groups of similar individual opinions unite to promote or defend their common interest. By offering leadership and by formulating specific proposals, organized interest groups are in a position to bring pressure to bear on points of political decision making, and thereby transform public opinion into public policy.

While still at this abstract level, however, it would be a mistake to assume that all the "interests" in any particular situation or on any particular issue need to be formally organized. Indeed, some of the most powerful interests in our society are those values or shared attitudes which are so widely held that no formal organization has to be organized to make their influence felt. Often they are reflected in the major institution of our society and although unorganized they can be regarded as potential interest groups capable of organizing if these share attitudes or values are regarded as being threatened or violated by the activities of any organized group. Truman states:

> These widely held but unorganized interests are what we have previously called the "rules of the game". Others have described these attitudes in such terms as "systems of belief", as a "general ideological consensus", and as "a broad body of attitudes and understandings regarding the nature and limits of authority." . . . Violation of the "rules of the game" normally will weaken a group's cohesion, reduce its status in the community, and expose it to the claims of other groups. The latter may be competing organized groups that more adequately incorporate the "rules", or they may be groups organized on the basis of these broad interests and in response to the violations. [8, pp. 512-13]

Such a conception helps us to move from the abstract to the concrete, and it gives us an insight into the history of our nation's public policy in labor-management relations. The earliest attempts of labor organization, collective bargaining, or protective labor legislation were viewed as threats to some of our society's most widely held attitudes on individualism, private property, and the laissez faire free market principle of economic liberalism. As a result, the more overt activities of the organized interests supporting the principles of unionism or protective legislation were often thwarted or greatly delayed not so much by better, more efficiently organized opposition groups as by the force of unorganized interest groups or potential interests whose strength lay in the widespread support their beliefs commanded in the society in general and in the courts in particular. Thus Brown and Myers state:

> Labor leaders, and others, have often placed much of the onus for obstructions to unionism upon the courts, upon judge-made laws. While it may be that the legal training of the judges, with its emphasis on precedent, as well as their social background, contributed to their dragging their heels, it is not unlikely that, for at least the greater part of the period prior to 1930, on the whole they reflected prevailing attitudes....the important determinants of policy may well have been the pervasive views with respect to property rights, on the one hand, and unionism on the other. [1, pp. 20-21]

Only when the increasing forces of urbanization and industrialization and the catastrophe of the Great Depression began to call into doubt the social efficacy of complete laissez faire and to introduce semi egalitarian considerations of material welfare as well as individual property rights into our value system did the "rules of the game" yield sufficiently to introduce new and also widely held attitudes into the institutional fabric of our society. In so doing, however, it must be recognized that much of the former "consensus" in the area of labor management relations broke down. Many of the existing interests in this field were transformed. Interests which previously had been unorganized or only potential interest groups began to reshape and increase their activities. Many existing interests became more highly organized both in terms of their formal structure and in the nature of the scope of their customary activities.

More will be said on this point later in the thesis, but for the present it is enough to point out that, at the present time, the area of labor-management relations is somewhat unique in the field of political activity in that no other area of governmental action has adversary pressure interests as highly organized as is the case here. Murray Edelman has noted:

> Management groups on the one side and organized labor on the other watch the governmental arena closely, ready to step into the fight or be drawn into it. In most areas of government activity, on the other hand, only one interested party (the railroads, the investment companies, the military services) is highly organized; its adversary is amorphorus. In some fields no interest is organized. [5, p. 52]

With regard to the implications of this fact, he has stated:

> Given two power groups which are organized, the struggle between them in the halls of State is certain to be more intense with respect to proposed public policies in which they have conflicting interests. To the extent that either can win majority legislative, administrative, or judicial support, there will be more action by the State designed to alter the balance of power from time than would have been the case if only one interest were organized. [5, p. 53]

The analysis might well explain the tendency we have seen toward more detailed regulation of labor-management relations. Each enactment seems to upset the power equilibrium between the contending parties, and with both sides highly organized, this immediately sets up pressures for further enactments either to restore the old equilibrium or to consolidate new gains into strength for even further gains.

The fact that both sides are well organized, combined with the fact that they are apparently fairly evenly matched in terms of the amount of influence they can command in Congress, also probably helps to explain the 12-year "jerkiness" we have previously noted in recent congressional enactments. Under these circumstances, only unusual events such as those cited earlier can break the deadlock long enough to give one side a sufficient advantage over the other to get any legislation enacted. But this process, by its very nature, seems to give undue influence to contemporary events in shaping long run labor policy. This in turn means that as contemporary events change there are new pressures for more modifications of policy, and again seems to imply that under present circumstances the tendency for increasingly detailed regulation seems irreversable.

If this is so, it should be fruitful to examine in more detail the political nature of the contending labor and management interests which are now engaged in this precarious balancing of the public policy seesaw in order to see to what extend we can expect it to change from the viewpoint of the contending parties. Therefore, the next chapter will examine the historical attempts of organized labor and its spokesmen to fashion a viable political influence in the area of labor - management policy, and the following chapter will do the same for American management. Then, Chapter V will examine the Post World War II period in more detail in an attempt to access the present situation with regard to the political dimension of labor - management relations.

REFERENCES - CHAPTER II

1. D. V. Brown and C. A. Myers, "Historical Evolution" in Shister (et. al.) editors, Public Policy and Collective Bargaining (New York: Harper and Row, 1962).

2. Frank Cantwell, "Public Opinion And The Legislative Process," American Political Science Review, October 1946, Vol. XL, pp. 924-935.

3. John R. Commons and J. B. Andrews, Principles of Labor Legislation (New York: Harper, 1936).

4. Edward S. Corwin, The President: Office and Powers, 1787-1957 (New York: New York University, 1957).

5. Murray Edelman, "Government and Labor-Management Relations", The American Journal of Economics and Sociology, October, 1950, Vol. 10, pp. 51-60.

6. Charles O. Gregory, Labor and The Law (New York: Norton, 1958).

7. Glen W. Miller, American Labor and the Government (New York: Prentice Hall, 1948).

8. David B. Truman, The Governmental Process (New York: Knopf, 1955).

9. U. S. Department of Labor, Growth of Labor Law in the United States (Washington: U.S. Government Printing Office, 1962).

CHAPTER III

HISTORICAL EXPERIMENTS IN POLITICAL ACTIVITY: ORGANIZED LABOR

As America began to industrialize, the functional differentiation of employers and employees, accompanied by different social and economic rewards attaching to these separate functions, permitted the development of attitudes and interests peculiar to each group. These interests often appeared to be in conflict with each other. Early employee attempts to organize together in an effort to modify the disrupting influences of industrialization and to gain a greater voice in determining their conditions of employment were often met by the associated opposition of employers who, as we have seen, relied heavily on the judicial institutions of government (particularly the convenient common law concepts of conspiracy) to combat worker threats to their unilateral rule making authority. A survey of labor's subsequent political activity seems to indicate a more-or-less pragmatic adjustment to changing environmental conditions. Much of labor's early political activity was sporadic and poorly organized. It tended to be local in character and was largely directed against social abuses. During most of the nineteenth century trade unions proved unable to survive economic adversity and employer hostility on a permanent basis. Workers in the industrial centers, therefore, usually relied on trade union activity during periods of economic prosperity, and then turned to political agitation during periods of depression when their unions collapsed or were destroyed.

This pattern began to change during the latter 1800's as American workers became more successful in establishing permanent or at least longer-lasting institutions. In discussing labor's modern political activity since the turn of the century, this chapter's discussion will focus almost exclusively on the activities of organized trade unions and their national federations. Even here, however, caution must be exercised, since the organized labor movement in the United States is, in reality, a polyglot of competing organizations. The activities of the national federations can be quite different in both purpose and technique from the activities of a constituent or independent national or local union. Despite many differences, however, there are some ties which link most of these organizations together; and although some generalizations are likely to be dangerous, they cannot be avoided at this broad summary level of analysis.

Since the first labor parties in the world appeared in the United States, it is perhaps somewhat of a paradox that the American labor movement today is probably the least political labor movement in the world. While it was possible for American labor parties to be founded ahead of those in other countries due to the fact that male workers had gained the right to vote in most states by the 1830's, the American trade union movement today is the only major movement in the democratic world not associated with a labor or socialist political party. Indeed, the modern American labor movement is definitely anti-socialistic in nature; and independent partisan activity has not been the only, or even the most predominant, type of political behavior exhibited by the American labor movement.

Historically, American labor has moved from an earlier identification with independent, partisan electoral activity to a more-or-less bipartisan approach, which also emphasizes the lobbying and other non-electoral activities employed by most interest groups now operating in our rather amorphous two party political system. A brief historical review of labor's role in the political process will indicate the relative significance of these different approaches in understanding the contemporary political activities of American labor unions.

Colonial and Revolutionary America: Relative Quiescence

Because of the property qualification for voting, labor, as such, played little if any role in colonial politics. After 1760, however, there were many workingmen in the so-called Whig Clubs. These Clubs aimed at the democratization of government, but they were usually led by young merchants, lawyers, and storekeepers. During the Revolution, these clubs became known as the Sons of Liberty, and labor was probably the largest constituent element in this organization. After the war, however, the leaders of the Sons of Liberty, who were voters, became more interested in how the new government functioned rather than in who voted for it. In addition to the lack of franchise, another reason for labor's slight political participation during the 40 years after the war was that for the most part they were satisfied with political conditions and they sympathized with the Jeffersonian Party's democratic tendencies. Thus, Morris notes:

> While labor had certain separate and distinct interests in the colonial and Revolutionary periods, its members were not precluded from making common cause with others, as, notably, in joining with the commercial interests to protest the British policy on the eve of the Revolution. [22, p. vii]

Early Nineteenth Century: Oscillation

After the war of 1812, however, a new political generation appeared, and labor was becoming aware of the fact that its status was being reduced from its colonial position of dignity as the handicraft stage of American industry gradually gave way to the age of "merchant capitalism". Rayback states:

> Workingmen who were of this new generation were caught up in the trend. With their living standards lowered by a depression and the merchant-capitalist system, they became conscious of a sense of inferiority and inequality. As one workman expressed it, "The laboring classes in our country, in consequence of inroads and usurpations of the wealthy and powerful, have for years been gradually sinking in the scale of public estimation". Manual labor had ceased to be respectable. Laboring men, particularly the skilled, began to develop a "Workingmen's Platform", intended to establish or restore the equality of esteem which had once been theirs. [26, p. 65]

By 1825 the Workingmen's Platform had been more or less generally evolved. It called for: a 10-hour day; universal male suffrage; equal and universal education; abolition of imprisonment for debt; abolition of the compulsory military system; mechanics lien laws, which would give workers priority in case of death, bankruptcy or defalcation of employers; and abolition of chartered monopolies and banks, which in labor's opinion encouraged monopoly enterprise and defrauded labor of wages by issuing paper money. The Workingmen's Platform took definite shape only gradually; but, since it was essentially a political program, labor turned to its allies in the Jeffersonian party. At first the Jeffersonians responded; but the merchant capitalists, who had little sympathy for workers' objectives, gradually assumed control of the party. As a result, workingmen began to engage in politics independently. Philadelphia and New York became the leading centers of activity.

The first labor party in the world was founded in 1828 when the Mechanics' Union of Trade Associations of Philadelphia launched the Workingmen's Labor Party in that city. By 1830 "worky" parties, supporting the Workingmen's Platform, had appeared in a host of other cities. Yet, by 1832 most of the workingmen's parties had disappeared. The reasons were numerous: internal dissension caused disgust; the Democrats, who had replaced the Jeffersonians, stole much of their platform; and, most important, the return of prosperity shifted the attention of labor to economic problems and trade unionism. The next major political movement by labor did not appear until after the Civil War, but labor's interest in politics was never completely abandoned after the dissolution of the "worky" parties, and there were several sporadic occurances of interest.

Labor leaders and many workingmen are believed to have

supported Andrew Jackson because they recognized him as the enemy of bank monopolies. While Jackson's war against the U.S. Bank no doubt won hearty labor approval, his Pet Bank policy probably aroused resentment because State Banks were as much disliked by labor as was the Bank of the United States.

In 1834 workingmen also began to urge the Democratic party in several eastern states to adopt the Gouge program which advocated free banking with no right of issue, the separation of federal and private funds, and it wanted to make hard money the normal circulating medium. This issue internally divided the Democratic party in some states. The most important struggle came in New York, where the workers formed the Equal Rights Party (nicknamed Loco Focos) and were just barely defeated by the Tammany machine in 1835. The panic of 1837 then broke and brought the bank war to a climax, after which the Loco Focos gained considerable influence in Democratic parties in many eastern states. The Independent Treasury bill was passed in 1849; and, in another act favorable to labor, President Van Buren simultaneously ordered the 10 hour day for all mechanics and laborers employed by the Federal government.

In addition to this labor attachment to the Democratic party after the collapse of the independent workingmens parties, there was a strong revival of trade union activity between 1833 and 1837, including a movement for a national organization of all trades. The National Trades' Union was created in 1834, and its main function was one of exhortation. It encouraged the creation of more local associations, and they attempted to push the Workingmen's platform upon the state legislatures. Their petitions also added a few planks to the platform to stop convict labor, and to correct the deplorable conditions which were developing with the increasing use of women and children in the "sweat shops" and the factories. The National Trades' Union also encouraged the free give away of public lands. In 1835 the National Trades' Union, acting as a pressure group for the 10 hour day in the Navy Yards, secured a concession from President Andrew Jackson in the Philadelphia Navy Yard.

The triumph of the workingmen in the struggle to secure influence in the Democratic party in the east eventually brought other results, and the workingmen's programs may also have made an impression on the Whig party. The Workingmen's Platform was gradually enacted in the northeastern states after 1836, and in 1842 it was a Whig Judge, Lemuel Shaw, who handed down the famous Commonwealth v Hunt decision.

Although much of the Workingmen's platform, which had been created in the 1820's was put into law by the 1860's, labor's national position was not greatly improved as a result. Many of the provisions were "uplift" in nature, and those which did attempt to help labor directly such as maximum hour laws were not enforced, and, as was mentioned in the preceding chapter, many subsequent laws were later declared invalid by various court decisions.

The financial panic of 1837 grew into a depression which continued until the gold discoveries of 1849 stimulated a business recovery. During this period workers became involved in schemes for utopian communities, producer's and consumer's cooperative movements, and finally a drive for land reform. Of these activities, land reform was the most significant.

The free land agitation of the NTU was expanded, and the "homestead movement" was born during this period. This movement, according to Selig Perlman, was a demand that the government "open an escape to the worker from the wage system into self-employment by way of free land" [24, p. 281]; and, along with the issues of the Civil War, it dominated American politics during the 1850's and 1860's.

If the first half of the 19th century was characterized by the oscillation of labor between political and economic activities the second half was characterized by a split within the labor movement itself as to which course of action proved most promising as a permanent course of action. This split was clearly highlighted during the brief existence of the <u>National Labor Union.</u>

Late Nineteenth Century: Dichotomy

The National Labor Union was an attempt to unite two subsequently incompatible philosophies: (1) the politically-conscious, humanitarian-reform philosophy which was carried over from the agitation of the 1820's and the many reform movements of the 1840's; and (2) the more restrictive, wage conscious, trade unionist philosophy which dominated the upsurge of unionism in the early 1850's. Following the Civil War, both Marxian and Lassalian Socialists also appeared for the first time in the American labor movement. Both groups were radical in that they wanted to overthrow the capitalist system, but the Marxists preferred to begin the class war through organized trade unions whereas the Lassalians preferred political action. These groups joined forced and created the Social Party in 1868 and became part of the N.L.U. They were never very influential, and this alliance was always on the verge of disintegration. The N.L.U., however, was the first sizeable national American labor organization to show a strong interest in the European labor movement, and it also created the first labor lobby in Washington.

The establishment of the National Labor Union was a response to a growing demand for unification of labor groups throughout the country. The issue which became the catalytic agent of the movement for national federation was the eight hour day which began to develop in appeal as Ira Steward put his personality behind it. In August, 1866, an attempt to unite the eight hour movement in Baltimore led to the creation of the National Labor Union. Basically a loose federation of city centrals, the N.L.U. also included some national and local unions as well as various social reform organizations. From the first meeting of the N.L.U. various issues created discord, but this internal disunity did not always cause conflict where the interests of the politically conscious and the trade unionists coincided.

The N.L.U.'s first congress announced three major demands: a universal 8-hour day, abolition of the convict labor system, and repeal of the Contract Labor Law of 1864, which had been written in response to employer demands for more labor during the war. There were some modest gains along these lines, and the political 8-hour movement was supported by the trade unionists. During the 1866 depression they also went along with producers cooperatives. The aims of these two groups did not always coincide, however, and the first clashes came over admitting women and negroes to membership. Then came a fatal clash over greenbacks, when currency reform again replaced land reform as the number one panacea on the American scene.

The driving personality behind the N.L.U. was William H. Sylvis of the moulders union, a politically conscious "humanitarian" who was a strong believer in cooperatives as a means of freeing workers from the "control" of the capitalist industrial system. Because cooperative enterprizes required capital and credit, labor switched from its earlier advocacy of hard money and was prompted to support various politically inclined farm groups in the "Greenback" movement which favored large issues of paper money and easy credit at low interest rates.

The trade unionists staunchly resisted the movement towards political action when the labor leaders favorable to greenback ideas sought to persuade the N.L.U. it should support a political movement in this direction. The "greenbackers" secured control of the 1870 congress, however, and they set up a political branch known as the National Labor Reform Party. This angered the trade unionists. They had lost the fight on admitting women and negroes and now this! No national unions sent delegates to the N.L.U. congress in 1871, and the National Labor Reform Party failed to survive the election campaign of 1872 after its original presidential candidate, Judge David Davis of Illinois refused the nomination. Only six delegates appeared at the 1872 congress. The N.L.U. had died, and the center of political insurgency shifted to the agricultural states of the Middle West.

Despite its failure, the N.L.U. represented the first strong effort to unite a fragmented labor movement. It served to focus and highlight the differences between the egalitarian, politically conscious labor philosophy and the self-centered, wage-conscious trade union philosophy which were destined to dominate the internal American labor scene during the last part of the nineteenth century. It oversimplified terms these differences were reflected in the battle between the Knights of Labor and the trade unions which formed the American Federation of Labor for the loyalty of the American workingman. This battle was further complicated by the second politically conscious element of largely European origin, which was strongly socialistic in nature. The divisiveness inherent in these three factions on the American labor scene was temporarily obscured by the "United Front Campaign" of 1886; but this campaign, which will be described in more detail later, also revealed the basic incompatibility of the three groups, and the last decade of the nineteenth century witnessed a decisive showdown between these conflicting elements.

The Noble Order of the Knights of Labor was originally founded as a secret society by Uriah S. Stevens in 1869. Membership in the organization grew slowly at first, but a sudden upsurge after the railway strike of 1877 and the question of how to respond to a proposed Greenback-Labor movement led to the creation of a national organization at the Reading Convention of January, 1878. Stevens resigned shortly after the Convention, and he was succeeded as Grand Master Workman by Terence V. Powderly.

The Knights represented an attempt to form one great labor union to speak for all labor. Secrecy was dropped, and membership in the local assemblies was open to any person regardless of race, sex, nationality, or skill who was over 18 and was working for wages or had worked for wages. No person who sold alcohol, no doctor, lawyer, or banker was to be admitted. The Reading convention announced three "cardinal principles" usually summarized in the words "organize", "educate", "cooperate". The ultimate goal of the Knights was to set up producers cooperatives, but Fine notes:

> Specific demands called for bureaus of labor statistics, productive and distributive cooperatives, public lands for actual settlers, "the abrogation of all laws that do not bear equally upon capital and labor," health and safety laws, weekly pay-days, and wages in legal currency, a mechanics' lien law, abolition of the contract system on public works, substitution of arbitration for strikes, no child labor, no contract prison labor, equal pay for equal work for both sexes, reduction of hours to eight a day, and a circulating medium issued directly by the government. At subsequent conventions, or sessions as they were called, the national body adopted additional planks for the prohibition by law of the Pinkerton Protective Patrol; abolition of the militia; restriction of immigration; the Australian

> ballot; the initiative and referendum; immediate possession by the government of the Union Pacific Railroad; and government ownership of the railroads and telegraphs. [13, p. 123]

During the six years following the Reading convention, the Knights were in a constant state of turmoil. A few strike victories and the adverse economic conditions of the early 1880's, however, led to a rapid increase in membership from about 50,000 in 1876 to approximately 700,000 by 1884. Although the Knights had started out to achieve their program through education and cooperation, their vast program of reform called for so much legislative action that they were drawn more and more into the use of political means of achieving it.

Several of the Knight's officers were Greenback-Labor candidates in 1878. Powderly himself was one of the most successful being elected mayor of Scranton, Pennsylvania, in 1878 and re-elected in 1880. Many local assemblies of the Knights also cooperated with the Greenback movement, and some supported independent tickets of their own. In 1884 the Knights began lobbying in state capitals and in Washington, D.C. to secure their legislative demands.

The rapid expansion of the Knights, together with the newspaper publicity which surround it, was accompanied by some tangible political results. Convict labor was abolished in several states, and in 1887 the Federal Government abolished convict labor. Seven states created Bureaus of labor statistics, and the Federal Government established its Bureau of Labor Statistics in 1883. Most of the Knight's political activity, however, was much less successful;

and the Knight's progress was abruptly halted by the rapid decline in membership due to the increased anti-labor sentiment following the Haymarket bombing in Chicago on May 4, 1886.

After their participation in the United Front Campaign later in 1886 came to naught, the Knights began to lose most of their non-socialistic membership in the cities. Its still declining strength lay in the small towns and rural areas. Thus, when the Populist movement began sweeping the middle west, the Knights were in the forefront of the drive and openly advocated independent political action on a national level. In 1891 Powderly sent out a call to the AFL, Railroad Brotherhoods, and independent unions for an organizing convention. Few responded, but the Knights went ahead and cooperated with the farmer organizations which founded the Peoples Party. In 1892 the People's Party ran General Weaver, the Greenback candidate of 1880, for president and in 1896 they backed the Democratic candidate, William Jennings Bryan. The Knights cooperated in both elections, but neither was fought on labor issues. The People's party ceased to exist after the 1896 elections, and the KOL, weakened by depression and AFL competition, never again gained any importance in either the political or labor fields.

Thus, the Knights of Labor gradually faded from the American labor scene. Their basic platform written at Reading in 1878, however, served as a model for much of the state labor legislation written between 1886 and 1900. Most of this legislation dealt with child labor; women's labor; factory, sweatshop, and mine safety; arbitration of industrial disputes; responsibility for industrial accidents; and the eight-hour day. The Knights were not directly responsible for the passage of the laws, but their agitation combined with that of the socialists and some AFL unions in the United Front parties of 1886-87 and later the Populists, and the humanitarian instincts of a public aroused by the condition of some labor elements did contribute to their enactment.

As we know, little of this legislation was effective. Employers were seldom willing to use the arbitration machinery, and most of the protective laws were poorly enforced and some were later invalidated. Nevertheless, this legislation formed a base upon which the more effective enactments of the progressive era were built.

During the period when the Knights were in ascendency, a small number of independent national trade unions of skilled workers continued to function independently. A number of these craft union leaders decided to cope with the development of industry's national expansion by uniting with other unions in a national federation. Accordingly, in 1881 the Federation of Organized Trades and Labor Unions of the U.S. and Canada was established. A five-man legislative committee, including Samuel Gompers of the Cigar Makers' Union (who became chairman of the committee in 1883) was established, and its objectives were outlined in the platform adopted at the organization's first convention. Selig Perlman has reported:

> The platform as adopted demanded: legal incorporation for trade unions, compulsory education for children, the prohibition of child labor before fourteen, uniform apprentice laws, the enforcement of the national eight-hour

> law, prison labor reform, abolition of the "truck" and "order" system, mechanics' lien, abolition of conspiracy laws as applied to labor organizations, a national bureau of labor statistics, a protective tariff for American labor, an anti-contract immigrant law, and recommended "all trades and labor organizations to secure proper representation in all law-making bodies by means of the ballot, and to use all honorable measures by which this result can be accomplished". [9, p. 324]

While seeking the election of persons sympathetic to its needs, and pressing for legislation they deemed favorable to the workers, however, the FOTLU did not establish an independent party or formally ally itself with any political party. This policy was continued when the organization joined the newly formed American Federation of Labor in 1886 and one of its leaders, Samuel Gompers, rose to a position of leadership in the new Federation. "The "United Front" compaigns of 1866 and 1887 only served to convince Gompers of the wisdom of this course of political action.

In the face of strong anti-labor sentiment following the Haymarket affair in May 1886, many workers turned to independent political action in several industrial localities. Several "united labor" parties sprung up and were supported by members of the Knights, the trade unionists from AFL unions, and representatives of various socialist groups. An attempt to combine these scattered parties into a national organization soon subsided, however, and the last important independent political movement of American labor in the nineteenth century disintegrated.

The most important of the 1886 political struggles were waged in New York and Chicago, but a host of minor ones were fought throughout the country. Samuel Gompers, himself, was active in the Henry George campaign in New York City. Aroused by a judicial decision against labor in a boycott case, the Central Labor Union of New York City invited all labor-reform organizations, labor unions, Knights, Greenbackers, anti-monopolists, socialists, and land reformers to a conference. The conference, attended by some 400 delegates from 165 organizations, formed the United Labor Party and nominated Henry George, the father of the single tax, as its candidate for the major of the city. George polled 67,930 votes to 90,456 for the Democratic candidate, Abram S. Hewitt, and 60,474 for the Republican candidate, Theodore Roosevelt. [13, p. 43] Labor hailed these results as a great victory and the state legislature apparently agreed, for several new labor laws were shortly forthcoming. Attempts to extend the United Labor Party statewide soon resulted in a split between the socialists and the single-taxers, however, and the 1887 state elections were a disappointment to both factions.

The 1886 political upheaval outside New York city temporarily had more favorable results. Labor tickets won municipal elections in several New England cities. In Chicago a United Labor party elected a state senator and six assemblymen in 1886, and a farmer-labor coalition elected a congressman, a state senator, and six assemblymen in Milwaukee. The spring elections of 1887 seemed to bear out the promise of the previous year, and labor tickets carried local elections in 19 midwestern communities. This surge quickly faded, however, and the same forces which destroyed the movement in New York appeared in other industrial centers. The movement invariably split into two wings - "conservative" and socialists. In most places the "conservative" wing captured control of the organization, leading to a socialists ouster or secession. Rayback quotes Joseph Buchanan's description of the situation as follows:

> Men representing a dozen different shades of opinion ...come together ostensibly to pool their issues and amalgamate the elements variously represented. When they...come to write the 'union' platform...each claimed that he had the cure-all.... The upshot of the business has been a few truces, and the stronger faction has written the platform, while the rest have gone home sore-headed. [26, p. 172]

Thus, while the results of the United Front Campaigns of 1886 and 1887 were a determining factor in the AFL's decision to hold fast to its pure and simple trade unionism and eschew independent political action, they were also a determining factor in persuading the Socialist Labor parties to adopt an uncompromising position of "going it alone" irrespective of trade union support.

Samuel Gomper's leadership in political and other matters was not unchallenged during the early days of the Federation, however, and many socialists still tried to "bore from within". After a long internal struggle, Gomper's report to the 1898 convention included a section on "Trade Unions - Their Philosophy". By adopting that report the convention declared itself conscious of the principles which Gompers had been evolving. Since these principles were to guide the Federation for many years after 1898, and, indeed, are still important today it may be well to summarize them briefly.

The new union philosophy was one of pragmatism and business-like methods. The AFL recognized a real conflict of interest between employers and employees, and reliance was placed on trade organizations of skilled workers, job control, and the negotiation of written labor agreements to improve the lot of the working man.

Taking to heart the lesson of a century of experience, the new unionism shunned direct participation in politics or support for any program to revamp the economic system. In sharp contrast to the Knights of Labor, the Federation principles involved strict autonomy for the affiliated national unions (no Federation control over their internal affairs), exclusive jurisdiction (one union for each craft, and no dual unions), avoidance of political alignments, and major emphasis on economic action, with the Federation lending support to the national unions in strikes and organizing activities.

Traditionally the AFL's political policy has been termed "non-partisan" and is summed up in Gomper's classic statement:

> The partisanship of Labor is a partisanship of principle. The American Federation of Labor is not partisan to a political party, it is partisan to a principle, the principle of equal rights and human freedom. We, therefore, repeat: Stand faithfully by our friends and elect them, Oppose our enemies and defeat them whether they be candidates for President, for Congress, or for other offices, whether Executive, Legislative, or Judicial. [3, p. 234]

Despite Gomper's strong leadership, these principles were not accepted by the Federation until after a long struggle between the Socialists within the AFL, who favored a labor political party, and those who adhered to Gomper's approach of rewarding friends and punishing enemies had been at least partially resolved.[1] During the early years of the Federation's existence, the delegates to the AFL conventions holding socialistic views upon political matters persisted in their efforts to secure an endorsement of these views from each convention of the Federation. With only one exception, the result was uniformly the same, and the AFL refused to pledge or advise the trade unions to take part, as such, in any movement in the nature of partisan politics.

The one exception, and the greatest success of the Socialists was in 1893, when the AFL convention by an overwhelming vote adopted a resolution endorsing the independent political policy

---

[1] The first of the socialist parties claiming to represent the true interest of the American working class, was Lassallean in its theoretical position. The Labor party of Illinois was founded late in 1873, and the Social-Democratic party of North American was born the following year. Both of these party's were less important than the Working Men's party of the United States founded by a gathering of socialist in Philadelphia in 1876. Late the following year, this became the Socialist-Labor party, which attained the height of its influence in the 1890's under the leadership of Daniel DeLeon.

Schisms in the socialist camp led to the creation of two new parties before the Socialist party of American was founded in July, 1901. The nucleus of its initial strength lay in former members of the Socialist-Labor party and recruits from the vanishing Populist cause. Until it was severely split by the issues created by the First World War and the Bolshevist Revolution, the Socialist party was roughly equivalent with the socialist movement in the United States, but Henry David notes: "the party's political strength was far less a product of conversion to socialism than of a widespread desire for 'honest' and 'good' government and of dissatisfaction with the major parties. It is significant that the response to socialist candidates was releatively greater in states that were not preeminently industrial." [10, p. 103]

of the British unions. A political program, including collective ownership by the people of all means of production and distribution, was submitted as a basis for a labor party, and the labor unions were asked to instruct their delegates to the next convention on this subject. At the 1894 convention, Gompers and his associates eliminated the socialist plank and defeated the proposal to form an independent party. In revenge the Socialists helped to elect John McBride of the United Mine Workers to the presidency of the AFL for a year's term, but Gompers regained the office in 1895 and admonished the convention: "Party politics, whether they be Democratic, Republican, Socialistic, Populist, Prohibition or any other, shall have no place in the Conventions of the American Federation of Labor." [1, p. 79][1]

The Socialists, nevertheless, continued to harass the delegates at each succeeding convention until it was finally decided that a decisive test should be made upon the issue of politics versus trade unionism at the Boston Convention of 1903.

Ten resolutions of a political nature were introduced by the Socialists at Boston, and the ensuing debate lasted nearly two days. The ultimate result was a resounding defeat for the Socialists

---

1 Prior to this skirmish, the Socialists greatest success over Gompers was in 1889, when he almost campaigned for a seat in the New York Senate. The Republican Party nominated him and a fraction of the Democrats gave him their support. The Socialists, however, refused to support him on an old party ticket, and Gompers withdrew from the race.

and their program. Gompers, himself, took great delight in leading the attack against his old enemies in the Federation. He concluded his attack against them in the following words:

> I want to tell you, Socialist, that I have studied your philosophy; read your works upon economics, and not the meanest of them; studied your standard works, both in English and German-have not only read, but studied them. I have heard your orators and watched the work of your movement the world over. I have kept close watch upon your doctrines for thirty years; have been closely associated with many of you, and know how you think and what you propose. I know, too, what you have up your sleeve. And I want to say that I am entirely at variance with your philosophy. I declare it to you, I am not only at variance with your doctrines, but with your philosophy. Economically, you are unsound; socially, you are wrong; industrially, you are an impossibility. [4, p. 198]

Thus, while the AFL's non-partisan policy was developed as a result of Gomper's desire to dissociate the economic movement of labor from the political movement of Socialism, it had the practical effect of giving local labor leaders the opportunity of playing ball with the dominant political machines in their communities and allowing every head of an international union to endorse the political party he chose. Furthermore, the AFL did not rule out all types of political activity.

We have seen that the AFL's predecessor, the Federation of Organized Trade and Labor Unions, set up a legislative committee; and Gompers himself represented the AFL before Congressional hearings from 1886 onwards. Because of his hatred of Socialism and state interference, however, Gompers vehemently opposed any effort to secure from the state what the trade unions could obtain for themselves in the economic field. Thus, closely aligned with his non-partisan political philosophy, was Gomper's philosophy of "voluntarism". These two concepts were closely related and often confused, but basically they referred to two different things. Non-partisanism was the <u>method</u> favored by Gompers to implement the AFL's political program. The actual <u>content of the program</u>, however, stemed from Gompers' philosophy of "voluntarism" which relegated political activity to a minor role in comparison to the primary economic objectives of trade unionism.

It was assumed that the skilled craftsmen possessed sufficient strength to take care of themselves if allowed to exercise their economic power without restriction from public authorities. Therefore, most of the AFL's legislative demands were "negative" demands for the removal of governmental restraints on the freedom to organize, to strike, to picket, and to bargain collectively. Gompers maintained that the chief purpose of political action was to secure a climate favorable to economic organizations. Where economic power was ineffective, however, or where gains through collective bargaining were not very likely, such as with women, children, government employees, and seamen, the Federation modified its general anti-interventionist position on the functions of government. The Federation also favored immigration restriction on the grounds that unlimited immigration interfered with the labor market and undermined their inherent economic power. But the AFL still held that a full blown program of social reform legislation would weaken the need for trade unions. They felt that labor could expect only minimum benefits from the state, and feared that a government bureaucracy providing welfare services would curtain freedom, and weaken the workers allegiance to trade unions. At a less philosophical level, there probably was also the fact that even in the small labor movement of this period it was easier to get agreement in opposing a measure than it was to get agreement in proposing a positive action. And there was also the danger that if unions began proposing positive legislative measures, the Socialists might get in with some of their proposals and create a greater pressure for independent political action.

In support of its limited and largely negative program the AFL tried to impress Congressmen with announcements such as the following resolution from the 1899 convention: "Candidates of any party who openly declare themselves in favor of the AFL platform of laws shall be endorsed." [2, p. 107] Karson, however, notes: "Congress paid little attention to the Federation's legislative demands because the legislator's knew that in actuality the AFL leaders were undertaking no serious action that might conceivably swing labor votes to particular congressmen." [17, p. 21] Thus, a student at the turn of the century summed up the AFL's political position in these words:

> The position of the American Federation of Labor, as gathered from its records, is that, while rejecting the proposal of political action by the trade-unions, as fundamentally opposed to the proper purpose of these

> bodies, it favors discussion and action upon legislative lines. In other words, it seeks to secure favorable legislation from the existing legislative bodies without reference to their political make up, leaving to the individual trade unionist, in his capacity as a citizen, the duty of voting as his experience and judgment dictate. [21, p. 316]

1900-1930: Non-Partisanism Emergent

By surviving the depression from 1893 to 1896 the AFL managed to accomplish what no other national labor organization had done before. In 1897, trade unionism was confined almost entirely to the four independent railroad brotherhoods (the Locomotive Engineers, Railroad Conductors, Locomotive Firemen and Engineers, and Railroad Trainmen) and to the 58 national unions affiliated with the AFL. Between 1897 and 1904, however, trade union membership in the United States experienced its sharpest percentage increase in history. The membership of AFL affiliates increased from about 265,000 to approximately 1,676,000 persons, and the total trade union membership increased from 440,000 to 2,067,000. After this four fold increase, which was probably boosted by the spirit of reform which dominated the "muckraking era", unions membership stabilized at around two million between 1904 and 1907 in the face of a sharp employer counter offensive and "open shop" campaign. Despite this upsurge, however, it must be kept in mind that at no time during this period were more than 10% of the organizable workers enrolled in the ranks of the trade union movement.

It has frequently been charged that the outlook and activities of the AFL craft unions during this period were narrow, selfish, and disregardful of the far greater needs of the increasing masses of unskilled workers, whose interests had to be taken up by the radical activities of such organizations as the Industrial Workers of the World (the only labor group in U.S. history to completely renounce all forms of political action). There may be some justification for these charges, but it must be remembered that unions still existed in a hostile environment of open shop employers and injunction judges, and at least their organization could show success and growth whereas more "idealistic" groups had perished on the shoals of disunity and economic adversity.

Continuing to follow Gompers' leadership and spurning the establishment of a separate labor party, the AFL began to lobby formally in national politics in 1895. Two years later the Federation moved its headquarters to the national capital, and shortly thereafter its Executive Council began to lobby directly for its legislative measures. Until 1906, however, whatever political pressure the AFL had been able to generate was directed toward individual legislators and the party organizations. For practical purposes, it played no role designed to affect the outcome of elections, and the returns from its political efforts were very thin indeed. Organized labor was being prosecuted under the provisions of the Sherman Act, and the labor injunction was being employed with increasing frequency and more injurious effects. At the same time the Washington lobby of the NAM was emerging and enjoying real success in killing proposed labor legislation. More will be said on the political activities of the NAM in a subsequent chapter, but the AFL itself has stated:

> In 1902 the NAM caused the defeat of labor supported 8-hour and anti-injunction bills before congress. And in the 1904 elections the NAM scored signal successes in its efforts "to cut off labor's influence at the source" by defeating congressmen and senators favorable to labor. [6, p. 8]

In consequence of this political impotence, the AFL was spurred to undertake a broader and more energetic campaign of political action. This action was probably encouraged by the developing atmosphere of the progressive movement and the tempting success of the organization which later became the British Labor Party in the 1906 elections in Great Britain. In March, 1906 Labor's Bill of Grievances was formulated which demanded governmental action to effect a long list of reforms. This document is felt to be of sufficient importance to warrant its inclusion as Appendix A at the end of this thesis.

In addition to the removal of governmental interference under the anti-trust laws and through the injunction procedure, the Federation also sought immigration restrictions, regulation of convict labor, protective legislation for American seamen, and effective enforcement of the 8 hour day for employees on government contracts. When Congress ignored these requests, the Executive Council decided to participate actively in the 1906 Congressional campaign. The non-partisan policy was reaffirmed, but steps were now taken to make it more effective. A labor Representation Committee was designed to run the campaign, and some modest provisions were made to raise funds for it. Subsequently, this committee became the Nonpartisan Political Campaign Committee; and after 1906, there were active steps to defeat labor's enemies in the elections of 1908, 1910, and 1912. (Labor seemed to be more interested in defeating enemies than helping friends during these years.)

In 1908 and again in 1912 the Democratic Party adopted labor planks proposed by the AFL, and following Woodrow Wilson's election in 1912 some favorable labor bills were passed. The reform sentiment of the "progressive era" also reached its peak during these years, and the Socialists candidate, Eugene Debs polled 6% of the votes cast for President in 1912. Several states passed laws regulating the employment of women and children in industry. The first effective workmen's compensation laws were passed in several states, and Congress established the department of labor as a separate cabinet post in 1913. The previously mentioned Lloyd LaFollette Act was passed in 1912, and the Clayton Act was enacted in 1914. In 1915 Congress passed the Seaman's Act, regulating the employment conditions of American sailors; and in 1916 the Adamson Act established the 8-hour day on the railroads. With the outbreak of the First World War, labor's political influence continued strong as their cooperation was sought in furtherance of the war effort. With the end of the war this influence was greatly reduced. The courts stripped away the illusory gains of the Clayton Act, several major strikes were lost, and in the "return to normalcy" following the Republican triumph in 1920 labor was again placed on the defensive.

The general ferment in the immediate post-war period gave rise to a wave of labor parties despite the fact that a committee of the AFL executive council and department officers was set up to combat a third party trend. The response of the AFL chieftans was to wage the non-partisan campaign of 1920 a little more vigorously than usual, and the Federation also let its principles of voluntarism slip a little when it grudgingly committed itself to the nationalization of railroads, mines, and public utilities. Despite Federation efforts, however, some officials and rank and file members of AFL unions, state federations, and central labor unions played key roles in these independent political movements.

Henry David has stated that"when the first convention of the American Labor Party met in Chicago in July 1920, 15 state labor parties were already in existence. The national organization changed its name to the Farmer Labor Party of the U.S." [10, p. 100] In the presidential election of 1920 the Farmer Labor candidate, Parley P. Christensen, ran well behind the state parties which scored a number of congressional successes. Shortly afterward, the rival, Communist-controlled Federated Farmer Labor Party appeared; and in 1922 the independent railway unions, together with other segments of the labor movement which wanted vigorous political action but not an independent labor party, created the Conference for Progressive Political Action.

The Conference established local conferences, and their purpose was to work either through the primaries of the old political parties or to nominate independent congressional candidates, as each local conference might deem appropriate. While the AFL did not affiliate with this movement, some of its national unions and state organizations did. When this organization made possible Senator Robert LaFollette's presidential candidacy in 1924, the AFL reluctantly made its only official endorsement of a presidential candidate until it openly backed Adali Stevenson in 1952. The Federation's announcement, however, made clear that the AFL was not identifying itself with the other supporting groups nor committing itself to third party action. LaFollette made a creditable showing by polling over 16% of the popular votes, but the temporary unity among western progressives, industrial workers, and agrarians had collapsed. Of all the state labor parties that followed after 1919, only the Minnesota Farmer-Labor Party remained a significant political force, and it merged with the Democrats in 1944.

On the radical front during this period, socialists elements with a revolutionary orientation were seeking to win labor's support through the Worker's Party, which was fused out of several competing organizations in 1921-22. This group substantially became the Communist party of the U.S., and was the American section of the Communist International until the later was dissolved in 1943. The Communist Party then took the form of a political association. It resumed its existence as a party after the Second World War but has not participated directly in national elections, although it strongly supported Henry Wallace on the Progressive Ticket in 1948.

Following their reluctant and unsuccessful support of

LaFollette in 1924, a reaction set in within the AFL. Even after Gomper's death shortly after the 1924 elections, the AFL leadership continued to rely on his principles of voluntarism. William Green continued to share his predecessor's convictions regarding the limited role of government in labor-management relations, even though the industrial environment of the 1920's was quite different from the environment of the late 1890's when the principles were originally formed.

In the face of a steadily declining membership, the Nonpartisan Political Campaign Committee continued to issue its appeals, but they produced only varying responses. It is probably safe to say that until very recent years the actual involvement of the Federation's rank and file membership in political activity was extremely slight. Prior to the 1930's, political activity was only a very limited part of the Federation's program, and it revealed a fairly bi-partisan pattern based strictly on candidate's records rather than party labels.

The records of office holders had been kept by the Federation since 1896, and any official action the AFL took was solely on the basis of these records. On the national scene it found that the Democratic Party listened more attentively to its platform demands than the Republican Party, but the Federation still insisted on maintaining its independence. Whatever alliances the AFL chose to make with political parties were made at the local level. In normal Republican states, the labor organizations tended to be Republican.

In normal Democratic states they were Democratic. In order to improve trade union relationships with the police force in strike situations and where local ordinances and practices affected the crafts, such as in the building trades, local unions tried to develop working relationships with whatever political machines were dominant in the community. It is only recently that the ideological content has been provided for local political participation by trade unions. Thus, the director of the AFL's information and publicity service could write in 1924:

> The American Federation of Labor leaves to the organizations in each election district the matter of making the choice of candidates to be supported. It may assist in fighting for the defeat or election of individual candidates, but it will do so only in accord with the wishes of the unions in the district or State. [30, p. 741]

During the complicated period of the 1920's and 1930's, however, changing industrial conditions appeared to be rendering much of the AFL's traditional policy obsolete. Despite the proven merits of "voluntarism" when well-organized skilled workers faced a relatively small employer in a competitive market, it was a different story when labor was increasingly confronted by large integrated corporations which relied on mass production techniques and had millions of dollars at their command. Philip Taft has observed:

> These corporations did not depend upon injunctions to combat organized labor. Company-supported unions, private police, and extensive system of industrial espionage could undermine a union even more rapidly

> than an injunction. To oppose an employer with such instrumentalities at his command required greater resources than many unions could muster. [29, p. 640]

Outside the mass production industries employers also began to present problems that most unions could not meet by economic action alone when they began moving their plants into non-union areas and undercutting their organized competitors in the old union strongholds.

The reason that the AFL was so slow and even reluctant in adapting to these changing conditions, even in the face of declining membership, can probably best be explained by the fact that the Federation's policy was strongly influenced and almost dominated by the traditionally conservative building trades unions. Taft notes:

> Not being in the main employed in industries with large aggregations of capital, these unions felt they had nothing to gain from government intervention in economic matters. They still believed, in the late twenties, that the demand for protection against the issuance of injunctions in labor disputes was the essential item of a labor program. ... Such questions as unemployment insurance, old age security, and the limitations of the hours of labor by legislative enactment were opposed by the American Federation of Labor on the grounds that they would open the door to government control of economic life and, incidentally, of labor unions. [29, p. 637-38]

The continuing influence of the Railway unions and the enactment of the Railway Labor Act in 1926, proved a glaring exception to the general decline in union influence during the 1920's. The more active union interest in politics on the railroads can probably be explained by the fact that the government had begun to regulate rates and, directly and indirectly, labor relations. Regardless of philosophy, these unions could not afford to be indifferent to politics. Following the disastrous shop craft strike in 1922, the railroad unions sought positive aid from the government to protect their right to organize. They were instrumental in the LaFollette campaign of 1924, and there were certain factors which also worked in their favor as effective instruments in the political process after this movement to independent political action collapsed. First, like the AFL, they set rather limited political objectives for themselves; but unlike the Federation they were not adverse to government action if if would promote their immediate interest. Second, they were forunate in having the bulk of their membership concentrated in rural areas where their influence was magnified in the districts which are overrepresented in Congress. Finally, the mores within the railroad industry tended to solidify the railroad workers, and a union endorsement meant more than in most industries. In addition to their official organs the railroad men continue to sponsor a newspaper, _Labor_, which is mainly a political sheet.

Post-1930: Nonpartisanism Reshaped and Revitalized

In the face of the social ferment and political unrest following the stock market crash in 1929, organized labor was compelled once more to examine the old issue of the most appropriate form of political action. Several local labor parties were formed following unsuccessful strikes during the early thirties, but at this juncture neither the socialist or communist parties could seriously claim that they were genuine political instruments serving the mass of American workers. In spite of some scattered local voting strength, the Communist vote in the 1932 presidential election, with conditions more favorable to the party's appeal than ever before, barely topped 100,000 out of a total popular vote of almost 40 million. David notes:

> The Communist Party, in short, had failed to establish a significant political bridgehead in the camp of labor. It had, moreover, won the enmity of most trade unions as a result of its name, its programs, and its attempts to capture control of the labor movement through the tactics of boring within and dual unionism. [10, p. 102]

The AFL indirectly supported the election of Franklin D. Roosevelt in 1932, but the early change in the Federation's political activity during the New Deal came not in its non-partisan political policy of rewarding friends and punishing enemies but rather in its traditional voluntaristic attitude toward the role of government in enacting social and labor legislation. The philosophy of voluntarism had been evolved in an environment quite unlike that of the 1930's. With millions unemployed and hunger a frightening reality, it became increasingly less tenable to maintain suspicion of a government that provided social or welfare services. The old attitudes changed only slowly, however, and even then with much reluctance and internal opposition. Therefore, organized labor can not really be counted as a driving force behind much of the New Deal labor legislation.[1]

The AFL leaders did not give their initial blessing to the principle of the Wagner Act without a great deal of fear that it might open the door to subsequent government intervention in the internal affairs of unions. (A fear which was not unfounded in the light of subsequent events.) A decision was made to support the bill fully, however, but after the CIO split in 1938 the Federation became increasingly critical of the Acts administration by the NLRB. The Federation's position on protective legislation was even less clear cut. Traditional AFL attitudes proved to be strongly resilient even in the face of the tremendous downward pressures exerted on labor standards by the existence of mass unemployment.

As late as the 1936 convention, President Hutcheson of the powerful carpenters union, made the following classic anti-legislation speech.

> The labor movement is going far afield.... When it comes to private employers, I say, establish your wages and hours by negotiation and not by law.... What they can give us they can take from us. [5, p. 719]

The first indication of a changing attitude, however, came in 1932 when the executive council reversed its long maintained position

---

[1] The most authoritative study of this period concludes that with regard to the NIRA, the Wagner Act, the Social Security Act, and the FLSA, organized labor was a relatively unimportant source of pressure for policy changes, although they did support these measures with varying degrees of enthusiasm and effectiveness. Since 1939, however, unions have exhibited a growing interest and influence in these areas. See [11] especially chapters 5, 6, and 7.

For another study that also emphasizes organized labor's lack of influence in affecting New Deal labor policy, see [12].

and recommended that the AFL work for unemployment insurance laws. The AFL also supported the Black 30 hour bill as a "spread the work" measure when it passed the Senate in 1933. This Act was allowed to die in the House when the Administration submitted the NIRA as a more comprehensive recovery program. In his testimony prior to the enactment of the NIRA, President Green confined his remarks to the desirability of section 7(a) and did not comment on the code's provisions for minimum wages or maximum hours. The AFL also supported the Social Security Act on its passage in 1935, but it did not originate this legislation nor act as its strongest supporter.

From its inception the CIO was more favorable than the AFL to protective labor legislation. Although John L. Lewis expressed some reservations about general wage fixing by the government, other CIO leaders less influenced by traditional AFL thinking, did not view government legislation as a threat or rival for union member loyalty so much as they saw it as a supplement to union activity in protecting labor standards in unorganized areas. CIO leaders were also more prone to see unions as more than mere bargaining mechanisms, and they envisioned organized labor as an effective pressure group in the political arena.

The 1936 elections marked a watershed in the political activities of organized labor, and it also marked a significant shift in the political alignment of social and economic interests in the nation's political parties. At the national level at least the 1936 election reflected the economic revolution which the New Deal Fostered.

The attack made by the Republican candidate on the Social Security Act and its vigorous defense by the President and his supporters made the election somewhat of a referendum on the New Deal and its concept of the role of the Federal Government in the nation's economic life. Not many previous elections had been fought along such clearly drawn economic lines, and the traditional attempts of both parties to appeal to all economic classes was severely modified by the sharp clash between the "New Dealers" and the "Economic Royalists".[1]

In 1935 a number of AFL, CIO, and independent unions formed Labor's Nonpartisan League to formulate and direct political action for the 1936 campaign. In contrast to the 1932 policy of the AFL in endorsing the candidacy of Roosevelt by indirection, the League clearly devoted itself to Roosevelt's reelection and conducted a vigorous campaign on behalf of the Democratic ticket. Since President Roosevelt was clearly labor's "friend", this activity did not necessarily break with the old non partisan approach of rewarding

---

[1] Even in 1936, however, not all labor leaders supported Roosevelt. The Carpenter's President, William Hutchinson, not only retained his traditional position as the Chairman of the Republican Labor Division, but emitted such firey broadsides as the following:

> "[Labor opposes]... the subversive forces present in the Roosevelt administration in the person of Rex Tugwell, Richberg, Hopkins and his other soviet sympathizers and Red tinged advisors Frankfurter and Jerome Frank slinking in the background."
>
> "[It is]... against John L. Lewis and his Committee for Industrial Organization with its radical Brophies, Hillmans and Dublinskys who are pleading for labor to vote for President Roosevelt so Communism can overthrow the American form of government."

Quoted in [16].

friends and punish enemies. The intensity of labor's 1936 campaign in comparison with the AFL's previous efforts, however, clearly differentiated the 1936 campaign from any which preceded it. Whereas most previous labor endorsements were implicit and frequently unsupported by active participation, Labor's Nonpartisan League clearly and explicitly endorsed Roosevelt, and reported political expenditures by interstate labor organizations ran to over $770,000. This exceeded by eight times the sum raised by the AFL for political purposes during the previous <u>thirty years</u>. [23, pp. 56-57]

The 1936 presidential election also marked a major change in the nature and the distribution as well as in the amount of organized labor's political expenditure. Louise Overacker's figures indicate that the AFL had expended a little over $95,000 between 1906 and 1925, but in 1939, she stated:

> Since 1925 no political funds have been raised. Almost all of this money was contributed by affiliated unions and was expended for postage, leaflets, and the expenses of speakers. In no instance were the general funds of the AFL used for political purposes, nor is there any record of contributions to the campaign fund of a party or candidate. [23, p. 57]

While some of the affiliated national and local unions no doubt deviated from this AFL pattern before 1936, Miss Overacker's figures show that the entire three-quarters of a million dollars which organized labor reported spending in 1936 went to the Democratic party, and a substantial part to the national committee of that party. Thus, five percent of all funds received by the Democratic National Committee in 1936 came from labor organizations. The greater part of this money came from CIO unions (the Mine Workers alone contributed $469,800), but many AFL affiliates also contributed varying amounts.

Although Labor's Nonpartisan League was primarily dedicated to the reelection of Franklin D. Roosevelt, it planned to continue as a permanent organization in order to augment the politcal effectiveness of the nation's liberal forces. After the 1936 elections, however, discord within the ranks of labor became apparent. In 1938, William Green urged AFL members to withdraw from the League, charging that it was a CIO agency manipulated by CIO leaders seeking to create an independent third party. Even before this date, the League and the Nonpartisan Political Campaign Committee of the AFL were operating as rivals, quarreling over the terms of the federal wage and hour law, over nominations, and over endorsement of candidates.

The League continued to function without AFL support, but it was further weakened in 1940 when it again supported Roosevelt only to have John L. Lewis throw his support to the Republican Candidate Wendel Wilkie, and then resign as president of the CIO when the "labor vote" did not follow his lead.

During Roosevelt's second term real differences developed between the AFL and CIO over the administration of the Wagner Act, and the AFL was much less enthusiastic than the CIO in its support of the FLSA. Indeed, the 1937 convention reprimanded President Green for going as far as he did in supporting the administration's original proposal, which was changed in several ways before it finally passed in

1938. The hostile reaction to Roosevelt's court packing threat, and the increasingly hostile public reaction to the alleged abuses of a growing and divided labor movement resulted in a relatively conservative Congress being elected in 1938, and the period of New Deal labor legislation came to an end. The events of these years, however, were to have a lasting impact on the outlook of the American labor movement toward things political.

Philosophical considerations aside, the AFL's old concept of voluntarism had been developed out of the social and economic conditions of a period when the government was hostile or at best grudgingly tolerant toward the interests of organized labor. With a government unfavorable to labor it is not surprising that labor wanted to keep the role of the government to a minimum. Furthermore it was not very realistic to expect that a labor movement which included only one of every ten organizable workers could be a very decisive political force in the governmental process outside of certain geographical regions in which the membership was concentrated. The decentralized nature of state legislation and the relative immunity of the judiciary from electoral pressure further militated against any real political success. The social and economic conditions of the 1930's, however, were quite different from those of any other period in our country's history.

In the face of an unprecedented amount of unemployment, all but the most secure craft unionists began to lose faith in their own unaided economic strength, and the AFL was forced to modify its policy of voluntarism, if not abandon it completely. Furthermore, the growth of industrial unionism under the governmental support of the NIRA and the Wagner Act gave the American labor movement a veritable blood transfusion.

The challenge of the CIO resulted in a revival of the AFL in the race to organize new members, and both federations developed a political program that tended to differ from the traditional policy of voluntarism--the CIO by deliberate purpose, the AFL by dint of gradual pressure and more or less reluctance. The essential difference between the attitude of the AFL and that of the CIO towards social and labor legislation during the late thirties was chiefly one of degree, and may be attributed in part at least to the fact that the depression fell more heavily on the mass production workers who made up the bulk of the CIO than it did upon the more favored craftsmen who traditionally dominated the AFL.

Just as the New Deal itself was a typically American, experimental and non-philosophical reaction to the catastrophe of the Great Depression, so was the modification of organized labor's political program a pragmatic adjustment to drastically altered environmental circumstances--although the CIO was apparently willing to carry its non-voluntary principles to much greater lengths than the AFL.

With the remedial and reform measures of the New Deal, organized labor acquired a new stake in politics, wages, hours, jobs, relief, unemployment insurance, a broad social security program, the conditions of organization and collective bargaining--all these were now affected with varying degrees of decisiveness by government policy. And increasing experience with the governmental bodies administering these laws gradually broadened most union leader's conception of the labor movement's political goals.

The constitutional revolution which accompanied and even made possible the economic revolution of the New Deal, also meant that the most crucial decisions affecting labor's fate were now centralized at the national level of government--a fact which greatly facilitated the focusing of the increased political pressure which an expanding membership base made possible. The 1930's also revealed the necessity of increasing political activity at the lower levels of government. In its first report the LaFollette Committee on Violations of Free Speech and the Rights of Labor summarized instances and methods of employer - police cooperation in strike breaking, which only reaffirmed many union organizers' convictions that strikes were broken by the police or with their connivance in state after state and county after county. When the experiences with local officials were compared with the actions of the federal administration, it was not hard for unionists to conclude that they could get equal protection only by active participation in local elections.

The increasing amount of restrictive state labor legislation after 1939, also aroused a fear of losing many New Deal gains, and maintained labor's interest in the Democratic party even after John L. Lewis' rebellion.

Lewis' early leadership of the CIO had encouraged an unusual degree of political activity by that organization. It was widely held, and often feared, that he had personal political ambitions of his own. These rumors (if they were only rumors) certainly did nothing to discourage the lesser CIO leaders from taking an active part in politics. If another CIO president had frowned on political activity as time wasted from organizing, it is unlikely that either the interest in or the actual practice of politics would have been as deeply imbeded in the CIO as they were in the late 1930's. This argument becomes stronger when it is noted that there was a relative hiatus in CIO political activity between 1940 and 1943 following Lewis' resignation; but this might be explained equally well by the subservience of economic issues to the preoccupations with wartime conversion during this period, and the necessity of breaking in Philip Murray as the new CIO President.

Nevertheless, the Damocles sword of restrictive labor legislation which Congress dangled above unions from 1941 onwards prevented any real lapse in labor's political interests, and there can be little question that the direct incentive for the creation of the CIO's Political Action Committee was the Smith-Connally Act. Roosevelt vetoed the bill, but Congress passed it over his veto in June, 1943. The CIO executive board met in July of the same year to consider the effect of the law.

Fearing that its New Deal gains were in jeopardy, the CIO set up its Political Action Committee—known as the PAC. It was made separate from the CIO because the Smith-Connally Act had prohibited contributions by labor unions in federal elections.

In its early years the PAC became the center of a great deal of controversy and obtained a great deal of publicity for itself despite repeated statements such as the following from its chairman, Sidney Hillman:

> We are not interested in establishing a third party, for a third party would only serve to divide rather than to unite the forces of progress. We are not an appendage of either major political party. Nor, as has sometimes been charged, have we any desire or ambition to "capture" either party. ... Like every other organization concerned with the affairs of government, we seek to influence the thinking, the program and the choice of candidates of both parties. [14, pp. 238-39]

As long as Roosevelt was the Democratic standard bearer, however, there was little reason for breaking the alliance by which labor bound itself to specific Democratic candidates and policies without officially supporting the party itself. It is not surprising, therefore, that most of the PAC's energy was spent in support of Roosevelt and New Deal candidates. Most of this support, however, was devoted largely to publicity rather than to the precinct aspects of politics. Henry David has stated that the PAC and AFL labored openly and behind the scenes at the Chicago Democratic National Convention in 1944. They were both committed to Roosevelt for a fourth term and both fought the vice-presidential candidacy of James F. Byrnes, but the CIO favored Henry Wallace while the AFL championed Harry S. Truman. [10, p. 107]

After Roosevelt's death it appeared that there might be a change in the attitude of the trade union movement toward the Democratic Party. President Truman seemed unable to fire the imagination of the trade union membership, and he did not follow the policy of frequent consultations with labor leaders which had been characteristic of Roosevelt. The election of the Republican 80th Congress in 1946, however, had a profound effect upon the political program and political ideas of both the AFL and CIO. The enactment by the 80th Congress of the Taft-Hartley law proved to be a severe jolt to the labor leaders who concluded that their failure to be effective during the 1946 election was responsible for the Republican victory, and who feared that a filure to regain lost ground in 1948 would bring further punitive anti-labor legislation.[1] The overwhelming support which the Taft-Hartley Law found from Republican Congressmen also served to make it difficult for labor leaders to identify themselves with the Republican Party. The AFL became so alarmed that it established Labor's League for Political Education (LLPE) as its counterpart to the CIO's PAC. In 1948 both groups set out to punish the members of Congress who had voted for the Taft-Hartley Act. The CIO officially endorsed President Truman, while the AFL withheld official endorsement and gave instead financial and tacit organizational support to the national Democratic ticket.

---

1 For a critical discussion of the role of the PAC in the 1946 elections see [18].

The 1948 platform of the Democratic Party and the unexpected Truman victory that year served to forge anew the alliance between the Democratic Party and American labor at the national level, and the failure of the Progressive Party in 1948 once again revealed the continuing futility of third party political activities by any part of the American labor movement.

In 1952, the AFL and the CIO both endorsed the Democratic candidacy of Adlai Stevenson, but they apparently had little voice in the Democratic Convention which nominated him, since Stevenson was at best organized labor's third choice behind Averill Harriman and Estes Kefauver. Other than the LaFollette endorsement in 1924, this was the only time the AFL ever officially endorsed a presidential candidate. Stevenson's endorsement was repeated in 1956 by the newly merged AFL-CIO, and this combined organization also supported Democrat John F. Kennedy in 1960.

The AFL-CIO Merger and Contemporary Political Activity

The AFL-CIO merger in 1955 was widely hailed as a milestone in American labor history, and the political potential of a "unified" labor movement was one aspect of the merger that was widely discussed in the popular press. Subsequent events, however, seem to indicate that most of the concern voiced over organized labor's political "potential" was ill founded or at least that this potential has failed to materialize.

Two of the twelve "objects and principles" of the merged

AFL-CIO, which are contained in Article II of the organization's constitution are particularly relevant with regard to the federation's political activities. They are the fifth and the twelfth, which provide the foundation for the organization's lobbying and electioneering activities respectively.

The fifth of the "objects and principles" states that the federation is: "To secure legislation which will safeguard and promote the principle of free collective bargaining, the rights of workers, farmers and consumers, and the security and welfare of all the people and to oppose legislation inimical to these objectives." [15, p. 236]

While the breadth of this mandate appears to be a far cry from the narrow philosophy of "voluntarism" which produced Labor's Bill of Grievances nearly a half-century earlier, a comparison of the actual efforts devoted to specific legislative proposals is likely to reflect a change in labor's economic and political environment as much as a change in the philosophy of the labor movement. A statement which probably serves as the contemporary document most closely comparable to the earlier Bill of Grievances is the twenty-point resolution adopted by the AFL-CIO Executive Council at a meeting on January 5, 1961, just prior to President Kennedy's innaugration. This resolution was later published in the February, 1961, issue of the American Federationist as "Labor's Goals for a Better America", and is reproduced as Appendix B where it can be compared with the earlier Bill of Grievances in Appendix A.

The scope as well as the content of some of the 1961 proposals, which range from aid to depressed areas to national defense, seem to indicate that the older fear that government action would weaken the worker's loyalty to his union has been abandoned in favor of a view which sees the trade union movement not as a rival to the government in dispensing benefits but rather as an instrument through which greater pressure might be exerted on government to secure benefits not only for oganized labor but for all workers regardless of their affiliation. It is important to remember, however, that the federation differs considerably in the degree of militancy and the degree of cohesion with which it supports some of these proposals. Indeed, Arthur Goldberg has stated:

> "The importance of public policy to the labor movement does not militate against the fact that the first business of the labor movement is collective bargaining.... Within the total framework of public policy, the labor movement will naturally give emphasis to those aspects of public policy that have an intimate connection with the movement's collective bargaining position." [15, p. 216]

Furthermore, it should be remembered that both within and outside the federation many individual unions also have independent programs of their own which they support in different situations. Jack Barbash, for example, has argued that in addition to the ideological roots of unions and union leaders, much of the contemporary union concern with government is simply a practical necessity of running a union in a society in which government plays an increasingly important part in economic and social affairs. He has stated:

> The difference between unions with respect to the utilization of political action are differences only in degree and articulatiness. This is another way of saying

> (1) that no union can function in modern society without seeking in one way or another to influence government; (2) that some unions utilizing government do it as part of a systematic philosophy; others just do it as a matter of run-of-the-mill union activity. Although there are differences in temperment and technique and emphasis in utilizing government, there is little evidence of much difference in the substance of what the unions seek to get out of government. [7, p. 78]

Marjorie Thines Stanley has also argued that the nature of a union's political activity may be explained by the nature of the product market in which the union operates. For example, she argues that much of the support given to the Employment Act of 1946 by the United Automobile Worker's Union (generally accepted as one of the most politically active unions in the United States) can be explained by the fact that the demand for automobiles is income elastic, and Mrs. Stanley concludes:

> Much of the UAW's political action and tactics (and similar activity on the part of some other unions) can be regarded not as a basic change in the direction of a major part of the American labor movement, but as one method of furthering job security. It is not a particularly novel method, having long been used by certain craft unions on a local level. [Witness the building trades unions and local building codes] It is novel, however, in its application on a national basis. The extension of collective bargaining to the national political arena is an instance of the scope of union action paralleling the scope of the product market, with the political activity itself a logical concomitant of economic forces at work within and upon the imperfectly competetive auto industry. [28, p. 47]

The second of the merged AFL-CIO's "objects and principles" which is of concern to us here is the twelfth of those listed in article II of the constitution. It states that the federation seeks

While preserving the independence of the labor movement from political control, to encourage workers to register and vote, to exercise their full rights and responsibilities of citizenship, and to perform their rightful part in the political life of the local, state and national communities. [15, p. 237]

Just as the fifth of the "objects and principles" sought to spell out the nature of the federation's political objectives, so does the twelfth thus outline in part some of the ways in which the federation hopes to have their political objectives realized. As stated it differs little from the old approach of "reward your friends" and "punish your enemies". Yet this method of electoral participation--particularly as practiced since 1936--has served to distinguish the labor movement from many interest groups in the American political process, and it has apparently also served to attract a disproportionate amount of publicity to their efforts.

William Ricker has stated that "Most pressure groups are distinguishable from parties not only by smaller size but also by use of different tactics. While parties organize votes, pressure groups merely lobby and propagandize." [27, p. 8][1] By this definition, organized labor is clearly a pressure group which seeks to transcend itself to take on party functions. While it would be a mistake to assume that organized labor is the only interest group

---

1 Another distinction which Ricker does not mention is that parties also take a position on a much wider range of issues than do interest groups or pressure groups. As pointed out above, however, the number of issues on which organized labor (or at least the federation) now takes a stand has increased considerably, and in this respect they also seem to approach party activity more than most American interest groups. The exact implications of this trend are easy to misinterpret, however, and more attention will be devoted to the question of a labor party shortly.

which does this, the techniques they have employed in election campaigns, the fact that election campaigns are more exposed to the public view than most phases of the political process, and the fact that the candidates supported by organized labor have generally not been the candidates supported by the popular press all have served to give an unduly large amount of publicity to organized labor's non-lobbying political activities. Whether all this publicity has been warranted by the actual results of organized labor's political performance, however, is a question that can be answered only after a more detailed examination of organized labor's post World War II political performance.

Such an examination will be undertaken in Chapter V, after next turning to a historical review of management's political activities. Before reviewing management's historical experiments in political activity, however, it might be well to briefly summarize this chapter's review of labor's historical experiments in political activity.

Summary and Concluding Comments

After a period of relative quiescence in colonial and revolutionary times, American workingmen in the eastern cities began to agitate for the Workingmens Platform which focused on relatively broad social reforms such as universal male suffrage and public education rather than specific conditions of employment. This agitation eventually led to the establishment of the first labor parties in the world beginning with the Workingmen's Labor Party of

Philadelphia in 1828. Most of these early labor parties were local in character and soon disentegrated from internal dissention, loss of planks to the established parties, and other forms of trade union activity during periods of prosperity.

Although many workingmen's representatives rose to a position of some influence in the Democratic Party in many eastern states, and many of the planks of the Workingmen Platform were eventually adopted in these states, the first half of the nineteenth century continued to be characterized by the oscillation of workingmen's organizations between broad gauged political reform movements and more narrowly oriented trade union activity. These oscillations largely coincided with the business cycle. Most of the political agitation occured during times of depression or economic adversity, with various forms of cooperative movements and land reform being the main goals of this agitation towards the middle of the century.

Following the Civil War, the American labor scene was characterized by a dichotomy within the labor movement itself as to which course of action promised to be the most rewarding as a permanent long run program. Those favoring relatively limited forms of trade union activity by skilled workers strong enough to organize and protect themselves were opposed by the advocates of broad based political reform movements. This latter group included not only the radical and revolutionary diciples of European socialism, but also a new generation of native American leaders attracted to the humanitarian - reform philosophy of the earlier cooperative and land reform movements. A federal easy money policy was added to the reform panaceas of this latter group in the greenback movement of late 19th century America.

The experiences of the short-lived National Labor Union gave clear evidence of the basic incompatibility of these different ideologies, and after the distintegration of the "United Front" campaigns of 1886 and 1887, the radical socialists continued to argue among themselves, agitate within the AFL, and remain a tiny but vocal element on the American Labor scene. The reform elements within the Knights of Labor became associated with the Populist movement which swept the middle west, and the trade unions associated with the AFL under Samuel Gomper's leadership rose to ascendency on the American Labor scene.

Underlying the AFL's political program was a basic philosophy of "voluntarism" which held that skilled craftsmen possessed sufficient strength to care for themselves if allowed to exercise their economic power without interference from restrictive judicial doctrines and injunction judges. Where economic power was ineffective, however, or where gains through collective bargaining were not likely, such as with women, children, government employees, and seamen, the Federation modified its general anti-interventionist position, but Gompers still held that a full blown program of social reform legislation would weaken the need for trade unions.

In support of his largely "negative" demands for the removal of governmental restraints on the freedom to organize, to strike, to picket, and to bargain collectively, Samuel Gompers began to lobby before Congress in 1886, and he relied on a non-partisan political policy of rewarding friends and defeating enemies to gain support for his rather limited legislative program. As a practical matter, however, the AFL usually did little more than publish the labor records of incumbent office holders, and for the most part it played no other role designed to affect the outcome of elections. When coupled with the AFL's other cardinal principle of strict autonomy for affiliated unions, the non-partisan political principle left each union free to make whatever political alliances it deemed most profitable. On the national scene it found that the Democratic Party listened more attentively to its platform demands than the Republican Party, but the Federation still insisted on maintaining its independence. Whatever alliances the AFL chose to make with political parties were made at the local level. In normal Republican states, the labor organizations tended to be Republican. In normal Democratic states they were Democratic. In order to improve trade union relationships with the police force in strike situations and where local ordinances and practices affected the crafts, such as in the building trades, local unions tried to develop working relationships with whatever political machines were dominant in the community.

The most dramatic attempt to apply the non-partisan principle on a broad scale during the first three decades of the twentieth century was the publication of Labor's Bill of Grievance and the creation of the Nonpartisan Political Campaign Committee within the AFL in 1906. There was some relatively modest labor legislation enacted during Woodrow Wilson's administration, but organized labor's political influence waned rapidly after their cooperation was no longer sought in maintaining the national war effort. The AFL executive council later tried to combat the rash of third party political movements that broke out in the United States immediately following World War I, but in the depths of the doldrums of the nineteen twenties the AFL itself endorsed the third party candidacy of Robert M. LaFollette in 1924.

This latter act, as much as anything else, typified the impasse that confronted the AFL's traditional policies in the face of a changing industrial America. In response to the events of the 1930's, however, the vast bulk of the expanding American labor movement did not move further toward the time worn old nostrum of independent third party action. Rather, the AFL's traditional non-partisan approach and its underlying concept of voluntarism, were reshaped and revitalized in a pramatic response to rapidly changing environmental conditions.

The adjustment did not occur without a substantial internal struggle within the house of labor, however, and one of the ironies of history is that labor itself had a relatively small influence in enacting the most sweeping and most favorable labor legislation in American history. The grudging acceptance of such principles as unemployment compensation and wage and hour legislation reflected the still powerful influence of the more conservative craft unions within the AFL, and the principles of the Wagner Act were not even accepted without a great deal of reservation in some labor circles.

Regardless of labor's influence in its enactment, however, the labor legislation of the New Deal gave organized labor a new stake in politics. Indeed, much of their subsequent political activity can be explained in terms of: (1) trying to protect the labor policies of this unusual period in American history in an increasingly hostile environment, and (2) trying to expand and enlarge the basic provisions of the protective legislation of this period in a society that has come in general to accept a larger role for government in the economic life of the whole nation, including the labor movement.

Increasing experience with the governmental bodies administering national and state labor laws appears to have gradually broadened most union leader's conception of the labor movement's political role, but it is interesting to note that this chapter's review of history indicated that the major new departures in organized labor's (non-third party) electoral activity have come after rather pronounced legislative setbacks. Thus, the AFL's formation of its Non Partisan Political Campaign Committee followed the inattention paid to its Bill of Grievances in 1906. The formation of the CIO's Political Action Committee in 1943 occured within a month of the Congressional passage of the Smith-Connally Act, and the

AFL organized Labor's League for Political Education in direct response to the enactment of the Taft-Hartley Act. Both of these pieces of legislation, incidentally, were passed over a presidential veto.

The only exception to this pattern of increased electoral effort following legislative or lobbying setbacks appears to be the creation of Labor's Nonpartisan League for the 1936 elections. In this case, the motivation of this electoral innovation would appear to have been an effort to insure early New Deal gains rather than to protest legislative adversity. This apparent exception may be overemphasized, however, when it is recalled that organized labor, at least at the federation level, was not the prime mover in much of the pre-1936 legislation, and when it is recalled that the League was really less of an innovation than the other departures previously mentioned. The League entailed none of the structural changes and enjoyed none of the organizational permancy of the other endeavors. It can be argued that Labor's Nonpartisan League merely represented a tremendously more vigorous application of the program of the AFL's Non Partisan Political Campaign Committee, and its short lived effectiveness can be explained in terms of the previously mentioned leadership and ambition of John L. Lewis. The League quickly faded as a militant electoral factor following Lewis' falling out with FDR in 1940 and the organization apparently lacked the structural foundation to survive a loss of leadership.

Regardless of how the League's experience is interpreted, it is probably safe to say that increased electoral activity on the part of organized labor in the United States during the twentieth century has flowed from legislative defeat or the threat of defeat rather than from overwhelming victory leading to a thirst for even more legislative conquests. The League, however, did bind organized labor's political efforts to the national Democratic party in an unprecedented manner. For the first time really substantial sums of money were contributed to the National Democratic Committee by strong independent national unions. The elections of 1936 also marked somewhat of a watershed in American political history as far as economic matters in presidential elections are concerned. The bitterness of the clash between the "New Dealers" and the "Economic Royalists" severely modified the previous attempts of both parties to appeal to all economic classes, and the overwhelming support which the Taft-Hartley and Landrum-Griffin laws found from Republican congressmen and a Republican President who was instrumental in having the latter bill passed in its final form has subsequently made it increasingly difficult for labor leaders to identify themselves with the Republican party at the national level.

The rather sharp economic clevarage between the parties on labor matters since the 1936 Presidential elections has thus greatly reduced labor's maneuverability in rewarding friends and punishing enemies, but it is important to note that the upsurges in electoral activity following the major legislative reversals of the twentieth century have not developed into third party movements. Indeed, Albert Blum has observed that within the contemporary American labor movement "at least for the present, the once exciting debate over the formation of a labor party has come to an end." [8, p. 631] The fact that independent, partisan political action of either a farmer-labor or radical reform bent has failed to win the continued support of the American labor movement, however, is no measure of the influence that these ideas and parties have had an organized labor or on the American political process. Henry David has noted:

> They have helped to sharpen political awareness and to spur organized labor to political action; they have conditioned the drafting of labor's political programs; and finally, they have contributed to the splits and schisms that have marked the history of the labor movement. [10, p. 104]

Perhaps the main reasons for the failure of a labor party to develop in this country have been the relative lack of cohesion within the labor movement and the relatively non-ideological character of the major American parties and their willingness to adopt labor programs that appear to have any chance for success. Perhaps more fundamentally, the whole tenor of the American value system, with its emphasis on equality and individual achievement based on competition, and the formal structure of our federal-state system of government have just not been conducive to the development of a formally recognized, class-oriented party. Seymour Lipset has stated:

> Much of the unique character of the American labor movement, as contrasted to that of northwestern Europe, clearly may be seen as a derivative or as a consequence of the value system. The lack of social and political class consciousness, with the opposite emphasis on furthering the self interest of the individual (and of specific crafts, or industries, at the expense of other workers if necessary), is, as Schumpeter noted but the application in the realm of working class life and trade unions of the general value system. Thus, it has always been difficult to build unions or create explicitly class-conscious parties in the United States. Indeed, the union movement has rejected class ideology and urged itself upward as a better way to higher economic returns. [20, p. 82]

Earlier, Selig Perlman listed the "Basic Characteristics of the American Community" which led to the disintegration of class-based political reform movement in this country. He cited: (1) the strength of the institution of private property; (2) the lack of class consciousness in American labor, which he traced to "the absence, by and large, of a completely 'settled' wage earning class", "the free gift of the ballot which came to labor to labor at an early date" and to immigration which resulted in "the most hetrogenous laboring class in existence--ethnically, linguistically, religiously, and culturally", and (3) the inadequacy of the political instrument in a federal system "which has broken up the political sovereignty into forty-nine disjointed pieces, setting going an eternal jealously between the largest piece, Congress, and the remaining forty-eight. Furthermore, each of the forty-nine pieces has been divided into three members, two houses of the legislature and an independent executive, all of whom must agree in order to make a law", and run by established parties which "are capable, if need be, of a flexibility of one hundred and eighty per cent in their platforms, with extraordinary dexterity at 'stealing the thunder' of the new party." [25, pp. 155-176]

Although the New Deal "revolution" of the 1930's considerably altered the class alignment of the national political parties on most economic issues as well as the relative powers between the state and the national governments, many of Perlman's insights still help to explain the failure of any permanent labor party to develop in the United States.

There are also some rather practical considerations militating against an operational labor party in this country even if by some stretch of the imagination one should develop. Theodore Levitt, for example, has argued that a labor party would not only create polarized ideologies and unreal issues, but that it would present real problems of internal cohesion. A successful government requires that a multitude of interests be served, yet a pressure-group government (whether labor or otherwise) could not afford to initiate and pursue policies that would appear to its supporters as violating the immediate aims of the group it represented. Levitt feels that running government must be left to professional politicians who are free to compromise and balance conflicting interests. Specific groups may try to influence them, but no group will ever make all of the professional politicians its servants. On this assumption that democratic government requires compromise, he states: "The logic of statecraft and the very nature of Democratic government, at least in the United States, would predestine failure on the part of any partisan pressure group that managed to capture the reigns of government". [19, p. 617]

In the absence of formally-organized third party activity, however, the American labor movement has definitely committed itself to active campaign activity on behalf of "favorable" candidates. This now includes not only formal and informal endorsements, but also efforts to register, "educate", and "deliver" the "labor vote" in addition to making financial contributions from "voluntary" funds. After the elections are over, there is also continuing reliance on permanently established labor lobbies for influence at key points of political decision making. How successful all this effort has been in the post World War II period will be examined in more detail after reviewing American management's historical experiments in political activity.

REFERENCES - CHAPTER III

1. American Federation of Labor, Report of the Proceedings of the Fifteenth Annual Convention, 1895.

2. _______. Report of the Proceedings of the Nineteenth Annual Convention, 1899.

3. _______. Report of the Proceedings of the Twenty-First Annual Convention, 1901.

4. _______. Report of the Proceedings of the Twenty-Third Annual Convention, 1903.

5. _______. Report of the Proceedings of the Fifty-Sixth Annual Convention, 1936.

6. American Federation of Labor-Congress of Industrial Organizations, "Union Political Activity Spans 230 Years of U.S. History," American Federationist, May 1960, Vol. 67, pp. 6-11.

7. Jack Barbash, "Unions, Government, and Politics", Industrial and Labor Relations Review, October 1947, Vol. 1, pp. 66-79.

8. Albert A. Blum, "The Political Alternatives of Labor", Labor Law Journal, September 1959, Vol. 10, pp. 623-631.

9. John R. Commons and Associates, History of Labor in the United States (New York: Macmillan, 1936) Vol. II.

10. Henry David, "One Hundred Years of Labor in Politics" in Hardman and Neufeld (eds.) The House of Labor (New York: Prentice-Hall, 1951).

11. Milton Derber and Edwin Young, Labor and the New Deal (Madison: University of Wisconsin, 1957).

12. Grant N. Farr, Origins of Recent Labor Policy (Boulder: University of Colorado, 1959).

13. Nathan Fine, Labor and Farmer Parties in the United States 1828-1928 (New York: Russell and Russell, 1961).

14. Joseph Gaer, The First Round: The Story of the CIO Political Action Committee (New York: Duell, Sloan and Pearce, 1944).

15. Arthur J. Goldberg, AFL-CIO: Labor United (New York: McGraw-Hill, 1956).

16. Lewis Goldberg, Organized Labor and Politics as a Factor in the 1936 Election (New York: ILGWU, 1937).

17. Marc Karson, American Labor Unions and Politics (Carbondale: Southern Illinois University, 1958).

18. Herbert J. Lahne, "The Failure of the PAC in 1946", in Joseph Shister (ed.) Readings in Labor Economics (New York: Lippincott, 1951).

19. Theodore Levitt, "Dilemmas and Dangers in an American Labor Party", Labor Law Journal, September 1955, Vol. 6, pp. 613 ff.

20. Seymour M. Lipset, "Trade Unions and Social Structure" Industrial Relations, October 1956, Vol. 1, pp. 75-89.

21. W. Macarthur, "Political Action and Trade Unionism", The Annals of the American Academy of Political and Social Science, September 1904, Vol. 24, pp. 316-330.

22. Richard B. Morris, Government and Labor in Early America (New York: Columbia University, 1946).

23. Louise Overacker, "Labor's Political Contributions", Political Science Quarterly, March 1939, Vol. 54, pp. 56-58.

24. Selig Perlman, A History of Trade Unionism in the United States (New York: Macmillan, 1922).

25. Selig Perlman, A Theory of the Labor Movement (New York: Macmillan, 1928).

26. Joseph G. Rayback, A History of American Labor (New York: Macmillan, 1959).

27. William Ricker, "The CIO in Politics, 1936-1946" (Unpublished Ph.D. Thesis, Harvard University, 1948).

28. Marjorie Thines Stanley, "The Amalgamation of Collective Bargaining and Political Activity by the U.A.W.", Industrial and Labor Relations Review, October 1956, Vol. 10, pp. 40-47.

29. Philip Taft, "Labor's Changing Political Line", Journal of Political Economy, October 1937, Vol. XLV, pp. 634-650.

30. Chester M. Wright, "Labor in American Politics", Current History, August, 1924, Vol. 20, pp. 741-747.

CHAPTER IV

HISTORICAL EXPERIMENTS IN POLITICAL ACTIVITY: AMERICAN MANAGEMENT

Robert A. Dahl has stated "For all the talk and all the public curiosity about the relations between business and politics, there is a remarkable dearth of studies on the subject." [19, p. 1] This being the case it will be necessary to quote more extensively from the few existing studies in this chapter on management's political activities than was the case in the preceding chapter's review of organized labor's political activities, where it was possible to paraphrase the better known conclusions of several standard works in labor history.

Presumably it is common knowledge that, like organized labor, "business has always been in politics". Yet this "knowledge" doesn't help much in attempting to understand what form this political activity has taken on what issues and with what degree of intensity. Clarence E. Bonnett has observed "Business men have organized from time immemorial whenever they have believed they had a common interest which could be promoted by group action." [5, p. 1] Today there are literally thousands of organized business groups, and many are vitally concerned with the political process. Recourse to the institutions of government by these groups results both from their desire for help in furthering their aims, and from their closely related desire for protection from the activities of economic and political rivals. Indeed, E. Pendleton Herring has stated that the major reason for the concern of these business associations with government action has been, not the promotion of their own interests per se but the defense of their interests, both by fostering legislation or regulation to control the activities of their rivals and by fighting legislation or regulation that operates to the disadvantage of their members. [25, p. 101]

"Businessmen" are a heterogeneous lot and their political interests range over a variety of activities such as tariffs, taxation, government procurement, and government regulation and antitrust action in addition to labor relations, and "business" groups can be found on opposite sides of many political issues such as reciprocal trade legislation or farm subsidies. While differences of interest among business groups are commonplace, however, it is nevertheless true that as "employers" businessmen and managers are capable of maintaining a relatively solid front on many basic issues of labor relations. Indeed it is often common to distinguish between different types of business groups with the term "trade association" used to designate an organization that deals with market relationships and trade practices, while for the term "employers' association" Clarence E. Bonnett offers the following definition:

> An employers' association is a group which is composed of or fostered and controlled by employers and seeks to promote the employers' interests in labor matters. [4, p. 509]

Thus defined, employers' associations are not particularly

modern organizations; and, as the following quotation shows, they have long been engaged in political activities.

> A stone tablet which has been unearthed among the ruins of ancient Sardis shows not only that employers' associations existed in the building trades of that day but that they appealed to governmental authorities to restrain certain practices by the workmen. The craft guild of the Middle Ages ordinarily functioned as an employers' association not wholly unlike associations of master craftsmen in the building trades of our own times. In the United States the craft guild functioned as an employers' association in the colonies of Massachusetts, New York and Pennsylvania. Thus an association was formed to resist the demands of the ship carpenter sailors. The early conspiracy cases against labor organizations were instituted by the associations of master cordwainers, master carpenters, master tailors, master hatters and so on... As early as 1880 a National Labor League was formed in Pittsburgh for the purpose of building up workingmen's organizations "to put an end to strikes", and employers were also advised to use the labor injunction. [4, pp. 509-510]

Not all business political activity has been on an association basis, however, and like individual unions and labor leaders, several companies or individual businessmen have their own political contacts. Charles P. Taft, the former Mayor of Cincinnati, has stated:

> Companies of any size have a trouble shooter, part or full time, who knows his way around in politics. He may also be the one who decides what campaign contribution is made to what politician by what officer—from his personal salary, of course. [45, p. 10]

Although both labor and management thus take an active role in political affairs, their techniques and tactics may differ. Not having the membership base nor desiring the publicity of the unions' often noisy electoral activities, most businessmen confine themselves to different forms of campaign participation—usually financial contributions or institutional advertising campaigns on selected issues. Like organized labor, however, there is usually a strong legislative lobby representing various business interests at all branches of the political process. More will be said on both organized labor and management lobbying activity later. For the present, a brief mention of the two most common forms of business campaign activity will be discussed, and the history of some of the major management political organizations will be traced.

With regard to financial contributions, Alexander Heard's detailed analysis of campaign spending in the 1952 and 1956 national elections found:

> An examination of the several types of selected organizations, in fact, indicates that only among business interests were high proportions of the officials studied found to have made contributions. Even among them, however, the proportion giving varies sharply from one organization to another. Organization policy toward this type of political action by its officials, the current intimacy of the group's concern with governmental decisions, differences in personal affluence and predisposition, and similar factors account for these differences. It is abundantly clear, nevertheless, that political contributing in large sums is an important form of participation by some classes of businessmen. The officials of organizations whose members have a visible and continuing stake in government policy and action—like members of the American Petroleum Institute and the National Association of Manufacturers—habitually engage in this form of political action. The incomplete data indicate that in two successive presidential election years upwards of one-fourth of the individuals in leadership positions in certain trade associations made at least one campaign gift of at least $500. This is a _characteristic_ form of political expression for such individuals and the groups of which they are a part. [24, pp. 99-103]

At the level of individual corporations a survey of 2,700 of the country's top executives made for the _Harvard Business Review_, by Dan H. Fenn, Jr., found that 32% of them reported making campaign contributions but not otherwise working in political activities, whereas

22% reported that they gave money and also worked in other ways and 3% said they worked but did not give money. [21]

Such political activity by corporation officials inevitably produced suspicion that company money is used for partisan purposes, particularly since one board chairman has publically stated that "A lot of corporation presidents just reach in the till and get $25,000 to contribute to political campaigns—just as labor unions do." [35, p. 238] More will be said on the politics of campaign contributions later, until then it might be best to reserve judgment on the political effectiveness of large financial contributions, since V. O. Key has observed that the "semicontractual" theory of contributions thrives on a dearth of evidence and the projective tendencies of most observers. He stated:

> Most speculation in this vein has been by professors and newspaper reporters, persons to whom $25 is a wad of money, and it is doubtful that they achieve a sophisticated comprehension of the motivation, attitudes, and expectations of persons who can blithely throw $5,000 in the pot to help elect old Joe, a college classmate, a drinking companion, and a fellow Rotarian, without being any the poorer. [27, pp. 470-71]

With regard to institutional advertising, Richard W. Gable has stated: "The public relations and propaganda programs of the NAM are the most intensive, comprehensive, and expensive means by which it attempts to influence the formation of public policy. [22, p. 262] It is known that private corporations also engage in this type of "indirect" lobbying to cultivate public opinion.

Fenn's survey found that 21.5% of the 2,700 executives questioned said that their companies took a stand on issues like "right to work" laws. [21, p. 8] In 1956 the Democratic majority of the Senate Privileges and Elections Subcommittee said there had been numerous instances of institutional advertising "either clearly political in nature or with definite political implications", and asked the Justice Department to investigate several specific cases. [16, p. 202] And, in 1950, the House Select Committee on Lobbying Activities under the Chairmanship of Frank Buchanan (D., Pennsylvania) sent a questionnaire letter to 173 business corporations requesting them to report on a voluntary basis details as to expenditures relating to attempts to influence legislation, directly and indirectly during the period from January 1, 1947, to May 31, 1950. With regard to institutional advertising "dealing with public issues having legislative significance" just 31 corporations reported expenditures of $2,013,370. [26, p. 183 and p. 250]

While the devices of individual campaign contributions and institutional advertising are thus two techniques of political influence that seem particularly well adapted to and widely used by the American business community, it is also well to recall the earlier observation that many companies and employers have a long history of associated as well as individual activity on labor matters. A brief review of some of the major employer organizations and activities designed to influence national labor policy will illustrate how some of these efforts have evolved over time.

The National Association Of Manufacturers

Any individual, firm, or corporation engaged in manufacturing in the United States, whose application is approved by the board of directors, may become an active member of the National Association of Manufacturers. "In practice", Gable has noted, "membership has been restricted almost to firms and corporations." [22, p. 257] Although the organization does not release membership lists even to those who pay dues, the Congressional Quarterly estimates that the NAM today speaks for 20,300 business firms. [18, p. 954] This represents less than 10% of the manufacturing enterprises in the United States, but the Association tends to be dominated by the spokesmen for some of the largest firms in the country in terms of size, output, wealth, and number of employees. [14, pp. 364-65]

The NAM was originally founded on January 24, 1895 to promote American commerce, particularly international trade.[1] But David Truman has noted "The NAM did not become a particularly significant group until it also became involved in labor questions in 1903. The change in emphasis and the subsequent growth of the organization almost justify the assertion that 1903 marked the beginning of a new association." [48, p. 81]

As a result of the upsurge of trade union membership after 1896, a number of local and state-wide associations of employers began in 1900 to develop and execute vigorous drives for the open shop, which was in a sense a symbol for insistence upon the unrestricted discretion of employers in establishing the conditions of employment in their plants. General leadership of this movement on a national scale was

---

1 For some of the personalities behind the formation of the NAM, see [2].

assumed by the NAM at its 1903 convention under the leadership of its president David M. Parry. President Parry's report to the convention noted:

> It is true that the fight against organized labor is, in a measure, a departure from our former conservative policy respecting labor, but it is an inevitable departure if the Association hopes to continue to fill the full measure of its possible usefulness to the manufacturers and people of the country. [36, p. 16]

Accordingly, the remainder of Parry's report was a strong indictment of the practices of labor unions which he felt were un-American in their "unwarrantable usurpation of rights and the disastrous industrial policy which characterizes them in their present associated capacity". [36, p. 17] He described the losses of the anthracite strike of the previous year as "enforced tribute exacted from the consumers of the country for the cause of organized labor", [36, p. 27] and the AFL was singled out for special mention as "the source whence proceeds such noxious emanations as the eight hour and anti-conspiracy bills. It is also the fountainhead of inspiration which breeds boycotters, picketers, and Socialists". [36, p. 50] Parry called for the formation of employers association in all centers of industry to be united under one national employers council so that the "un-American institution of trades unionism" could be pulled up "root and branch". [36, p. 59]

Parry's report was printed and circulated at the convention, but it was not read to the assembly. The business session of the meeting, however, was highlighted by a paper read by John B. Kirby, Jr. of Dayton, Ohio, who later became president of the NAM. Kirby denounced labor unions even more vigorously, if that were possible, than had Parry.

Parry continued to agitate for his program, however, and although its primary membership included only individual firms the NAM set up a series of satellite, though nominally independent, groups made up of employer associations concerned with labor matters to facilitate its activities in labor relations. To coordinate these activities, the Citizens Industrial Association of America was formed in Chicago on October 29, 1903, and Parry himself was elected president of the new group. The C.I.A.A. was succeeded in 1907 by the National Council of Industrial Defense (later called the National Industrial Council). This organization "sought then to unify the action of national and local associations on matters relating to industrial legislation both national and state". [3, pp. 374-75] The NAM was also instrumental in organizing the United States Chamber of Commerce in 1912 (to be discussed later in this chapter), but it later resigned from this organization in 1922. The National Industrial Conference Board was created in 1916 to supply research data to all of these groups.

The shift in the orientation of the NAM from international trade to labor problems occurred at the same time that the AFL was formulating labor's "Bill of Grievances". Both sides soon became more deeply embroiled in the political process, and in these early days the NAM was much more apt to engage directly in campaign activity than it has been in more recent years. Richard Gable has stated:

> The NAM openly and vigorously entered the political arena in 1906. Between that date and 1912 practically all public officials who won the enmity of the AFL were supported and all public officials noted for their support of labor measures were opposed. A reprint of the "white list" of the AFL was used as a "blacklist" by the NAM...

> In the 1906 and 1908 elections agents of the NAM personally went into certain Congressional districts and took part in the campaigns. In support of certain candiates "protective associations" made up of workingmen were formed and then dissolved after the election...
> The Association no longer publically endorses or condemns candidates for Congress by name or actively participates in election campaigns. However, before the 1946 elections the voting records of members of Congress were published for the "information" of NAM members. [22, p. 266]

Not only was the NAM originally active at the Congressional level of national politics, Clarence Bonnett has noted "the Association took more than ordinary interest in the appointment of the judges of the Supreme Court of the United States; in fact, it gives the highest endorsement to the appointments by President Taft of Charles E. Hughes and Horace H. Lurton." [3, pp. 329-30] He also states "In 1906 [Theodore] Roosevelt was endorsed in the very highest terms, but later condemned as a dangerous demagogue." [3, p. 330] The NAM took a very active part in the 1908 presidential campaign, first in the Republican Convention and then out on the hustings. The Association's president James W. Van Cleve, whose company was later involved in the famous Bucks Stove case, is quoted as having said, among other things, "The result of the convention has made it the duty of the employing interests regardless of party to bury Bryan and Bryanism under such an avalanche of votes that the work will not have to be done over again in 1912." [3, p. 327] Indeed, Bonnett has indicated that some of the NAM's early literature, though not always consistent, may even have toyed with the idea of an "NAM Party". He stated:

> Its leaders have solicited members to break party lines, to forget party affiliations, yet at times have advocated the formation of a new political party based on the principles of

> the Association. They, however, decided that the undertaking was too great for the time being, and after the Republican Party, apparently frightened by this threat, had adopted a "sane" platform and nominated a "safe" candidate for president in 1912, they satisfied themselves by making a severe condemnation of the Democratic and Progressive parties, and an unqualified endorsement of the Republican Party platform and candidates. [3, pp. 331-32]

The NAM toned down many of its political activities following an investigation of its lobbying practices in opposition to the Underwood tariff bill in 1913.[1] It was revealed that the chief page of the House of Representatives and the confidential secretary of Congressman James T. McDermott were in the employ of the NAM. The House Select Committee, which conducted the investigation, registered its "severest censure" upon all persons connected with this arrangement. The action was characterized as "a violation of all the proprieties". McDermott was declared guilty of "acts of grave impropriety, unbecoming the dignity of the distinguished position he occupied" when it was found that he had supplied a room in the basement of the Capitol where NAM representatives could meet in secret with the chief page, and also permitted the Association to use his franking privilege. What made these revelations particularly inconderous was the fact that McDermott was a "Congressman from the stockyards district of Chicago, a member of a labor union, and elected through labor's support." [46, p. 114]

Despite this "exposure", the NAM continued to retain its interest in governmental affairs in general and labor relations in particular; and in 1914, the Association adopted a resolution to support

---

1 See [25, pp. 43-46].

its friends and oppose its enemies for public office. As mentioned previously, however, the NAM has always relied most heavily on its "educational" or propaganda programs. This has been true despite a fairly significant shift in the composition of the membership during the ferment of the 1930's.

Clarence E. Bonnett has noted that following the sharp turn in NAM policy toward unions after the 1903 convention, "The loss of conciliatory members was more than offset by the addition of belligerent members—the Association is said to have doubled its membership in a year. [3, p. 302] The NAM continued to expand during the second decade of the century, fluctuating somewhat with shifts in the business cycle and the aggressiveness of labor unions. During the post World War I decade, however, the organization did not grow appreciably. After 1926 its financial position declined, and its memberships soon followed. By 1933 the number of members had dropped about 75 per cent from the peak of 5,350 established in 1922. [39, p. 165]

David Truman has stated:

> The reasons for this shift are of particular interest. In the first place, the active membership—and presumably the entire roll, though this cannot be ascertained, since the organization does not release membership lists even to those who pay dues—was limited almost entirely to relatively small firms. The officials represented only those firms presumably not large enough alone to oppose the union organizations as they were then constituted. For the big, mass-production industries, especially those that developed after World War I, were, as we have seen, beyond the grasp of organized labor in the 1920's. Neither the possibility that their workers would become organized nor the threat of labor activity through legislation was enough to bring these corporations into an organization like the NAM. Consequently, when the depression hit in 1929 and a number of the small firm members withdrew for reasons of economy, the association

suffered acutely.

This situation was dramatically altered after 1933. With the upturn in labor union membership and the organization after 1935 of the mass production workers along industrial lines, and with the passage of national legislation favorable to labor consequent upon a shift in the relative influence of major political groups, the association began again to grow. The new recruits, moreover, included increasing numbers of large corporations in automobile and electrical goods manufacture, chemical products, and similar industries. The "independence" that these firms had easily maintained in the 1920's had been sufficiently threatened to bring them into the fold, and they led in building the membership, especially after passage of the National Labor Relations Act of 1935, up to a claimed sixteen thousand in 1948. The entire association was reorganized in 1933, and since then it has been led primarily by representatives of "big business". Its political activities, moreover, have shown no diminution, but rather a considerable increase. [48, pp. 83-84]

With regard to the NAM's publicity campaigns Richard Gable has stated:

The NAM's public relations and propaganda programs can be classified according to the audience as external, indirect, and internal. The audience of the external appeal is the general public. The indirect approach covers educators, churchmen, women's club leaders, agricultural leaders, and similar community leaders who in turn mold specific publics. Internal programs are directed at state and local associations affiliated through the National Industrial Council as well as the NAM membership. Their purpose is to induce and assist members and affiliates to conduct community public relations programs using manuals and materials supplied by the Association.

To reach these audiences the NAM avails itself of almost every media and channel of communications: house publications, newspapers and magazines, the public platform, billboards, radio, television, and film. The country is blanketed with literature that ranges from the handsome brochure to the gaudy comic book. Sometimes the NAM has failed to identify the materials as coming from the Association. In some cases it has arranged for the sponsorship of its literature by another group to hide the NAM's authorship, because the NAM felt that material issued over its by-line "is naturally discounted"...

The themes and trends of the Association's public relations and propaganda campaigns have reflected changes on the political and economic scene. Both open shop drives (1903-1913; 1919-1926) on the public relations side were

> consciously organized efforts directed specifically against the rising tide of unionism. The Industrial Conservation Movement (1913-1919) vowed the broader purpose of giving the American people a better understanding of their responsibility to industry and of the relevance of industrial prosperity to their welfare. This movement was in response to the social legislation of Woodrow Wilson's administration, and the improved position of labor resulting from the advances made during World War I under the leadership of the AFL.
>
> A new campaign was launched in 1933. The capitalist system had to be acquitted of any blame for the depression. The "cultivation of public understanding" was the strategic solution NAM proposed to cure the economic ills of the day. At the same time an extensive effort to inform the country about the disadvantages of the National Labor Relations bill became a tactical public relations objective. After its passage, the evils of labor unions and the NLRB became the focus of the Association's programs. [22, pp. 262-64][1]

During the mid 1930's, the NAM was joined in its publicity campaign by the American Liberty League, which was founded by several prominent industrialists from the Du Pont and General Motors organizations. Neither organization met with much success, however, and the Liberty League quietly faded from the scene following FDR's reelection in 1936. [40][2]

Following World War II, with the scent of a changing political tide in the air, the NAM attempted to reshape its program from one of "defensive public relations" to a more "positive" approach. The President, Ira Mosher, announced to the membership that a decision had been made to

> project industrial management into a hard-hitting, constructive force—transforming management from its traditional

---

1 For a fairly detailed accounting of the opposition to the Wagner Act and the NLRB by the NAM and other employer groups see [31, pp. 281-91].

2 For a brief discussion of the League's National Lawyers Committee and its attack on the Wagner Act also see [50, pp. 24-5] and [31, p. 295].

> defensive position of continuously answering the allegations of the collectivists... Henceforward, NAM's representation of management will be at its proper station--on the offense --with a direct, positive, constructive approach to every problem that arises. [39, p. 165]

How much the NAM's underlying policy on labor issues changed during this alternation in its publicity program, however, is a matter of some conjecture. In 1903 the NAM put forth its "Declaration of Labor Principles". This manifesto expressed opposition not to organizations of labor as such, but to "boycotts, blacklists, and other illegal acts of interference with the personal liberty of employer or employee... Employers must be free to employ their work people at wages mutually satisfactory, without interference or dictation on the part of individuals or organizations not directly parties to such contracts." The next year NAM added a plank expressing its "unalterable antagonism to the closed shop", and with minor changes this stood as the Association's labor platform until what it regarded as its historic labor statement of 1946.[1]

---

[1] For a detailed discussion of the evolution of the NAM's labor policies before 1928, as well as a description of the Association's internal policy making apparatus see [46].

> With regard to the NAM's policies on: "(1) the abstract right of labor to organize, without resorting to either militant action or collective bargaining; (2) the maintenance of the open shop", Taylor states:
>
> "The Association does not object to collective bargaining carried on with organizations similar to company unions or shop committees. It objects strenuously, however, to collective bargaining with trade unions. If one considers, therefore, that the Association not only denounces some of the important practices of unionism which have been generally considered legal by the courts, and also denies to it the exercise of the prime function of collective bargaining, it will

(continued on following page)

In 1946, the NAM's Industrial Relations Program Committee, under the chairmanship of Clarence B. Randall of Inland Steel, submitted a report on "The Basic Principles Behind Good Employee Relations and Sound Collective Bargaining". This report was approved by the Board of Directors on December 3, 1946. As the title implied, this document recognized collective bargaining with independent unions to a far greater extent than any preceding NAM pronouncement, and it stated, "When the collective bargaining relationship has been established, both employers and employees, quite aside from their legal obligations and rights, should work sincerely to make such bargaining effective". The 1946 statement, however held firm in the NAM's historic opposition to union security clauses in these words:

> No employee or prospective employee should be required to join or refrain from joining a union, or to maintain or withdraw his membership in a union, as a condition of employment. Compulsory union membership and interference with voluntary union membership

---

(Footnote 1 continued from preceding page.)

> be apparent that the assertion of the abstract right to organize is without significance...
>
> "Moreover, the 'open shop' as advocated by the National Association of Manufacturers means either frankly or implicitly an anti-union shop." [46, pp. 162-63]

both should be prohibited by law. [14, pp. 369-71][1]

Since yellow dog contracts and employer interference with union organization were already outlawed by the Norris La Guardia Act and the Wagner Act, the last sentence quoted above clearly called for new legislation only in the area of outlawing compulsory union membership. The NAM now had apparently accepted the principle of government participation in labor relations as a means of preserving its traditional values and interests. Gable has stated:

---

1 With regard to the 1946 pronouncement, Fortune reported:

"In its desire to see some changes made in the federal labor laws, NAM was surely on the side of the angels, or at least the majority of the voting public of the U.S. This was a good opportunity for the association to fatten its account in the bank of public opinion, but from all reports it was almost funked. As the time for the 1946 annual meeting drew near, a movement was started to draw up a formal, positive NAM platform on labor, the first statement of its kind since the hallowed pronouncement of 1903. But the progressives struck a snag. 'Let's be honest,' said the tories—and it's hard not to admire them for it—'We don't like the Wagner Act and would like to throw it to hell and gone out the window, so why not say what we think, and fight it with everything we've got.' To which the progressives replied, 'We've got to go along with the times, and take the kind of stand that has a reasonable chance of being enacted into law.' In the resultant compromise the progressives emerged with the lond end of the stick, and the platform beginning, 'The right of employees to join or not to join a union should be protected by law,' reached a new high in NAM statesmanship. NAM considers the Taft-Hartley law 'a step in the right direction,' but it favors the prohibition by law of industry-wide bargaining." [39, p. 168]

> The symbol of free enterprise was used to sell labor policies that advocated increased government intervention in industrial relations...
> The Association's attempt to disprove the validity of labor's right to organize and bargain collectively was replaced by limited approval. Attention was then directed to injustices that resulted from a law which guaranteed these rights. The injustices were characterized as violative of the rights of employees' and employers' and destructive of the welfare of society. The solution was to modify the Wagner Act along lines proposed by the Association...
> In 1947 the public relations program was expanded to proportions that surpassed any previous year. [22, pp. 264-65]

In 1947, the year the Taft-Hartley Act was enacted, Fortune reported:

> NAM disbursed $2,258,865 on its public-relations program, which is just about one-half the money that NAM gets and spends in a year. In the past NAM has had two main sources of revenue--its dues, and its voluntary contributions to the public-relations program. Beginning in 1948, dues and contributions were merged into a single schedule. [39, p. 166]

As this quotation indicates, much of the money spent on the 1947 Taft-Hartley campaign was solicited through the NAM's National Industrial Information Committee for the Association's public relations program. In December, 1947, the board of directors voted to discontinue the National Industrial Information Committee. Since then the NAM has collected enough under its revised dues schedule to support all its activities, including public relations. Having abolished the NIIC, the NAM was able to report to the Clerk of the House as required by the Federal Regulation of Lobbying Act of 1946: "The NAM does not 'solicit, collect, or receive' any money for the purpose of influencing legislation." [22, p. 263] More information on the NAM's unsuccessful attempts to have the Lobbying Act declared unconstitutional is contained in Appendix C, which will be discussed later. Although the Association has had its representatives register under the law, the NAM has never reported any lobbying expenditures under the Act's provisions.

During the Congressional debate on the Taft-Hartley proposal several Congressmen charged that the NAM wrote the bill. The NAM thought enough of these charges to issue a mimeographed denial, and in this connection, Gable notes:

> In spite of the remarkable similarity between NAM proposals and the Taft-Hartley Act, the decision in Congress involved adjustment and compromise among the divergent demands of various interest groups that streamed toward Congress. The voice of the NAM was not the only one heard, because conflicting claims upon government are always numerous. The NAM's success lay in its ability to identify its special interests with these various intersts that flowed toward Congress. Actually, the real influence the NAM exerted over the preparation of the Taft-Hartley Act resulted, not so much from direct pressure upon Congress, but from accepting the concept of government intervention in employee relations and from engaging in the most extensive public relations campaign in its history to secure approval for specific proposals within this general frame of reference. The NAM was confident that its public relations programs were responsible for the enactment of the law. [22, p. 272]

Following the Taft-Hartley battle, the NAM continued its campaign to outlaw all types of union security provisions and to eliminate industry-wide collective bargaining. After the revelations of the McClellan Committee and the defeat of the Kennedy-Ives bill in 1958, the Association issued a pamphlet Labor Law Reform, which included six objectives:

> ...The restoration of basic power and authority over their affairs to the members of labor organizations, where it

> rightfully belongs but where today it rests only in theory...
> ...The restoration and protection of the right of each individual to decide for himself whether or not he wishes to join a labor organization and a ban on making membership or non-membership in a labor organization a condition of employment in any industry or activity.
> ...A prohibition against organizational picketing to force recognition of a union and against violence, coercion, boycotts and all other forms of activity designed to force individuals to join unions.
> ...A restoration by act of Congress of the right of state authorities to act in labor-management matters properly within their jurisdiction...
> ...A prohibition against nationwide or industrywide union monopolistic practices whereby collective bargaining is dominated by national or international unions without regard to the situation at the local level...
> ...An effective ban on the use of union funds and union staff manpower for political activities in behalf of particular parties or candidates, even though such activities may be disguised as "political education", "citizenship education" or under some similar high-sounding label...

Not all of these objectives were included in the Landrum-Griffin Law of 1959 but in reporting the NAM's legislative results in 1959 Congressional Quarterly stated:

> The NAM said "industry's legislative program fared extraordinarily well during the First Session of the 86th Congress." It praised the labor bill and hailed the refusal of Congress to heed "multi-billion dollar spending demands from New Dealers." The NAM attributed "the favorable outcome" of the 1959 Session to "an irresistible upsurge of public opinion against wasteful Government spending and against union corruption; the sharp upturn in business conditions, which completely deflated the New Deal contention that big Government spending was imperative to lift the economy out of a recession; President Eisenhower's veto power." But the NAM cautioned its members: "Failure to pass many measures opposed by industry may be but a reprieve until next year..." [17, p. 674]

Before attempting to assess the overall political influence of the NAM we will examine the political activities of other business groups and corporations.

The Chamber Of Commerce Of The United States

The second of the major national business federations, the Chamber of Commerce of the United States, has a much more complex membership structure than does the NAM. Basicially, however, the Chamber is a federation of Chambers of Commerce and trade associations; and in 1961 Congressional Quarterly reported that the national organization spoke for 3,400 local and state Chambers of Commerce. [17, p. 954][1]

Regarding the Chamber's origins, David Truman has stated:

> It is frequently asserted that the Chamber of Commerce was founded as a result of the encouragement of the Government and that it was sponsored by the NAM. Such accounts say both too much and too little, because so narrow a set of sources is insufficient to account for an association of the chamber's scope. As in most major inventive developments, social as well as technological, the stimulating circumstances were so general as to produce initiating actions from a number of sources. Prior to 1912 several preliminary efforts

---

1 In his early study of the Chamber Harwood Childs stated: "The by-laws of the Chamber of Commerce of the United States as now in force provide for three basic types of membership: organization members, individual members, and associate members. The first of these three types comprises three classes: first, business organizations constituted on a geographical basis, such as local or state chambers of commerce; secondly, trade associations whose membership is confined to a trade or group of trades; and, finally, special associations or organizations elected to membership by the Board of Directors... Individual and associate members comprise persons, firms, and corporations which are members in good standing of some organization member of the Chamber." (These last two groups are distinguished by the fact that the associate members pay considerably higher annual dues.) [13, pp. 22-24]

had been made by such organizations as the Boston Chamber of Commerce and the Chicago Association of Commerce either to reorganize the National Board of Trade into a more representative body or to supplant it. Among the obstacles to these efforts was the problem of securing appropriate sponsorship. Childs indicates that this problem was solved by a decision to have an organizing meeting called by the President of the United States. Thus the Government's role was a reflection of efforts on the part of a small, initiating group. Persuasion of the President undoubtedly was made easier by his previously expressed desire for an organization that could regularize the relations between the Government and business associations in the field of foreign commerce...

At a preliminary meeting in the Department of Commerce and Labor in February, 1912, the National Association of Manufacturers was represented, along with the San Francisco Chamber of Commerce, the Southern Commercial Congress, the Boston Chamber of Commerce, and the District of Columbia Board of Commerce. This meeting resulted in issuance by the Secretary of Commerce and Labor of an invitation to the organizing meeting in April, attended by about seven hundred delegates. The entire course of this development not only illustrates the circumstances under which such groups emerge but indicates as well the involvement of the association, from its inception, with governmental affairs. [48, pp. 85-86][1]

Following its organization in 1912, the Chamber immediately began publishing what is now its regular monthly magazine Nation's Business, and its membership in all classes increased steadily until 1921. Following the depression in that year, however, Childs noted that organization and individual memberships showed a great deal more cyclical sensitivity than did associate memberships. [13, pp. 27-29] Among the organization members, the Chamber has found that those formed on a geographic basis are a more reliable source of support, since the specialization of trade associations built on a particular line of business apparently militates against their becoming completely effective units within the Chamber's structure. The previously mentioned

---

1 For a less scholarly tracing of the Chamber's origin back to a group of New York Merchants in 1786, see [43].

tendency of organization members to fluctuate with the fortunes of the business cycle and the Chamber's subsequent policy of concentrating on individual and associate memberships, however, has meant that the Chamber has concentrated on those best able to pay individual as well as organization dues, since both individual and associate members must also belong to member organizations. This in turn has meant that, as in the NAM, the larger or at least the financially better off elements have tended to exert a disproportionate influence within the Chamber.

To help overcome the image of minority dominance (which really seems to characterize all group, business, labor, social, or other alike) the Chamber has made wide use of the referendum technique of policy formulation. Rather than serving as a means of formulating policy, however, the referendum technique as used in the Chamber and elsewhere, is more apt to serve like a strike vote as a means of internal propaganda in winning support for predetermined policies and presenting a show of unity to make the policy more effective externally. Regarding the Chamber's referendum procedure, Paul Studenski has observed:

> The questions are answered by organization (constituent society) members and often by organization secretaries, who may or may not consult their group before replying. In either case the matter is given only cursory consideration. Furthermore, the questions are frequently framed in the referendum in such a way that there can be little doubt in the mind of the representative of the average chamber as to how he should vote upon them.
>
> The secretary of a local chamber ordinarily draws up resolutions which obtain automatic endorsement. Committee reports are drawn up hastily, usually by the secretary of the organization, whose business it is to see that no action

is recommended which may stir up a controversy and cause a loss of members. [44, p. 328]

Unlike the NAM, the Chamber did not appear to emphasize labor problems early in its career nor did it become as directly involved in the electoral process.[1] The early concerns of the Chamber seemed to center on problems of business regulation and the promotion of foreign trade. Its formal by-laws outlined two principle lines of endeavor: "first, the encouragement of domestic and foreign trade; second, the development of co-operation among business organizations in the interest of efficiency, uniformity, and equity in business usages and laws, and the proper consideration by the government of questions affecting business and civic interest." [13, pp. 65-66] These by-laws have been supplemented by periodic publications of a book entitled the Policies of the Chamber of Commerce of the United States of America, which compiles various resolutions adopted at annual meetings and propositions which have been approved through referenda.

---

1 Childs' early study stated: "The Chamber does not undertake to support officially the candidacy of any person or persons, apparently preferring to take the officials as they are selected and bring organization pressure to bear upon them. This is not to intimate, however, that the influence of the Chamber is not felt at election time. By focusing the attention of the Nation on certain problems of a business and governmental character, by developing a group psychology and a set of attitudes toward major issues, it consciously or unconsciously directs the voters toward the standard bearers of Chamber policies." [13, pp. 195-96]

The first referendum passed in 1912 advocated a national budget system for the federal government, and at its first annual meeting the Chamber favored the creation of a federal tariff commission. The Chamber also early supported the Federal Reserve Act of 1913, the creation of the Bureau of Foreign and Domestic Commerce in the Department of Commerce, and the creation of a privately-owned and operated American merchant marine. The earliest clear statement on its labor policy by the Chamber, which the writer has been able to find, is the following, which is unfortunately available only in this abbreviated form:

> The right of workers to organize is as clearly recognized as that of any other element or part of the community ...Wages should be adjusted with due regard to the purchasing power of the wage and to the right of every man to an opportunity to earn a living at fair wages, to reasonable hours of work and working conditions, to a decent home, and to the enjoyment of proper social conditions. [43, p. 18]

The "right to organize" portion of this statement is ambiguous in this form. In the following year, however, a referendum was passed by the Chamber which aligned the organization with the NAM and the American Bankers Association in leading the anti-union offensive of the 1920's known as the "American Plan".[1]

---

1 Perlman and Taft have stated: "The American Plan purported to abolish the 'un-American' closed shop, but as in previous open shop crusades, the destruction of unionism was the real objective. Neither effort nor money was spared in this crusade." [15, p. 491] How unified the national leadership of this drive was during the '20's, however, is hard to say. Taylor has stated: "The National Association of Manufacturers established a wide affiliated interest through its membership in the Chamber of Commerce of the United States. Although the Manufacturers' Association aided much in the formation of the Chamber of (continued on following page)

The 1920 resolution, which passed by 1,664 votes to 4, declared that:

> The right of open shop operation, that is, the right of employer and employee to enter into and to determine the conditions of employment relations with each other, is an essential part of the individual right of contract possessed by each of the parties. [34, p. 17]

With regard to this resolution, Savel Zimand stated:

> The U.S. Chamber of Commerce, which in the past claimed to be an institution for education without propaganda, made in 1920 a change in its policy. Mr. Frederick Foster, former president of the San Francisco Chamber of Commerce, who played an important role in the fight against trade unionism in San Francisco, received a prominent position with the Chamber of Commerce. [52, p. 31]

In 1934 when it was proposed that a National Labor Board be established to implement Section 7(a) of the NIRA, the Chamber joined the NAM and other employer representatives in attacking the proposal "as class legislation, imposing restraints on employers but not on unions, as tending toward compulsory unionism, and as unconstitutional". [31, p. 24]

After the Wagner Act was passed over business opposition in 1935, and to the great surprise of the business community was upheld as constitutional in 1937, the Chamber of Commerce of the United States immediately began a campaign for amendments to the Act to add regulation

---

1 (Footnote 1 continued from preceding page.)
Commerce and consequently expected much from it, the heterogeneous composition of the latter often caused the interests of the two organizations to be at variance with one another, and led to the formal withdrawal of the National Association of Manufacturers in 1922." [46, p. 28]

of certain unfair labor practices for employees. This contrasted to the belated official acceptance of the amendment rather than the repeal position by the NAM in 1946. A resolution adopted by the Chamber on April 29, 1937 recommended "equalizing" amendments to the Wagner Act and state and federal legislation to regulate union activity. [10]

As has been previously mentioned, however, except for the Smith-Connally Act, federal action on labor legislation was postponed until after the war effort of World War II. As the war moved toward its close in 1945, an effort was made under the leadership of Eric Johnston, then president of the Chamber of Commerce of the United States, to secure agreement by industry and the two labor federations on a charter of principles to promote full production and industrial peace. This effort came to naught when the AFL executive council, under pressure from the carpenters and others, decided that it would not sit with the CIO in joint sessions and when it was disclosed that a joint NAM-Chamber of Commerce Committee was working on a program of restrictive legislation.

At its May, 1947, meeting the Chamber adopted a labor program going beyond its earlier pronouncements. Millis and Brown note:

> It now put major emphasis on protecting the public from interruption of operations, called for limitations on strikes, for the outlawing of any coercion and of compulsory union membership, for control of monopolistic practices of unions, exclusion of foremen from bargaining, accountability at law for any injurious conduct by employees and unions as well as by employers, and in general for "equality" of the laws and equitable administration. It called on the states as well as the federal government to act on these and other points. [31, p. 290]

Following the passage of the Taft-Hartley Act, the Chamber continued to advocate certain amendments. In 1953 the Chamber printed and distributed in pamphlet form some of its congressional testimony detailing 23 specific recommendations for changes in or strengthening and retaining certain provisions of the Taft-Hartley Act. These 23 recommendations focused on five areas of concern:

> 1. The exercise of monopolistic power by labor leaders acting through union organizations should be restrained by legislation. Those exercising such power or seeking to acquire it should be denied the facilities of the National Labor Relations Board or should be made subject to the anti-trust laws, or both.
> 2. All forms of compulsory unionism should be barred...
> 3. New legislation is necessary to cope with communist infiltration or domination of labor unions...
> 4. The constitutional right of free speech should be fully preserved.
> 5. The National Labor Relations Board should be reconstituted so as to eliminate pro-union bias... [11, pp. 2-3]

Like the NAM, the Chamber sought to employ the anti-corruption sentiment surrounding the McClellan Hearings to get some basic changes in the law affecting the labor-management power structure of collective bargaining. An editorial in the January 1959, Labor Relations Letter of the Chamber's Labor Relations and Legal Department, for example, was entitled "'Labor Reform' is More than 'Union Democracy'". To quote a paragraph:

> An effective labor bill will not stop at "union democracy", it will cover union violence, racket picketing, secondary boycotts, featherbedding, forced union membership, restrictive practices, extortion, the diversion of dues money for political and social purposes, and the monopoly power of the labor boss. [12, p. 2]

Following the defeat of the Kennedy-Ives Labor reform bill in 1958, both the NAM and the Chamber continued to push for "strong" legislation. When Secretary of Labor James P. Mitchell originally presented the Eisenhower Administration's labor reform proposals before the AFL-CIO Convention at Atlantic City in December 1957, however, he firmly stated that:

> this Administration will not propose and in fact will vigorously oppose any legislation designed to bust unions ... We will not recommend a so-called national right-to-work law and we will oppose such legislation if it is proposed. [47, p. 14]

Mitchell also indicated that he would not support any attempt to apply anti-trust laws to unions. Following the 1958 elections, however, Mitchell had a rougher time pushing his "moderate" proposals through a predominately business oriented cabinet. While he advocated tightening up the Taft-Hartley picketing and secondary boycott curbs, Mitchell had to battle down "conservative" elements in the Administration, which sought to put drastic curbs on political activity and spending by unions. The U.S. News and World Report wrote:

> The labor message which President Eisenhower sent to Congress January 28 represents a personal triumph for Secretary of Labor James P. Mitchell, While House aides report. They say the Secretary had to battle hard before the message was approved. [49, p. 21]

In 1959, however, the American Retail Federation, a group representing 70 state and national federations with a total membership of 800,000, was strongly behind the Administration's picketing and boycott curbs, and they supported Mitchell's "no man's land" provisions with particular vigor. Their concentration on these issues, and their apparent willingness to forgo the more sweeping demands for a federal right to work law and anti-trust applications to unions, blazed the trail which eventually won almost unanimous support from the rest of the business community. This eventual compromise of business and Administration forces, combined with labor's continued intrangence, succeeded in winning the support of enough "middle-of-the-road" Congressman to eventually pass the Landrum-Griffin bill.

All of this brings us to the fact that there are other business groups besides the NAM and the Chamber which sometimes take a stand on labor and other political matters. This fact raises the question: "how well do these groups represent the business community in labor matters?"

Other Business Spokesmen And The Representativeness Of The Major Business Lobbies

It might be expected that the aforementioned heterogeneity of the business community on most issues would tend to limit the dominance of the best known national federations. David Truman, for example, has stated:

> It is generally recognized that the superficiality and generality of the programs put forward by the Chamber of Commerce of the United States are due largely to the heterogeneity of the membership that it claims. Its affiliated units do not necessarily keep in line with its policy pronouncements...
>
> The National Association of Manufacturers, often popularly assumed to be a monolithic political force, perhaps because of its advocacy among its following of "unit thinking and unit action," has probably achieved a maximum of unity because its political efforts have been largely defensive in character. Nevertheless, it has experienced criticism from its rank and file for its opposition to the renewal of price-control legislation in 1946 and for the dominance of "big business" in the organization's affairs. Its leaders admit, moreover, the necessity for internal compromise on policy matters in order to achieve effective unity.
>
> Groups that attempt, like the Chamber of Commerce, to

speak for "American business" or "American industry" as a whole, both members and nonmembers, are at great pains to avoid situations in which the interests of "little" business differ sharply from those of "big" business. They have, for example, left to the specialized trade associations the struggles between the retailers and the chain stores and mailorder houses. From time to time, however, cleavages of this sort have come out in the open and have resulted in the formation of competing groups, more often than not shortlived. For example, in the spring of 1946 during the struggle in Congress over the renewal of price-control legislation, to which both the Chamber and the NAM were opposed, there appeared a group calling itself the New Council for American Business. An outgrowth of the Business Men for Roosevelt organization that participated in the 1944 presidential campaign, the New Council asserted that "business is not properly represented by the NAM and the U.S. Chamber of Commerce". The group claimed its support from among "small" businessmen who are "more vulnerable to a depression than big NAM people." Although its exact membership is unknown, the roster of its officers suggested an additional line of cleavage accounting for the group's existence, namely, that between the manufacturing and large commercial enterprises and the service and light consumer goods enterprises... This group raised a competing, if feeble, voice in opposition to the chamber and the NAM. Other businessmen's groups, such as the Committee for Economic Development, have had a somewhat similar origin. [48, pp. 183-85]

With regard to labor legislation at the time of the Taft-Hartley Act, Millis and Brown have stated:

A word should be said about other groups who did not follow the line of the NAM. The American Management Association, with its background of interest in scientific management and personnel administration, in its annual meetings considered rather practically matters of how to deal sensibly with problems which arose under the new national policy, and much good advice was given by experienced men. While different points of view were expressed, the net effect must have been to promote acceptance of collective bargaining and a realistic consideration of the needs of the future. Somewhat similarly the Committee for Economic Development in its statement on national policy early in 1947 put emphasis on ways of making collective bargaining work better on a voluntary basis. It presented a limited program for legislation to supplement existing policy by supporting free collective bargaining, outlawing interferences with it,

> and outlawing such union activities as jurisdictional strikes, strikes to compel violation of laws, and union monopolies which are clearly evasions of the antitrust laws. But it is doubtful whether these organizations had as much influence upon employers, or certainly upon the public, as did other groups with their extreme campaigns for a change in national labor policy. [31, p. 291]

The Committee for Economic Development mentioned in both of the preceding quotations has been described in the following words:

> The Committee for Economic Development is a nonprofit, nonpolitical organization dedicated to research on private and public economic policies that would strengthen and perpetuate economic freedom by helping to make free enterprise fully compatible with economic growth and stability. As an educational association, the CED does research and puts out policy statements for purposes of public education. Professing not to be a lobby, CED does not represent any particular group of businessmen, and its major objective is the public welfare. CED studies are made available to the public and to the press. Members of the Committee for Economic Development Research and Policy Committee present their views to Congress only when requested to do so. [28, p. 37]

The CED was founded on September 3, 1942, by a group of businessmen who were concerned with the problems of the still-distant postwar reconversion. Paul Hoffman, the President of the Studebaker Corporation, and the others associated with the project were convinced that the proposed investigations should not be conducted by the Chamber of Commerce, the NAM, or any trade or industry organization, because, "the impartiality of the research must be above question, which it certainly would not be if it were conducted by official spokesmen for business". [41, p. 18] While the Chamber and the NAM agreed to this proposition, these established organizations were wary of allowing a permanent rival to appear on the scene, and Schriftgiesser states:

> the Chamber and the NAM exacted a so-called "gentleman's agreement" to the effect that any organization of the kind

> proposed should be set up for the duration of the war only. Once its immediate postwar objectives had been achieved it was to be dissolved. This solemn but unwritten pact was to cause some difficulties in later years. [41, p. 22]

The difficulties alluded to began late in 1945 and early in 1946. On February 12, 1946, the CED trustees met and dissolved the Committee's field division after a plan to have these activities absorbed by the Chamber of Commerce of the United States had failed. The trustees, however, voted to continue the work of the Research Division "for another 18 months, perhaps as long as three years." [41, p. 75] Differences between some of the individual businessmen in the CED and the established employer groups came out in the open in 1946 when Chairman Hoffman and others, following the CED's self-imposed restraint on lobbying, nevertheless testified in behalf of the Employment Act of that year; while, at the same time, the NAM, the Chamber, the Farm Bureau Federation, and the Committee for Constitutional Government had united under the leadership of Donaldson Brown, vice-president of General Motors and a Director of the NAM, to lobby against the bill.[1]

"As the postwar reaction to liberalism set in", Schriftgiesser

---

1 The complete legislative history of the Employment Act of 1946 is traced in [1]. One of the most interesting dilemmas faced in the CED's position on this bill was that of Eric Johnston, then president of the Chamber of Commerce who had already failed to get the Chamber to incorporate the CED's Field Division, and who was one of the 13 members of the CED's Research Committee at a time when most of the local Chambers of Commerce were the most vociferous opponents of the bill.

noted, "The Economic Club of Detroit heard an important industrialist declare that Paul Hoffman, Eric Johnston, and Beardsley Ruml were three of the most dangerous men in America." [41, p. vi] Despite shots such as this from within the business community, the CED trustees unanimously voted to continue the research activities of the Committee on a permanent basis in May of 1948.

On the basis of its continued policy pronouncements, the CED has since become identified as "the more progressive and liberal wing of Big Business".[1] Despite its general liberal leanings within the business community, however, when one of the CED's independent study groups published its recommendations on national labor policy late in 1961 and recommended, among other things, repeal of Taft-Hartley's Section 14 (b), this group was wryly referred to as a "wholly disowned subsidiary" of the Committee. The CED has subsequently abandoned its policy of automatically publishing all of the independent study papers prepared for its consideration, although it still continues to publish its own policy statements based on these study papers.

In commenting on how well the national business groups represent the prevailing sentiment within the business community,

---

1 William Benton, one of the early driving forces behind the formation of the CED, has been quoted as saying: "In retrospect, it seems clear to me that the greatest single service rendered by the CED has been the education of its members from the business community in politics and economics. Most of them however, ... have remained loyal to the Republican Party—although many of these...are somewhat suspect within it." [41, p. 71]

Lenhart and Schriftgiesser state:

> The organizations through which business management functions in the political sphere are often staff run and are sometimes little more than propaganda machines. Their policy pronouncements run the gamut from a series of staff written resolutions hastily passed at annual conventions to carefully researched policy papers.
>
> Too often a policy pronouncement is a composite of the prejudices and biases the staff think are held by members of the organization rather than the carefully thought out views of the businessmen based on a real understanding of the issues. [28, p. 40]

And, commenting on the official labor pronouncements of the NAM, Brown and Myers have noted:

> We sense little resiliency, little awareness of a world on the move. Rather, we have the sensation of a television production in which most of the characters stay immobile while the backdrop moves across the stage. Fortunately or unfortunately for the survival of American management ideology, the characters appear to act in one way in their private lives and another in their stage roles. (A study by the AFL-CIO indicates that, of 171 companies represented on the directorate of the NAM in 1955, 93 had contracts with AFL-CIO affiliates; of the 71 in states permitting union-security provisions, 59 had such clauses.) [7, p. 94]

It might be added, however, that it is difficult to determine if the character's actions in their private lives really reflect their latent desires in the area of labor-management relations - (probably the easiest of all issues on which to get management cohesion) or whether they merely reflect the dint of economic necessity, which would be readily changed if given the opportunity, or at least the hope of opportunity. In this connection, Gable has noted:

> The fluctuations of membership indicate that the NAM's labor policies have been essentially reflective of member's desires, because membership has swollen during campaigns of union opposition and fallen off after their successful completion. [22, p. 260]

If it is the case, however, that the members turn to the NAM for results in the political sphere (e.g., the open shop or a right to work law) which they cannot obtain on their own in the economic sphere, then the situation becomes somewhat incongruous. This is so because one of the five main points in the "code of conduct under which both organized labor and industry can serve the nation better and more efficiently", which Charles R. Sligh read to George Meany at the Congress of American Industry in 1955, was the following: "5. Keep politics out of labor-management relations and avoid trying to obtain by political pressure that which cannot be justified economically." [33, p. 19]

While most people would agree with these sentiments, a careful reading of the history of labor and management in the political process would seem to show that, dutiful tributes to Laissez faire and "voluntarism" aside, both labor and management have turned to the institutions of government when it was felt that governmental action would aid their cause; and likewise both sides have most strongly urged non-intervention when it was felt that governmental action would aid their opponents. A survey of "American Management-Labor Relations and Management Attitudes" by the Department of Manufacture of the Chamber of Commerce of the United States arrived at this conclusion as far as management was concerned, but also expressed the hope that it would stop in these words:

> History reveals also a great change in management's conception of the role government should occupy in management-labor relations. Until the New Deal era, management for a number of years, perhaps unwittingly, placed great

> reliance on government by reason of ability to solve many unpleasant labor relations problems through use of court injunctions. Today, however, management recognizes that, 'reliance upon government to solve labor-management problems is unsound.' Management has seen it demonstrated that government solutions of such problems are not basic in their effect. They are subject to change according to what administration is in power. At the same time, management sees clearly that unless management-labor problems are solved, there will be more rather than less government control--a result detrimental to both management and labor. Management's hope today, therefore, is that management and labor can find some reasonable means to solve their own problems--to 'work together and stay free.' [9, p. 31]

The fact that one year after these words were written the Chamber strongly supported the Taft-Hartley Act, which brought the government into labor-management relations more than ever before, however, seemed to indicate that the "reasonable means" sought still remained to be found.

A glance at the activities of private corporations and individual businessmen will complete this review of management's role in the political process.

Political Activities Of Corporations And Individual Businessmen

The age of the "robber barons" and the founding of modern corporate empires in the late nineteenth century survives in American folklore as the epitome of business influence in the political process. Whether this influence was ever as great as it is now presumed to have been is difficult to say. Nevertheless, the Sherman Act notwithstanding, the rapid growth in the wealth and power of the railroad, banking, steel, oil refining and other industries was accompanied by fierce outcries against business malpractices in the political as well as the economic sphere; and William R. McIntyre, has noted:

> A series of articles by David Graham Phillips in the _Cosmopolitan_ in 1906 and 1907 ("The Treason of the Senate") came to the startling conclusion that 75 of the then 90 senators served the railroads, the Beef and Sugar trust, Standard Oil, and steel interests. The Hepburn Act in 1906 prohibited railroads from giving free passes, long a favorite source of political influence, except under strict limitations. Then in 1907, after strong urging by President Roosevelt, Congress for the first time made it unlawful for a corporation to make "a money contribution in connection with any election" involving candidates for federal office. [29, pp. 764-65]

The subsequent attempts to regulate corporate and labor political activity will be examined in more detail in the next chapter of this thesis and in appendices C and D which discuss the Federal Regulation of Lobbying Act and the Federal Corrupt Practices statutes respectively.

With regard to lobbying activities, many corporations maintain Washington offices in addition to belonging to one of the national business federations discussed above. In 1950 the Buchanan House Committee found that 38 of the 173 corporations they polled had reported $776,466 under the Federal Regulation of lobbying act between January 1, 1947 and June 30, 1950. Thirty-seven of the corporations polled indicated that they had expended another $406,787 to influence legislation not otherwise reported in addition to 66 corporations reporting $227,257 for travel expenses incurred in attempts to influence legislation, 7 reporting $346,808 for the maintenance of a Washington office, 65 reporting $2,189,152 in expenditures for printed or duplicated matter dealing with public issues, 31 reporting $2,013,370 for advertising services in the same area, and 125 reporting $26,941,453 in tax exempt contributions _not_ made to charitable or eleemosynary institutions. [26]

The fact that only $776,466 (2.4%) of the total of $32,124,827 reported to the Buchanan Committee by these 173 corporations over the 3-1/2 year period covered was reported under the Federal lobbying law during the same period gives some indication to the completeness of the figures reported by all the groups covered by this legislation. It should be pointed out, however, that the Buchanan Committee's definitions of attempts to influence legislation were much broader than those later laid down by the Supreme Court in interpreting the federal lobbying statute.

With regard to the bans on corporate spending which have been in effect at the federal level with various modifications since 1907, only one firm has ever been convicted of violations; and that was under the Public Utility Holding Company Act of 1936 not under the Federal Corrupt Practices Act. In 1959 about 30 states also limited the right of corporations to give money to candidates or their supporters. The provisions varied, some extending only to certain classes of corporations, such as insurance companies and public utilities.

Despite these prohibitions, however, Alexander Heard has stated:

> It is not unusual for corporate funds to make up 10 per cent of the campaign fund of a candidate for state or local office, and the percentage has gone higher. In all, in a presidential election year, several million dollars of corporate money finds its way by one process or another into political campaigning. [24, p. 130]

Aside from establishing lobbies and making campaign contributions, however, most corporate executives have not traditionally been overactive in the political process. Lenhart and Schriftgiesser have stated "Business leaders, to a greater extent than is perhaps widely realized, have tended to remain aloof from active party politics and instead have sought their political advantages through their costly and effective lobbies and through captive legislators." [28, p. 35] Likewise Michigan's former Governor Williams has stated:

> Another reason I believe many businessmen have a somewhat warped view of government and politics is simply that they get their government and politics secondhand. The businessman does not participate in government or politics directly but through paid agents or lobbyists. [51, p. 105]

Working the other side of the street, Senator Barry Goldwater in a plea for "warm bodies to ring doorbells", has stated that "it's still hard to convince businessmen that the least of our problem is money." [17, p. 58] As mentioned above, the Harvard Business Review mailed out a questionnaire on business and politics to a cross section of 10,000 of its subscribers in 1959. The responses to selected questions by 2,700 top executives with regard to their personal views and company policies in this area were then published in the Review. With regard to individual participation, 54% of the respondents reported giving money in the 1958 campaign, and 25% reported that they personally "worked" in the 1958 campaign. A further breakdown indicated that 32% gave only, 22% both gave and worked, and 3% worked but did not give. [21, p. 8][1]

---

1 This study found that, among those who did work in the 1958 campaigns, participation tended to drop off as the size of the company increased. In other words direct participation and size of firm were inversely related, and most of the active participants were from the smaller firms.

TABLE 1 - Executive Responses to Selected Questions on Business and Politics*

Question	Percent of Total Answers
1. In which of the following activities does your company engage?	
Urge employees to register and vote	70.1%
Belong to any organization designed to make the political climate more favorable to business	43.9
Belong to any organization designed to improve the efficiency of government operations	36.4
Participate actively in formulating trade association political policy	25.2
Take stands on issues like "right to work" laws	21.5
Encourage employees to participate actively in campaigns	21.1
Urge executives to serve as elected officials in the city where plant is located	16.1
Encourage campaign contributions by employees	15.0
Carry articles on current public issues in the company paper	14.6
Have top managers make talks on important issues	14.3
Allow candidates to come into the plant and meet employees	13.8
Invite elected officials to meet with the management group	13.3
Employ specialists to deal with elected officials	13.0
Perform services for politicians	12.1
Give employees time off to work on campaigns	11.6
Invite elected officials to talk to employee groups	5.5
Consider political activity in recommendations for promotion	3.0
2. Do you think that the influence of business on political affairs in general since 1950 has . . .	
declined considerably	17.1%
declined a little	18.3
stayed the same	13.2
increased a little	33.4
increased considerably	18.0
3. Do you think that the influence of your company on political affairs since 1950 has . . .	
declined considerably	4.5%
declined a little	7.1
stayed the same	61.6
increased a little	20.6
increased considerably	6.2
4. Do you believe that businessmen should be more active in politics?	
yes	88.8%
no	5.6
no opinion	5.6

*Based on replies of 2,700 Harvard Business Review subscribers.

Source: Harvard Business Review, May-June 1959, Vol. 37, p. 8.

Table 1 reproduces other responses in tabular form, showing the percent of the 2,700 answers to each question with regard to company activities and individual opinion. In light of the responses on individual participation and the fact that almost 90% of the respondents felt that business should be more active in politics, the report concluded "In short, the record shows a fairly low degree of active participation in political affairs in relation to the high enthusiasm and interest reported." [21, p. 10] But the report also added "In all fairness to the respondents, it should be remembered that there is not a great deal of active participation in politics in this country in any segment of the population." [21, p. 10][1]

With regard to company activities, aside from associated activities with other firms and encouraging employees to register and vote, Table 1 shows that the largest response indicated that 21.5% of the companies took stands on issues. Coming right after the 1958 election campaigns this response may be significant, since William R. McIntyre, writing before the elections, had stated:

---

1 Perhaps the main reason for this lack of more active participation was the fact that Table 1 shows 64% of the respondents felt that business influence on political affairs had not declined since 1950 and the corresponding figure for their own company was even higher, being over 88%. A breakdown of these responses, however, indicated that those respondents who had actually worked in the 1958 campaign took a less rosy view of the political influence of business as a whole, but these people also felt that their own companies were doing much better than those who did no work.

> The only instance in recent years in which business groups have shed the non-partisan cloak and carried their case vigorously to the voters have concerned referendum issues rather than contests for office. In such campaigns, business has worked hard, and often successfully, using some of the same techniques labor employs to influence the electorate.
>
> In at least four of the six states where right-to-work laws are to be considered at the polls this year, major corporations, in addition to some chambers of commerce and manufacturer's associations, are publicly campaigning for voter approval. [29, p. 763]

After describing the right-to-work activities of the Boeing Airplane Company in the states of Washington and Kansas, the Timken Roller Bearing Company in Ohio, and the General Electric Company in California, McIntyre continued with regard to the latter campaign:

> Any preference for candidates is explicitly disclaimed, although in the gubernatorial race the right-to-work proposal has been a major issue from the outset, with Sen. William F. Knowland (R) for and State Attorney General Edmund G. Brown (D) against.
>
> A few corporations thus have begun to speak out on issues confronting voters, but it is noteworthy that the great majority still refrain from direct participation in political campaigns. [29, p. 763]

Much of the increased corporate involvement in the 1958 election campaigns may be attributed to the businessman's traditional antipathy toward union security, but there is also some evidence that many corporations may have been attempting to take a significant new tack in their political course. The late 1950's witnessed a veritable flood of speeches, pamphlets, magazine articles, and books stressing the theme "businessmen must get into politics". In view of what has preceded in this chapter, this must seem a little incongruous for there is ample evidence that business is now and always has been involved up to its ears in the political process. Nevertheless, the Employer's

Labor Relations Information Committee was able to issue an annotated bibliography containing reference to no less than 78 magazine articles and 51 books, pamphlets, or printed speeches on management's political activities published during the 13 months from July 1958 to August 1959. [20] As nearly as can be determined, most of this sudden outpouring dating from about mid-1958 stems primarily from two sources which can be identified for convenience, by the persons of Andrew Hacker and Archie D. Gray.

Andrew Hacker is now an Associate Professor of Government at Cornell University, and in September 1958 the Fund for the Republic published his study of Politics and the Corporation. Hacker's study sought to probe the question of "how compatible the imperatives of corporate employment are with the requirements of democratic citizenship." [23, p. 3] He concluded that the growth of corporate employment tended to replace local community citizenship with a national "corporate citizenship", and this tended to eliminate active political participation by a large segment of the middle class upon which democratic governments have always relied so heavily. Hacker felt that the foundations of our democratic political system were being weakened by corporations which "have erased the need for political participation on the part of the very people who have always been the prime participants in the political process." [23, p. 13] Given these philosophical considerations, it logically followed that one way in which a corporation could help to strengthen democracy would be to encourage its middle class executives to actively participate in party politics at the local level.

In the same month that Hacker's study was published, Archie D. Gray, a Senior Vice President of the Gulf Oil Corporation, used that company's publication The Orange Disc, to sound another, more pragmatic, call to political action on the part of corporation executives. In a widely-quoted statement, already cited on the first page of this thesis, Gray observed:

> If we are to survive, labor's political power must now be opposed by a matching force, and there is no place in the United States where such a force can be generated except among the corporations that make up American business. [42, p. 41]

Gray's analysis became emeshed with Hacker's analysis and apparently struck a responsive chord in the hearts of many American businessmen. The flood of literature annotated in the previously cited EIRIC report indicates the volume if not the effectiveness of the immediate response to these appeals. Since the pleas of Hacker and Gray were logically as well as physically separate, however, the upsurge of activity in the late 1950's was not entirely homogeneous. Indeed, two basically different kinds of company program seemed to be involved. One type aimed only at stimulating the civic consciousness of employees; the other frankly advocated a stronger voice for business and public affairs.

It is interesting to note, however, that before either Andrew Hacker or Archie Gray had published their thoughts, some individual corporations had already sponsored programs along both of these lines. In 1951 the Johnson and Johnson Corporation established a Sound Government Committee to arrange panel discussions among white collar workers on company time to discuss public issues and encourage employees to become active in politics. In 1959, however, the Congressional Quarterly

Weekly Report indicated that this committee was no longer operating and that the company felt that it had "done its job". [8, p. 491]

Another more permanent pioneer in the field of corporate political education was the General Electric Company. For many years this corporation has stressed the principle of "corporate citizenship" and it has long given much publicity to its views on public issues as well as its own labor negotiations. In early 1959, a GE spokesman estimated that between 4,000 and 5,000 of the corporations 300,000 employees had taken or were taking a course in practical politics. [8, p. 491] In the preceding year the company organized a special Government Relations Service to serve as a clearinghouse for all of the organizations political, legislative, and government relations activity. A month before either Hacker or Gray published their views, General Electric Vice President Lemuel R. Boulware was stating that politics was "The Businessman's Biggest Job in 1958" [6], and in the company's annual report for that year the chairman of the board, Ralph J. Cordiner, said that GE's political "awakening" was the company's major event in 1958.

Another of the more publicized recent program seeking to emphasize both individual and corporate political participation is that of the Ford Motor Company. [38] Not only have individual companies tried to encourage the spread of such programs, the Effective Citizens Organization (ECO), which was established in 1955, has recently increased its efforts in this area and now holds workshops on college campuses for corporate executives. A private consulting firm, Public Affairs Counselors, has been established to assist companies and employer associations set up political education programs. Both the NAM and the Chamber of Commerce of the U.S. have made available courses in practical politics and McIntyre has noted "The Committee on State Sovereignty recently published a 44-page handbook acknowledged by its editors to be basically a condensation of COPE's How to Win." [29, p. 759] In addition to G.E., Gulf Oil, and Ford, some of the other large companies which have begun to speak out on political issues and to encourage employees to become more active politically are the American Can Company, Caterpillar Tractor Co., Chase-Manhatten Bank, Chrysler Corporation, General Dynamics, Monsanto Chemical Co., Shell Oil, Sears and Roebuck, Standard Oil Co. (N.J.), U.S. Steel, and F. W. Woolworth.

McIntyre has stated:

> Revival of company interest in open politicking has consisted so far mainly of efforts to educate management personnel in the art of politics and encourage active participation in party work at the neighborhood level. Many corporations have instituted seminars in practical politics and made it a custom to acquaint executives below the top level with the company position on political issues...
>
> Current advocacy of participation in local politics is intended to supplement, not replace, the long-time corporation stress on political contributions. A chief aim of the present movement is to get candidates with business sympathies nominated for office...
>
> Gulf Oil appears to be the only company actively interested in political education which has said it intends to distribute voting records outside of its plants... No other large company or business association has announced plans comparable to the labor technique of distributing information about candidates to large numbers of voters. [29, pp. 758-61]

Since this latter statement was made, however, the Americans for Constitutional Action has been formed as a conservative nonpartisan group with plans to screen and endorse candidates favorable to business.

This group was founded with Ben Morell, retired chairman of the Jones and Laughlin Steel Corporation, as its head; and other prominent businessmen were announced as trustees for ACA.

The recent upsurge in business political activity, thus, seems to be aimed at more participation in the electioneering and campaign aspects of politics than is usual for business groups, and much of it appears to be independent of the activities of the traditional spokesmen for the employer community in the political process. Some of the basic premises and some of the possible implications of this "movement" will be examined in more detail in subsequent chapters following a brief summary of this review of managements past efforts in politics.

Summary And Questions For Further Consideration

Like organized labor, American management has a long history of active participation in the political process. Due to basic differences in the nature of the membership base and the economic and social position of these two groups, however, American management traditionally has relied for the most part on tactics that shy away from the more visible electioneering aspects of politics and has relied primarily on campaign contributions and institutional advertising in addition to formal lobbying by individual companies and business organizations.

With regard to labor matters, the most visible business or employer groups have been the National Association of Manufacturers and the Chamber of Commerce of the United States. The NAM was originally founded in 1895 to promote American commerce and international trade. A change in policy that turned the Association's primary attention to labor matters in 1903, however, resulted in a significant increase in membership, and since that date the NAM has been an active participant in the political process on labor and labor-related issues. In its formative years the NAM was much more predisposed toward direct participation in specific election campaigns than it has been in more recent times, and the Association participated quite vigorously in the election campaigns of 1906 through 1912. Indeed, there was even some talk of an "NAM Party" in 1912, before the Republican party platform finally espoused most of the NAM program after the "Bull Moose" split in that year.

The NAM toned down many of its political activities following the "expose" of its efforts during the Underwood Tariff Debates of 1913, however, and the Association has relied increasingly on a vast communications program with its own members, with education, church, and civic groups, and with the general public, to maintain its influence in the political process. The Association's membership climbed to a peak of about 5,350 firms in 1922, but during this period membership tended to be confined to relatively small firms who dropped their affiliation rapidly following the economic collapse of the early 1930's. There was a second major reorganization of the Association as the result of the New Deal labor legislation of the 1930's. Following the enactment of the Wagner Act of 1935, the NAM's membership not only increased substantially, but it also began to consist of and be dominated by the large industrial giants of the American business community. Today's NAM membership is estimated at over 20,000 firms.

Despite changes in the size and composition of its membership over the years, however, the main thrust of the NAM's communications and public relations efforts has been strongly opposed to some of the most basic labor union activities and programs. Indeed, much of the NAM's "program" has traditionally been in opposition to the programs of other groups--particularly organized labor. Despite a conscious attempt to develop a "positive" program in the immediate postwar period, the NAM's official labor policies appear to have changed little over the years, but the Association does seem to be increasingly willing to seek more government intervention in labor-management relations to see its policies implemented. The NAM strongly supported the Taft-Hartley Act, and the Association has continued to advocate other measures such as national prohibition of all union security clauses, outlawing industrywide collective bargaining, more state-level jurisdiction in labor-management affairs, and prohibition of all union funds in political campaigns.

The Chamber of Commerce of the United States, which was organized in part by the NAM and other groups in 1912, did not evidence the almost single-minded concern with labor problems that characterized the NAM immediately after 1903, nor did it undertake the direct participation in election campaigns that characterized the earlier days of the NAM. Following an "open-shop" referendum in 1920, however, the Chamber became more outspoken on labor matters and was an ardent champion of "the American Plan" during the 1920's. Today the Chamber, which is basically a federation of Chambers of Commerce and trade associations, has over 3,000 state and local Chambers of Commerce at the heart of its rather complex membership structure. Although the NAM and the Chamber reached a parting of the ways in 1922, both organizations opposed section 7-a of the NIRA. They also opposed the Wagner Act vigorously, but following the Jones and Laughlin decision upholding the Act's constitutionality in 1937, the Chamber began a campaign for "equalizing" amendments whereas the NAM argued for outright repeal until 1946, on the grounds that the government should not intervene in labor-management relations. With the sharp shift in public sentiment concerning unionism during the strike wave of 1946, both organizations accepted the principle of more government regulation to control union power. Thus, despite the more conciliatory efforts of Chamber President Eric Johnston, both organizations were influential in the enactment of the Taft-Hartley Act in 1947. Since 1947 the Chamber's labor program has been very similar to that of the NAM, emphasizing the need for complete prohibition of "compulsory unionism" and the need to "place labor under the anti-trust laws".

Both the NAM and the Chamber advocated stronger measures than President Eisenhower's Secretary of Labor, James P. Mitchell, during the debates leading to the Landrum-Griffin Bill in 1959, but other business groups and administration forces combined to have this legislation enacted with the ultimate support of the major business lobbies. Today, however, both the NAM and the Chamber continue to advocate more stringent labor policies than those currently in existence or currently practiced by a large part of their membership;

and the fact that a business or firm bargains collectively with a national union representing its employees, often with union security clauses in its contract, apparently still doesn't prevent it from supporting organizations advocating labor policies that would reduce these obligations.

In addition to the NAM and the Chamber, of course, there are other national business organizations which from time to time become concerned with the political aspects of labor-management issues. The American Retail Federation for example, played a key role in the enactment of the Landrum Griffin Act, and the Committee for Economic Development has voiced opinions that differ from the Chamber and NAM line, although the CED is not organized for political action in the same sense that these other national organizations are. Also, in addition to the national spokesman for the business community, many individual corporations and businessmen are known to undertake political activities on their own. It is difficult to measure the exact extent of these "independent" efforts, but there are some signs that they may be on the increase.

A survey of Harvard Business Review subscribers in 1959 indicated that about one of five companies took stands on issues such as "right to work laws", and some of the nation's largest companies played active roles in the state referendum campaigns on this issue in 1958. The decisiveness with which these referendums were defeated and the unusually large numbers of Democratic congressional victories in 1958 appeared to arouse a fairly widespread concern within the business community that their position was being undermined by organized labor's political efforts, and there was a rash of speeches, magazine articles, pamphlets, and books emphasizing the theme that "business must get into politics". This apparent upsurge in management attention to things political accounts in large part for the concern with the political dimension of labor management relations expressed in the first chapter in this thesis. A closer examination of this "movement", however, reveals that its most direct antecedents pre-date the November 1958 elections and that it is compounded of at least two main streams of thought. One stream of thought, which seems to find its intellectual foundations in works such as Andrew Hacker's study Politics and the Corporation, is aimed at stimulating the civic consciousness of corporate employees and encouraging them to become more active in local political affairs. The other main stream seems to find its sources in the writings and speeches of management executives such as Archie D. Gray of Gulf Oil and Lemuel Boulware of General Electric, and is based on the proposition that increased management political activity is necessary to offset the increasing political influence of organized labor.

The merging of these streams has resulted in an apparent increase in emphasis on the campaign and electioneering aspects of politics by several prominent companies which advocate "educating" management and other personnel in the art of politics and acquainting them with the company position on political issues. Both the U.S. Chamber and the NAM have developed courses in practical politics to encourage such efforts, and several new business groups such as the Effective Citizen's Organization, and Public Affairs Counselors have been established to assist companies and employer associations to set up political education programs.

Given this sudden upsurge in action as well as talk about more business in politics, one can ask how widely based is this movement? It is being established on a firm foundation that will insure lasting permanency, or is it just a fad that will soon fade? Will it really work and give management a more effective influence in political affairs, or will it simply antagonize rival groups in the political process and spur them to greater and more effective action? It is an attempt to supplement the activities of the traditional business spokesmen in the political process, or will it serve to some extent to replace or substitute individual corporate activity for the work of such groups as the NAM and the Chamber?

Since one of the major premises of this movement appears to be the feeling that management is doing badly and that organized labor is doing well in the political process, it may be best to review in some detail the actual postwar political performance of both groups before attempting to answer these questions in more detail. This will be the task of the following chapter.

REFERENCES - CHAPTER IV

1. Steven K. Bailey, Congress Makes A Law (New York: Columbia University, 1950).

2. Wallace F. Bennett, The Very Human History of "NAM" (New York: The Newcomen Society of England, American Branch, 1949).

3. Clarence E. Bonnett, Employer's Association In The United States (New York: Macmillan, 1922).

4. Clarence E. Bonnett, "Employer's Association", Encyclopaedia of the Social Sciences (New York: Macmillan, 1931) Vol. V, pp. 509-514.

5. Clarence E. Bonnett "The Evolution of Business Groupings", The Annals of the American Academy of Political and Social Science, May, 1935, Vol. 179, pp. 1-8.

6. Lemuel R. Boulware, "Politics - The Businessman's Biggest Job in 1958", Labor Law Journal, August 1958, Vol. 9, pp. 587-594.

7. D. V. Brown and C.A. Myers, "The Changing Industrial Relations Philosophy of American Management", Industrial Relations Research Association, Proceedings of the Ninth Annual Meeting (Madison, 1957).

8. "Businessmen Getting into Practical Politics", Congressional Quarterly Weekly Report, April 3, 1959.

9. Chamber of Commerce of the United States, American Management-Labor-Relations and Management Attitudes (Washington, 1946).

10. ________. Federal Regulation of Labor Relations (Washington, 1937).

11. ________. Labor Law in the Public Interest (Washington, 1953).

12. ________. Labor Relations Letter, January, 1959.

13. Harwood Childs, Labor and Capital in National Politics (Columbus: Ohio State University, 1930).

14. Alfred S. Cleveland, "NAM: Spokesman For Industry?" Harvard Business Review, May 1948, Vol. 26, pp. 353-371.

15. John R. Commons and Associates, History of Labor in the United States (New York: Macmillan, 1935), Vol. IV.

16. Congressional Quarterly Almanac, 1957, Vol. XIII.

17. _______. Almanac, 1959, Vol. XV.

18. _______. Almanac, 1961, Vol. XVII.

19. Robert A. Dahl, "Business and Politics: A Critical Appraisal of Political Science" in Social Science Research on Business: Product and Potential (New York: Columbia University, 1959).

20. Employers Labor Relations Information Committee, Management's Political Activities: An Annotated Bibliography (New York: 1959).

21. Dan H. Fenn, Jr., "Problems In Review: Business and Politics", Harvard Business Review, May-June, 1959, Vol. 37, pp. 6ff.

22. Richard W. Gable, "NAM: Influential Lobby or Kiss of Death?", Journal of Politics, May 1953, Vol. 15, pp. 254-273.

23. Andrew Hacker, Politics and the Corporation (New York: The Fund For the Republic, 1958).

24. Alexander Heard, The Costs of Democracy (Chapel Hill: University of North Carolina, 1960).

25. E. Pendleton Herring: Group Representation Before Congress (Baltimore: John Hopkins, 1929).

26. House Select Committee on Lobbying Activities, Expenditures by Corporations to Influence Legislation, House Report 3137, 81st Congress 2nd Session (Washington: U.S. Government Printing Office, 1950).

27. V. O. Key, Jr. Southern Politics in State and Nation (New York: Knopf, 1949).

28. R. F. Lenhart and Karl Schriftgiesser, "Management in Politics", Annals of the American Academy of Political and Social Science, September, 1958, Vol. 319, pp. 32-40.

29. William R. McIntyre, "Corporations and Politics", Editorial Research Reports, October 8, 1958.

30. "The Misuse of Organization", Guntons Magazine, June, 1903, Vol. 4, p. 475.

31. H. A. Millis and E. C. Brown, From the Wagner Act to Taft Hartley (Chicago: The University of Chicago, 1950).

32. National Association of Manufacturers, Labor Law Reform: The Faults in the Kennedy-Ives Bill: What is Needed to Protect Working People and the Public (New York; 1958).

33. _______. "What Organized Labor Expects of Management" by George Meany and "What Management Expects of Organized Labor" by Charles R. Sligh, Jr.,(New York, 1956).

34. Nations Business, September 1920, Vol. 8.

35. Duncan Norton-Taylor, "How to Give Money to Politicians", Fortune, May, 1956, Vol. 53, pp. 113 ff.

36. D. M. Parry, "Annual Report of the President", NAM, Proceedings of the Eighth Annual Convention, 1903, Vol. 8.

37. The Public Interest in National Labor Policy (New York: Committee for Economic Development, 1961).

38. T. R. Reid, "Management Programs to Encourage Political Participation", Industrial Relations Research Association, Papers Presented at the 1960 Spring Meeting, (Madison, 1960).

39. "Renovation in NAM", Fortune, July 1948, Vol. 38, pp. 72 ff.

40. Frederick Rudolph, "The American Liberty League, 1934-1940", American Historical Review, October, 1950, Vol. 56, pp. 19-33.

41. Karl Schriftgiesser, Business Comes of Age (New York: Harper, 1960).

42. Horace E. Sheldon, "Businessmen Must Get Into Politics", Harvard Business Review, March-April 1959, Vol. 37, pp. 37-47.

43. Earl O. Shreve, The Chamber of Commerce of the United States of America, (New York: The Newcomen Society in North America, 1949).

44. Paul Studenski, "Chambers of Commerce", Encyclopaedia of the Social Sciences (New York: Macmillan, 1930) Vol. III, pp. 325-328.

45. Charles P. Taft, "Should Business Go in for Politics?" New York Times Magazine, August 30, 1959, pp. 10 ff.

46. Albion G. Taylor, Labor Policies of the National Association of Manufacturers (Urbana: University of Illinois, 1928).

47. Time, December 16, 1957.

48. David B. Truman, The Governmental Process (New York: Knopf, 1955).

49. U. S. News and World Report, February 6, 1959.

50. Clemet E. Vose, "Litigation as a Form of Pressure Group Activity", Annals of the American Academy of Political and Social Science, September 1959, Vol. 319, pp. 20–31.

51. G. Mennen Williams, "Can Businessmen be Democrats?", Harvard Business Review, March–April, 1958, Vol. 36, pp. 102–106.

52. Savel Zimand, The Open Shop Drive (New York: Bureau of Industrial Research, 1921).

CHAPTER V

A DETAILED LOOK AT THE POST WORLD WAR II LABOR-MANAGEMENT POLITICAL SCENE

Despite their different and changing approaches to political activities both organized labor and management have sought to influence the course of federal legislation over a wide range of issues during the post World War II period. Each side has sought to exercise this influence through formal lobbying efforts in the nation's capital and through a variety of campaign techniques designed to influence the composition of the executive and legislative branches of government upon which their lobbying efforts are brought to bear. This chapter will attempt to examine labor and management lobbying and campaign efforts in some detail with respect to both money spent and results obtained.

Unfortunately, any attempt to discuss financial involvement in the political process must first cut through much complex legislation and litigation surrounding lobbying and election expenditures. While it might be easier to avoid this legal morass than try to follow the modern equivalent of Theseus' thread in the Labyrinth, the figures involved have no real meaning out of their proper context. Appendix C outlines federal attempts to regulate lobbying activity and to establish reporting requirements through the 1946 Regulation of Lobbying Act, and Appendix D describes federal attempts to regulate financial contributions and establish reporting requirements in national elections.

Lobby Expenditures

Bearing in mind the limitations outlined in Appendix C, Table 2 breaks down the lobbying expenditures reported by various groups under the Federal Regulation of Lobbying Act from 1947 through 1960. This table indicates that the total amounts reported by all groups increased annually from 1947 through 1950, but dropped sharply after the Act was first declared unconstitutional by a lower court in 1951. The overall totals have remained fairly stable at a much lower level following the Supreme Court's decision upholding the Act but sanctioning a narrow definition of "lobbying" in the Harriss case in 1954.

The number of labor and employee groups reporting under the Act has increased substantially relative to the total number of groups reporting during the period covered in Table 2 (from 17 of 256 in 1949 to 38 of 289 in 1960). The number of business groups reporting, however, was about the same in 1960 as it had been in 1949.

The amount of lobbying expenditures reported by labor and employee groups has also increased substantially as a percentage of the total amount reported (from 3.2 percent in 1949 to 27.1 percent in 1960). This trend is the result of both an increase in reported labor expenditures and a decrease in the expenditures reported by other groups. These figures, therefore, seem to lend support to the contention that organized labor has shown an increasing political

TABLE 2 - Amount and Percent of Reported Lobby Expenditure by Group Classification, 1947-1960

Year	Labor and Employee Groups		Business Groups		All Groups*	
	Number Reporting	Amount and (%) Reported	Number Reporting	Amount and (%) Reported	Number Reporting	Amount Reported
1947	Not Available				154	$ 5,191,856
1948	Not Available				222	6,763,480
1949	17	$ 257,301(3.2)	140	$3,280,278(41.2)	256	7,969,710
1950	30	518,413(5.0)	141	3,410,054(33.1)	340	10,303,204
1951	30	581,488(6.7)	117	3,089,742(35.5)	295	8,711,097
1952	22	466,733(9.7)	96	2,215,591(45.9)	257	4,823,981
1953	23	453,000(10.2)	102	2,660,141(59.8)	197	4,445,841
1954	21	656,149(15.3)	132	2,289,539(53.4)	225	4,286,158
1955	Not Available				274	4,365,843
1956	30	748,320(18.9)	150	2,031,933(51.3)	264	3,957,120
1957	32	836,189(21.9)	149	1,854,490(48.6)	269	3,818,177
1958	31	842,557(20.4)	144	2,047,657(49.5)	263	4,132,719
1959	34	1,217,361(28.4)	151	1,761,556(41.1)	280	4,281,468
1960	38	1,044,142(27.1)	144	1,497,662(38.9)	289	3,854,374

* The number of group categories in addition to business and labor has varied in different years and different issues of the Almanac. Most recently five other categories have been used: Citizens, Farm, Military and Veterans, and Professional.

Source: Congressional Quarterly Almanac, 1948-1961.

awareness in recent years. The largest labor expenditure reported in Table 2 occured in 1959, the year the Landrum-Griffin bill was enacted.

Going beneath the aggregate figures in Table 2, we will now examine the reported lobbying expenditures of labor and business groups in more detail before turning to an examination of the legislative "batting averages" of these groups.

Organized Labor

Immediately following the merger convention in 1955, the AFL-CIO established a Department of Legislation under the co-directorship of William C.Hushing and Robert Oliver. Hushing was the former director of the AFL Legislative Committee and Oliver had directed the work of the CIO Legislative Department. Hushing retired and Oliver resigned to enter into private legislative practice in 1956, and they were replaced by former Congressman Andrew J. Biemiller as the single director of the department.

The AFL-CIO Legislative Department, of course, is not the only labor or employee group appearing before Congress. Table 3 shows the amounts of money the national headquarters of the AFL-CIO has reported spending to influence federal legislation under the Federal Regulation of Lobbying Act since the merger. These figures are expressed as a percentage of the total money reported by all labor and employee groups, and as a percentage of the total amount reported by all groups filing the reports under the act. Table 4 then lists the amounts reported by the ten labor and employee groups reporting the largest expenditures in 1960, the last year for which complete reports are available.

TABLE 3 - Lobby Spending Reported by the AFL-CIO As a Percentage of Lobby Spending Reported by Other Groups, 1956-1960

Year	Amount Reported By AFL-CIO National Headquarters	AFL-CIO as % of Amount Reported By All Labor and Employee Groups	AFL-CIO as % of Amount Reported By All Groups
1956	$ 145,182	19.4	3.67
1957	134,986	16.1	3.54
1958	133,348	15.8	3.23
1959	132,053	10.8	3.08
1960	129,157	12.4	3.35

Source: Congressional Quarterly Almanac, 1957-1961

Table 3 shows that the amount reported as lobbying expenditure by the AFL-CIO has declined every year since the merger — from $145,182 in 1956 to $129,157 in 1960. Since reported lobbying expenditures by all labor and employee groups have increased during this time — from $748,320 in 1956 to $1,044,142 in 1960 — the percentage of total labor expenditures reported by the AFL-CIO has fallen from 19.4% in 1956 to 12.4% in 1960

The total expenditure by all groups reporting under the federal lobbying act fell from 1956 to 1957, but then increased in 1958 and 1959 before falling to below the 1956 level in 1960. As a result, the percentage of total lobbying expenditure which was reported by the AFL-CIO fell from about 3.7% in 1956 to about 3.4% in 1960.

TABLE 4 - The Ten Labor and Employee Groups Reporting the Largest Expenditures Under the Federal Regulation of Lobbying Act in 1960

Group	Amount Reported
AFL-CIO (National Headquarters).	$ 129,157
International Brotherhood of Teamsters	95,766
National Federal of Post Office Clerks	85,261
International Ass'n of Machinists District Lodge No. 44	72,734
Brotherhood of Locomotive Firemen and Engineers	67,793
National Ass'n of Letter Carriers.	66,693
Railway Labor Executives Ass'n	56,000
AFL-CIO Industrial Union Dep't.	55,731
Seafarers Section, Maritime Trades Dep't. (AFL-CIO)	48,299
Retirement Federation of Civil Service Employees of the U.S. Government.	37,332
28 Others	329,376
TOTAL	$1,044,142

Source: Congressional Quarterly *Almanac*, 1961, pp. 961-62

As Table 4 indicates, however, the AFL-CIO *national headquarters* is only one of several AFL-CIO groups reporting. All told, eight of the ten labor and employee groups reporting the largest expenditures in 1960, and 20 of the total of 38 groups reporting in this year, were affiliated with the AFL-CIO in one way or another. The other groups represented various governmental employee associations and several independent unions.

Despite the fact that its reported lobbying expenditures have been declining both in absolute terms and as a percentage of the spending reported by labor and other groups, however, the AFL-CIO national headquarters has ranked as the largest single spender reporting under the Lobbying Act in three of the five years from 1956 through 1960. This is also true despite the fact that the merged organization has reported less total spending than the totals reported by the two separate federations before merger, and despite the fact that their combined totals would have ranked them first in only two of the seven pre-merger years from 1949 through 1955. This is shown in Table 5, which compares combined AFL and CIO lobby spending with the spending of the other groups reporting the largest annual expenditures.

As indicated in this table, it was not always possible to get an exact figure for the combined AFL and CIO lobby expenditures for every year since 1947, because in certain years the Congressional Quarterly Almanac published the individuals reporting figures for only a certain number of the largest spending groups, or for groups reporting above a certain amount.

If we assume that the smallest spender of the two labor federations (interestingly enough, the CIO in every case) spent the maximum possible without being listed, the highest possible ranking which could have been attained by the combined expenditures of the two groups can be determined. Thus, the figures in Table 5 show that the national labor federations have consistently ranked among the highest spending groups during the postwar period, and their relative

TABLE 5 - Groups Reporting the Largest Annual Lobby Expenditures, and Reported Lobby Expenditures of National Labor Federations, 1949-1960

Year	Name of Largest Spending Group and Amount Reported		National Labor Federation Expenditure			
			AFL	CIO	AFL-CIO Total	Rank Among Groups
1949*	American Medical Association	$1,225,028	$ 56,859	$ 36,126	$ 92,985	11
1950	American Medical Association	1,326,078	116,027	NA, under $100,000	216,026**	7***
1951	American Farm Bureau Federation	878,813	104,257	NA, under 100,000	204,256**	9***
1952	Natl. Assn. Electric Companies	477,941	105,537	NA, under 50,000	155,536**	5***
1953	Natl. Assn. Electric Companies	547,789	123,608	48,425	272,033	4
1954	Natl. Milk Producers Federation	185,496	125,996	120,119	246,115	1
1955	Natl. Assn. Real Estate Brokers	131,006	114,080	111,788	225,868	1
1956	AFL-CIO	145,182			145,182	1
1957	Campaign for 48 States	138,331			134,986	2
1958	AFL-CIO	133,348			133,348	1
1959	Intl. Brotherhood of Teamsters	242,952			132,053	3
1960	AFL-CIO	129,157			129,157	1

* First nine months only.

** Not actual expenditures, but the highest possible expenditures since CQ did not list groups reporting less than certain amounts in these years.

*** Not actual rank, but the highest possible rank based on the explanation above.

Source: Congressional Quarterly Almanac, 1950-1961

ranking has advanced in the more recent years. This, however, has not been because of increased expenditures by the national labor federations, but, rather, because of the relative decline in the reported spending of other groups.

To briefly summarize these figures on reported lobbying expenditures by organized labor groups, several conclusions appear to stand out from the data presented in the preceding tables:

1. Over the postwar period, the number of labor and employee groups reporting lobbying expenditures has increased relative to the total number of reporting groups.

2. The amount of lobbying expenditures reported by labor and employee groups has increased as a percentage of the total amount reported by all groups. This trend is the result of both an increase in reported labor expenditures and a decrease in expenditures reported by other groups.

3. Since the AFL-CIO merger, the national headquarters has reported considerably less lobbying expenditure than reported by the separate AFL and CIO prior to 1956, and the amount reported by the AFL-CIO has declined every year since the merger. The even faster decline in reported spending by other groups, however, has raised the relative ranking of the AFL-CIO among all groups reporting lobbying expenditures to one of the top three positions in every year since 1953. Prior to 1951, the combined totals of the AFL and the CIO would never have ranked higher than fifth among all the groups reporting lobbying expenditures.

4. Within the labor groups reporting lobby expenditures, the amount reported by the AFL-CIO has not only declined absolutely in every year since the merger, but it has also fallen as a percentage of the increasingly larger totals reported by all labor and employee groups (from 19.4% in 1956 to 12.4% in 1960).

5. An examination of the 38 labor and employee groups reporting lobbying expenditures in 1960, however, revealed that 20 of these groups are affiliated with the AFL-CIO in one way or another. The other 18 groups represented various groups of government employees and several independent unions.

Again it should be emphasized that all of the above figures are based on the rather ambiguous requirements of the Federal Regulation of Lobbying Act. Indeed, the limitations of the data available under this Act become more apparent if we turn our attention to the lobbying expenditures reported by employer or business groups under its provisions.

Business Groups

As indicated by the figures in Table 2, more groups consistently report as "business" lobbies than in any other single category. These lobbies, as a group, also consistently account for a larger amount of the total expenditures reported than any other single classification. The "business" lobbies covered in Table 2, however, spread their interest over a wide range of issues, and may even work in opposition to each other. Furthermore, the National Association of Manufacturers and the Chamber of Commerce of the United States, which were described in Chapter IV as the leading national employer spokesmen on Labor issues, are not conspicuous in the influence they exert on the figures shown in Table 2.

As indicated in Appendix C, the National Association of Manufactuers has waged a long struggle against the Federal Regulation of Lobbying Act. Although its attempts to have the law declared unconstitutional failed, the NAM continues to claim that its "principal purpose" is not to influence legislation, and it has never reported any lobbying expenditures under the law. The Chamber of Commerce of the United States, however, has reported expenditures in every year except 1954, but the amounts of its reported spending have dropped substantially since the Harriss case in that year. This is indicated in Table 6, which shows the Chamber's reported expenditures as a percentage of the total expenditures reported by all business groups. (A column expressing the Chamber's reported expenditures as a percentage of the total reported by all groups as was done for the AFL-CIO in Table 3 has been omitted since the figure would be less than 1% in all cases.) Outside the area of direct lobbying activity now covered by federal law, it is probably true that the NAM and the Chamber spend a much larger percentage of the total business outlay for indirect advertising and publicity campaigns related to political issues, but there are no reliable figures to verify this.

Lobby Results

In attempting to assess the performance of the major labor and business lobbies during the post World War II period, data were

were collected to measure each lobby's success with respect to its position on the major legislative issues to come before Congress from 1947 through 1961, and to compare these records with other major lobbying groups. In this latter connection the two best known farm lobbies (The American Farm Bureau Federation and the National Farmers Union, Farmers Educational and Cooperative Union of America) were selected as best representing non labor and management groups with broad, continuous legislative records over the entire period under consideration.

TABLE 6 - Reported Lobby Spending by the Chamber of Commerce of the United States, Expressed as a Percentage of the Total Lobby Spending Reported by All Business Groups 1949-1960

Year	Amount Reported by the Chamber	Chamber as % of Amount Reported by All Business Groups
1949	$ 71,391*	2.2%
1950	109,926	3.2
1951	116,383	3.8
1952	93,297	4.2
1953	90,988*	3.4
1954	No Report	NA
1955	31,208	NA
1956	30,209	1.5
1957	28,235	1.5
1958	30,852	1.5
1959	33,432	1.9
1960	25,029	1.7

* First nine months only.

Source: Congressional Quarterly *Almanac*, 1950-1961.

In selecting the issues and the groups to be used for comparison, the Congressional Quarterly Almanac was consulted for each legislative year from 1947-1961. The index headings "Major Legislative Issues" and "Lobby Stands" were used for the years 1947-1953; the heading "Lobby Scorecard" was used for the years 1954-1956; and the heading "Lobby Roundups" was used for the years 1957-1961. A list was made of the five or six major bills at each legislative session and the position of each lobby group on each bill was compared with the final disposition of these bills by Congress or by the Executive in cases of vetoes not later over-ridden by Congress. The results of this tabulation are shown in Table 7. Since the AFL and the CIO did not pursue identical legislative programs prior to the merger in 1955, the years 1947-1955 and the years 1956-1961 are tabulated separately, as well as a total tabulation for the entire 15-year period 1947-1961.

Examination of the work sheets on which Table 7 is based (now shown because of cumbersomeness) indicates that the AFL and the CIO took opposite stands on only two major pieces of legislation between 1947 and the merger late in 1955. These bills were the St. Lawrence Seaway Bill, which was opposed by the AFL and favored by the CIO, and the New Military Reserve Plan of 1955, which was favored by the AFL and opposed by the CIO. The St. Lawrence Seaway Bill was defeated in 1952, but enacted in 1954, and the New Reserve Plan was passed in 1955.

Within the business community, the Chamber of Commerce of the United States and the National Association of Manufacturers have taken similar positions on all of the bills on which both groups took

TABLE 7 - "Batting Averages" of Selected Lobbies on the Major Bills Before Congress, 1947-1961

	Major Bills Supported			Major Bills Opposed			Totals		
Lobby Group	No.	No. Passed	Percent Success	No.	No. Passed	Percent Success	No. of Major Bills	No. of Favorable Action	Percent Success
					1947-1955				
AFL	33	16	48%	14	8	57%	47	24	51%
CIO	35	16	46%	16	7	44%	51	23	45%
C of C	19	13	68%	25	17	68%	44	30	68%
NAM	11	5	45%	20	15	75%	31	20	65%
AFBF	16	12	75%	21	14	67%	37	26	70%
NFU	30	13	43%	9	3	33%	39	16	41%
					1956-1961				
AFL-CIO	32	6	19%	3	1	33%	35	7	20%
C of C	3	3	100%	32	26	81%	35	29	83%
NAM	3	3	100%	30	24	80%	33	27	82%
AFBF	3	3	100%	30	24	80%	33	27	82%
NFU	29	6	21%	2	0	00%	31	6	19%
					1947-1961				
AFL + AFL-CIO	65	22	34%	17	9	53%	82	31	38%
CIO + AFL-CIO	67	22	33%	19	8	42%	86	30	35%
C of C	22	16	73%	57	43	75%	79	59	75%
NAM	14	8	57%	50	39	78%	64	47	73%
AFBF	19	15	79%	51	38	75%	70	53	76%
NFU	59	19	32%	11	3	27%	70	22	31%

Source: Congressional Quarterly Almanac, 1948-1962

a stand, with the single exception of a bill to increase highway building in 1956. The Highway Bill was passed in 1956 with Chamber support, while the NAM opposed this legislation. The relative unanimity within the labor and business lobbies, however, stands in marked contrast to the dichotomy between the Farm Bureau Federation and the Farmers' Union, where these groups opposed each other on 50 of the 61 measures on which each group took a stand during the postwar period. Each farm group also took a stand on nine other bills on which the other farm group did not take a position. The Farmers' union most frequently lined up with organized labor, and the Farm Bureau Federation usually lined up with the major business lobbies on the issues that separated the business and labor positions.

With this information as background, Table 7 indicates several points of interest. During the period 1947-1955, the CIO took a stand on a few more of the major bills before Congress than did the AFL, but the older federation's lobbying efforts were slightly more successful than those of its younger counterpart—particularly in having measures it opposed defeated. The "batting average" of the merged AFL-CIO fell drastically during the years 1956-1961, however, and was considerably below the "batting average" of either the AFL or the CIO during the earlier period.

Within the business community, the Chamber of Commerce of the United States took a stand on more of the major issues than did the NAM, and the Chamber did significantly better than the NAM in getting favored measures enacted, but the NAM had a slight edge in having measures it opposed defeated over the entire 1947-1961 period. The record of the Farmers' Union corresponds very closely to the record of organized labor and the record of the Farm Bureau Federation is very similar to the record of the business lobbies over these years.

The over-all totals for the 15 years covered in Table 7 indicate clearly that the business lobby did much better than the labor lobby, both with respect to having favored bills enacted and with respect to having opposed bills defeated. There was also a sharp increase in the business "batting average" after the AFL-CIO merger in 1955, corresponding to the decline in labor's "batting average" noted above. Indeed, there appears to have been an increased "polarization" on the major legislative issues after 1955. This is indicated by the fact that the percentages between the different lobby groups on the selected issues and almost exact reciprocals in the latter period. This means that the selected lobbies have lined up diametrically opposed to each other on practically all of the key issues since 1956, whereas the figures from 1947 through 1955 indicate that there was at least some overlap or mutual support between the lobbies on some key issues during this earlier period.

Table 7 indicates that organized labor tends to favor most of the major legislation on which it takes a stand, whereas the business lobbies tend to oppose far more legislation than they support. Since it is far easier to defeat legislation than it is to have major bills enacted, this helps to explain part of the wide discrepancy between the over-all batting averages shown in Table 7 for the entire

1947-1961 period. But, again, the figures show that business was far more successful than organized labor both in having favored legislation enacted and in having opposed legislation defeated, particularly since 1956. And the postwar period included the enactment of both the Taft-Hartley Act and the Landrum-Griffin Bill, neither of which organized labor was able to stop or modify greatly despite the advantages that accrue from being on the defensive in the legislative process.

The "batting averages" in Table 7, however, obviously have to be interpreted with a great deal of care. The fact that a lobby supported a measure which was eventually enacted or opposed a bill which was ultimately defeated or vetoed of course does not always mean that it was solely responsible or even a prime mover in the eventual outcome. The entire results or outcome of the complex legislative process can rarely be traced to a single source. Also, each session of Congress is treated separately in arriving at the total figures shown in Table 7. Thus, a bill is counted each time it comes up in a different session of Congress. This procedure can be somewhat misleading in the case of a measure, such as the Depressed Areas Bill, which was defeated or vetoed five times before it was finally passed on the sixth try. The final passage of such a measure probably indicates a greater degree of success for its advocates than a one-for-six average (17%) would indicate.

On the other hand, it is even more misleading if each issue arising at any time during these years is counted only once. For example, in the area of housing legislation, there were two federal housing bills passed during this period. If each issue were counted only once, does the passage of two bills in the same area mean that the lobby has been 200 per cent successful? In this case, and in general, it was felt that a situation in which a housing bill was sought six times and passed twice was best represented by an "average" of 33 per cent, even though, as has been pointed out, this method may somewhat understate the success of a lobby supporting the legislation that takes several attempts to become enacted. On the other side of the fence, it may also overstate the success of a lobby that defeats a bill several times before it is finally enacted, because the apparent success on a year-to-year basis in defeating legislation may, in the long run, turn out to be simply forestalling the eventual passage of a strongly opposed measure.

The element of compromise has also been glossed over in the data presented in Table 7. Since it seemed impossible to determine to what extent the final draft of a bill really fulfilled the intent of the sponsors or overcame the objections of its opponents, it was simply recorded whether a bill was enacted or defeated in any specific area. Thus the ultimate support of the NAM and the Chamber for the Landrum-Griffin Act in 1959 was counted as a "victory" for them, even though both groups would have preferred even more stringent regulations of certain union activities. And the same bill was counted as a "defeat" for organized labor, even though the unions in the construction industry actually obtained an easing of the NLRB election provisions, and some of the more stringent regulatory proposals were modified before the Landrum-Griffin Act was finally passed by both houses of

Congress. Related to this element of compromise is also the problem that some bills are more important than others as far as the different lobbies are concerned. A victory on a "minor" issue doesn't "balance" a loss on a "major" issue. For practical purposes, however, the writer could think of no objective way to conveniently assign different weights to different measures; and so all bills have been treated the same in computing the percentages in Table 7.

Another weakness of looking only at the major bills that have come before Congress is the fact that some of the legislation most sought or most opposed by a particular lobby may never get to Congress for a vote, and thus would really be more significant than the "victories" or "defeats" indicated in Table 7 as far as the different lobbies are concerned. For example, labor's campaign to repeal the Taft-Hartley Act was counted as a "major issue" only twice in computing the averages in Table 7, although this was the chief proposal in labor's political program for several years. Likewise the attempts of the NAM and the Chamber to make Taft-Hartley more stringent were counted only two times in Table 6 although they have waged a more or less continuous campaign against "labor monopoly" and "compulsory unionism".

Given all of these qualifications, the data presented in Table 7 may still be significant. If it could be quantified, the "multiple attempt" or "just forestalling" factor mentioned above would probably raise labor's batting average and lower management's. But the "weighting" of the Taft-Hartley Act and the Landrum-Griffin Act would probably lower labor's batting average and raise management's. Thus it could be argued that these two adjustments would still leave us not far from where we started. In any case, the same qualifications, including the inability to measure degrees of compromise, would apply to both the 1947 through 1955 and the 1956 through 1961 period (especially since the "weight" of the Taft-Hartley Act in the former and the Landrum-Griffin Act in the latter period would be similar), and the increased polarization and the drop in labor's effectiveness after 1956 still stand out as two of the main trends in Table 7 as far as the purpose of this thesis is concerned. This is so because Chapter III indicated that the most significant increases in organized labor's political efforts have been spurred by legislative adversity, not relative success, and Chapter IV indicated that much of the thrust behind the recent "get business in politics" movement is based on the assumption that management has been doing badly vis-a-vis organized labor in recent years. Given these conclusions, the data in Table 7 would seem to indicate that the drop in organized labor's political effectiveness since 1956 might lead them to launch even more vigorous political efforts, and the increase in the reported lobby expenditure by labor and employee groups shown in Table 2 may be evidence of just such a move. As far as employers are concerned, the record of Table 7 seems to indicate that they have been doing increasingly well, and that much of the apparent concern with labor's superiority in political affairs may be mistaken.

Each of these points, however, requires further evaluation

before any definite conclusions can be drawn. The increased polarization between labor and management lobbies and the decline in organized labor's batting average between 1956 and 1961 does not offer a very long time span for generalization, and these years were characterized by the revelations of the McClellan Committee plus the fact that there was a Republican administration in the White House during five of these six years (a key nationwide speech by President Eisenhower was largely responsible for the Landrum-Griffin Bill passing in the form it did, and Ike's two vetoes of depressed area legislation after it had been approved by Congress did nothing to improve labor's legislative batting average). Given these conditions, one could argue that the decline in labor's batting average was not as bad as it might have been, and that the increase in business influence was not as great as they might have anticipated. Indeed, the business community apparently views their recent "successes" as only partial victories that simply recover some lost ground and do not really represent any new gains. Analysis of the NAM's long-run legislative record, for example, indicates that the years 1903 to 1933 saw only two major pieces of legislation opposed by the NAM enacted during this entire thirty-year period. They were the Clayton Anti-Trust Act and the Norris-LaGuardia Act. Between 1933 and the end of World War II, however, almost the exact opposite was the case. Alfred Cleveland has calculated that "Of 38 major legislative proposals enacted into law between the years 1933 and 1941, the NAM opposed all but seven, sometimes on the basis of their objectives, and sometimes on the basis of particular provisions therein," [14, p. 357] and the only labor legislation enacted prior to the end of World War II of which the NAM approved were certain provisions of the Smith-Connally Act.

The increase in the NAM's batting average since 1947, and particularly since 1955, thus still doesn't compare with its pre-1933 record, but it is significantly better than its performance during the 1930's. One's evaluation of the business lobby's success, then, depends on the frame of reference selected. There have been no major new legislative enactments in the area of "protective" labor legislation since the late 1930's, but none of the basic proposals, such as Social Security or minimum wages, so strongly opposed by the NAM have been "rolled back" either, and there have been periodic "liberalizations" of these laws which may have been postponed but have not been defeated.

Thus, the data in Table 7 are not necessarily inconsistent with the hypothesis that we are witnessing an increase in the political dimension of labor-management relations, because organized labor feels that it is losing influence and must make its traditional response of shoring up its political efforts in the face of adversity, while at the same time management feels that in light of the favorable circumstances of recent years it has not succeeded as much as it should or could have because of the increasing political efforts of organized labor.

Labor and management attempts to increase their political influence through campaign activities will be discussed in some detail in the next section of this chapter, but it might be noted that the increase in lobby spending reported by organized labor and employee groups shown in Table 2 has occurred during the period of relative adversity shown in Table 7, while the total lobby spending reported by all business groups during this period has declined except for the one year, 1957. Obviously, there does not appear to be a direct relation between reported lobby spending and political influence, and in the case of the passage of the two major postwar labor bills (the Taft-Hartley Act of 1947 and the Landrum-Griffin Act of 1959) there is some evidence that organized labor, if anything, overspent, overpressured, and generally did not make effective use of its lobby resources.

Writing after the passage of the Taft-Hartley Act, Max M. Kampelman stated, "Too many labor unions have still not learned that lobbying is a profession which calls for the development of an expertise and is not merely a reward for past services performed." [29, p. 172] And some 12 years later, after the Landrum-Griffin Bill had passed through its critical stages in the House, Sar A. Levitan noted, "The spokesmen for organized labor were as much responsible for the House-approved labor reform bill as were any of its proponents." [34, p. 675]

Along these lines, the AFL-CIO is known to have brought in reinforcements to help labor's regular legislative staffs during the Landrum-Griffin debate, and in all they probably numbered around 100. Some of the union huskies who helped choke the capital corridors and fill the galleries became the butt of some derisive comment, but the complaints were not so much against their lobbying per se as they were against their indiscreet lobbying. Thus, a Senator, reported as being friendly to labor, told of hurrying to chamber when the bells rang for a vote. A regular union lobbyist supposedly hailed him with the injunction: "You had better vote for this, Senator, or we won't forget it." To which the Senator shot back: "I don't know what it is, but now I have to vote 'no'." [45, p. 8]

Throughout the whole procedure Levitan has stated:

> "Until the last week prior to the House approval of the Landrum-Griffin Bill, lobbying by AFL-CIO representatives lacked any coordination. In some cases, they even worked at cross purposes. It was alleged that some railway union spokesmen concentrated their efforts to secure exemption for unions subject to the Railway Labor Act. Similarly, building trade representatives devoted their attention to securing pet provisions of special interest to their unions. These cross-currents among labor lobbyists certainly failed to make friends for labor's cause." [34, p. 678]

Perhaps the best known of labor's indiscretions in 1959, however, was the "Carey letter." Just as the Senate and House Conferees were about to start work on reconciling two different versions of labor reform legislation James B. Carey, President of the IUE and a vice president of the AFL-CIO, wrote a fairly crude letter threatening the 229 Representatives who had voted for the Landrum-Griffin Bill in the House with reprisals in the 1960 elections. The reaction to Carey's letter was immediate. On August 20, Representative Homer H. Budge (R., Idaho) called it a "cheap effort at intimidation." On August 21, however, Carey said, "The bitterness of the reaction to my letter... indicates that my criticism has struck home. I threatened nobody. There was no intimidation." [18, p. 1168]

The fact that Carey's action was completely independent of

any official AFL-CIO approval only served to reveal once again the lack of cohesiveness and coordination within the labor lobby, and the only real effect of this letter appears to have been to add grist to the mills of labor's opponents. Herbert Lahne has observed, "Even a politician does not like to be black-jacked publicly--there is some pride in every man--even if he yields to pressure privately time and again." [31, p. 135]

There is no doubt that business lobbies are also occasionally guilty of blatantly crude maneuvers that violate more or less understood rules of circumspection, but in general they appear to do better than organized labor on this score. Joseph Loftus, for example, noted that during the 1959 Landrum-Griffin debates in the House, "The American Retail Federation brought in strangers from the midwest and elsewhere. They blended inconspicuously with the capitol decor." [45, p. 8] The generally higher social standing of business executives and their legislative representatives also helps to facilitate alliances, or at least cooperation with other lobby groups in crucial situations, whereas organized labor apparently has more difficulty on this score.

David Truman, for example, has stated: "On most matters, for example, the American Farm Bureau Federation and the Chamber of Commerce of the United States would find it easier to secure allies than would the Congress of Industrial Organization." And he reported:

> "The National Association of Manufacturers, being a fairly vulnerable minority and lacking a mass following of its own, has made a variety of alliances with groups having equal prestige and larger publics...A somewhat less formal understanding was reportedly developed between the NAM and the

> American legion in 1940. This arrangement established a cooperative committee to carry on 'educational' activites, including the distribution of NAM literature through the legion's hierarchy." [59, p. 252]

The fact that the largest farm lobby in Washington, the American Farm Bureau Federation, which claims to represent 1.6 million farm families, often lines up with the major business lobbies on labor issues was noted in discussing Table 7. This has some real advantages given the disproportionate influence of rural and farm voters in Congress.[1] During the Landrum-Griffin debates in Congress, Charles Schuman, President of the NFBF, not only supported the management position on labor reform, but also sent telegrams to all state farm bureaus urging them to support the "strong" House version of the legislation that went to the joint Senate-House Conference Committee. Labor could not drum up any such influential support among its farm friends, and a study of the testimony before the Congressional committee considering labor-reform legislation in 1959 indicates that organized labor's position was supported almost exclusively by labor affiliated groups (John Rayber of the Indiana Farmer's Union being one of the few exceptions), whereas the business position was supported by a whole host of spokesmen of groups not normally associated with labor legislation. This latter group included such organizations as the American Hotel Association, the National Restaurant Association, the Associated General Contractors of America, the National Small Businessmen's

---

1 See [55].

Association, the National Auto Dealers' Association, and the National Association of Refrigerated Warehouses, as well as spokesmen for individual companies and state chambers of commerce. This indicates that even though many of the "business" groups reporting lobby spending in Table 2 are not normally associated with "labor" issues as are the Chamber and the NAM, they are nevertheless available in the "pinch".

Finally, still focusing on the passage of the Landrum-Griffin Act, which was by far the most decisive labor-management showdown in recent years, the influence of the Republican administration also played a key role in the enactment of the bill in its final form. Not only was President Eisenhower's nationwide TV address of August 6, 1959, widely regarded as a determining factor, but the general "influence of office" including patronage from Postmaster General, Arthur Summerfield, also helped to sway the final verdict.[1]

Indeed, in the last analysis, a lobby's effectiveness can be no greater or no less than its ability to gain "access" to the centers of political power at the time of crucial decision making, and success in direct lobbying activities is not independent of a group's other political skills, including indirect lobbying or "education" and election campaign activities. Thus, we will now turn to an examination of these more indirect efforts to increase the effectiveness of a group's lobbying desires.

---

1 See [19, p. 14494]

Electoral Activity and Indirect Lobbying

As in the above section on lobby expenditures, this section on election activities and indirect lobbying will begin with an examination of organized labor's political efforts and then turn to the activities of the management community before summarizing the results of this chapter's examination of the postwar labor management political scene.

Organized Labor

When the AFL-CIO merger was ratified on December 5, 1955, the new federation's Committee on Political Education was formed through the merger of Labor's League for Political Education, the political arm of the former AFL, and the Political Action Committee of the former CIO. At the national level, COPE began operations under the co-directorship of James L. McDevitt, former LLPE director, and Jack Kroll, former PAC director. At the lower levels of organization, equally pragmatic compromises were worked out.

One of the first problems facing the new COPE was the merger of existing state and local groups engaged in trade union political activity. It was generally agreed that merged political effort need not wait upon the complete organic merger of the existing state federations and industrial union councils. This policy worked fairly well, since fewer problems were attendant upon the merger of political effort than upon organic merger, and the pressure of a forthcoming national election was imminent. Following the 1956 election campaigns, on March 1, 1957, COPE co-director Jack Kroll retired. AFL-CIO

President and COPE Chairman George Meany then appointed James McDevitt the single national director of COPE and named Alexander Barkan as deputy director.

Like its immediate predecessors, COPE's entrance into politics tries to form a source of electoral finance for organized labor's increasingly comprehensive legislative program. In addition to its financial participation in election campaigns, however, COPE also tries to encourage union members to register and vote, and it tries to provide them with "educational" information so that their vote can be an "intelligent" one. The problem of what is an educational expenditure and what is a political expenditure, however, has been one of the thorny legal questions arising out of the relatively recent attempts to regulate the financial participation of labor groups in national elections. Therefore, we will briefly review the legal aspects of organized labor's financial participation in election and education campaigns before turning to an analysis of the actual spending figures reported and an examination of labor's efforts to register, educate, and get out the labor vote.

Campaign Activity: Legal Aspects -- As we have seen, third parties aside, organized labor's electoral activity has historically taken different forms. The traditional AFL nonpartisan approach consisted of little more than an official endorsement based on the candidate's voting record and a written plea to members to consider these endorsements in making their voting decisions. A minimum of financial involvement in actual campaigns was characteristic. With the advent of Labor's Nonpartisan League in 1936 and the CIO's

Political Action Committee in 1943, however, more emphasis was placed on financial support of particular candidates, and the amount of "educational" electoral propaganda directed at both union members and non-members alike was stepped up in an unprecedented manner. Indeed this political activity on the part of organized labor attracted so much attention that for the first time legal restraints were placed on the allowable forms of labor's financial participation in national elections.

The first attempt to regulate union political expenditures by the Federal Government came in 1943 when the War Labor Disputes (Smith-Connally) Act extended Section 313 of the Federal Corrupt Practices Act to cover labor organizations for the duration of the Second World War. Section 313, as extended temporarily by the Smith-Connally Act, made it unlawful for a national bank, a corporation "or any labor organization to make a contribution in connection with any [federal] election".

Section 304 of the Taft-Hartley Act made permanent the wartime extension of Section 313 to unions. It also expanded the coverage of the prohibition on both union and corporate spending to include political "expenditures" as well as "contributions", and it made the restrictions applicable to primaries as well as to regular federal elections. The 1947 provisions read:

> "Sec. 313. It is unlawful for any national bank, or any corporation organized by authority of any law of Congress, to make a contribution or expenditure in connection with any election to any political office, or in connection with any primary election or political convention or caucus held to select candidates for any

> political office, or for any corporation whatever, or any labor organization to make a contribution or expenditure in connection with any election at which Presidential and Vice Presidential electors or a Senator or Representative in, or a Delegate or Resident Commissioner to Congress are to be voted for, or in connection with any primary election or political convention or caucus held to select candidates for any of the foregoing offices, or for any candidate, political committee, or other person to accept or receive any contribution prohibited by this section. Every corporation or labor organization which makes any contribution or expenditure in violation of this section shall be fined not more than $5,000; and every officer or director of any corporation, or officer of any labor organization, who consents to any contribution or expenditure by the corporation or labor organization, as the case may be, in violation of this section shall be fined not more than $1,000 or imprisoned for not more than one year, or both. For the purposes of this section 'labor organization' means any organization of any kind, or any agency or employee representation committee or plan, in which employees participate and which exists for the purpose, in whole or in part, of dealing with employers concerning grievances, labor disputes, wages, rates of pay, hours of employment, or conditions of work."

This amended version of Section 313 has been codified as section 610 of Title 18 of the U.S. Code. From the time of enactment it was generally understood that these amending prohibitions applied only to the use of general corporate funds and union dues money. They were not interpreted as applying to "individual" political contributions by corporate officials or "voluntary" funds solicited from union members by independent labor committees specifically established for political purposes. Thus, when the CIO created the PAC as its political "arm" in 1943, the Political Action Committee took the form of a series of independent committees at all levels superimposed on the existing CIO machinery. Each committee had its own treasury separate from the general union funds raised through dues assessments.

Although, all of the PAC's direct contributions in federal elections came from voluntary funds, however, some general union funds were used to cover the overhead and administrative costs of these committees and to finance their "educational" activities. Indeed, a detailed explanation of the PAC's early organization and operation goes something like this:

When the PAC was formed early in July, 1943, approximately $650,000 in general union funds (dues money) was contributed to the PAC treasury by CIO unions and the national federation itself. Until July 23, 1944, a little over $370,000 of these funds were used to set up offices, assemble a staff, pay for office equipment and materials, and conduct an "educational" campaign strongly supporting the policies of FDR. After the Democratic convention nominated Roosevelt for a fourth term on July 23, the unexpended balance of these funds were "frozen" until after the November election. From July 23 to November 7, PAC appealed for voluntary contributions of $1 or more from members of the CIO unions to finance all of its activities. One-half of the $750,000 thus raised went into a separate PAC bank account, the other half remained with the local union's political committee which solicited the money. Another $90,000 in voluntary funds was contributed to the CIO-PAC by non-union members in addition to the separate funds raised by the National Citizens' PAC (about $280,000).

Once the 1944 elections were over, the PAC "defrosted" its trade union contributions account and used these funds, along with additional trade union contributions, to pay its bills until

September 3, 1946, the date arbitrarily set by the PAC as the beginning of the 1946 election campaign. In 1946, as in 1944, a voluntary drive for individual contributions financed the PAC activities during the campaign. This drive supplied the national PAC with approximately $130,000 for its activities in September and October. Roughly two-thirds of the committee's expenditure in 1946 were made before September, however, and thus were covered with general union funds.[1]

Prior to 1947, then, the PAC operated on the principle that the War Labor Disputes Act did not ban the use of general funds in primary campaigns, and they felt that union funds could be used to make political contributions to candidates and political committees for use at any time except during the actual course of a federal election campaign. Although they did not follow it in practice, they also felt that general funds could be used during these campaigns for indirect political expenditures which were not directly contributed to a candidate for federal office. After the Taft-Hartley Act, however, both these questions were called into doubt, although it was still recognized that general funds could be used in state elections unless prohibited by state law.[2]

---

1 For an extended discussion of the organization and operation of the PAC see [23].

2 At the state level, the most restrictive law ever attempted occurred in Wisconsin in 1955 when the legislature passed a law sponsored by State Assembly Leader Mark Catlin, Jr. (R) which was modeled after the Federal Corrupt Practices Act, but designed to ban all forms of labor campaign spending at the state level, including "voluntary" funds contributed by union members to labor political committees. (Continued on following page)

Following the enactment of the Taft-Hartley Act in 1947, the AFL created Labors' League for Political Education, along much the same lines as had been used by the CIO in forming the PAC. By this time, however, the Taft-Hartley ban on political "expenditures" as well as political "contributions" further complicated the issue, since the distinction between a legal "educational" expenditure previously financed by general corporate and union funds and the now illegal "political" expenditure was not clear, and since it was felt that a ban on indirect corporate or union expenditures as opposed to direct contributions might violate the constitutional guarantees of freedom of speech and freedom of the press.

The Taft-Hartley Act had been on the books less than a week when the CIO executive board resolved to test the constitutionality of the ban on political expenditures. Anxious to force a Supreme Court ruling before the 1948 campaign got under way, the CIO publically disclosed its intention of violating the new version of section 313 by endorsing candidates in special elections to fill vacancies in the House of Representatives. The July 13 issue of the CIO News carried a statement by Philip Murray entitled "Test of Political Freedom", which urged the election of Judge Edward A.

(Footnote 2 continued from preceding page.)
This so-called "Catlin Act" was later repealed in 1959, and at the present time only four states prohibit the use of union dues money in state elections. These laws are discussed in [7] and in the issue of Congressional Quarterly mentioned in Appendix D.

Garmatz in a Baltimore Congressional election. To remove all doubt that the expenditure of general union funds was involved, 1,000 extra copies of the paper were printed and distributed in Maryland's Third Congressional District.

Despite this early attempt to test the constitutionality of the amended version of Section 313 of the Corrupt Practices Act, however, the Supreme Court has not yet squarely faced the constitutionality of these provisions. There, nevertheless, has been no dearth of complex and sometimes confusing litigation. Although a corporation has never been indicted under Section 313, at least six labor organizations have been brought to trial. One of the labor groups pleaded nolo contendre and was fined, but no labor organization has ever been convicted of violating the law.[1] Beginning

---

1 When Assistant Attorney General Warren Olney III testified before a Senate committee in 1956, he submitted a memorandum stating that between 1950 and 1956 the Justice Department received 54 complaints alleging that these provisions of the Corrupt Practices Act had been violated. Of these, 39 involved labor organizations, 11 involved national banks and corporations organized under federal law, and four involved private corporations.

These complaints were such that investigations were made in 49 instances, and 14 of these were presented to grand juries. Two indictments were obtained against two separate labor organizations, but both cases resulted in acquittals. These cases will be reviewed in the text along with four others arising outside the time period covered in Olney's report. For his findings see [62, pp. 562-65].

with the previously mentioned case of U.S. v CIO, we will briefly review the various labor cases arising under this section of the law as well as a recent case arising under the Railway Labor Act which has important implications in this area and may signal a new departure in union electoral activity involving both "educational" and "political" expenditures.

After the front page editorial endorsing Judge Garmatz, Murray and the CIO were arraigned on February 20, 1948. They pleaded not guilty and filed a motion for dismissal, alleging that these provisions were unconstitutional. The district court agreed with them and dismissed the case brought by the government as a violation of the First Amendment, particularly the freedoms of speech and press clause. The government then appealed to the Supreme Court. Acting with uncharacteristic rapidity, the court handed down its decision on June 21, 1948, but it avoided the constitutionality question in ruling that the law did not outlaw such a publication.

It should be pointed out that the Government's case did not make much use of the fact that 1,000 extra copies of this issue of the CIO News were circulated to persons not regularly entitled to receive the publication. Thus, by emphasizing that the CIO News was published regularly and circulated among organization members and subscribers, the Court held that Congress did not want "to prohibit the publication, by corporations and unions in the regular course of conducting their affairs, of periodicals advising their members, stockholders or customers of dangers or advantage to their interest from the adoption of measures, or the election to office of men espousing these measures". [57, p. 457]

At no time were the provisions prohibiting the use of union funds for campaign contributions questioned. The key consideration was the meaning of a political "expenditure" as opposed to a political "contribution", and four members of the Supreme Court noted that the Congressional debates on the 1947 amendments resulted in a "veritable fog of contradictions".

In the first session of the 81st Congress, Senator Taft introduced a bill seeking to continue the prohibition on labor union "contributions" but to eliminate the prohibition on "expenditures". The bill passed the Senate by a vote of 51-42 on June 30, 1949, but later failed in the House. Meanwhile, a 1949 circuit court decision in the case of U.S. v Painters Local Union No. 481 cited the CIO decision in holding that a union financed political advertisement in the Hartford Times and a local political radio broadcast were not prohibited by Section 313. In this case the court noted "this small union owned no newspaper and a publication in the daily press or by radio was as natural a way of communicating its views to its members as by a newspaper of its own". [32, p. 731]

The next case involving a government prosecution of a union for violation of Section 313 occurred in 1951. In this case the union was acquitted by a district court for lack of sufficient evidence in U.S. v Construction and General Laborers' Local Union, and the court more or less openly acknowledged that minor violations of the expenditure ban would be tolerated under some sort of implicit de minimis rule. Joseph Tanenhaus states:

"A twelve-count indictment alleged that the union's automobiles, employees, and funds had been used illegally in support of its president, Theodore Irving, in his campaign for election to Congress in the fall of 1948. Defendants, who offered no testimoney, attacked the adequacy of the indictment and the constitutionality of the law. The court dismissed nine counts as based on insufficient and unsatisfactory evidence. The three remaining counts, charging that union checks for $60.20, $59.00, and $20.00 had been paid to its employees as compensation for services rendered in connection with Irving's campaign, were ultimately dismissed as failing to state a violation of the law. The statute, if strictly construed, the court openly asserted, would prescribe this activity, but the judge could not believe that Congress intended section 304 to be interpreted literally." [57, pp. 460-61]

The second major Supreme Court interpretation of Section 313 came in the case of U.S. v UAW. A Michigan grand jury indicted the UAW for using general union funds to pay for a television broadcast urging the election of candidates for Congress in the 1954 elections. A district court dismissed the indictment on the ground that it did not allege a statutory offense. This issue was taken to the Supreme Court, where it was ruled that such activities, if proven, would constitute a violation of Section 313. The Court drew the following distinction between the case and its earlier CIO decision.

Thus, unlike the union-sponsored political broadcast alleged in this case, the communication for which the defendants were indicated in CIO was neither directed nor delivered to the public at large. The organization merely distributed its house organ to its own people. The evil at which Congress has struck in [section] 313 is the use of corporate or union dues to influence the public at large to vote for a particular candidate or a particular party. [32, p. 732]

Although the majority of the Court avoided the constitutional questions in deciding this issue, it was indicated that after a trial and a conviction it could further consider the Constitutional questions in the light of the then facts of record. Such an opportunity was never provided, however, for a Michigan jury acquitted the UAW in the district court.

While the UAW case was still in litigation, the Senate Subcommittee on Privileges and Elections held hearings into the conduct of campaign financing in the 1956 elections. At these hearings both labor and management testimony had offered a rather broad interpretation of what was permissible legal expenditure.

The Congressional Quarterly Almanac reported that representatives of labor testified that general union funds legally could be used to:

> Systematically organize drives for registration of voters; carry out a systematic program of political education, including organization of schools where political questions are discussed, and the compilation and distribution of voting records; and exercise the right of free speech by expressing their views on political questions in print and by means of television and radio and otherwise. [15, p. 189]

The Almanac also reported that committee testimony indicated that corporations had been advised that they legally could:

> Pay salaries and wages of officers and regular employees while engaged in political activities; publish opinions and arguments of a political nature, expressed as the views of the corporation, in any house organ or other printed document circulated at the expense of the corporation; purchase radio and television time or newspaper space for the presentation of the corporation's political views; use any other means of expressing the views of the corporate management, publically or privately; encourage people to register and vote, and disseminate information and opinions concerning public issues without regard to parties and candidates. [15, p. 189]

At these hearings the UAW proposed several reforms in the

Federal Corrupt Practices Act, and they also stoutly maintained both corporations and labor unions had the constitutional right to spend money to express their own points of view without restriction. This right would not embrace paying for a candidate's or a party's opportunity to express its point of view, but would contain no restrictions on labor or corporate campaigning in their own name. A union pamphlet resulting from this testimony contains the following statement:

> It is difficult, if not impossible, to limit expenditures by persons or groups wishing to express their views on candidates and elections. Any such attempt seems to us subject to serious Constitutional doubts and our union has urged that position before the courts. We believe that we, that John Doe, that General Motors Corporation and that Henry Ford all have a Constitutional right to express, under our and their own name and auspices, our and their views on the most important issue before any citizen. We believe that we can exercise this right of free speech either as individuals or as regularly organized groups. [61, p. 38]

As we have seen the constitutional aspects of this contention still remain to be tested, although the statement previously quoted from the Court's decision in the subsequent UAW case indicated that, if proven, such practice is illegal under the present law.

This might be a good point to briefly summarize the major findings of the three most important cases under Section 313 of the Federal Corrupt Practices Act up to 1957: From the time of its initial application to unions, Section 313 was understood to prohibit the direct "contribution" of general union funds (dues money) to candidates for federal office and to their political committees, and this prohibition has not been the subject of any legal contention. It was also understood, however, that Section 313 did not prevent voluntary political contributions by union members. By supporting their "political" activities (as distinguished from their "educational" activities) from the voluntary contributions of union members, separate union political committees were permitted to function and make legal "contributions" and "expenditures" in federal elections. Such "contributions" and "expenditures" would be illegal, however, if the funds had been involuntarily exacted from union members. General funds, however, could be used for "educational" activities, providing they remained within the legal restraints on non-voluntary union funds, which up to 1957 were:

Regular union periodicals or newspapers financed from dues money could contain political material and be distributed to those accustomed to receiving copies since this involved a "house organ" not directed to the public at large.

At least in the Second Circuit a union without a regular periodical could buy advertising or radio time to endorse Congressional candidates.

A union could <u>not</u> "expend" union funds for commercial television broadcast or other political activities with the intent of influencing the general electorate in federal elections, since this involved "the evil at which Congress struck in section 313" namely "the use of corporate or union dues to influence the public at large to vote for a particular candidate or particular party".

At the end of 1957, however, the constitutional aspects of these prohibitions had not received Supreme Court consideration. In one case (<u>U.S. v. CIO</u>) the Court narrowed the coverage of Section 313 to avoid the dangers of unconstitutionality, and in another (U.S. v. UAW) it avoided facing the constitutional question pending the outcome of a jury trial which did not result in a conviction. The constitutional questions still remain to be answered, and so one can still speculate as to whether the protections of the first amendment apply only to persons or whether they also extend to corporate or union entities which have a separate legal existence apart from their owners or members.

Following the UAW case in 1957, there was a hiatus in litigation under Section 313 until the spring of 1961 when two different U.S. district courts were confronted with cases arising under these provisions, and the U.S. Supreme Court handed down a decision in a case arising under the Railway Labor Act which may have far reaching repercussions in the use of general union funds in the previously broadened area of legal "educational" expenditures.

The government won its first half-way victory in its attempts to convict a union under Section 313 of the Corrupt Practices Act when Teamsters Local 405 in St. Louis, Missouri, was charged with having made a contribution to a candidate directly from its general fund in a 1958 election campaign. The local pleaded nolo contendere and was fined $1,000. Later in the same year, however, the government's record of never securing a court conviction under the act was kept intact when the U.S. District Court in Anchorage, Alaska, granted a motion of acquittal following a jury trial on finding that "voluntary" funds were used to pay for four union-financed political telecasts during Alaska's first Congressional elections in 1958.[1] The telecasts in question in the latter case were part of a regularly-sponsored union television series "Building and Serving Anchorage" which had been regularly broadcast each week since 1955, but the thing which distinguishes this decision was the view of "voluntarism" applied by the U.S. District Judge Walter H. Hodge. Traditionally the test had been applied to the way the money was obtained from the individual union member, but in this case involving the Anchorage Central Labor Council, the Judge was impressed by the way in which this body obtained its funds from the affiliated local unions. Since each union affiliate decided by membership vote whether it would contribute to the T.V. fund and how much, the Judge held that this was a voluntary expenditure and not subject to the prohibition on union political spending.

This case seemed to shift the test of a voluntary contribution from an individual decision on whether to contribute to a specific union political committee to a majority decision by a local union on whether it wished to spend its dues money for political purposes. Any tendency for this interpretation to become widespread, however, was apparently nipped in the bud by the Supreme Court itself only a little over one month later when in a majority decision in the case of Machinist v. Street it ruled that the 1951 union shop amendment to the Railway Labor Act denied railroad unions the power

---

1 Both of these cases are discussed in [8].

to use an individual member's dues money for political action to which he was individually opposed.

This case originated with a group of Southern Railway employees who objected to the use of dues money for political purposes by railroad unions in which they were required to maintain membership. The Georgia courts upheld their contention and enjoined the enforcement of the union shop contract. The Supreme Court, however, held that such a blanket injunction was not an appropriate remedy and sent the case back to Georgia to have a remedy fashioned. The court also suggested some possible alternatives from which such a remedy might be chosen.

In writing the majority opinion in this case, Justice Brennan carefully pointed out that the Court was not outlawing the union-shop contract nor curtailing railroad unions' traditional political activities. He stated "Our construction therefore involves no curtailment of the traditional political activities of the railroad unions. It means only that those unions must not support those activities, against the expressed wishes of a dissenting employee, with his exacted money."

As to a proper remedy in the case at issue, Justice Brennan declared:

> One remedy would be an injunction against expenditures for political causes opposed by the complaining employee of a sum, from those moneys to be spent by the union for political purposes, which is so much of the moneys exacted from him as is the proportion of the union's total expenditures made for such political activities to the union's total budget. The union should not be in a position to

> make up such sum from money paid by a nondissenter, for this would shift a disproportionate share of the costs of collective bargaining to the dissenter and have the same effect of applying his money to the support of such political activities. A second remedy would be restitution to an individual employee of that portion of his money which the union expended, despite his notification, for the political causes to which he had advised the union he was opposed. There should be no necessity, however, for the employee to trace his money up to and including its expenditure; if the money goes into general funds and no separate accounts of receipts and expenditures of the funds of individual employees are maintained, the portion of his money the employee would be entitled to recover would be in the same proportion that the expenditures for political purposes which he had advised the union he disapproved bore to the total union budget. [9, p. A-2]

As yet, the Georgia Courts have made no subsequent decision on the exact formula to be used, but the issue raised in this case is an interesting one and apparently goes beyond the preceding litigation on educational vs. political expenditures, since presumably if a member objected to the educational material used in a union's political program he could prevent his dues money from being used to finance such activity whether or not it is permissable in the legal sense.

Thus, while litigation on union political expenditures rolls on, our review of this experience to date reveals that Section 313 and its subsequent court interpretation has not eliminated organized labor's financial participation in federal elections--particularly with regard to the voluntary funds collected by union political committees. Indeed, Table 8 lists the National Political Expenditures Financed by Voluntary Contributions Reported by the CIO-PAC, the AFL-LLPE, and the AFL-CIO-COPE for the Years 1944-1960.

TABLE 8 - National Political Expenditures Financed by Voluntary Political Contributions Reported by the CIO-PAC, the AFL-LLPE, and the AFL-CIO-COPE 1944-1960

Year	CIO-PAC	AFL-LLPE	AFL-CIO-COPE	Totals
1944	$ 470,852			$ 470,852
1946	151,693			151,693
1948	512,455	$ 312,196		824,651
1950	511,386	556,252		1,067,638
1952	505,722*	249,258		754,980
1954	415,042*	485,082		900,124
1956	23,220*	148,080	$ 670,985	842,285
1958			709,813	709,813
1960			795,140	795,140
Totals	$2,590,370	$1,750,868	$2,175,938	$6,517,176

* Additional educational expenditure also reported during these years.

Source: 1944 and 1946, Joseph Tannenhaus [57, p. 462].
1948-1960, Congressional Quarterly Almanac, 1949-1961.

Campaign Activity: Financial Aspects -- As indicated in Appendix D, the election expenditures reported under the provisions of the Federal Corrupt Practices Act do not represent the total amount spent on federal elections. Table 8, for example, represents only the reported expenditure of the national labor federation's from voluntary union funds. As the note in the Table indicates, the

CIO-PAC reported additional political education expenditures in three of the years covered. Other labor groups beside the ones shown in Table 8 also reported collecting and contributing voluntary political funds from their members during these years, and the figures in Table 8 do not include all of the expenditures by state and local political committees of PAC, LLPE, or COPE, because these groups are not considered subsidiaries of the national committee's for reporting purposes. Keeping these limitations in mind, one can observe that with the exception of 1946, which was apparently a year of widespread apathy, the CIO-PAC was able to raise roughly half a million dollars in voluntary contributions in each election year from 1944 through 1954. The AFL-LLPE seems to have been able to raise more money in off-year elections than during presidential years by requesting $2 rather than $1 contributions in these years, but even their highest year before 1954 never went much over half a million dollars, indicating that labor's ability to raise political funds via appeals for _voluntary_ contributions has fairly definite limits. Following the transition year of 1956, which shows the remnants of the PAC and the LLPE making political contributions as well as the newly formed COPE, COPE's reported contributions in 1958 and 1960 appear to be significantly less than the amounts raised by the separate political committee prior to the merger. The COPE data cover too short a time period to generalize much, but there certainly doesn't appear to be any significant increase in the reported campaign spending of the merged national labor federation as many had hoped or feared prior to the merger.

Congressional Quarterly began analyzing all federal election reports filed with the Clerk of the House under the Federal Corrupt Practices Act in 1948, and they have published their results in the Congressional Quarterly *Almanac* every two years since 1949. Although *Congressional Quarterly* has changed the format of their presentation from time to time, comparable figures are available for each election year since 1950 in most cases, and from 1948 in some instances. Using these data to go beyond the figures reported by the National Labor Federation in Table 8, Table 9 shows the number of national political committees (Republican, Democratic, Labor, and "Other") reporting federal election expenditures in each presidential election year from 1948 through 1960. Since the national committee expenditures are not the only expenditures reported, the total amounts reported by the individual Congressional candidates have been added to the amounts reported by the national committees to get a grand total of all election expenditures reported in the presidential election years covered. Table 10 presents the data reported for the non-presidential election years, 1950 through 1958, in the same manner as the data reported in Table 9 for the presidential election years. The adding of committee and candidate reports in Tables 9 and 10, may result in some duplication since some money may be transferred from a national committee to a particular candidate and then reported by both. Most of the money spent by the candidates comes from other sources, however, and as mentioned previously, much of the money actually spent in federal elections does not have to be reported at all. Therefore, despite some duplication, it would be generally agreed that the total figures shown in Tables 9 and 10 greatly understate

TABLE 9 - Total Federal Campaign Spending Reported in Presidential Election Years, 1948-1960*

Reported by:	1960		1956		1952		1948		Total
	No. Comm.	Amount	No. Comm.	Amount	No. Comm.	Amount	No. Comm.	Amount	
National Committees	154	$28,074.7	112	$23,090.5	133	$20,424.4	144	$13,563.9	$85,153.5
Republican	43	12,950.2	31	13,348.7	42	12,229.2		NA	NA
Democratic	29	11,801.0	22	7,189.4	22	5,121.7		NA	NA
Labor	60	2,450.9	43	1,805.5	35	2,070.4	13	1,291.3	7,618.1
Other	22	872.6	16	746.8	34	1,003.1		NA	NA
Congressional Candidates		$ 4,821.6		$ 6,169.6		$ 2,640.0		$ 2,980.9	$16,544.7
Republican		2,523.9		3,287.7		1,585.8		NA	NA
Democratic		2,249.7		2,857.0		1,038.1		NA	NA
Other		48.0		25.0		16.1		NA	NA
Total Reported Spending		$32,896.3		$29,260.1		$23,064.4		$16,544.7	$101,765.5
Labor Committee Spending as a % of Total Reported Spending		7.45%		6.17%		8.98%		7.80%	7.48% Average expenditure $1,904.5

* All dollar figures are in thousands. Columns may not total due to rounding.

Source: Congressional Quarterly Almanac, 1949, 1953, 1957, and 1961.

TABLE 10 - Total Federal Campaign Spending Reported in Non-Presidential Election Years, 1950-1958*

Reported by:	1958		1954		1950		Total
	No. Comm.	Amount	No. Comm.	Amount	No. Comm.	Amount	
National Committees	64	$8,675.5	147	$10,616.5	75	$8,158.7	$27,450.6
Republican	14	4,657.7	48	5,663.7	14	3,176.2	13,497.6
Democratic	7	1,702.6	41	2,361.8	12	2,971.2	7,035.7
Labor	32	1,828.8	41	2,057.6	31	1,618.6	5,505.0
Other	11	486.4	17	533.3	18	392.6	1,412.3
Congressional Candidates		$3,283.7		$ 3,045.9		$2,777.3	$ 9,106.9
Republican		1,670.9		1,596.0		NA	
Democratic		1,600.1		1,436.6		NA	
Other		12.6		13.3		NA	
Total		$11,595.1		$13,662.4		$10,935.9	$36,557.5
Labor Committee Spending as a % of Total Reported Spending		15.29%		15.06%		14.8%	15.06% Average Labor Expenditure $ 1,376.3

* All dollar figures are in thousands. Columns may not total due to rounding.

Source: Congressional Quarterly Almanac, 1951, 1955, and 1959.

actual election spending.[1]

---

[1] One piece of evidence in support of this point is the abnormally high amount of Congressional campaign spending reported in Table 9 for the 1956 House and Senate elections. Most of the huge difference between the reported spending in 1956 and that reported in preceding years can probably be explained by the more complete job of investigating reports in 1956. In that year the previously mentioned Senate Privileges and Elections Subcommittee undertook an exhaustive compilation of all reports filed with state and local agencies as well as the national reports. In addition to the official reports filed by the candidates, the Senate subcommittee also sent out supplementary questionnaires, and direct testimony was taken during five days of public hearings.

After all of this research, the Subcommittee's findings revealed that approximately $33 million was spent directly on federal elections in 1956 (as opposed to the $29.3 million reported in Table 9). The Subcommittee still felt that even the $33 million figure was incomplete, however, since only a limited period was intensively covered and since no study was made of primary elections or nominations. Neither did the Subcommittee attempt to cope with the problem of non monetary expenditures of time and effort by unpaid individuals or the whole area of non federal elections.

In addition to this evidence gathered in 1956, a specialist in the field of election finance, Alexander Heard of the University of North Carolina, has estimated that in 1952 the cost "in out-of-pocket cash expenditures for nominating and electing all public officials in the United States was around $140,000,000." [27, p. 2] In a subsequent and more comprehensive publication, Heard explains in detail how the above estimates were arrived at, and guesses that "1956 expenditures at the outside were around $155,000,000." [26, p. 8] In 1961, the Congressional Quarterly Almanac stated "Some individual estimates of the entire cost of the 1960 primaries and elections for all offices have gone as high as $175 million." [17, p. 1078]

Analyzing the spending reported in presidential and non-presidential years separately indicates that the number of labor committees reporting election expenditures in presidential years has increased each year from 1948 through 1960 with very large increases between 1948 and 1952 and between 1956 and 1960. Most of this latter increase is associated with the Teamster Union's formation of DRIVE, after the passage of the Landrum-Griffin Act in 1959. Despite the increase in the number of labor committees reporting, however, the amount of reported spending fell in 1956, the first presidential election year following the AFL-CIO merger.

Turning to the non-presidential election years between 1950 and 1958, Table 10 shows a drop in both the number of labor committees reporting and the amount of federal election expenditures reported between 1954 and 1958. The large number of "right to work" referenda appearing in state elections during 1958, however, may have diverted some union election funds from the federal campaigns in this year.

If the presidential election years and the non-presidential election years are combined, there does not appear to be any consistent trend in the amount of labor committee spending reported in federal elections. Total spending reported by national labor political committees has ranged between slightly over one and a quarter and slightly under two and a half million dollars in the last seven national elections. The average expenditure tends to be higher in presidential years for both labor and non-labor political committees, but non-labor committees seem to step up their presidential spending more than the labor committees. Thus, Table 9 shows that in the four presidential election years from 1948 through 1960 national labor committees reported spending an average of $1,904,530 per election, but this was only a little less than 7.5% of the total spending reported and less than nine per cent of the total spending reported by all national political committees during these years. On the other hand Table 10 shows that during the three off-year congressional elections between 1950 and 1958, reported labor spending averaged $1, 376, 254; but this lower average expenditure equalled over 15% of the total spending reported and just over 20% of all the expenditures reported by national political committees during these years.

The figures reported as labor spending in Tables 9 and 10 are presumably for the most part contributions made to candidates for federal office from voluntary funds. It is known that some "educational" expenditures from general union funds are included in these totals, but it is not likely that more than a small fraction of these expenditures are included, since such reports are not required by law.[1]

---

[1] In some years Congressional Quarterly's presentation of the data from the labor reports permitted a partial breakdown between voluntary contributions and non-voluntary educational expenditures and in some years it did not. For example, it is known that a total of $841, 385 in funds from the CIO-PAC education account is reported in the totals for the three elections from 1952 through 1956. The Machinists Non Partisan Political League has also reported a total expenditure of $242,908 from its general fund in the 1954, 1958, and 1960 elections, but beyond this the information is spotty.
(Continued on following page)

The change in the number of labor groups reporting from year to year, and a more detailed breakdown of the 60 labor groups reporting the $2,450,873 spent in the 1960 national elections, reveals some of the same diversity which we earlier noted characterized labor's spending on lobbying activities. Nineteen of the 60 committees reporting in 1960 were affiliated in one way or another with COPE. The national headquarters reported spending $795,140, while five international unions having COPE connections (Communication Workers, Chemical Workers, IBEW, IUE, UAW) reported spending $254,080, and 13 other local and regional COPE's in various parts of the country affiliated with various international unions or various geographical federations reported spending $69,668.

(Footnote 1 continued from preceding page.)

In 1952, Congressional Quarterly broke down the $2,070,350 reported by 35 national labor political committees in the following manner: $352,117, went as contributions to various Congressional races, and the other $1,718,233 went "for presidential campaign expenditures and other general educational and organizational spending such as registration drives, state gubernatorial and legislative campaigns as well as the presidential race."

In 1956 the detailed investigations of the previously mentioned Gore Committee revealed that national labor political committees had used $941,271 for direct campaign expenditures in federal election and in addition had contributed $1,078,852 in voluntary funds to candidates running for federal office. This Gore Committee total of $2,020,123 for labor groups exceeds the total of $1,805,482 reported by national labor committees through the regular reporting channels in 1956 just as the Gore Committee's total estimate of $33 million exceeds the total of $29 million officially reported from all sources in the 1956 elections.

Another group of 16 committees reported for the first time in 1960 in connection with the Teamster Union's new political organization Democratic, Republican, Independent Voter Education (DRIVE). The national headquarters of DRIVE reported spending $50,435 in 1960, while 15 local and joint council groups reported spending $22,030. In addition to these two large groups of committees, 14 separate international unions reported spending $1,131,471 through their own independent political committees and their affiliates. The remainder of the reported spending ($267,412) was reported by various other labor groups such as the Labor Committee for the Election of Kennedy and Johnson, the Ohio Telephone Education Committee, etc.

Despite the fact that the number of labor political committees reporting election expenditures has varied from year to year, a certain "hard core" of national committees account for the bulk of the expenditures. Some of these groups have a continuous record of political spending going all the way back to 1948, the first year in which Congressional Quarterly began analyzing spending reports. Ten of these committees in addition to the national federation committees themselves and the amounts they have reported in each election since 1948 are shown in Table 11. This table shows that of the total of $13,123,133 reported by all labor committees in the seven elections since 1948, $11,504,510 has been reported during the six years for which we have detailed breakdowns of labor political committees expenditure reports. During these six years, $10,215,997, or about 89% of the total labor expenditure, has been reported by these ten

TABLE 11 – Federal Political Spending Reported by Continuing Labor Political Committees, 1948-1960*

	1960	1958	1956	1954	1952	1948
AFL-LLPE			148.1	485.1	249.3	312.2
CIO-PAC Contributions Account			23.2	415.0	505.7	512.5
Educational Account			8.1	400.0	433.3	
AFL-CIO COPE						
Individual Contributions Fund	795.1	709.8	671.0			
Amalgamated (Clothing Workers) Political Action Committee	81.3	44.7	64.6	18.1	43.1	35.1
Hat Cap and Millinery Workers	11.8	NR	5.5	4.0	13.8	NR
ILGWU	315.7	107.7	149.5	44.8	265.3	240.5
Machinists' N-P Political League						
Educational Fund	73.5	70.5	55.2	37.1	20.8	33.0
General Fund	119.7	79.7	NR	43.4	NR	NR
Railway Labor's Political League	88.2	78.8	104.5	82.9	88.6	84.4
TWUA-Political Education Fund	29.1	35.1	21.0	6.0	14.5	4.2
Trainmen's Political Education League	9.7	14.3	9.7	12.8	13.7	5.8
UAW-CIO-PAC	61.4	243.8	245.1	255.2	135.0	16.5
Carpenters' Non-Partisan Committee	49.0	5.5	6.0	0	34.5	18.3
United Steelworkers Pol. Act. Fund Individual Contributions Account	239.5	192.1	184.8	185.0	NR	NR
Total, for Selected Groups	1,874.1	1,582.0	1,696.3	1,989.7	1,817.6	1,262.3
All Other Labor Groups Reporting	576.9	246.8	109.2	68.0	252.7	29.0
TOTAL LABOR SPENDING REPORTED	\$2,450.9	\$1,828.8	\$1,805.5	\$2,057.6	\$2,070.4	\$1,291.3
Selected Groups as % of Total	76.46%	86.51%	93.95%	96.70%	87.79%	97.75%

* All dollar figures are in thousands. Columns may not total due to rounding. Detailed breakdowns are not available for 1950.

Source: Congressional Quarterly *Almanac*, 1949, 1953, 1955, 1957, 1959, and 1961.

committees, plus the national labor federations. Their relative percentage of total reported labor expenditures, however, has shown a tendency to decline during the most recent elections. This tendency is similar to the lobby spending figures reported earlier which indicated that the influence of the national federations was declining as a percentage of the total lobby spending reported. Unlike the figures on lobby spending shown in Table 2, there does not appear to be any marked increase in the total amount of campaign spending reported by labor groups in recent years, except for the sharp increase between 1958 and 1960 associated with the Teamsters' formation of DRIVE. The amount of campaign spending reported by the AFL-CIO COPE increased by some $85,327 (12%) between 1958 and 1960, again unlike the decrease shown in Table 2 for AFL-CIO lobby spending during these years, but COPE's percentage of the total campaign spending reported by all labor groups fell from about 40% to about 32% between 1958 and 1960, despite its increase in absolute terms. Aside from the Teamsters, the largest increases in reported campaign spending between 1958 and 1960 were by the ILGWU, $207,960 (193%), the Clothing Workers, $36,568 (86%), and the Steelworkers, $47,327 (24%). The biggest drop between 1958 and 1960 was by the UAW, down $182,359 (75%).

To sum up this data on union campaign contributions the $13,123,133 seven-year total of reported labor spending represents an average expenditure of $1,874,733 a year for each of the election years since 1948. Ignoring the previously mentioned variations between presidential and non-presidential years, this represents an annual election year average of 11.65% of the total reported committee expenditure and an average of 9.49% of the total reported expenditure during these years. While not overwhelming, these figures represent a substantial amount of electoral involvement. Some perspective can be gained on their relative magnitude, however, if it is considered that in 1956, a year in which 43 labor committees were reporting election expenditures of $1,805,482, twelve of the richest families in America alone accounted for contributions of $1,153,735, and the known contributions of $500 or more by 199 executives of the country's 225 largest corporations totaled $1,936,847. Comparable figures on family spending are not available for 1952, but in that year 35 labor committees reported spending $2,070,350, and the known contributions of $500 or more by 92 officers and directors of the country's 100 largest corporations totaled $1,014,909.[1]

---

1 More will be said on the executive contributions in the following section on business political activity. The figures on the twelve family political contributions in 1956 are published in [15, p. 212]. They show the du Ponts contributed $248,423 in 1956 followed alphabetically by these families: Field $33,500; Ford $36,899; Harriman $38,850; Lehman $39,500; Mellon $100,150; Olin $53,550; Pew $216,800; Reynolds $49,609; Rockefeller $152,604; Vanderbilt $64,400; and Whitney $121,450. As might be expected, most of the money contributed by the 12 families in 1956 went to the Republicans: $1,040,526 (90.19%). $107,109 (9.28%) went to the Democrats, and $6,100 (53% went for miscellaneous purposes.

Since state and local committees are not considered as subsidiaries of national bodies for reporting purposes, however, there is no way of knowing exactly how much is contributed by all labor groups. The Gore Committee in 1956 made the most comprehensive compilation of this information ever attempted, however, and their summary of political contributions by 217 state and local labor groups in the 1956 national elections appear in Table 12.

TABLE 12 - Disbursements of State and Local Political Committees, September 1 - November 30, 1956

No.	Type of Committee	Total Disbursement
	State*	
20	Committee on Political Education (COPE) Affiliated with State Labor Councils	$137,538
23	Labor's Leagues for Political Education (LIFE) Affiliated with State Federations of Labor	105,702
27	CIO-Political Action Committees (PAC) Affiliated With State Industrial Union Councils	196,351
	Totals for 70 AFL-CIO State Political Committees	439,591
27	Machinist's Non-Partisan Leagues	52,002
8	Miscellaneous	42,107
	Local	
112	All types - Located in the 100 Largest Counties	296,644
217	TOTALS	$830,344

* At the time of the 1956 campaign, state AFL and CIO groups had merged in some states and not in others. In a few instances, the reporting organization was the labor organization itself (e.g., a state industrial union council) rather than its political committee. In some states, both CIO-PAC's and COPE's were active. In those cases, the COPE's are reported with the LIFE's as affiliated with the AFL.

Source: Alexander Heard, [26, p. 183].

The total of $830,344 revealed in this table would appear to constitute about a 46% addition to the $1,805,482 reported by the national political committees in 1956, but the internal transfer of funds among labor political groups results in some duplication and Alexander Heard has concluded: "Crude though they are, these estimates from independent data are sufficiently consistent to fix the probable outer limits of labor's voluntary contributions for the 1956 elections at about $2,200,000." [26, p. 93] This figure would represent about 7.3% of the total of $33,000,000 estimated as <u>direct</u> election expenditures by the Gore Committee in 1956.

Clearly, organized labor is in no position to dominate American election finance through its access to funds voluntarily contributed by its members for political purposes. Indeed, its position apparently is no better than that of a handful of the nation's wealthiest families or the executives of America's 225 largest corporations. But there is one thing that the American labor movement has which the wealthy families or corporate executives do not have, and that thing is members--large numbers of members. Thus we are reminded that campaign contributions from voluntary funds are not the only source of campaign support in organized labor's attempts to elect legislators favorably disposed to its lobbying aims. Registration drives, "educational" material, union endorsements, and other devices are also employed in an attempt to influence the "labor vote" on which much of organized labor's implied political power supposedly rests, and there is no evidence that the financial aspects of these programs (even though financed from dues money) are any indication of their total impact on the American political process.

There is no way to put a price tag on the whole range of union political activities designed to register, inform, and influence the votes of union members; but Alexander Heard, who made a detailed analysis of the UAW, perhaps the most politically conscious of all American unions, has stated:

> Campaign-connected expenditures from union treasuries may be made under at least 13 different headings... The 13 categories are: (1) donations, (2) political department, (3) citizenship program, (4) education and information, (5) communications, (6) public service activities, (7) public relations, (8) research, (9) legislative activities, (10) legal department, (11) expense accounts, (12) general administrative cost, and (13) salaries. [26, p. 206]

After examining each of these areas in detail, Heard concluded:

> If 25% of the UAW international's editorial, radio, research, and educational activities, and all of its citizenship activities, are arbitrarily declared to have been campaign-connected, expenditures in 1956 would have come to less than $1,500,000. If an equal amount was spent by UAW locals--also nothing but a guess--the total for this union would have been about $3,000,000, or less than $2.50 per member. This represents an outside figure for one of the most aggressive of all unions; for the 17,385 members of the labor movement resident in the United States, the per capita average would be a small fraction of it.
>
> Crude though all of this is, the conclusion seems inescapable that labor money in politics from all sources pays a much smaller share of the nation's campaign-connected costs than union members constitute of the population of voting age. [26, p. 208]

Whether these union members exert any non-financial influence through the weight of their sheer numbers alone is a question to which we will now turn our attention.

Campaign Activity: Registration, Education, And The "Labor Vote" -- The so-called "labor vote" is one of the more widely discussed concepts in our contemporary political folklore. Sometimes referring to all labor voters, but most often used in the context of only trade union voters, speculations vary as to both its size and its cohesiveness, but little note is usually taken of its distribution in determining its political effectiveness. Ignoring the distribution problem for a moment, a fairly common procedure for "estimating" the "potential" labor vote by hopeful and fearful alike is to take the number of union members and multiply it by a fairly healthy "family factor" to arrive at a conclusion like the one cited in the following statement: "... the unions have grown enormously both in numbers and prestige and now are decidedly to be reckoned with politically--on the theory that this 25% of the workers--15 million people--can control or influence 60 million voters." [21, p. 29]

Such "estimates" suffer on several grounds. Several million union members are minors and other aliens not eligible to vote, and many others are disqualified by residence requirements and in some southern states by the poll tax. But, as Edwin Witte has pointed out, more than offsetting the union members who are not eligible are the wives of members, retired former members, and nonmembers who go along with the unions. Witte then goes on to make a potential estimate of his own which does not consider the distribution of the total vote in determining its significance. He states: "The total vote which the unions might potentially control may be as high as

25,000,000 but probably is considerably smaller. This is a large block of potential voters, but less than a third of the total number. [65, p. 414] The word "potential" is a key word in this estimate, since the problem of getting union members registered and informed is a crucial one as far as labor's political activities are concerned. Before turning to these considerations, however, a word on the distribution of trade union membership is in order.

When the Bureau of Labor Statistics of the United States Department of Labor published its Directory of National and International Unions in the United States in 1957, it reported that there were 189 American national and international unions in this country with about 18,477,000 members in some 77,000 locals. Seventeen million three hundred and eighty-five thousand of these members were living in the continental United States, and they comprised approximately 25% of the United States' labor force and about 34% of those employed in nonagricultural establishments. Some 3,191,000 of these members were affiliated with unions which are not now in the AFL-CIO. As might be expected, these members were not evenly distributed among the different unions. In fact, almost two-fifths of the membership was concentrated in the seven largest unions, and roughly one-half of the membership was affiliated with one of the twelve largest unions.

For purposes of effective political influence, the distribution of trade union membership in different national unions is of considerable importance, because, although COPE was established as a staff department responsible to the AFL-CIO Executive Council, its effectiveness is dependent upon the support and cooperation of member unions. And, of course, not all unions are members of the federation. The political vitality of organized labor is thus rooted in the attitudes and actions of individual unions; and the organizational structure, political activities, and even the partisan preferences of American unions are considerably more diverse and disunited than the limited facade of unity at the federation level would lead one to believe.

Our earlier figures on lobby spending and campaign contributions indicate that, within the federation, the largest unions are not always the most politically active. Further, the building trades unions often act in concert, as do the railroad unions (through the Railway Labor Political League), which gives them greater cohesion and often makes them politically more effective than some of the larger individual unions. Some of the national unions within the federation, which have their own independent political organizations, do not work through COPE. These include such unions as the Machinists, the IUE, the International Ladies' Garment Workers, the Glass Bottle Blowers, and the Retail Clerks. Other affiliated unions such as the Auto Workers, the Steelworkers, and the Amalgamated Clothing Workers also have political organizations of their own; but they do most of their work through COPE. Outside the federation, the independent United Mine Workers now operates through its own political organization, Labor's Non-Partisan League; and, as noted above, the Teamsters' Union, expelled from the AFL-CIO in 1957, has also set up an independent political action committee known as DRIVE. Beneath these national organizations, both inside and outside the federation, lie a myriad of state and local political action committees of varying scope and composition.

Probably even more important than the distribution of trade union members among the different national and local unions, however, is the geographical distribution of trade union membership. This is true because most political offices are determined on a geographical basis, not along the industry lines for which unions are organized for the purposes of collective bargaining.

The most comprehensive estimate of the geographical location of trade union members by states was compiled by Leo Troy in 1953. [58] Since union membership in this country hasn't grown greatly in the past decade, the figures for 1953 are probably still useful. Table 13 shows Troy's information on the numerical strength of union membership in each state in 1953, and the percentage of nonagricultural employment organized in each state in 1953. Then, using these data, Alexander Heard combined it with United States Bureau of Census' estimates of the population of voting age in each state in 1952, and computed the third column of Table 13 which shows union membership as a percentage of the population of voting age in each state. It can be seen that the geographical distribution of trade union membership is by no means uniform. In fact, over two-thirds of the union members in 1953 were concentrated in 10 states, and another 10% were located in seven additional states, thus placing

TABLE 13 - Labor Unions Membership and Percentage of Voting Population by States, 1953

State	Union Membership in (thousands)	% of Non-Ag. Employment Organized	Union Memb. As % of Pop. of Voting Age	State	Union Membership in (thousands)	% of Non-Ag. Employment Organized	Union Memb. As % of Pop. of Voting Age
Alabama	168.3	25	10	New Jersey	645.4	35	19
Arizona	55.7	28	12	New Mexico	25.0	14	7
Arkansas	67.9	22	6	New York	2,051.8	34	20
California	1,392.5	36	18	North Carolina	83.8	8	4
Colorado	114.2	28	14	North Dakota	17.3	16	5
Connecticut	232.1	27	17	Ohio	1,162.6	38	22
Delaware	25.8	18	12	Oklahoma	86.7	16	7
Florida	135.9	16	7	Oregon	201.5	43	20
Georgia	135.8	15	6	Pennsylvania	1,540.7	40	22
Idaho	29.1	22	9	Rhode Island	82.8	27	16
Illinois	1,358.7	40	23	South Carolina	49.7	9	4
Indiana	569.6	40	22	South Dakota	17.4	14	4
Iowa	159.2	25	9	Tennessee	187.3	23	9
Kansas	130.8	24	11	Texas	374.8	17	8
Kentucky	155.1	25	9	Utah	56.9	26	14
Louisiana	135.8	20	8	Vermont	19.6	19	8
Maine	58.9	21	11	Virginia	156.1	17	8
Maryland	203.6	25	13	Washington	393.6	53	26
Massachusetts	546.1	30	18	West Virginia	223.9	44	19
Michigan	1,062.0	43	25	Wisconsin	418.7	38	19
Minnesota	327.6	38	17	Wyoming	24.2	29	14
Mississippi	50.0	15	4	District of Columbia	107.8	21	—
Missouri	510.5	40	19	Not distributed by state	458.5	—	—
Montana	72.5	47	20	United States	16,217.3	33	17
Nebraska	68.6	20	8				
Nevada	21.8	30	19				
New Hampshire	43.1	25	12				

Source: Alexander Heard, [26, p. 174.]

TABLE 14 - States in Which Union Membership Was Concentrated Both As A Percentage of the Voting-Age Population and As A Percentage of the Non-Agricultural Labor Force in 1953*

State	Union Membership (in thousands)	Per Cent of Non-Agricultural Employment Organized	Union Membership As Percentage of Population of Voting Age
New York	2,051.8	20	34
Pennsylvania	1,540.7	22	40
California	1,392.5	18	36
Illinois	1,358.7	23	40
Ohio	1,162.6	22	38
Michigan	1,062.0	25	43
New Jersey	645.4	19	35
Indiana	569.6	22	40
Massachusetts	546.1	18	30
Missouri	510.5	19	40
TOTAL (10)	10,839.9	—	—
Wisconsin	418.7	19	38
Washington	393.6	26	53
Minnesota	327.6	17	38
West Virginia	223.9	19	44
Oregon	201.5	20	43
Montana	72.5	20	47
Nevada	21.8	19	30
TOTAL (7)	1,659.6	—	—

*The first group contains the ten states with the largest number of union members. The second group consists of the remaining seven states in which the percentage of voting-age population who were union members equaled 17 or more and the percentage of non-agricultural employees who were union members equaled 30 or more.

Source: Alexander Heard, [26, p. 176].

approximately three-fourths of the union members in approximately one-third of the states. These 17 states are shown separately in Table 14, which includes all of the states in which 30% or more of the nonagricultural employees are organized and in which at the same time the percentage of union members among persons of voting age matched or exceeded the national average of 17 percent.

These figures certainly show that the trade union political potential is not evenly distributed throughout the nation, but even these figures must be further qualified. For example, trade union membership within these states tends to be concentrated in the urban areas and not evenly spread throughout the state; and the composition of union membership by national union varies considerably from state to state.

Moving from the state level to individual congressional districts, in 1957 Congressional Quarterly identified 52 "labor districts" in which more than 60 percent of those employed were "blue collar" workers. This classification made no attempt to distinguish between union workers and non-union workers, however, but simply used the 1950 census results to compute "the percentage of employed persons in each Congressional district who held blue-collar jobs: craftsmen, foremen, machine operators, private household help, service employees, and all laborers except those who work on farms." [15, p. 812] The Congressional Quarterly noted:

> "While in the average Congressional district, 48.9% of the workers were in blue-collar jobs, there are 52 districts where more than 60% of those employed were blue-collar workers. These districts [are] the biggest

'labor' districts in the country. [15, p. 812][1]

While this definition cannot stand as an iron-clad definition of a labor district in the sense of a trade union district, 42 of these 52 Congressional districts are in the states with large union memberships cited in Table 14. While far from being a majority of the 435 Congressional districts, these districts nevertheless are the ones in which a potential "labor vote" is most likely to reside.

Regardless of where the potential "labor vote" resides, it is of little practical value unless it can be registered and informed (or instructed, as some would say) and brought to the polls on election day. In this connection, Walter Reuther, President of the United Automobile Workers and Vice-President of the AFL-CIO, has stated:

> Politics is the everyday housekeeping job of democracy. In a democratic society, politics is the people's business. Two basic problems confront labor in the field of political action:
>
> 1. We must do the practical day-to-day organizational work necessary to mobilize people and get them to register and then get them out to vote on election day...
>
> 2. We must carry on a comprehensive educational campaign to develop an understanding among the people of the basic issues on which political decisions are being made

---

1 The 52 districts identified as having more than 60% of the workers in blue-collar jobs were: Alabama (9); California (19, 23); Connecticut (5); Illinois (1, 5, 7, 24); Indiana (1); Maine (2); Maryland (3); Massachusetts (3, 7, 9, 14); Michigan (1, 13, 16); New Hampshire (1); New Jersey (8, 14); New York (8, 9, 16, 18, 23); North Carolina (9, 11); Ohio (18, 19, 20, 21); Pennsylvania (1, 3, 4, 11, 12, 14, 15, 20, 21, 22, 23, 25, 26, 30); Rhode Island (1, 2); South Carolina (4); West Virginia (1, 5, 6).

> and where the interest of the people lies. Millions of workers have not yet learned the relationship between the bread box and the ballot box. [51, pp. 71-72]

Reuther's feeling that the question of voter registration is indeed a problem for labor political action has been confirmed by many voting studies which show that the percentage of eligible voters who actually register and vote is generally much smaller in districts where most of the working people live compared to the better residential areas in the cities, in the suburbs, and in rural areas. Gus Tyler, the chief political adviser of the ILGWU, has described an LLPE study which

> "Politically dissected a typical city with ten silk-stocking and ten organized labor precincts. In the silk-stocking districts, there were 18,400 eligible voters, 17,000 of whom registered and 15,965 of whom voted; in the labor districts, there were 43,400 eligible voters, 11,103 of whom registered and 8,622 of whom voted. The silk-stocking areas with 18,000 eligible voters outvoted labor districts with 43,000 eligible voters by almost two to one.
>
> Labor's prime task is to turn non-voters into voters." [60, p. 124]

Given an awareness of the registration problem, some of the more politically conscious elements in the American labor movement have made increasing efforts in this direction, and they have apparently met with some moderate success. Angus Campbell and H. C. Cooper found that union members voted more often than non-union persons in the same occupations in 1948, 1952, and 1954 [12, pp. 31-32], and in its report to the AFL-CIO convention in 1957, COPE estimated that its efforts had increased the overall average of registration among trade-union members by 5-6% [1, p. 109].[1]

In perhaps the most comprehensive study of trade union voting behavior ever made, Kornhauser, Sheppard, and Mayer found that in 1952 Detroit members of the UAW registered and voted in about the same proportions as the public at large. They noted that this was "a phenomenon not usually observed in blue collar groups. This would indicate that union efforts to get out the vote may have had some degree of success. One-third of the membership did not vote, however, even though the great majority of these non-voters were legally eligible." [30, p. 73] The authors also indicated that they were not studying a typical union. They indicated that "Within the whole of American labor, the UAW is probably the union most fully committed to political action on the national level and most influential in the use of its political arm in relation to broad economic and social policies." [30, p. 14]

---

1 Despite this estimate of a 5-6% increase in union member registration, however, the same report later on stated:

> "Registration remains one of the major problems of our organization in this field. In an effort to meet it, the Executive Council of the AFL-CIO in January, 1957 adopted a resolution setting forth the views of our organization on the subject and calling upon affiliated organizations to take steps to establish permanent registration committees as standing committees of the local union...
>
> This program of activity has been followed up by the Committee on Political Education. We are happy to report that 61 international and national unions now have specific programs dealing with this subject." [1, p. 113]

When it is remembered that the AFL-CIO had 144 affiliated unions in 1957, however, this record of 61 participating unions is probably not overly impressive, even though it no doubt covered most of the larger unions.

Going beyond the problems of voter registration and "get-out-the-vote" campaigns, there is the question of voter "education" and trade union information in political campaigns. While there is no precise way to estimate the total amount of this activity, some insights are possible.

Since the earliest days of the CIO-PAC it has been traditional that the executive board of the national labor federations and their national political committees formally endorse candidates only for the Presidency and Vice Presidency. This endorsement, which has always gone to the Democratic candidates, usually follows previous endorsements by the affiliated national unions. The national Federation does not officially endorse Senatorial, Congressional, state, or local candidates; but it is generally recognized that initiative and leadership are more likely to flow downward than upward in affiliated unions and political committees, even though most of the endorsements are formally made by the latter groups. The records of official labor endorsements prior to the AFL-CIO merger are incomplete, but in 1956 State and local AFL-CIO bodies, or both, endorsed 282 candidates for the House, and 30 Senatorial candidates. In 1958, with "right-to-work" laws on the ballot in six states, 12 candidates for governor were endorsed along with 294 candidates for the House and 30 candidates for the Senate. In 1960 state and local COPEs endorsed 19 Senatorial candidates, 258 House candidates, and 19 Gubernatorial candidates.

Once these endorsements have been made, there is the question of publicity and passing this information on to the union members and others. At this juncture much of the diversity within the American labor movement begins to exert itself. Even those unions having an active political program are not able to excite all of their local officers or members about political affairs. Some of these key persons may even resent an active political program. Hudson and Rosen, for example, made a detailed study of a large regional Machinists' union in the St. Louis area. The official policy of the union studied was limited to candidates for state and national offices, and it consisted of promoting voter registration, endorsement of candidates, collection of money for campaign purposes, and campaigning for candidates among the membership. When asked whether they thought the union should take an active part in politics, 79% of the members felt that this should be done at least sometimes whereas 86% of the stewards and local offices felt the union should be active in politics at least sometimes. In this respect, however, the fact that 14% of the local officers and stewards, supposedly the "backbone" of the union, felt that the union should not be active in politics is probably very significant for the ultimate effectiveness of the union's official political program. Indeed, Hudson and Rosen concluded:

> While official policy on political action is definite, we have no evidence that all union officials firmly suscribe to it. And it almost certainly would take a "back seat" should a choice between success in politics and success in collective bargaining be called for. [28, p. 411]

Thus, the fact that the local union is the basic unit of organization as far as the actual contacts of the vast majority of union members are concerned, only multiplies the opportunities for diversity and inconsistency in the effectiveness of national political programs. This is particularly true of local union endorsement procedures when "one of the boys" wants to run for office. The ex-journalist and late Senator Richard L. Newberger, has stated:

> Business groups would be ridiculed if they were compelled to boost every candidate who ran a grocery store or movie theater, but labor is often put in this position when union members get the itch for office... But all union people must be endorsed regardless of their qualifications. [44, p. 674]

It should be made clear, however, that not all of the diversity is confined to the local level. William "Big Bill" Hutchenson's life-long attachment to the Republican Party is well known, though an admitted exception among most union presidents. A more recent example occurred shortly after the official AFL-CIO endorsement of Adlai Stevenson in 1956, when Dave Beck, then the still unsullied leader of the nation's largest union, let it be known that he had voted for the Republican presidential candidate in each of the preceding two elections. Edwin Witte also noted: "While the endorsement of Stevenson was reported as having been a unanimous vote, several prominent union leaders supported Eisenhower in the campaign." [65, p. 413]

Finally, even in the most politically active unions, it must be remembered that the officers already have full time jobs in other areas. In this connection, Gus Tyler has noted:

> Most trade union leadership--paid and unpaid, full time or part time--is involved with the daily grind of organizing, bargaining, and above all enforcing contracts. This pure and simple trade union work is, of necessity, so absorbing that it leaves minimal time for discussion of public issues. Hence, the burden of issue education falls on the shoulder of union journals, generally monthly publications, with some allocation of space to political matters. [60, p. 135]

Until recently there were no really exhaustive studies of trade union periodicals which could estimate how much these journals emphasized political matters. In the summer of 1960, however, the University of Michigan's Bureau of Industrial Relations initiated a project to make a detailed analysis of the political content of 43 major trade union periodicals during the first eight months of 1960, a presidential election year.

Using a rather broad definition of "politics", this study found that political news and viewpoints made up 25.84% of the total column inches available in 43 leading union periodicals during the first eight months of 1960. Interestingly enough only 6.6% of the total available column inches in the papers studied were devoted to the forthcoming presidential election, and more than three times as much space (22%) was given to matters of public welfare, health legislation, aid to education, housing, depressed areas, and aid to the aged, under consideration in Congress or proposed for enactment. Not much attention was given to other elections, such as those of Congressmen or various state officials, either. The study noted:

> Only 1.9% of all political news, only one-half of one percent of all column-inches available in these key union papers, was devoted to influencing elections of legislators...when it came to getting on page one of an

> important union newspaper, candidates and issues in non-presidential elections ranked lower than almost every other category of item in editorial emphasis. [54, p. 1]

The fact that this study terminated on September 1, 1960, probably limits some of the above conclusions, but it does provide some interesting insights into the different amounts of interest in political matters expressed by various national unions. Based on their analysis of this point Shedd and Odiorne concluded:

> Papers circulated among predominantly industrial workers had a significantly higher amount of political news than those of craft unions...
>
> Another observable difference between the national industrial union papers and those of the craft unions was the emphasis on the election of the president or of congressmen. The industrial unions, in addition to having a greater political content, generally devoted more space to this subject than did the craft union papers. [54, pp. 3-4]

Aside from the content of these union periodicals there is also the problem of getting them circulated to and read by potential voters.

With regard to the circulation of trade union periodicals, which are without uniformity of appearance or circulation, one can only guess, but Tyler has stated:

> If we assume that, on the average, each of the 16,000,000 workers in the United States is exposed to a trade union journal about once every two weeks, then we can arrive at a rough calculation of about 8,000,000 readers weekly, or about a million plus daily readers. Needless to say, this is only a drop in the ocean of American journalism, something less than the circulation of several major dailies in New York City alone. [60, p. 135-36]

In addition to regularly published union periodicals, union political committees also resort to special publicity and literature campaigns as election day approaches. In its report to the 1959 AFL-CIO convention, COPE stated:

> During 1958 and the first half of 1959, 33 different items of literature were printed and distributed with a total circulation in excess of 31 million...
> In the late summer of 1958 approximately 11,250,000 copies of the 1957-58 voting record of members of the House of Representatives and United States Senate were sent to the various states for distribution to members of the AFL-CIO. [2, pp. 280-81]

If all of this literature and educational material is to be effective in gaining support for labor endorsed candidates, however, it must be read and used as the basis for action by the recipients. Indeed, successful propaganda of any type must pass through three stages: the propagandists' message must be perceived; this perception must stimulate attitudes appropriate to the propagandist aim; and these attitudes must result in the type of action the propagandist desires.

With respect to the first of these stages, the study by Kornhauser, Sheppard, and Mayer found that only 31% of the Detroit auto workers they studied had read about the election in any magazines or papers other than regular newspapers. Only 7% of this group said that they read the union publication during the 1952 presidential campaign. (More Stevenson voters read this literature than did union members who voted for Eisenhower.)

After examining all sources of campaign influence and their relative importance as reported by the auto workers, the authors concluded:

> The union was mentioned spontaneously by only a very small minority of workers as: 1) a source of most of their information about the campaign; 2) the most important source; 3) a source of publications about the election; and 4) as an organization whose ideas they wanted before election day. [30, p. 93]

This last point moves beyond the mere perception of union political messages to the next stages of the propaganda process--the stages which consider the initial attitudes of the persons who perceive the message and the extent to which these attitudes are changed or activated. Kornhauser, Sheppard, and Mayer presented a list of six groups to the auto workers they studied in 1952 and asked them to indicate the groups they particularly trusted with regard to their voting recommendations. The same procedure was followed for groups which were not trusted. They concluded:

> The findings on this entire question indicate that the most generally accepted position among UAW members is one of trusting union voting recommendations and distrusting those offered by Business and Newspapers. The declarations of trust and distrust, along with the reasons assigned, leave little doubt that a large sector of the membership (approximately one half of all members) feels that they have political interests opposed to those of Business and Newspapers, interests that they can protect and advance by supporting the union's position on the political front. At the same time it is clear that a small but significantly numerous group in the union holds dissenting opinions and does not trust union political recommendations; they include a minimum of one in eight who *express* distrust (and presumably some others who refrain from stating their views). The remaining 30 to 40% of the members are the uncommitted--people who are not prepared to declare themselves as either trusting or distrusting political endorsements by labor groups. Most of them fall into the 41% of respondents who refrained from naming *any* group they do not trust. They constitute a considerable portion of the union, the politically less aroused and less partisan, who presumably will go along with the union in any particular election or will not, depending upon the social forces and cross-pressures affecting them at the time. [30, p. 110]

This finding of a minority more or less opposed to the union's political endorsements with a farily large undecided element separating them from those who approved tends to be corroborated by the results of an attitude study made among the members of a large regional machinist union in the St. Louis area at about the same time the Detroit study was made. On the basis of this study, Hudson and Rosen concluded that:

> "It would appear that the immediate political power of unions at the polls is fairly limited... Present political strength of the unions seems limited more by members lack of positive enthusiasm or by their uncertainty than by a strong disapproval of political activity." [28, p. 418]

Much the same conclusion was reached in an earlier survey of union member attitudes in a study of Teamster Local 688 in St. Louis, done by Arnold M. Rose in 1949. Rose found that 77.3% of the members of this local felt that the union should tell members which candidates are "friendly" to labor, but only 35.0% felt that the union should "advise" members how to vote. He concluded:

> The discrepancy between the proportion of workers who wish to be "advised" on how to vote and the proportion who simply wish to be told which candidates are friendly to labor has another important implication. It suggests that the workers will not necessarily accept any candidate, regardless of his merits and general reputation, whom the labor leaders support. Workers say they will listen to the political information provided by their union leaders, but they do not say they will always follow their advice. As in other matters, workers distinguish their obligations and loyalty to their union from their other obligations and loyalties. [52, pp. 83-84]

The fact that union members have other attachments and loyalties outside their union affiliation is of course an obvious one, and raw voting figures, classed only by union membership, are not likely to be an adequate reflection of all of the complexities that go into a political decision, due to the phenomenon which David Truman has called "overlapping membership." He states:

> No tolerably normal person is totally absorbed in any group in which he participates. The diversity of an individual's activities and his attendant interests involve him in a variety of actual and potential groups. Moreover the fact that the genetic experiences of no two individuals are identical and the consequent fact that the spectra of their attitudes are in varying degrees dissimilar means that the members of a single group will perceive the group's claims in terms of a diversity of frames of reference. Such heterogeneity may be of little significance until such time as these multiple memberships conflict. Then the cohesion and influence of the affected group depend upon the incorporation or accommodation of the conflicting loyalties of any significant segment of the group, an accommodation that may result in altering the original claims...
>
> Organized interest groups are never solid and monolithic, though the consequences of their overlapping memberships may be handled with sufficient skill to give the organization a maximum of cohesion. [59, pp. 508-10]

One of the things that makes it difficult to isolate the influence of union voting recommendations on the actual performance of union members is the fact that several of the comprehensive studies that have been made of American voting behavior have indicated that most workers vote Democratic whether they are union members or not.[1] In this situation, with unions explicitly or implicitly endorsing Democratic candidates in the vast majority of cases, does the fact that a union member votes for a particular Democratic candidate mean that he followed the advice of his union leader or that he simply voted

---

1 See [36, p. 285], [33, p. 20], and [37, pp. 333-34].

as he would have in any circumstances? If a labor-endorsed candidate is elected, does this mean that the union "delivered" the vote of its members, or does it mean that the leadership simply reflected the members' wishes in endorsing the candidate who would have been elected anyway? Then, there are also the questions of special circumstances. Is there a "labor vote" at some times and not at others? If so, what circumstances tend to promote a labor vote, and what circumstances are not conducive to cohesive voting by union members?

Probably the best known instances of the "labor vote" not being "delivered" are John L. Lewis' unsuccessful attempt to drop FDR and support the Republican Wendell Wilkie in the 1940 Presidential election and the more widely-based effort on the part of the labor movement to unseat Ohio's Republican Senator Robert A. Taft, co-sponsor of the Taft-Hartley Act, a decade later. In both of these cases, a study of union voting behavior is available. Organized labor's attempt to unseat Republican Senator Barry Goldwater in 1958 also received a good deal of publicity, but no one really expected the popular Arizona conservative to be defeated, and no serious study was made of this election.

In the case of John L. Lewis and Wendell Wilkie, Irving Bernstein made a study of the reaction of CIO officials and editors and the reaction of working class voters to Lewis' endorsement of the Republican Presidential candidate in 1940. His study included an analysis of 63 counties and 14 towns, selected as best representing CIO voting behavior, and his conclusions were:

> In the election returns there is little evidence that John L. Lewis' action moved any appreciable number of CIO workers, their families, or their sympathizers to vote for Wilkie... There is evidence, however, that he exerted an influence in a few individual localities. [5, p. 245]

Fay Calkins made a detailed study of the CIO's participation in the 1950 Ohio Senatorial campaign, and noted that an inability to get union members registered and interested in the Democratic primaries left the CIO-PAC with a candidate it did not really admire, and she stated:

> As a result of this rank-and-file inertia, PAC had to bestir itself considerably to get CIO members registered and out to vote. It had hoped that 80% of the 500,000 CIO members in Ohio would register and that 8-1/2 out of 10 would vote for Ferguson. November returns indicated that about 70% had voted, and that 7 out of 10 had voted Democratic. This amounted to about 245,000 CIO votes which followed PAC's endorsement. But many of these unionists would have voted Democratic anyway, and the same vote could not be counted upon for internal or third-party action. The actual concern of CIO members thus sets narrow limits to the influence of PAC and the relationship it can establish with the parties. [10, pp. 35-36]

Turning to more comprehensive studies of American voting behavior and the influence of union membership on voting decisions in Presidential elections, however, seems to indicate that union members as a whole may tend to vote more Democratic than non-members in the same occupational positions, and that the more "active" the union member the more likely he is to exhibit this characteristic. In a study of the 1948 Presidential elections in Elmira, New York, Berelson, Lazarsfeld, and McPhee concluded:

> "Union members vote more Democratic than non-members (of the same occupation, class, education, age, religion, or selected attitudes). The more that union members are committed to unionism, in general or in particular, the more Democratic their vote." [4, p. 53]

Subsequent nationwide studies by the University of Michigan's Survey Research Center have indicated that the same tendency may also be true of members of union households, but to a lesser degree.

The percentage of union members voting for the Democratic Presidential candidate fell from 87% in 1948 to 61% in 1952 and to 57% in 1956, while the percentage of persons in union families voting for the Democratic Presidential candidate during these years fell from 81% to 56% to 52% respectively. Concentrating on the "distinctiveness" of the union vote rather than its absolute level, the Michigan researchers computed a "Democratic distinctiveness rating" as "the deviation in per cent Democratic of the two-party vote division from the comparable per cent among the residual non-member portion of the total sample. A positive deviation indicates that the group was more Democratic. [11, p. 302]

Using this method, it was found that in 1948 union members and members of union households (the categories were not separated in the 1948 study) voted 35.8% more Democratic than the two-party vote division among non-union members and their households. In 1952, however, union members had a Democratic "distinctiveness rating" of +24.9 and the comparable rating for voting members of union households was only +19.8. Eisenhower's increasing popularity in 1956 cut the union members' pro-Democratic "distinctiveness rating" to +21.4, and the Democratic "distinctiveness rating" of the members of union households fell to +18.1 in 1956. Unfortunately, similar results for the 1960 Presidential election have not yet been published.

While most of the national election analyses have been confined to the Presidential vote, the 1952 study of the Detroit auto workers also covered other election contests. This study found that 75% of the workers covered in the sample voted for Stevenson rather than for Eisenhower in 1952. This percentage was considerably above that given to the Democratic candidate by all union members combined in that year, but it was well below the 89% vote these same auto workers said they gave Truman in 1948; and, in 1952 the Democratic candidates for the governorship and the U.S. Senate ran well ahead of that party's Presidential nominee among the auto workers--85% of the UAW vote was cast for G. Mennen Williams in the gubernatorial contest and 81% for Blair Moody in the Senate race. How much of this decisive vote was due purely to union influence, however, is difficult to say. Kornhauser, Sheppard, and Mayer stated:

> "One other test of whether union members voted in accord with union recommendations was afforded by a ballot on proposals for reapportionment of voting districts in the State. The UAW conducted a vigorous campaign on this issue. Our results on members' voting and information about the issue indicate that large numbers remained poorly informed and unaware of the importance of the question. Only 57% were able to state how they had voted (21% of registered voters did not vote on the issue). Nevertheless, on the positive side of the union's accomplishment, those workers who did vote cast their ballots overwhelmingly for the proposal supported by the union (51% of the 57%). [30, p. 75]

The variation in the UAW members' votes on the candidates and issues endorsed by the union in this case seems to indicate what the earlier observations on union member attitudes would lead one to expect: namely, that factors other than the union's endorsements influenced the voting behavior of the UAW members.

Thus, the extent to which the auto workers' other associations reinforced or conflicted with the political policies of the UAW no doubt had an influence on their ultimate voting behavior. The question then becomes "Is it possible to isolate the influence of the union from that of the other groups and forces influencing its members?"

In this connection, Harold Wilensky examined a politically active UAW local in Chicago and found that union "activity" was independent of social-economic status, religion, sex, ethnicity, and race in influencing the political behavior of its members, but that the number of "actives" in the union was by no means a majority of the total membership (43 of a total of 160 persons in his sample). [64]

The Survey Research Center at the University of Michigan also tried to isolate group membership from other life situations in analyzing the previously mentioned distinctiveness ratings for several selected groups in the 1956 Presidential elections. They isolated a control group of non-members on several important aspects of life situations except for the fact of group membership.[1]

---

1 With respect to the life situations controlled, the authors stated:

> "The various aspects of life situation could be elaborated infinitely. Construction of such a control group presumes that we know which aspects are of real significance in the responses of the individual to politics. As empirical work proceeds our knowledge improves accordingly, but there may always be a dimension of importance that we have not yet discovered. In general, however, over

(Continued on following page)

The findings on trade union membership and membership in trade union families in 1956 brought the union members' pro-Democratic distinctiveness rating down from +21.4 to +20.4 with other life situations controlled, and the members of union households' Democratic distinctiveness rating fell from +18.1 to +17.1. This still leaves these groups with a distinctive voting behavior and their ratings changed less than those of the other groups studied. (Catholic and Negro Democratic distinctiveness diminished more than union distinctiveness with life situation controlled, and Jewish distinctiveness increased under these controlled conditions). Like the other studies, the Survey Research Center's analysis of the 1956 elections also found that when they took all members of groups that voted

---

(Footnote 1 continued from preceding page.)
a period of time we become increasingly confident that we know how to control the most important effects of life situations.
We know, for example, that the sharpest discontinuities in partisan political behavior occur between the South and the remainder of the country. Since our secondary groups are not evenly distributed between the two great political regions of the country, we must create the same balance in the control group. The differences between residence in metropolitan areas, towns, and rural districts need similar attention. Also, the stability of party identifications requires that we take account of the past residence of individuals with regard to region and to urban-rural differences. Though we shall find later that social class was not an important factor in the vote in 1956, it is still sure to influence other dimensions such as general involvement in politics. Therefore, we will control all of the major status dimensions as well: education, income, and occupation. In addition, we will control age and number of generations that the informant's family has spent in the United States. Finally, since it is our thesis that membership in certain social groupings creates additional forces on behavior, we shall take into account any overlap in personnel of our test groups. If one third of all Catholics are union members, we shall want the same union representation in the Catholic-control group." [11, pp. 304-05]

distinctively Democratic, the persons who were highly identified with these groups voted even more distinctively Democratic than members who were less highly identified. For example, the members of union households who were highly identified with the labor movement in 1956 gave 64% of their vote to Stevenson whereas those who were weakly identified gave only 36% of their vote to the Democratic candidates. The study found:

> The same effect appears when we look at a range of other political behaviors and attitudes. High identifiers in these groups vote more distinctively Democratic at all levels of government; they are more frequently Democratic in their party identification. They also react differently to political issues than low identifiers. For example, labor union members in general are more likely to feel that the government should provide for full employment than are members of a control group matched with them. But among union members, the strong identifiers are even more distinctive in their views about full employment than those who identify less strongly. [11, p. 308]

This study also found, however, that fewer union members were strongly identified with their group than were Negroes or Jews. Members of union households and Catholics were slightly less strongly identified with their groups than were union members. The results did show, however, that there was a substantial relationship between the strength of union identification and the length of membership in a union.

The "proximity" of a group to the political process was also found to be a factor in members' voting behavior in 1956. The authors hypothesized that as the proximity between the group and the world of politics increases, the political distinctiveness of that group would increase; and, also, at the individual level, as perception of proximity between the group and the world of politics becomes clearer, the susceptibility of the individual member to group influence in political affairs increases. As a general test of these propositions, they compared the 1956 voting behavior of members of unions formerly affiliated with the CIO with the voting of members of former AFL unions on the assumption that CIO unions had a greater proximity to the political process than did AFL unions. They found:

> If we make a simple division of our union members according to their one-time AFL or CIO affiliation, we find that our AFL respondents voted 51% Democratic, whereas 60% of the CIO members favored Stevenson. This is not a large difference, but differences of almost exactly the same magnitude have emerged in the voting patterns of the two groups in every presidential election covered by nationwide surveys since the time of the original schism in 1935. It has never been clear whether this difference stemmed from differences between the groups as agents of influence or from differences in the life situation of members. For example, the AFL is made up of craft unions with skilled workers who might be expected, on status grounds alone, to be less Democratic than the unskilled members of the CIO. But the difference between the two organizations in 1956 withstands all such tests. Furthermore, the distinctions in vote cannot be traced to variation in cohesiveness; AFL members are almost identical with CIO members in their aggregate strength of identification with the group. Finally, the necessary perceptual conditions are present. More CIO members saw their union leaders as intending to vote Democratic than was the case with AFL respondents. [11, p. 312]

To sum up, these voting studies are all based on the sample survey technique, and thus are subject to both the strengths and weaknesses of this type of research design. They seem to indicate that although the total "labor vote" may not be available for "delivery" by the union leadership, union political programs do seem to have some effect on their members voting behavior over and above other influences to which the members are naturally subjected in the course of their daily existence. The real influence of these programs, however, seems to vary according to the degree of political activity undertaken by different unions, and it also seems to be strongest on that part of the membership which is active in the union or identifies with the union and approves of its political efforts. Like all organizations, the "active" group does not constitute a majority of the membership, however, and unions seem to be less cohesive than some racial or nationality groups in influencing their members voting behavior. Voting members of union families seem to follow the voting patterns of the breadwinner, but with some deviation in the non-union direction.

Although the American public is apparently not oversensitive to issues in election campaigns, the studies at the Survey Research Center also indicate that

> While union people did not differ from the rest of the population in the extent of their concern with parties or candidates, they were clearly more likely to be concerned with issues... Union people (who made up 27% of the total population [surveyed]) contributed 31% of the people who were in the strong issue-oriented category and only 17% of those weakest on issue orientation. [13, p. 154]

Given this finding, it is likely that as issues change from election to election, the number of union members who identify with the union position may change--particularly if union-centered or economic issues are concerned and considered more important than other issues affecting the members' status outside the union. This may therefore account for the heavy union vote for Truman in 1948, when the Taft-Hartley Act was an issue, and the sharp dropoff in the number and percentage of union members voting for the Democratic candidate in 1952 and 1956, when there were no real "labor issues" at stake. The 1958 State and Congressional elections, when "right-to-work" laws were up for referendum in several industrial states, may also be a case in point. It is also likely that as issues closer to the union's own security or immediate interest arise in the political process, the leaders will make a greater effort to influence their members' political behavior.[1]

Over and against the influence a union can exert on the political behavior of its members, of course, must be considered the influence that these activities have on non-members in the electorate. This second consideration has not been studied to anywhere near the extent that the former has; but it seems likely that a union endorsement of a candidate may not only rally labor sympathizers to his cause, it may also arouse anti-labor elements to new heights of opposition. Indeed, in earlier times a CIO-PAC endorsement was sometimes referred to by the rather unflattering sobriquet "kiss of death".

In a study of the differential influence of various political groups in the state of Washington prior to the 1950 elections, Freeman and Showell found that business, political, and veterans'

---

1 A detailed account of organized labor's efforts in the 1958 "Right-to-Work" campaigns is contained in [2, pp. 193-200]. The AFL-CIO's continuing campaign against this type of legislation is also described in [3, pp. 176-80].

associations exerted the widest positive political influence, while labor and church organizations exerted the narrowest. Unions, like the Catholic Church, apparently achieved a high saturation of a small target, but this positive influence was confined to their own membership. In fact, labor's hypothetical endorsement had a negative effect on candidate preferences among non-union members surveyed, and this study indicated that perhaps the more political a union the more negative is its influence on non-members, since the CIO was ranked higher than the AFL in the amount of negative influence it generated among non-members. [23, p. 712]

To the extent that organized labor's political influence on non-union members is based on the community status of union leaders, Orme W. Phelps has systematically documented the gross under-representation of labor union officials among honorific biographical listings and appointments to public offices, boards of foundations, university boards, and service clubs. [49] William H. Form confirmed these findings in a case study of Lansing, Michigan, and concluded:

> An overall-appraisal of union power in various community segments from high to low would result in the following rank order: economic bargaining, welfare, education, political parties, elective municipal offices, city appointive boards, religion, and mass communication. In all these sectors labor is heavily outweighted in terms of representation and power by businessmen and professionals. [22, p. 539]

All things considered, then, the matter boils down to the crucial question: Do union endorsements, get-out-the-vote drives, and other forms of publicity (in addition to the direct campaign contributions discussed above) exert enough positive influence on union members to overcome the possibilities of negative influence on some members and non-members and result in a net addition to the number of votes that the labor-supported candidate would normally receive? A related question, of course, concerns whether or not any extra votes thus obtained prove to be crucial in determining the result of any particular election--an extra 500 votes means little if the candidate wins by 100,000, or loses by a similar margin.

On the basis of this test, the ultimate payoff of union political efforts should show itself most in those closely contested election districts where union members are concentrated enough for the "positive" effect of union political efforts on "active" union members to offset the problems of overlapping group memberships for "non-active" members and to overcome the possibility of "negative" influence on non-members in such a way that the union supported candidate wins. The number of election districts which meet this test, however, is difficult to specify; and the number no doubt changes from year to year. Nevertheless, we will now turn to an analysis of the postwar election results in the states shown in Table 14, which are known to have a larger than average concentration of union members, as well as the 52 election districts identified above as "labor" districts, in addition to studying the fate of the candidates known to have personally received labor contributions in federal elections.

There is no doubt some overlapping in these categories, but we will begin by looking at the electoral success of the candidates receiving labor campaign contributions, and then look at the electoral success of candidates running with labor endorsements in those districts believed to contain a large part of the "labor vote".

Campaign Activity: Results -- The first point that becomes apparent with respect to organized labor's reported campaign contributions is the fact that the overwhelming majority of these funds are known to go to Democratic candidates, but tracing the specific funds reported by the different labor groups to particular candidates is no easy task. As indicated in Appendix D, national political committees and individual candidates are required to file separate reports under the provisions of the Federal Corrupt Practices Act, but due to the provisions of the Act there is no reason why the total contributions reported by national political committees should equal the amount received by individual candidates. Indeed, different funds are usually involved. An example of this situation occurred in 1954 when Congressional Quarterly made a detailed investigation of the reported contributions of 11 labor committees to only six Senatorial candidates. This study revealed that the labor committees reported contributing $118,000 to these candidates, but these same six candidates reported total personal receipts of only $23,253 from all sources. The only possible (legal) explanation is that much of the labor money was contributed to committees working on the candidates' behalf rather than to the candidates themselves. As mentioned previously, if these candidate committees are not subsidiaries of national political committees, if they confine their operations to one state, and if they operate without the formal legal approval of the particular candidates, they do not have to report their receipts or expenditures under federal law. This, for example, is what happened in the Ohio Senatorial elections in 1950, where it was widely known that organized labor was making an all-out effort to support Joseph Ferguson in opposition to Robert A. Taft. Ferguson's federal report of his personal receipts showed that none were received from labor unions. Figures filed with the Ohio Secretary of State, however, indicated that the Ferguson for Senator Committee, Farmers for Ferguson, Independent Citizens Committee, Church Civic League, and the Labor League, reported a combined total in labor receipts of $79,030 from CIO unions and $126,075 from other labor sources in 1950. [10, p. 19]

Given this situation it is not possible to examine the labor contributions reported by individual candidates and account for the total amount of organized labor's campaign spending reported in Tables 9-10. And, as a practical matter, it is not possible to trace all of the funds reported in these tables to individual candidates, either. In only one year--1958--did Congressional Quarterly attempt an exhaustive analysis of all of the 32 national labor committee reports filed in that year. They concluded that $702,456 (38%) of the total amount of $1,828,778 reported in that year went to 231 candidates or their committees, $630,650 went to "labor committees or others" in specific states, $130,893 went to Democratic committees in specific states, $35,055 went to Liberal Party committees in New York State, and the remaining $329,724 was either spent at the national level or in such a manner that its ultimate destination was not clear.

The 231 candidates reported as receiving labor contributions in 1958 were running in less than half of the some 470 House and Senate elections held in that year.

In 1954, Congressional Quarterly attempted a similar analysis of the reports of only 11 of the 41 labor groups reporting in that year. They found that $609,228 (30% of the total of $2,057,613) of reported labor expenditures in that year was listed as going to 226 different candidates. Thus, again, labor-supported candidates were reported in less than half of the congressional election races.

A detailed examination of these two reports was compared with the election results in 1958 and 1954 to compile Table 15, which shows how the candidates reported as benefiting from labor contributions fared in these two years. In 1954, 109 (48%) of the 226 candidates supported by organized labor won election. All five of the labor-supported Republicans won, compared to 104 of the 221 Democrats supported. Labor-supported candidates for the Senate also appear to have fared better than labor-supported House candidates during this year.

In 1958, organized labor's election batting average increased substantially when 152 of the 231 candidates supported were elected. Only five of the nine Republicans supported in this year won, however, compared to 147 of the 222 Democrats. Labor's batting average in supporting Senate candidates continued to exceed its performance in supporting House candidates.

TABLE 15 – Contributions to Individual Congressional Campaigns Reported by Labor Political Groups, 1958 and 1954*

	1958		1954		Totals	
No. of House Candidates	829		870		1,699	
No. and Amt. of Contributions Reported by Labor Groups	197	$339.7	198	$260.7	395	$ 600.4
Republican Winners	4	5.1	4	3.5	8	8.6
Republican Losers	2	.8	0	0	2	.8
Democratic Winners	124	213.7	88	133.2	212	346.9
Democratic Losers	65	119.7	105	123.9	170	243.6
"Other" Losers	2	.5	1	.1	3	.6
No. of Senate Candidates	75		93		168	
No. and Amt. of Contributions Reported by Labor Groups	34	$362.8	28	$348.5	62	$ 711.3
Republican Winners	1	7.0	1	3.0	2	10.0
Republican Losers	2	1.3	0	0	2	1.3
Democratic Winners	23	317.6	16	222.5	39	540.1
Democratic Losers	8	37.0	11	123.0	19	100.0
Total No. of Cong. Candidates	904		963		1,867	
Total No. of Contributions Reported by Labor Groups	231	$702.5	226	$609.2	457	$1,311.7
Republican Winners	5	12.1	5	6.5	10	18.6
Republican Losers	4	2.0	0	0	4	2.0
Democratic Winners	147	531.2	104	355.7	251	886.9
Democratic Losers	73	156.7	116	246.9	189	403.6
"Other" Losers	2	.5	1	.1	3	.6

* Reports of 32 groups examined in 1958, only 11 groups examined in 1954. All dollar figures are in thousands. Columns may not total due to rounding.

Source: Congressional Quarterly *Almanac*, 1959 and 1955.

On balance then, 261 (57%) of the 457 labor-supported candidates were elected, and $905,534 (69%) of the $1,311,684 in reported labor contributions went to winning candidates during the two elections covered in Table 15. These averages, however, are pulled up substantially by the results in 1958, which is widely regarded as labor's most successful election effort in the entire postwar period. Even in this year, however, the 128 successful House candidates filled considerably less than half of the seats in the 435-member House of Representatives and, of course, one-third of the Senate was up for election in this year, although labor-supported candidates did win 24 of the 34 available seats.

If we turn from a detailed examination of the labor committee reports to an examination of the reports filed by the individual candidates, data are available for a larger number of years, but even less of the total amount of campaign spending reported by labor committees can be accounted for, and some of these funds may be from labor sources not reporting as labor committees in the preceding tables. An exhaustive analysis of the individual candidate's receipts and expenditure reports published by the Congressional Quarterly for each election from 1948 through 1960 reveals that detailed breakdowns of these data can be tabulated for the years 1950, 1956, 1958, and 1960. The results of this analysis are shown in Table 16.

As can be seen, fully 85% of the amounts reported in Tables 9-10 above as campaign contributions by national labor committees during the years covered is not accounted for in the reports

TABLE 16 - Personal Receipts and Personal Labor Receipts Reported by Congressional Candidates 1960, 1958, 1956, and 1950 *

	1960		1958		1956		1950	
No. of House Candidates	891		829		828		808	
No. of House Candidates Reporting Personal Receipts, Amount Reporting	649	$3,183.7	580	$2,012.1	N.A.	$2,549.7	N.A.	$1,635.3
No. of House Candidates Reporting Personal Labor Receipts, Amt. Reporting	168	$ 336.6	135	$ 230.6	188	$ 294.0	126	$ 119.8
Republican Winners	1	1.5	4	5.3	6	4.1	4	5.3
Republican Losers	0	0	1	1.1	1	.5	0	0
Democrat Winners	80	140.1	75	125.6	77	145.4	49	44.1
Democrat Losers	86	192.8	54	98.1	104	144.0	72	70.2
Other Losers	1	2.3	1	.5	0	0	1	.3
No. of Senate Candidates	81		75		72		75	
No. of Senate Candidates Reporting Personal Receipts, Amount Reporting	56	$1,011.7	66	$ 662.0	N.A.	$3,221.3	N.A.	$ 881.8
No. of Senate Candidates Reporting Personal Labor Receipts, Amt. Reporting	8	$ 55.4	12	$ 74.3	13	$ 75.0	6	$ 21.2
Republican Winners	2	1.3	0	0	0	0	1	3.6
Republican Losers	0	0	1	.9	0	0	0	0
Democrat Winners	2	32.1	8	59.3	4	41.0	0	0
Democrat Losers	4	22.1	3	14.0	9	34.1	5	17.6

* All dollar figures are in thousands. Columns may not add due to rounding.

Source: Congressional Quarterly *Almanac*, 1961, 1959, 1957, 1951.

of the individual candidates in Table 16. Nevertheless, the candidates' reports do indicate that only 656 (18%) of the 3,659 candidates running for election in 1960, 1958, 1956, and 1950, reported receiving labor contributions. It is impossible to know how many other candidates may have received labor money through non-personal committee contributions during these years, but it is likely that most of the committee money would go to the same candidates receiving personal contributions. Assuming that all elections in which labor contributions were reported were contested elections and that labor never contributed to both sides in the same election, this would mean that personal labor contributions were received in only about 36% of the some 1,876 election races during these years.

Indeed, since many House districts are so-called "safe" districts, and since there are many one-party states influencing Senate elections, the apparent fact that organized labor makes no attempt to influence all Congressional elections is probably not too surprising--particularly since money spent in primary elections does not have to be reported. It would seem most probable that the largest amount of labor financial support would tend to flow to states with large numbers of union voters to encourage pro-labor candidates, or to close elections where the labor funds might be decisive in a narrow contest. In this connection, Alexander Heard has stated:

> "Labor money, like other political money, is more likely to follow than to create political opportunity. Maine is a state of modest labor membership that formerly attracted little labor money. The Democratic revolution led by Edmund S. Muskie has changed things. Of slightly over $96,000 reported spent on behalf of Democratic candidates

in 1958, $35,000 came from labor groups, much of it from outside the state. Another $17,500 was transferred in from national-level Democratic committees." [26, p. 188]

With regard to the geographical distribution of the labor receipts reported in Tables 15 and 16, a list of the ten states in which the largest amount of labor receipts were reported was compiled for each of the five election years for which detailed data are available (1950, 1954, 1956, 1958, and 1960). Four states--Illinois, Ohio, Pennsylvania, and Michigan--were in the top ten states in each of the five years, and three other states--California, Missouri, and West Virginia--have ranked in the top ten states in four of the five election years covered. All seven of these consistently top "labor-receipt-reporting" states are among the 17 states having a union-membership which constitutes a larger percentage of the potential electorate than the national state average or a union membership of 17% of the state's voting age population. (See Table 14 above.)

With regard to the effectiveness of the labor money reported in Table 16, a total of 656 Congressional candidates reported receiving labor receipts during the four elections covered. Six-hundred and seventeen were candidates for the House and 39 were candidates for the Senate. Twenty-one were Republicans, 632 were Democrats, and three were third party candidates (Liberals in New York). Three-hundred and thirteen (47.7%) of these candidates won election, while 343 of the candidates reporting labor receipts were defeated. Of the total of $1,206,897 in reported labor receipts, $608,552 (50.4%) went to winning candidates, and $598,345 was reported by losing candidates. Recalling our earlier conclusion that organized labor does not appear to make financial contributions in a majority of the Congressional races, these figures further indicate that organized labor has been successful only about half of the time in those races in which candidates have reported the receipt of labor contributions. (These total figures also seem to be pulled up by the one exceptionally good year for labor candidates in 1958--the only year in the table in which more labor-supported candidates won than lost.)

In addition to the differences in labor's overall success from one election year to the next, which shows in Table 16, the data also indicate variations in success between labor contributions to the different political parties and between the candidates for the House and the Senate.

Although the overwhelming amount of labor money reported in Table 16 went to Democratic candidates (about 98%), that which did go to Republican candidates was more successful in the sense that a greater percentage of labor-supported Republicans won than did labor-supported Democrats. Eighteen (86%) of the 21 Republican candidates reporting labor receipts in Table 16 won election, and these candidates reported $21,023 (89%) of the $23,498 total labor receipts reported by Republican candidates. Only 295 (47%) of the 632 Democratic candidates reporting labor receipts in Table 16 were elected, but these candidates received $587,529 (almost 50%) of the $1,180,349 total in labor receipts reported by Democratic candidates in 1960, 1958, 1956, and 1950. None of the handful of Liberal party candidates receiving labor support in Table 16 were elected.

Labor's relative success in backing House candidates as opposed to Senate candidates in Table 16 shows that 48% of the House candidates reporting labor receipts were successful whereas about 44% of the labor-supported Senate candidates were successful.

This conclusion appears to be the exact opposite of the one shown in Table 15, which is based on a detailed examination of labor committee reports rather than on the reports of the individual candidates. In the two years shown in Table 15, 56% of the House candidates receiving labor contributions were elected compared to 66% of the labor-supported Senate candidates who were elected during these years.

For the sake of comparing the two different methods used in compiling Table 15 and Table 16, the one year of 1958 is covered in both tables. Using the candidates' reports of Table 16 in 1958, the best year for labor in the whole table, labor successfully supported 87 (59%) of 147 candidates, and $190,248 (62%) of the $304,817 in reported labor receipts went to winning candidates. The comparable figures from Table 15 for the same year show that 152 (66%) of the 231 labor-supported candidates won, and that $543,331 (77%) of the reported $702,456 in labor contributions went to winning candidates. The percentage differences between the two tables for the same categories in 1958, thus, are 7% higher for successful candidates supported and 15% higher for money contributed to winning candidates in Table 15, indicating that if labor reports rather than candidate reports were available on labor contributions for each year, labor success would probably be greater than indicated in Table 16. But a one-year sample doesn't offer a very firm basis for generalization, particularly if that year is an unusual as 1958 appears to have been.

This detailed analysis of the available data on organized labor's national political contributions, however, does appear to lead to two conclusions: First, it appears that in most election years organized labor does not make reported contributions in a majority of the Congressional races. Labor appears to be most likely to make financial contributions in states with a larger than average percentage of union members in the voting population; and, in those campaigns in which it does contribute, labor tends overwhelmingly to support Democratic candidates, although the few Republicans who do receive labor support usually win.

The second conclusion is that, overall, approximately half of the Congressional candidates receiving labor contributions win election in any given year with some year to year variation, but with no consistently clear difference between House candidates and Senate candidates.

Candidates do not live by bread (or money) alone, however, so before a final evaluation of organized labor's campaign influence can be made, we should also try to estimate the results of organized labor's other non-contributory campaign activities designed to influence the "labor vote".

If the effectiveness of union endorsements since the AFL-CIO merger (adequate records of endorsements prior to this date are not completely available) are considered irrespective of the districts in which the candidates reside, they show that: (1) In 1956, 282 House candidates were endorsed, and 151 (54%) were elected; 30 Senate candidates were endorsed and 15 (50%) were elected [1, p. 111]; (2) In 1958, 294 House candidates were endorsed, and 182 (62%) were elected; 30 Senate candidates were endorsed and 23 (77%) were elected; 23 Gubernatorial candidates were endorsed and 17 (74%) were elected [2, p. 254]; (3) In 1960, 258 House candidates were endorsed, and 157 (61%) were elected; 19 Senate candidates were endorsed and 15 (79%) were elected. [3, p. 260] In this last year, however, the AFL-CIO report stated:

> Candidates endorsed by state and local COPE's for state or federal office fall into one of two categories: (1) those with a reasonable chance of winning who are given maximum assistance by their respective COPE organizations, and (2) candidates with almost no chance of success who are endorsed as a protest against their opponents. [3, p. 260]

Only the endorsements in the first category are reported in 1960, that is why the percentage figures for this year seem to be so successful compared to the 1958 results, which were widely hailed as the best in labor's history. All things considered, organized labor appears to have lost ground in the 1960 Congressional elections even though the Democratic candidate won the presidency with AFL-CIO support. Labor's 1960 performance, however, is even less impressive if the first efforts of the Teamsters' political organization, DRIVE, are considered. DRIVE did not support John F. Kennedy and with regard to the Teamsters' influence in the Congressional races, Congressional Quarterly noted:

> The plans of James R. Hoffa...to wield his union as a political power suffered a setback in the 1960 elections.
>
> Hoffa, in November 1959, announced that the Teamsters would work for the defeat of 56 Members of the House of Representatives. The 56 were singled out, Hoffa said,

> because they all had voted for the Landrum-Griffin bill and had been elected to the House in 1958 by margins of 5% or less of the vote in their districts. Of the 56, only 40 were actively opposed by the Teamsters in 1960 and 39 of these were reelected. Of the remaining 16, one was elected to the Senate, 5 retired and the other 10 were all reelected.
>
> Net result: one defeat of the 56 opposed by the Teamsters: Francis E. Dorm (R., New York).
>
> The Teamsters listed campaign contributions to 14 candidates for House seats. Of the 14, five were incumbents. The five incumbents...were reelected, but the nine non-incumbents supported by the Teamsters all were defeated. All ran against members of the '56 Club'. [16, p. 769]

A simple record of labor-endorsed candidates elected, however, doesn't show how decisive the "labor vote" was in securing their election, but some insight into this question may be gained by looking at the states and Congressional districts where the "labor vote" is believed to be concentrated.

Table 17 shows the postwar presidential election results in the 17 states identified in Table 14 as the ones in which union membership was concentrated in 1953. This table indicates that nearly 70% of the popular vote has been concentrated in these 17 states in the four postwar presidential elections. It also indicates that Truman carried 11 of these states in 1948, whereas Stevenson carried only one of these states in 1952 (West Virginia) and one in 1956 (Missouri). Kennedy then won nine of the 17 states in 1960. Only in 1960 did the Democratic percentage of the vote in these states exceed the national average for the candidate of that party. This indicates that even though the studies cited earlier indicated that union voters were "distinctively" more Democratic than the rest of the electorate, the labor vote in these states where over three-fourths of America's union membership is concentrated was not influential enough to consistently overcome the votes of the other members of the electorate. Thus, even if the "labor vote" is "distinctive", it apparently is not always influential enough to consistently carry presidential elections, even in those states having a disproportionate share of union members.

TABLE 17 - Post-War Presidential Election Results in 17 States Where Union Membership was Concentrated in 1953

No. of States Won By:	1960		1956		1952		1948	
Dem.	9		1		1		11	
Rep.	8		16		16		6	
2 Party Vote For Pres.*	No.	%	No.	%	No.	%	No.	%
17 States								
Dem.	23,626.0	50.6	17,846.1	41.6	18,709.7	44.3	17,398.2	51.0
Rep.	23,111.2	49.4	25,052.1	58.4	23,527.5	55.7	16,614.8	49.0
Total	46,737.2	100.0	42,898.2	100.0	42,237.2	100.0	33,923.0	100.0
All States								
Dem.	34,221.3	50.1	26,029.8	42.2	27,315.0	44.6	24,105.8	52.3
Rep.	34,108.5	49.9	35,590.5	57.8	33,936.2	55.4	21,970.1	47.7
Total	68,329.9	100.0	61,620.2	100.0	61,251.2	100.0	46,075.9	100.0

* All Numbers in thousands. Columns may not total due to rounding.

Sources: Table 14 above, and Richard M. Scammon, America Votes (Pittsburgh: Government Affairs Institute) Various Years. Selected Pages.

Turning to the postwar Congressional races for the United States' Senate and the United States' House of Representatives in these same 17 states, a complete record of official union endorsements are not available, but an analysis by political party is probably a rough guide of the influence of trade unions' strong Democratic leanings. Table 18 shows that a total of 44 Democratic Senators have been elected from these states during the postwar period, compared to 45 Republican Senators, but the Democrats have won a majority of the Senate seats in these states in each election year since 1954. This more or less reflects national trends since the Democrats have had a majority in the United States' Senate since 1954. In terms of the United States' Representatives, the majority of these states have elected a predominantly Republican delegation in every postwar election except 1958, despite the fact that nationally the Democrats have had a majority in the House of Representatives every year except 1946 and 1952. The national Democratic majorities are somewhat illusory, however, since they include many Southern Democrats whose political behavior on labor issues is quite likely to be distinct from that of most of the Democrats who are elected from the states covered in Table 18.

The more detailed breakdown of the Congressional results shows that over 55% of the total House seats are located in these 17 states, but that over 76% of the total Republican House seats have usually been won in these states during the postwar period, compared to less than 45% of the total Democratic House seats usually won in these states. More information on particular congressional districts

TABLE 18 - Post-War Congressional Election Results in 17 States Where Union Membership was Concentrated in 1953

	1960	1958	1956	1954	1952	1950	1948	1946
No. of States Won By U.S. Senate Candidates Who Were:								
Democrats	6	13	6	6	5	3	4	1
Republicans	2	2	5	2	10	8	4	12
No. of States With U.S. House Delegations Having a Majority of								
Democrats	7	10	6	3	2	5	6	0
Republicans	8	6	10	12	14	11	10	16
Even Split	2	1	1	2	1	1	1	1
No. of House Candidates Elected From These States Who Were								
Democrats	125	133	107	107	88	109	125	62
Republicans	133	125	151	151	169	147	131	194
Other						1	1	1
Composition of Total U.S. House								
Democrats	262	283	234	232	213	234	263	188
Republicans	175	154	201	203	221	199	171	246
Other					1	2	1	1

Source: See Table 17.

in these states will be considered below, after next looking at the intra-state election results in these 17 states believed to have a concentration of union members.

Table 19 shows that in the gubernatorial elections, which are not held in the same year in all the states and vary from two year to four year terms, a majority of Democratic governors was elected in these states in four of the eight years shown. A total of 42 Democratic governors and 45 Republican governors have been elected in these states during the postwar period with the Democrats gaining ground during the more recent years.

The limited data available indicates that the Democrats have gained ascendency in most of the state legislatures after the 1958 elections, but that the struggle has been harder in the State Senates than in the State Houses of Representatives, where they seem to have fared better even during the pre-1958 period of Republican dominance.

While the figures in the last three tables might be further refined for other purposes, they certainly point to the overall conclusion that, whatever their political influence on members or non-members, the trade unions certainly have not dominated the politics of the states in which most of the union members in America are concentrated.

Going from the state level down to individual Congressional districts within the various states, it was noted previously that no accessable figures could be found on union membership classified in this manner. The Congressional Quarterly classifications of 52 "blue

TABLE 19 - Post-War State Election Results in 17 States
Where Union Membership Was Concentrated in 1953

	1960	1958	1956	1954	1952	1950	1948	1946
*No. of States Won By Gubernatorial Candidates Who Were:								
Democrats	6	9	5	6	4	3	8	1
Republicans	4	2	6	5	7	8	3	10
**No. of State Senates Having A Majority of:								
Democrats	8	8	4	2	3	NA	NA	NA
Republicans	7	8	10	13	13	NA	NA	NA
Even Split	1		2					
**No. of State Hos. of Rep. Having a Majority of:								
Democrats	9	14	7	7	2	NA	NA	NA
Republicans	7	1	9	8	14	NA	NA	NA
Even Split		1						

*Gubernatorial elections are not held in the same years in all states and the terms vary from 2 to 4 years. Therefore the totals will not reach 17 in any given year. New Jersey holds its state elections in odd numbered years 1959, 1957, 1955, etc. These have been included as 1960, 1958, 1956, etc.

**One state, Minnesota, elects its state legislature on a non partisan basis; and, again, New Jersey's odd year elections 1959, 1957, etc. are included as 1960, 1958, etc. except for the state legislature results in 1953 (1954) which are not available.

Source: See Table 17.

collar" districts, listed above may give some insight in this area, however, particularly if they are combined and considered in conjunction with the state figures on membership concentration used above.

Although the Congressional Quarterly classification "blue collar" district is simply based on a population of 60% or more employed in the occupations enumerated above (p. 257) these districts are also likely to contain a high percentage of union members. Table 20 shows the Party affiliation of the Presidential and Congressional winners in these districts for each election since 1952.

TABLE 20 - Party of U.S. House and Presidential Winners in 52 "Blue Collar" Districts by Percent Of Vote Received, 1952-1960

	Election Years							
No. of Districts Carried by 55% or More and Won by:	1960		1958	1956		1954	1952	
	Cong.	Pres.	Cong.	Cong.	Pres.	Cong.	Cong.	Pres.
Democrats	41	36	43	35	17	39	34	30
Republicans	6	5	6	8	21	4	8	7
No. of Districts Carried by Less than 55% and Won by:								
Democrats	3	5	1	7	7	4	8	7
Republicans	2	6	2	2	7	5	2	8
TOTAL	52	52	52	52	52	52	52	52

Source: Congressional Quarterly Almanac, selected years, various pages. Richard M. Scammon, America Votes, selected years, various pages.

(Due to the Congressional redistricting following the 1950 census many of these districts were not in their present form before 1952 and many will not continue as they are presently constituted in the 1962 election due to the present redistricting following the 1960 census.) Most of these districts are urban districts located in large cities. Table 20 is also designed to show in a rough way the margins by which the winning candidates were elected, so some idea can be gained as to how many of these districts are relatively closely contested (won by less than 55% of the votes cast) and how many are "safe" districts (won by 55% or over of the votes cast in each election).

The table shows most of these districts are not "fighting" districts as far as winning by less than 55% of the votes cast goes, but that more of them are closely contested for Presidential elections than for the races for the U.S. House of Representatives. The Democratic House candidates regularly won between 42 and 44 of these 52 districts from 1952 to 1960, but the Democratic Presidential nominee won only 37 in 1952, 24 in 1956, and 41 in 1960.

As was mentioned above, 42 of these 52 "blue collar" districts are located in one of the 17 states reporting a concentration of labor union membership. If we use these 42 districts to separate the "union vote" from the "worker vote", Table 21 indicates that even fewer of these districts are closely contested as far as Congressional races are concerned, but again slightly more of these districts are closely contested in presidential elections than in congressional elections.

TABLE 21 - Party of U.S. House and Presidential Winners in 42 "Blue Collar" Districts Located in One of the 17 States in Which Labor Union Membership Was Concentrated in 1953 by Percent of Vote Received, 1952-1960

	Election Years							
No. of Districts	1960		1958	1956		1954	1952	
Carried by 55% or More and Won by:	Cong.	Pres.	Cong.	Cong.	Pres.	Cong.	Cong.	Pres.
Democrats	34	32	35	30	15	33	30	26
Republicans	5	3	5	6	17	4	5	4
No. of Districts Carried by Less Than 55% and Won by:								
Democrats	2	4	0	4	6	3	5	6
Republicans	1	3	2	2	4	2	2	6
TOTAL	42	42	42	42	42	42	42	42

Source: See Table 20.

The Democrats consistently win between 34 and 36 of these 42 districts in Congress or about the same percentage of "blue collar and union" districts as of "blue collar" districts alone (about 83%). In presidential elections, however, the 3-year presidential average in "blue collar and union" districts ($\frac{89}{126}$ = 70.6%) is higher than the average in "blue collar" districts alone ($\frac{102}{156}$ = 65.4%).

Going beyond the number of districts to the popular vote in these districts, Table 22 indicates that the 42 blue collar districts in the 17 states having a disproportionate concentration of union members vote slightly more Democratic in presidential elections than do the 52 blue collar districts in general, which, in turn, tend to vote considerably more Democratic than the nation as a whole. But, as was mentioned previously, the total vote in the 17 states where labor union membership is concentrated has been less Democratic than the nation as a whole in three of the last four presidential elections. This again may be due to the influence of the South in the national figures, or it may reflect a situation in which the non-working districts still register and vote a larger percentage of their potential voters than the "blue collar" areas.

TABLE 22 - Percentage Vote for President in 52 "Blue Collar" Districts, 42 "Blue Collar" Districts in "Union" States, and in the Nation As A Whole, 1952 - 1960

Party	1960			1956			1952		
	Union B. C.	Blue Collar	Nation	Union B. C.	Blue Collar	Nation	Union B.C.	Blue Collar	Nation
Dem.	61.5	60.2	50.1	50.6	49.0	42.2	56.7	55.0	44.6
Rep.	38.5	39.8	49.9	49.9	51.0	57.8	43.3	45.0	55.4
Total	100.0	100.0	100.0	100.0	100.0	100.0	100.0	100.0	100.0

Source: See Table 20.

The one conclusion which seems to stand out from this analysis of the results of organized labor's attempts to influence federal elections in a way that might tend to strengthen its lobbying efforts and improve its legislative batting average is that they have been only moderately successful. One never knows what results might have been attained had labor not made the efforts it did; but the facts are that, despite direct campaign contributions averaging some 9.5% of the total contributions reported from all sources, and despite substantial efforts to influence the political behavior of its large membership, the labor endorsed candidate won only 2 of the last 4 presidential elections and organized labor has never had more than 128 members of the 435 member U.S. House of Representatives elected with reported labor contributions, and no more than 182 labor endorsed members have ever been elected to the House in any given year. Furthermore, both of these high water marks were achieved during the 1958 elections, and did not prevent Congress from passing the very restrictive Landrum-Griffin Act in 1959.

Indeed, the fact that a congressman is elected with labor support, even labor contributions, does not guarantee that he is "in the bag" on a crucial vote, as labor found out during the decisive showdown on the Landrum-Griffin Bill. Of the 128 elected Representatives officially recorded as receiving union campaign contributions in 1958, only 118 opposed substituting the Landrum-Griffin Bill for the original House Labor Committee Bill. Eight of these "friends" of labor voted to support Landrum-Griffin and the other two were among the four votes not recorded in the largest House vote in history. Later the Landrum-Griffin Bill passed the House by a vote of 303-125.

Of course, some aspects of labor's legislative program, or

at least several bills that labor supports, also pick up votes from Congressmen who do not receive official labor backing at election time.

Shortly before the 1960 elections COPE evaluated the voting records of the 86th Congress. In the House, COPE selected 10 key roll call votes taken during 1959 and 1960. In the Senate, it also selected 10 key roll calls of the 1959-60 session by which to judge the candidates.

According to these records, 216 House members had voted "right" at least half the time they answered roll calls on the 10 COPE-selected issues, whereas 215 House members had voted "wrong" at least half of the time. In the Senate, 51 members voted "right" on at least half of the selected votes, and 47 Senators voted "wrong" most of the time.[1] Naturally, the fact that several different bills were involved means that these figures did not maintain in every case. Indeed, as the earlier figures on the AFL-CIO's lobbying activities indicated, not half of labor's bills passed during these years, let alone by a one vote margin in the House and a five vote bulge in the Senate.

Thus, following Chapter III's description of organized labor's historical efforts in the political process, the largest part of this chapter has concentrated upon the postwar political activities

---

1 For a list of the votes selected on the COPE score card, see [16, p. 769].

of the American labor movement at the national level of government. We have seen that, despite relatively high reported lobbying expenditures, the official legislative programs of the national labor federations have enjoyed limited success compared with the records of some other national lobbying groups. The different nature of the legislative programs of the different groups, however, may blunt some of these comparisons. Nevertheless, the records show that organized labor's relative effectiveness has declined since the AFL-CIO merger. Much of this decline can no doubt be attributed to the adverse publicity surrounding the Senate investigations of a few corrupt unions which ultimately led to the Landrum-Griffin Bill in 1959, and to the fact that during much of this period the White House was occupied by an administration which was not overly sympathetic to labor's interests or its legislative program. The attempts of organized labor to improve its legislative performance by facilitating the election of candidates friendly to its program have been examined both in terms of labor's direct financial contributions to congressional and presidential campaigns and in terms of organized "educational" campaigns to encourage labor union members to vote for candidates receiving official union endorsement.

Although labor, at the national level at least, has gone through the motions of following its traditional non-partisan pronouncements in these programs, the public position of the national Democratic party on labor questions has certainly corresponded to the official views of organized labor to a much greater extent than those of their Republican counterparts. This has left organized labor little choice in its search for a political ally. Max Kampelman has stated that the developing relationship between the labor movement and the Democratic party "is based on a marriage of convenience and compatibility of ideas. The extent to which the marriage if formalized, however, varies from state to state depending upon both the nature of the state party organization and the nature of the local trade union movement." [29, p. 173][1]

As with lobbying efforts, unions vary in the extent to which they pursue these campaign activities, and since not all union members or even officers are overwhelmingly enthusiastic about organized labor's political efforts, legislation has been enacted which prohibits the use of union dues money for direct political contributions or "expenditures" in federal elections. A series of court decisions and actual union practice has removed many union political "education" programs from these strictures, and only four states prohibit the use of dues money in state elections. All labor money contributed directly to a candidate for federal office however must be voluntarily solicited from union members by special political committees which have been established for this purpose. The use of

---

1 Fay Calkins [10] offers five different case studies showing how different relationships were worked out between the CIO-PAC and the Democratic party in various circumstances. These relationships varied from fighting the Democratic machine in Chicago, to balancing power between Democratic factions in Steubenville, Ohio, to supplementing a Democratic Senatorial campaign in Ohio, to actually entering the party apparatus at the county level in Rockford, Illinois and at the state level in Michigan. For another case study see [38].

union dues money to "educate" the membership on a political issue in a manner which is opposed by a union member recruited under a union security program raises questions of majority and minority rights in an organization primarily devoted to non-political activities but upon which certain political issues have a large impact. Such a case is now awaiting a lower court disposition following a Supreme Court decision that general funds cannot be used in this manner.

The records show that approximately one half of the Congressional candidates receiving voluntary labor contributions in any given election win office. The number of successful candidates receiving official labor endorsements or having favorable voting records on labor's legislative program is somewhat higher, but there appear to be definite limits upon both the amount of voluntary funds and the amount of membership voting support which labor can "deliver" to candidates favorable to their program.

The geography of union membership location and the geography of the division of the Democratic party also seem to place definite limits on the amount of consistent support labor can hope to command in Congress, and these limits fall short of a majority in most cases. This of course continues to be reflected in labor's rather modest legislative batting average, except in the sense that it is impossible to know who would have been elected or what legislation might have passed had these activities not been undertaken.

In light of these general findings, then, organized labor's

political power appears to be largely overrated by many people in their attempts to assess labor's political influence without taking a detailed look at the record. The reasons for this appear to be several: (1) it is extremely difficult to get objective and accurate information in this area; (2) the American labor movement is not the homogeneous, unified entity that one might assume simply by looking at the public activities of the national federation; and (3) it is all too easy to mistake noise and publicity for influence in the political process.

The implications of these conclusions in terms of some of the basic questions posed in Chapter I will be examined in the next chapter, which is the concluding chapter of Part I of this thesis. Before turning to these considerations, however, we will attempt a more detailed analysis of business attempts to improve its legislative "batting average" through campaign activity during the postwar period.

Business Groups

Turning to business attempts to improve their lobbying effectiveness through campaign activities, the preceding chapter on management's historical role in the political process indicated that after an early attempt by the NAM to take a direct and vigorous role in election campaigns, most business organizations gradually adopted less visible forms of participation such as individual campaign contributions and more or less indirect "communication" or "education" programs. Recent years, however, have seen an apparent attempt on the part of some spokesmen from the business community, and certain firms in particular, to pay more attention to the election aspects of politics. We will now attempt to determine how effective these efforts might be in improving management's legislative "batting average", which the earlier part of this chapter indicated has already been improving in recent years.

In this effort, as with the earlier attempt to examine management's historical role in the political process, however, we are confronted with the fact that not nearly as much data are available on management's political activities as were available on the union activities examined in the previous section.

With regard to the legal aspects of corporate money in federal election campaigns, the Federal Corrupt Practices Act's prohibition on the direct expenditure of corporate funds has not been subjected to nearly as much litigation as the ban on general union funds discussed earlier. As mentioned in Chapter IV, only one firm has ever been convicted of violating the election contributions provisions of a federal statute, and that was under the provisions of the Public Utility Holding Company Act of 1936, not the Federal Corrupt Practices Act. Alexander Heard, however, has stated:

> There is a whole catalogue of instances of corporate checks illegally sent to campaign treasurers and of corporate contributions inadvertently reported in states where they are illegal. Usually the error is courteously called to the attention of the offenders with the suggestion that adjustments be made. [26, p. 108]

But he concludes:

> None of this means that limitations on corporate political gifts and expenditures have been without effect.

> The statutes have made corporate financial activity in politics considerably more awkward and inefficient than it would otherwise have been. The amount of corporate money that shows up in nomination and election campaigns is without doubt greatly reduced because of them. Respect for law is not enhanced by the evasions that occur, but, given the ambition of the effort, the results are probably no worse than could reasonably be expected. By the standards of other nations, an attempt to prevent corporate contributing is incredibly bold. [26, pp. 134-35]

Heard then goes on to discuss contemporary corporate practice in election campaigns given the ambiguities of the present regulatory statutes. The following is a condensation of this discussion taken directly from his book.

> The Practice -- Two broad types of corporate expenditures can be distinguished: money spent openly by corporations for purposes they usually claim are not or cannot constitutionally be prohibited by statute; and political costs borne indirectly by corporate funds, more likely to be thought contrary to the plain language of section 610...
>
> In the first category, institutional advertising looms large... Closely allied are the publication and dissemination of political views in corporate publications or by other means paid for by corporate funds. In the climate of uncertainty that has prevailed, expenditures for these purposes are also thought to possess good prospects for constitutional protection should they be challenged.
>
> In all campaigns, and between them, corporate personnel spend time during business hours on politics... Some corporate personnel devote full time to the nomination and election of candidates, and this aid can only be interpreted as direct financial participation in politics by their employers.
>
> ...The techniques of indirect corporate political participation here listed do not characterize all business enterprise in the United States but illustrate the kinds of activities that take place under present statutes.
>
> 1. Expense accounts permit reimbursement for outlays that individuals normally make from personal funds...for many miscellaneous costs connected with political action.
> 2. Contributions in kind are made. Bill boards, furniture, office equipment, mailing lists, stamps, company planes, permanent hotel suites, and other facilities can be lent for the period of a campaign...

> 3. Advertisement in political journals paid for from corporate funds constitute indirect contributing...
> 4. Payments to persons in public relations easily find their way into electoral channels...
> 5. Fees to lawyers and others whose services are retained by a corporation are said to be passed on as campaign contributions...
> 6. Salaries and bonuses to corporate personnel may carry the expectation that the recipients will do their political share...
> 7. Payments to other organizations, such as trade associations, may wind up in political channels.
> 8. Funds straight from the corporate treasury are spent under some circumstances, not always in small enough amounts to be called petty cash, but presumably with some means of cover up. [26, pp. 131-32]

While it is impossible to put a precise price tag on many of the activities outlined above, one of the most obvious links between modern corporate organizations and the election process is the contributions made to political campaigns by corporate officials. These gifts, of course, take the form of voluntarily personal contributions; but the Gore Committee in its previously mentioned detailed analysis of the 1952 and 1956 election campaigns found that certain groups in certain corporations had an unusually high level of financial participation in election campaigns. Despite some industry variations, the top executives of the nation's largest corporations were generally found to be the most active.

Table 23 shows that in 1952, 92 of the 100 largest corporations were found to have officers or directors who made a known political contribution of $500 or more to some nomination or election campaign somewhere in the country. Table 24 shows that in 1956, 199 of 225 of the nation's largest firms had officials whose names turned up in the files of large contributors in that year.

TABLE 23 - Known Gifts of $500 and Over by Officers and Directors of the 100 Largest U.S. Corporations in 1952 Federal Elections

Type of Corporation	No. of Firms	Number with Known Contributors*	Totals of Known Contributors*		
			Total	To Rep.	To Dem.
Manufacturing........	27	26	$ 384,360	374,260	10,100
Commercial banks.....	28	24	298,948	253,948	45,000
Transportation.......	12	12	143,416	127,916	15,500
Life Insurance.......	16	15	86,065	85,065	1,000
Trade................	1	1	22,500	13,000	9,500
Public utilities.....	7	7	20,100	20,100	0
Savings banks........	3	1	4,020	4,020	0
Finance and investment	6	6	55,500	54,000	1,500
Totals	100	92	$1,014,909	932,309	82,600

Source: [26, p. 115].

TABLE 24 - Known Gifts of $500 and Over by Officers and Directors of the 225 Largest U.S. Corporations in 1956 Federal Elections

Type of Corporation	No. of Firms	No. with Known Contributors	Totals of Known Contributions			
			Total	To Rep.	To Dem.	To Other*
Manufacturing.......	100	96	$1,136,247	1,050,197	73,750	12,300
Commercial banks....	25	25	259,275	253,775	5,500	0
Transportation......	25	24	321,375	315,900	5,475	0
Life insurance......	25	20	107,625	102,125	4,000	1,500
Trade...............	25	17	86,525	69,300	14,500	2,725
Public utilities....	25	17	25,800	25,300	500	0
Totals	225	199	$1,936,847	1,816,597	103,725	16,525

* Miscellaneous political groups not affiliated with either major party.

Source: [26, p. 115].

These tables indicate that the gifts made by the officials of the largest corporations go overwhelmingly to the Republican party or to Republican candidates, and Heard has stated: "Despite diversities of interests, officials of America's biggest businesses display remarkable homogeneity in their political giving." He also goes on to add, however, that:

> Democratic money must come from somewhere, and as the economy is constructed, most of it must originate with persons engaged in business. Democratic backing may be slight at the top of the nation's corporate structure, but lower down support for the parties divides more evenly. To make the kind of analysis of smaller enterprises that was made of the largest ones is, at least for those who have tried so far, impracticable. The names of officials are too difficult to identify and too numerous to check against known contributors. By examining contributors to particular political committees, however, indications are found. Persons engaged in manufacturing provide significant sums to the national committees of both parties. Among Republicans in 1952, 60% of money given by manufacturers came from persons associated with the nation's 400 largest industrial firms. The comparable Democratic percentage was 38. [26, pp. 120-21]

This latter 60 - 38 split tends to more nearly reflect the general pattern of Republican and Democratic national political expenditures, and serves to emphasize that the bulk of American campaign finance is undertaken by persons engaged in some form of business activity or other. "Business" in this generic sense is probably too inclusive a term to be of very sharp analytical significance when compared to the larger and more dominant corporations. With regard to the larger and presumably more influential firms, a 1955 study of the party allegiances of 1,000 of the chief executives of American corporations tends to reinforce the fact shown by the large individual campaign contributions, namely that the larger the company of which a man was an officer, the greater likelihood that he was a Republican. The results of this study are shown in Table 25.

TABLE 25 - Relationship between Size of Firm and Political Party Allegiances of Corporation Executives-1955

Size of Firm	Republican	Democratic	Independent
More than 10,000 workers	84%	6%	10%
1,000-9,999	80	8	12
100-999	69	12	19

Source: Lipset [36, p. 287]

Despite the party affiliation and party contributions of most corporation executives, however, Chapter III's report of the 1959 Harvard Business Review survey indicated they have not themselves been overly active as direct participants in the political process. Barring any major increase in direct participation, how effective are large campaign contributions in exerting influence in political affairs? Other than noting that almost all of the executives' contributions went to Republican candidates, there are no data available to permit the tracing of these funds to particular candidates as was attempted with the union funds. In attempting to assess the influence of these contributions, however, we should recognize that individuals, perhaps more than groups, may give money to politicians for varied reasons. Whatever motivates the giving, however, access to key points of decision making in government can result. But as we have seen with regard to some of labor's funds, "access" doesn't necessarily guarantee "results". The whole concept of "access" is thoroughly discussed in Truman's book. He states:

> Except where a donation is purely a matter of personal friendship, the central objective of contributions is access to the power of the elected official. Such access may mean merely the representation in legislative and executive circles, of a general point of view toward government policies, or it may mean an "inside track" on lucrative contracts or jobs. It may imply merely a chance to argue a particular point of view or it may signify effective leverage for or against administrative or legislative action respecting taxes, regulation, and the spending of public funds. It may indicate that the recipient is virtually the agent of the donor or merely that the latter has hopefully climbed aboard the band wagon of an obvious winner. [59, p. 309]

Financial contributions are obviously not the only means of access to governmental decision centers, and equally obviously they cannot be effective unless they are made to winning candidates or parties. Nevertheless, Heard has stated:

> Access is the concept most frequently used by practical politicians to describe the objectives of large contributors. Sometimes they call it entree, or the chance to get a hearing, or the right to get on the inside when necessary, or as one person not a politician put it, a "sense of camaraderie."... It does not equate to decisive influence, but it means the opportunity to make one's case at crucial times and places. [26, p. 88][1]

---

[1] Heard later stated:
"Cash is far more significant in the nominating process than in determining the outcome of elections. Many factors unrelated to finance affect whether and how people vote. Few individuals can seriously seek a nomination, however, without assurance of the essential funds necessary to get a campaign under way. Those who can guarantee or withhold these assurances occupy an important strategic position in American politics." [26, p. 123]

Even given the rather ambiguous influence of large campaign contributions on successful candidates, the fact that most of the large contributions covered in Tables 23 and 24 went to Republican causes and the fact that aside from the widely based popularity of Dwight D. Eisenhower the Republicans have by no means had a controlling voice during most of the postwar period seems to rule out the possibility that this route provides the way to management dominance in the political aspects of labor-management relations. But the legislative batting averages cited earlier in this chapter do indicate that management has been more than holding its own during the postwar period. As a practical matter, it seems fairly clear that much of this record has been fashioned by Republican Congressmen in coalition with conservative Southern Democrats, who apparently receive campaign funds from neither organized labor nor executives of large corporations.

Turning from individual campaign contributions to more indirect means of political influence, Chapter IV emphasized the traditional reliance business groups have placed on indirect advertising and "education" campaigns to create an atmosphere more receptive to their programs in labor-management relations. In this area, however, the data for analysis are even more skimpy than that regarding direct campaign contributions. In addition to the figures cited in Chapter IV, W. H. Whyte, Jr.'s study of the NAM's vast "Free Enterprise" campaign during the early 1950's stated:

> "All in all, the Free Enterprise campaign is shaping up as one of the most intensive "sales" jobs in the history of industry--in fact, it is fast becoming very much of an industry in itself. At the current rate, it is accounting

> for at least $100,000,000 of industry's annual advertising, public relations and employee-relations expenditures. More to the point, it is absorbing more and more of the energies expended by the top men in U.S. management." [63, p. 7]

Even lacking more complete or comprehensive figures, one can recognize that, regardless of how much is spent on these efforts, all publicity campaigns are subject to the limitations mentioned in the preceding section with regard to the internal propaganda efforts of labor unions: the propagandist's message must be perceived; this perception must stimulate attitudes appropriate to the propagandist's aim; and these attitudes must result in the type of action the propagandist desires. When one carefully considers the difficulty entailed in these three stages it is clear that propaganda of any sort is not a device which can function independently of other political skills or the general status of the intended propagandist in society.

The previously cited voting study by Lazarsfeld, Berelson, and Gaudet, for example, pointed out that many people read, listen to and believe only what they want to read, listen to and believe. These authors stated: "Voters somehow contrive to select out of the passing stream of stimuli those by which they are more inclined to be persuaded. So it is that the more they read and listen, the more convinced they become of the rightness of their own position." [33, p. 82] The study by Kornhauser, Sheppard and Mayer also indicated that the autoworkers they interviewed discounted much of what they read in the newspapers as biased information, which no doubt accounts for the fact that the NAM and other groups sometimes don't identify themselves as the source of their publications and publicity. Nevertheless, given the very nature of the management community, they are the one element in our political system most apt to make use of the devices of widespread public relations techniques in behalf of their economic and political programs. First, even if all of the top business executives in the country could ban themselves into a cohesive voting machine, their numerical size and geographical dispersion would make them an insignificant political force unless they could align other broad segments of the public with their program. Secondly, businessmen as a group enjoy a tremendous natural advantage in access to all the conventional media of mass communications since the owners of most of these media are businessmen themselves and since the technique of advertising and bulk mailings are part of the everyday operation of many businesses. Finally, the generally high prestige of successful executives in our society tends toward a more effective use of these techniques for business groups than for others which might try to use the same approach to the political process.[1]

For example, the Freeman and Showel study cited above found "Business, political and veterans associations appear to exert the widest positive political influence; labor and church organizations the narrowest positive influence." [23, p. 713] And in 1954, the

---

1 For a sophisticated discussion of variations in propaganda advantages see [59, pp. 260-65].

Opinion Research Corporation of Princeton, New Jersey, conducted a nationwide survey of 1206 members of the general public and 445 clergymen and social science teachers for the NAM. This survey followed a similar survey in 1949, and found that among the "informed public" (people who say they have heard of the NAM and can name one or more ways in which they have heard of it) 58% thought "favorably" of the Association in 1954 compared to 53% in 1959. Only 11% thought "unfavorably" of the NAM in 1954 compared to 19% in 1949. The other respondents gave qualified answers or had no opinion. Forty-eight percent of the teachers and clergymen responding to the survey in 1954 felt that business leaders did a better job of presenting their views to the American people compared to 29% who felt that union leaders did a better job. The others gave qualified answers or had no opinion and no comparisons with the 1949 survey were possible on this question. [42][2] As was mentioned previously, the generally high prestige of the business community in our society also facilitates alliances with other interest groups in both propaganda and more direct lobbying activities.

---

2 This report did not say what proportion of the total respondents were in the "informed public" or how many of the 445 clergymen and teachers responded to the survey. Interestingly enough this survey found that the informed public had a much higher opinion of the NAM's influence on public opinion than the Association's own membership did. Yet these members continue to support expensive public relations programs. Perhaps this is because they want to overcome what they feel is a bad situation rather than to capitalize on what they feel is an advantage.

To the extent that the success of the national business groups in the political process is dependent upon the prestige of the business community, it must be recognized that this prestige is subject to variation as different elements in our not entirely consistent national ethos rise and fall with the tide of events.

While the business community seems to have identified itself with the institutions of private property, individualism, liberty, and freedom, which are a deeply ingrained part of our cultural fabric, they also seem to have been much less successful in associating themselves with other elements of this whole cloth such as sympathy for the underdog, humanitarianism, and equalitarianism.

In this respect, Frederick Rudolph, has stated that during the 1930's "Both the [Liberty] League and the New Deal were constructed of American materials, but those which went into the New Deal, given the facts with which they were intended to cope, built a more durable structure." [53, p. 32]

The "What Helps Business Helps You" campaigns of the 1930's by the Chamber of Commerce and other business groups were not conspicuous in their success.[1] And William H. Whyte's more recent writing on the "Great Free Enterprise Campaign" indicated that business efforts to merchandise ideas in the same manner that it

---

1 See [6] and [48].

sells products failed because they did not talk in human terms to human beings. [63][1] This sentiment is also reflected in Bernard D. Nossiter's analysis of "Management's Cracked Voice". [47]

Nevertheless, the lobbying figures cited above indicate that management seems to be doing better legislatively in recent years. But, aside from the Taft-Hartley Act and parts of the Landrum-Griffin Act, it was also mentioned that much of the business lobby's success in defeating labor-supported legislation on a year to year basis during this period may only have served to delay the eventual passage of some legislation such as minimum wage increases and depressed areas legislation. And some of industry's more stringent proposals for further regulating union activities still seem to lack widespread support.

Given these results, the question still remains, have the business lobbies been leading opinion or following opinion over all these years. Obviously the effect runs both ways, and in evaluating the overall political effectiveness of the national business groups

---

1 This article contains many comments critical of the NAM's Free Enterprise advertising by NAM people themselves and states:

> "Some of the most highly touted of the "education" projects have so provoked the unions into countermeasures that the net effect has often been to make Joe Doakes more suspicious than he may have been before. The "Freedom Forums" the Arkansas Crusader stages for corporations are a case in point. Almost joyously, one would suspect, union locals have seized on the programs ("Freedom Forum Fascist Front," "Operation Gas Chamber," etc.) as a peg for drumming up P.A.C. activity, while the national C.I.O., with exultant humor, has set up a "Captive Audience Department" to handle workers' complaints." [63, p. 8]

it is also probably necessary to make some allowance for what they want and what they realistically expect to get. For example, shortly after the ban on industry-wide bargaining and other "strong" provisions were being removed from the Hartley Bill in the joint House-Senate Conference leading to the final version of the Taft-Hartley Act, Congressman Hartley was quoted as saying:

> Confession being good for the soul, I can say now that we deliberately put everything we could into the House bill so we could have something to concede and still get an adequate bill in the end. [46]

Nevertheless, the long run big business record of defensive retreats in the face of the Norris-LaGuardia Act, the Social Security Act, the Fair Labor Standards Act, and their subsequent amendments indicates that business' economic and social influence can be transformed into political effectiveness only at a discount of varying size depending upon the surrounding circumstances. It also indicates that, since most of the sentiments voiced so fervently by the business community were formed and made sacrosanct in an earlier and simpler age, many of their positions have had to be adapted and modified at least tacitly to meet changing conditions in order to retain their political viability.

This, then, brings us to the upsurge of publicity surrounding the recent "business in politics movement" noted in Chapter IV. Just as our summary of labor's political efforts noted that it is often easy to mistake noise for influence or effectiveness, we should attempt to probe the depth of the actual activity underlying the outpouring of articles, books, pamphlets, and speeches in 1958-59 noted in that chapter.

There is little doubt that a few major companies, such as General Electric, Gulf Oil, and Ford Motors, launched new and continuing political programs during this period. Beyond this, however, the evidence is less clear. The results of several published surveys seem to indicate that, to date, the corporation in politics movement continues to be concentrated in a relatively small number of large and very articulate firms. It is difficult to determine a trend in this type of activity following the sudden upsurge surrounding the 1958 elections, but the movement may be leveling off after the publicity of the early days.

The results of the Harvard Business Review survey in Table 1 indicated that as of mid 1959 most of the companies responding to their questionnaire were still not doing much outside of belonging to associated organizations except urging employees to register and vote. Furthermore, while a vast majority of the respondents felt that business should be more active in politics, most of them did not see a pressing need in the sense that they did not feel that business in general or their company in particular had been losing political influence. This survey did find, however, that those respondents who were the most concerned were also the most active.

In another survey published later in the same year, the National Industrial Conference Board reported that among the 198 manufacturing firms participating in their monthly survey of business practices "while the majority of the companies surveyed are in agreement on the principle of company participation in the political process, there is a substantial disagreement as to the extent and nature of company participation, and the means to be employed." [39, p.424][1] The reasons given by the respondents for political participation were: 1. "responsibility of citizenship", 2. "the welfare of most companies is dependent to a considerable extent on the actions of federal, state, and local governments", 3. "industry, unless it becomes active, will be at the mercy of legislative bodies controlled by aggressive minorities which lack sympathy or concern for the problems of industry", 4. "industry has a right to see that its tax payments are used wisely". Those respondents who argued against participation made the following points: 1. "strictly speaking, a corporation, as such, does not really represent anything or anyone", 2. "any position taken by the company would probably be in conflict with that favored by some of our owners (stockholders)", 3. "If business takes one position and labor another, we will eventually give the rest of the population a choice between a labor party and a business party... However, I do not believe that either is in a position to deliver, for most of their activities are self-centered, and more often than not do not cover the complete scope of the political field", 4. "such efforts would be ineffective", 5. "fear they

---

1 Unfortunately this survey reports none of its findings in tabular form and uses words like "a majority", "most", "several", without giving any clearer indication of the exact number of firms or percentages involved.

might appear to be coercing their employees". [39, pp. 425-31]

These responses from businessmen themselves more or less cover the main points of the debate surrounding the announcements of the new political programs mentioned above.[1] Turning from the arguments for or against corporate political participation, the NICB survey found:

> Many of the companies participating in this month's survey state that, until recently, their policy has been "to stay out of politics," but that "it is going to be necessary for companies to take a more active part in the political and governmental process." [39, p. 431]

Whether the increased participation anticipated in this last paragraph has in fact taken place on a broad scale, is difficult to ascertain from a more recent and briefer survey reported in the February 1962 Management Record. Whereas the 1959 survey quoted above found "A number of programs to encourage employee political participation are described by survey participants", the 1962 survey, which reported the responses of 204 manufacturing companies found "Slightly more than half of the participating companies attempt to educate employees in the mechanics of political action. Many of these firms make their programs in practical politics available only to management and supervisory personnel, often because of the cost involved. [25, p. 26]

---

[1] For a more detailed treatment of some of the main arguments in this debate see Taft [56], Reagan [50], and Levitt [35] for examples of some of the main objections raised concerning the "business in politics" movement. The single article which attempts to answer all of the critics at one sitting was written by Willard Merrihue [41].

While not particularly comprehensive, another survey for the Yale Law Journal indicated that by 1961 some firms at least had firmed up their policies with respect to management participation in party and political affairs. One hundred and fifty corporations were solicited in this survey but only thirty-two replied. Of the thirty-two firms responding, ten did not fill out the questionnaire offered but did supply some information. Supplementing the responses to this questionnaire with knowledge from other sources the writer of this comment stated:

> Corporate political affairs programs take three forms: (1) attempts to create public support for selected legislative goals, specific legislation, or particular candidates, (2) maintenance of training programs designed to develop the political skills and interests of employees; and (3) provisions for employee participation in political activity during business hours...
>
> Of the companies which responded to the Questionnaire, slightly more than half permit employees on all levels to participate; the others at present restrict enrollment to salaried and supervisory personnel...
>
> To permit employees actively to participate in political campaigns, a few companies have adopted an express policy permitting absences during regular business hours. Responses to the questionnaire showed that six of the nine companies which permit such absences compensate the employee for the time spent in political activity. Only one company extended the 'released time' privilege to production line employees, the rest granting absence only to supervisory and salaried personnel. Several companies encourage their employees to seek political office. Staff and management employees are granted leaves of absence with or without pay (depending upon the term of the office) and, where applicable law permits, without loss of vacation privileges, service awards, insurance, and other 'fringe benefits'. (Statements of policy supplied by respondents to questionnaire. These statements indicate an awareness of the problems posed by Corrupt Practices Acts and Conflict of Interest statutes.) [20, p. 822-28]

For reasons to be discussed in more detail later, the volume of articles and speeches about business and politics seems to have dropped off substantially since the preceding article was published in 1961. As the novelty and publicity surrounding these efforts wears off, it is difficult to say how these programs will fare over the long pull. In addition to the brief quote from the NICB report above, the only other published article which permits a comparison over time is a brief article in the November, 1961 *Nation's Business*, which reports on some of the companies that have made use of the U.S. Chamber of Commerce's "Action Course in Practice Politics." Table 26 is derived from this article. This table shows that those employees who participated in the Chamber's course under company auspices became more active in politics immediately after completion of the course. One company, Monsanto Chemical, also interviewed nontakers and found that their interest and participation in politics had also increased even though it was generally lower than that of the participants to start with. The article did not say how many employees were in the different programs shown in Table 26, and the types of employees (hourly, salary, management, etc.) was not indicated. Neither was there any indication of which party the graduates were becoming active in, or whether this activity was supporting the company's point of view on particular issues.

Lacking this kind of information, it is extremely difficult to evaluate either the scope or the effectiveness of the new business in politics movement. It is not likely, however, that the kind of detailed information needed for a systematic evaluation will become available under the present conditions.

TABLE 26 - Changes in Political Participation of Employees of Selected Companies Using the U.S. Chamber of Commerce's "Action Course in Practical Politics"

Company Offering Course and Type of Activity if Specified	Percent of Employees Graduating from Course "Actively Participating in Politics"*	
	Before Course	After Course
Armstrong Cork Co.	20%	65%
Caterpillar Tractor Co.	26%	67%
American Can Co.		+18% increase after course (actual before and after % not given)
Ford Motor Co.		
Working for Party Organization	16%	30%
Contributing Money to Pol. Party	38%	59%
Having Party Membership	65%	85%
Monsanto Chemical Co.**		
Contributing Money to Pol. Party	13% (6%)	39% (11%)
Membership in Political Clubs	7% (4%)	26% (6%)
Attendance at Pol. Meetings and campaign events	30% (26%)	50% (30%)
Did 1960 Election-Day Chores		36% (18%)

* Not otherwise defined unless specified in the table.

** Activity percentage of employees who did not take the course are given in parentheses.

Source: "Political Action: Training Pay Off," Nation's Business, November, 1961, Vol. 49, pp. 62-63.

As we have seen, the present Federal Corrupt Practices Act provides even less information on corporate political activities than it does on labor activities, but in both cases substantial programs now operate outside the present scope of the Act. Whether the present Act could be tightened without violating the free speech provisions of the Constitution remains to be tested, but there do not appear to be any serious moves in this direction.

Beyond the Corrupt Practices Act, an attempt by a General Electric shareholder to get that company to reveal the nature and cost of all of its political activities as part of its proxy mailings on shareholders proposals, was held by the Securities and Exchange Commission not to be a "proper subject" under rule 14a-8(a) of the SEC 1954 proxy rules. [20, p. 843][1] Therefore, shareholders proposals don't seem to be a source of additional information at this time either.

This lack of information has prompted some persons to press for ways of obtaining more data in a way that may prove objectionable to the businesses engaged in this activity. One writer, for example, has argued:

> "The novelty of corporate political affairs programs argues against the application of more stringent legal controls before there is an opportunity to examine their effect upon shareholders, managerial personnel, hourly rated employees, and the public... But as long as corporate managements do not account separately for the cost of their political activities and do not disclose their efforts in detail, neither legislatures, courts, nor shareholders can be expected to act realistically to occasional revelations of political activity or to determine what, if any, additional legal controls are needed to supplement the present means of supervising corporate political activities.

---

1 This rule holds that management is required to include in its proxy solicitation materials all shareholder proposals it knows will be presented at the annual meeting <u>unless</u> the proposal is to promote "general economic, political, racial, religious, social or similar causes" or if the proposal recommends management action concerning the "ordinary business operations of the company".

> Disclosure might be compelled by the Securities and Exchange Commission under [Section] 13(a) of the Securities and Exchange Act of 1934 which requires every issuer of a security registered on a national securities exchange and every receiver required to file a registration statement to file such reports as the Commission may prescribe as necessary or appropriate for the protection of investors. The commission might require annual reports filed in compliance with regulations now in effect, to include a statement of the cost of political training programs, the amounts paid to employees under released time programs, and the amounts spent directly or indirectly (through contributions to business leagues, trade associations, and "educational" organizations) to influence the political views of shareholders, customers, employees, and the public." [20, p. 860-61]

The fact that the publication of this proposal for more detailed corporate reports on their political activities was followed by an almost complete hiatus in the barrage of discussion on corporate political activities may or may not be significant. Beyond this, this chapter's analysis of trade union political influence indicates that to whatever extent the motivation behind the business in politics movement was instigated by fear of labor dominance in politics, this fear does not appear to have been well founded. Management's realiziation of this fact following the 1958 elections and the passage of the Landrum-Griffin Act in 1959 may account for some of the cessation of discussion if not actual activity after 1960. The two relatively close recessions of 1958 and 1961 may also have caused some firms to cut back on some of its publicity and political activity, and the revelations of "the great electrical conspiracy" involving blatant price fixing by the General Electric Company and other electrical manufacturers may have put a crimp in some plans to publicly defend the basic free enterprise system from the evils of political encroachment.

Considering each of these points in turn, the 1958 elections, particularly the right to work referenda, indicated that even if management fears of organized labor's political power had been well founded, vigorous corporate attacks on union security clauses in industrial states did not seem to be the best way to combat it. Our survey of the unions' political efforts indicates that organized activity on the part of labor leaders and political cohesion on the part of union members tends to be strongest when the unions are clearly on the defensive. The fact that 1958 was a recession year with abnormally high unemployment may also have helped to accentuate workers' economic interests as opposed to their other interests and make the labor vote somewhat more cohesive than usual.

Despite the 1958 elections, however, 1959 did see a very restrictive labor law enacted over vociferous union opposition. This fact in itself may have cooled some companies concern for the need for more militant political action. Writing at the height of the business in politics movement in 1959, for example, Horace Sheldon cited the lack of a comprehensive labor reform bill in 1958 at the conclusion of the McClellan Committee hearings as one of the main reasons why business should get into politics. The fact that 1959 saw the enactment of a measure far more comprehensive than any bill seriously considered in 1958 may have blunted this appear.

Another factor which may account for the apparent drop off in publicly enunciated enthusiasm for corporate political affairs programs is the fact that the relatively severe 1958 recession was followed by another downturn in business activity in 1961. Political affairs are definitely a staff or non-operating activity in the organization of most companies. Given two severe jolts within three years and a continuing concern over a "profit squeeze", many companies may have felt the need to cut costs. It is traditional that most cost cutting programs quickly focus on staff or non-operating areas--if not in actual reductions at least in the prevention or postponement of expansions. Also, it may be difficult to run company sponsored political action programs while you are laying off workers because of a decline in business.

Finally, the revelations surrounding the conviction of several prominent executives in the electrical conspiracy cases, may have discouraged some management publicity programs during the early 1960's. How important each or all of these factors are in explaining the post 1960 cessation of the publicity given to corporate political affairs programs is difficult to say. But one thing which does seem clear is that the sharp increase in the attention shown to these programs from 1958 through 1960 hasn't yet changed the basic framework of the political dimension of labor-management relations, and the efforts of the national organizations such as the NAM and the Chamber of Commerce of the United States continue to function in the more or less normal manner.

The next chapter will attempt to analyze and interpret all of this experience in more detail and offer some tentative answers to the questions raised in the first chapter of this thesis.

Summary

This chapter has attempted a detailed analysis of the political activities of both labor and management groups. This analysis has been based on the reported lobby spending and campaign activities and the results achieved by these groups during the post World War II period.

Due to the nature of the reporting requirements of the Federal Regulation of Lobbying Act and the Federal Corrupt Practices Act, it is difficult to get reliable figures on political spending in the United States. The figures which are available on reported lobby expenditures, however, seem to indicate that the national labor federations have consistently ranked high among the groups reporting the largest amounts of lobby spending. The amounts reported by the AFL-CIO national headquarters, however, have actually declined every year since the merger, but the number of labor groups reporting lobbying expenditures has increased relative to the total number of reporting groups, and the amount of lobbying expenditures reported by all labor groups has also increased as a percentage of the total amount reported by all lobby groups during the post-World War II period.

Although more groups consistently report as "business" lobbies than any other classification, and although these lobbies consistently account for a larger percentage of the total reported lobby spending than any other classification, they usually represent many diverse interests and most of the "business" lobbies are not primarily concerned with labor matters. Indeed, the two lobbies most concerned with labor matters before Congress have taken advantage of the litigation surrounding the Federal Regulation of Lobbying Act to report a minimum of spending in the case of the Chamber of Commerce of the United States and no spending at all in the case of the National Association of Manufacturers, although both of these groups are known to be two of the most active organizations in the nation's capital.

Turning from reported lobby spending to actual legislative results, an examination of the final disposition of some 90 pieces of major legislation before Congress between 1947 and 1961 indicates that the two major business lobbies did considerably better than the labor lobbies, both with respect to having favored bills enacted and with respect to having opposed legislation defeated during this period. There has been a particularly sharp drop in organized labor's "batting average" since the AFL-CIO merger late in 1955, which may be related to a change in the overall legislative environment. Most of organized labor's post-merger activities have had to content with the adverse publicity of the McClellan hearings and the fact of a Republican Administration in the White House. There also appears to have been an increased "polarization" on the major legislative issues since 1956 with organized labor and management groups lining up diametrically opposed on more major legislative issues during this period than was the case from 1947 through 1955.

Although this "major issues" approach may overlook some of the lobbies' most favored proposals which do not become key bills before Congress, and although it may not clearly reflect the degree of compromise inherent in the legislative process, it does seem to indicate a trend in favor of business and against labor in recent years. Whether this trend will be reversed now that the Democrats again have control of the White House remains to be seen, but there appears to be little evidence for the proposition that organized labor's political influence has dominated, or even increased in, the U.S. Congress in the postwar period.

Of course, it is impossible to say what legislation might have passed had organized labor not been as influential as it has been, but the record does seem to indicate increased management influence at the national level. Again, however, there is no guarantee that this increase in management's "batting average" is as great as the business community might have hoped for or expected. Compared to the 1930's, the improvement in management's postwar "batting average" is impressive, but is still far short of the legislative record of American business before the Great Depression.

Despite the relative adversity that has befallen organized labor's legislative program in recent years, however, there does not appear to be any marked increase in AFL-CIO efforts to step up their election campaign activities to bolster their lobbying efforts as was the case with the formation of the AFL Non-Partisan Political Campaign Committee following the disregard shown "Labor's Bill of Grievances" in 1906 or the formation of the CIO-PAC following the Smith-Conally Act's prohibition of the use of union funds in federal elections, and the extension of this prohibition through section 304 of the Taft-Hartley Act. This extension amended Section 313 of the

Federal Corrupt Practices Act to prohibit national banks, corporations, or any labor organization from making a "contribution or expenditure" in connection with any convention, primary, or general election selecting candidates for a federal office. It has been generally understood that this prohibition does not apply to "individual" political contributions or expenditures by corporate officials or to the contribution or expenditure of "voluntary" funds solicited from union members by labor committees specifically established for soliciting such funds. It is also clear that corporate funds and union dues money cannot be contributed directly to candidates for federal office.

Beyond this, efforts to clarify the ban on the use of general corporate and union funds for political expenditures and to test its constitutionality, have not been successful in obtaining a decisive decision from the U.S. Supreme Court. In the case of U.S. v CIO the Court ruled that the ban did not apply to endorsements of political candidates in regular trade union or corporate publications, but in the case of U.S. v UAW the Court held that it did apply to the use of "corporate or union dues to influence the public at large to vote for a particular candidate or a particular party." The constitutionality of whether or not these interpretations violate the first amendment's guarantee of free speech has not been tested by the Supreme Court, and there have been some lower court decisions modifying these interpretations of what is now permissible in special situations.

Following a landmark decision in the case of Machinists v Street in 1961, however, the Supreme Court did make clear that in cases where union shop provisions are involved, no individual member's dues money can be used in any way to support political activities to which he is personally opposed. In turning this case back to the Georgia Courts for an appropriate remedy, Justice Brannan suggested that one of several possible remedies might be the refunding of a certain percentage of the member's dues in proportion to the percentage of total union funds spent on political activities. While the practical implementation of this decision remains to be worked out, it calls attention to two points:

First, the best estimates available indicate that in the most politically active of all unions, the UAW, any dissenting member would receive a maximum refund of $2.50 a year. In most unions, the refund would be a small fraction of this amount. How many union members would make an issue for this kind of money is still unknown.

Second, if members don't file for a refund, does this mean they are "voluntarily" contributing a portion of their dues money for political purposes? If this question is ever answered, and if the answer is "yes", it would be ironic indeed, for then a decision which seems to have tightened the ban on a union's use of dues money in politics might, in fact, loosen it.

Finally, the whole question of whether or not corporation and unions, as organizations, have rights of free speech just as individuals have these rights is not clear. But, if they do, all restriction on expression of the "organization's" point of view may be unconstitutional.

At present, there is no way of knowing if some of these legalities surrounding the use of labor money in politics will ever be resolved, but it does seem clear that there are rather definite limits to the amount of "voluntary" funds that unions can raise for political purposes.

As with the lobby spending figures discussed above, it is generally recognized that the campaign spending figures reported under the Federal Corrupt Practices Act leave much to be desired. Nevertheless, an examination of these reports indicates that all organized labor groups have reported spending an average of $1,874,733 during each of the seven federal election campaigns from 1948 through 1960. This represents about 9.5% of the total federal election spending reported during these years. During the presidential election years, the average labor expenditure of $1,904,530 has represented only about 7.5% of the total spending reported, while during the off-year congressional elections the average labor expenditure of $1,376,254 represents slightly over 15% of the total spending reported.

Within the labor groups reporting campaign spending, a "hard core" of only 10 groups, in addition to the national labor federations, have accounted for almost 89% of the campaign spending since 1948, but there has been some tendency for their percentage of the total spending reported by all labor groups to decline since 1954. Despite the general increase in the number of labor groups reporting, however, there is no clear trend in the amount of campaign spending reported by all labor groups. During presidential years, there has been an increase from 1948 to 1952, a drop between 1952 and 1956, and then an increase from 1956 to 1960. In off-year Congressional elections, there was an increase in the total amount of campaign spending reported by national labor committees between 1950 and 1954, but a drop for 1954 to 1958.

While it is extremely difficult to trace the exact allocation of all of the funds reported as labor contributions, *Congressional Quarterly* data indicate that, if we use the labor committee reports themselves, organized labor makes financial contributions to candidates in slightly less than half of the House and Senate races in any given year. Further, only about half of these labor-supported candidates win. Thus, a detailed examination of labor committee reports in 1954 and 1958 indicated that labor financed candidates won 230, or about 26%, of the 870 House seats up for election in these years. In the Senate, labor-financed candidates won 41, or almost 59%, of the 70 seats contested in these years. These figures are believed to be higher than the average for the entire postwar period due to the unusual success of labor financed candidates in 1958.

If we turn to the personal campaign receipts reported by individual Congressional candidates (the only data available for most postwar election years) the amount of labor contributions accounted for and the number of candidates reporting labor contributions drops sharply. In 1958, for example, only 147 candidates reported personal labor receipts while the labor committees mentioned above reported contributions to 231 candidates or committees working in their behalf. The figures for this one year in which a comparison from both types of reports is available indicates that 87 or 59% of the candidates reporting personal receipts were elected, whereas 152 or 71% of the candidates covered by the labor committee reports were elected. Whether this same tendency for individual reports to indicate less success would persist if both types of data were available for all of the postwar elections is not known, but an examination of the individual candidate's reports for the years 1950, 1956, 1958, and 1960 indicates that personal receipts were reported by candidates in less than 40% of the election races during these years, and that only a bout 48% (313 of 656) of these candidates were elected. Further, 1958 was the only year in which more candidates reporting personal labor receipts were elected than defeated.

Labor appears to be most likely to make campaign contributions in the states with a larger than average concentration of union members. Some 98% of the reported labor contributions went to Democratic candidates during the postwar period, but the few Republicans who did receive labor support won more often ($\frac{18}{21}$ = 86%) than did their more numerous Democratic counterparts ($\frac{295}{635}$ = 46%).

In addition to the voluntary funds contributed directly to candidates in federal elections, there is also the whole range of union activities designed to register, inform, and influence the votes of union members. While the total financial cost of these programs is relatively small compared to the costs incurred by other groups in the political process, the influence of these programs probably extends beyond the sheer dollar and cents involved yet it does not appear to be overpowering, even in those states where over three-fourths of American trade union members are located.

There is some evidence that union registration and get-out-the-vote campaigns bring more union members to the polls than non-union workers of the same occupations. Since most other occupational groups register and vote in greater proportions than workers to start with, however, only the most active unions, such as the UAW, have been able to get their members registered and voted in approximately the same proportions as the public at large. This still leaves about one-third of the membership in the non-voting category; and, of course, few unions are as active in the political sphere as the UAW. Indeed, in 1957, the AFL-CIO reported that only 61 of its 144 affiliated unions had formal registration programs.

On the question of "informing" or "educating" the "union vote," the degree of activity apparently varies widely from union to union. Yet a study of 43 major trade union periodicals during the first eight months of 1960 found an overall average of only 6.6% of total column inches available devoted to the forthcoming presidential election. Only 1.9% of the available space was devoted to the election of legislators, and most of this political information did not receive a very prominent place in the papers. This study also found a wide variation among individual union journals in the amount of emphasis given to political matters. While the AFL-CIO publications were found to be highly-oriented toward politics, the papers circulated among industrial union members had a significantly higher amount of political news than those of craft unions, and the industrial union journals tended to emphasize the election of the President or Congress, whereas many craft unions simply urged their members to register and vote.

Aside from their content, the average trade union member in the United States is exposed to a trade union journal only about once every two weeks, but these journals are usually supplemented by special publications and other appeals as election day approaches.

How much of this material is actually read by union members and used by them to act in a way different than they would have acted otherwise is difficult to say. A study of Detroit autoworkers during the 1952 Presidential election campaign found that only 7% of the union members said that they had read the union publications during the campaign, and only a similar minority spontaneously mentioned the union as the source of most of their information about the candidates.

Going beyond the mere perception of the union's propaganda, there is also some evidence that not all members react favorably to this type of activity. Several different attitude surveys have indicated that only a small minority (approximately 20%) actually dislike their union's endorsement of candidates, but that a large number of generally apathetic members (approximately 30 to 40%) separate them from the other large group of union members who might be expected to react favorably to union political blandishments.

Whether they actually do react favorably, of course, is another question; and one also has to consider the counter effect that union endorsements might have on the minority of members who oppose this activity and on non-union members who resent these activities on the part of the labor movement. There have been no systematic studies on this latter point, but one attitude survey in the state of Washington did indicate that labor endorsements had a negative effect on candidate preferences among non-union members surveyed.

Studies of actual voting behavior in presidential elections, which have tried to isolate the influence of union appeals from the other appeals normally influencing a union member in his customary life situation, have had to contend with the fact that most workers, union members or not, tend to vote more Democratic than the rest of the population. Nevertheless, several studies at the Survey Research Center of the University of Michigan and elsewhere have indicated that union members do tend to vote more Democratic than non-members with other selected life situations held constant. In 1956, for example, it was found that union members, with other things constant, had a pro-Democratic "distinctiveness rating" of +20.4 and members of households headed by union members had a pro-Democratic "distinctiveness rating" of +17.1% more Democratic than the two-party vote of the residual non-member part of the sample. These studies also found that, holding other things constant, union members tended to be slightly more issue-oriented than non-members, that "active" union members tended to vote more Democratic than "inactive" members, and that members of former CIO unions were more Democratic than members of former AFL unions.

Given this evidence that there may indeed be a pro-Democratic "union vote", the crucial questions are: Does it change in size as issues and candidates change? Is it big enough to overcome the "anti-union" vote? Is it geographically situated in such a way that it might be decisive in the political process? Unfortunately, one does not have all of the data one might like to answer these questions, but there are some indications that the union vote tends to be most cohesive when economic issues loom large in electoral contests or when it appears that the unions' customary way of doing things are being attacked as with the 1948 elections following the enactment of the Taft-Hartley Act or the 1958 elections when "right-to-work" referenda were on the ballots in several industrial states.

An examination of the election results in the 17 states in which over three-fourths of the trade union members in America are concentrated, however, indicates that in only one of the postwar Presidential elections (1960) did the Democratic vote in these states, which have an average of about 70% of the total popular vote in the country, exceed the average Democratic vote in the nation as a whole. Thus it would appear that the Democratic "distinctiveness" of the union vote in these states has not been sufficient to consistently overcome the Republican votes of non-members. In four presidential years, the Republican presidential candidate has carried one of these

17 states 46 times, while the Democratic candidates have done it only 22 times.

The races for the U.S. Senate in these states have been closer, with 45 Republican Senators and 44 Democratic Senators being elected in the postwar period; and the Democrats have been gaining ground in recent years. With regard to the U.S. House of Representatives, a total of 1201 Republicans have been elected from these states since 1946, and a total of 856 Democrats. These totals represent over 55% of the total House seats available during these years, but over 76% of the total House seats won by Republicans have been won in these states during the postwar period, compared to less than 45% of the total Democratic House seats usually won in these states. Only in one year, 1958, were more Democratic Congressmen elected in these 17 states than Republican Congressmen, and only in 1958 did a majority of these states have a House delegation with a Democratic majority. The rest of the postwar years have seen more of these states with a majority of Republican House delegates than with a majority of Democratic representatives.

It seems pretty clear from these figures that the "union vote" has not dominated the national elections in the 17 states where over three-fourths of the union members in America are concentrated. If we attempt to go below state totals and look at individual Congressional districts, it becomes impossible to get data on union membership by Congressional districts. But, using the districts created following the 1950 census, Congressional Quarterly did identify 52 "blue collar" districts in which over 60% of the population were non-farm laborers. Forty-two of these 52 "blue collar" districts are in one of the 17 states having a concentration of union membership.

An analysis of these 42 districts indicates that much of the union vote is probably concentrated in large urban areas which are not closely contested in Congressional elections. An average of only four or five of these 42 districts were won by less than 55% of the vote cast in the five elections from 1952 through 1960, and Democratic Congressmen consistently won between 34 and 36 of these 42 House seats. These same districts, however, seem to be slightly more closely contested in presidential elections than in Congressional races and the Republicans have also done a little better in the Presidential contests than in the House races. An average of about ten of these districts was won by less than 55% of the vote cast in the three presidential elections between 1952 and 1960, and the Republicans won an average of about 12 of these 42 districts during these years, with Eisenhower's good showing of 21 districts in 1956 pulling the average up considerably.

One never knows what results might have been attained had labor not made the election efforts it did during the postwar period, but the facts appear to indicate that their efforts have been only moderately successful. The labor endorsed candidate won only 2 of the last 4 presidential elections. There have never been more than 128 members of the 435 member U.S. House of Representatives elected with reported labor <u>contributions</u>, and no more than 182 labor <u>endorsed</u>

members have ever been elected to the House in any given year. Furthermore, both of these high water marks were achieved during the 1958 elections, and did not prevent Congress from passing the Landrum-Griffin Act in 1959. Indeed, only 118 of the 128 Congressmen elected with reported labor contributions voted against substituting the more restrictive Landrum-Griffin Act for the original House Labor committee bill.

The fact that organized labor's campaign efforts have not resulted in political dominance, however, does not mean that management's efforts have.

Most elections don't swing on clear cut labor-management issues, and most of the major bills coming before Congress are not primarily labor-management bills. Although there has been an increased tendency for the labor and business lobbies to line up on opposite sides of most of the major bills before Congress in recent years, other forces have to be considered; and these forces may be of greater importance than the labor and management positions in many cases. Thus, while the "batting averages" cited earlier indicate that management's legislative performance has been improving in recent years, it is difficult to attribute this improvement directly to business-backed campaign efforts.

There is considerably less information available on business campaign activities than is its case with organized labor. Data on election contributions, for example, cannot be compiled on a time series basis or traced to particular candidates; but we do know that in one year, 1956, the executives of 199 of America's largest corporations <u>alone</u> made personal contributions that totaled more than the amount of federal campaign contributions reported by 43 labor committees in this year. Almost all of this money has gone to the Republican party, however, and the Republicans, as such, have not dominated Congress during the years that the increase in management's "batting average" was observed. Furthermore, contributions even to successful candidates usually assure only "access" to the key points of legislative decision making. "Access" does not always guarantee "results", particularly if the contributions cannot be backed up with other assurances of support in the form of the key currency of politics, i.e., votes.

Management's attempts to influence votes as such are limited by their own small numbers. The generally high position of businessmen and executives in our society's social system, and their natural familiarity with mass advertising and communications techniques, however, seems to have resulted in a rather heavy reliance on massive "educational" programs to win the public to a business point of view on certain programs or specific issues.

While there is a dearth of information on the cost and the efficacy of these programs, it is quite reasonable to assume that they are quite expensive and of variable influence depending upon the current standing of the business community and the degree to which its programs want to move from the prevailing consensus of attitudes on any given subject.

An opinion survey in 1954, for example, found that the NAM was regarded more favorably in 1954 than it had been in 1949. This may give some insight into the improvement in the Association's legislative record noted above, but their labor proposals for a national right to work law and outlawing industry wide collective bargaining still seem far away from becoming major issues in Congress, let alone being enacted.

Also, as was mentioned previously much of management "success" in opposing minimum wage increases and depressed areas legislation on a year to year basis seems to have served only to postpone their eventual enactment. In all of this analysis of labor and management legislative positions it is also difficult to assess what the parties ask for and what they realistically expect to get. That is, it is hard to say how much compromise material is put into the initial proposals for bargaining purposes and the appearance of moderation in an attempt to reach agreement.

In addition to the "educational" programs of the national business spokesmen such as the Chamber and the NAM, the sharp increase in the amount of publicity given to the new political affairs programs of several large corporations surrounding the 1958 elections is also difficult to assess. The most widely discussed of these different corporate programs usually involve at least three things: a forthright statement of the company's position on key issues; an attempt to offer courses in practical politics to company employees in order to stimulate their interest in political affairs; and, in some cases, the provision of released time to company personnel (usually management personnel) who become active in the political process. As a practical matter there is no really adequate information on how widespread these activities of individual corporations have become, but they appear to still be confined to a relatively small number of very large and articulate firms. There also has been a notable hiatus in the amount of publicity and public discussion given to these programs since about 1960.

Just as it is difficult to judge the scope of this new business in politics movement, so is it difficult to determine its effectiveness. Several surveys published in 1959 and 1960 indicated that the vast majority of corporate executives still had not become very deeply involved in actual political work other than contributing to campaign funds, and there are no comprehensive figures on how many employees have gone through company-sponsored practical politics courses or what influence this has had on their political behavior. With regard to forthright statements on key political issues, however, it is clear that the active support given to the 1958 right-to-work referenda by Boeing in Washington, Timken Roller Bearing in Ohio, and General Electric in California did not prevent the decisive defeat of these proposals and the candidates identified with them.

The implications of all of these events will be summarized and interpreted in the following chapter.

REFERENCES - CHAPTER V

1. American Federation of Labor-Congress of Industrial Organizations. Proceedings of the 2nd Constitutional Convention, 1957, Vol. II.

2. _______. Proceedings of the 3rd Constitutional Convention, 1959, Vol. II.

3. _______. Proceedings of the 4th Constitutional Convention, 1961, Vol. II.

4. Bernard R. Berelson, P. F. Lazarsfeld, and W. N. McPhee, Voting (Chicago: The University of Chicago, 1954).

5. Irving Bernstein, "John L. Lewis and the Voting Behavior of the C.I.O.," Public Opinion Quarterly, June, 1941, Vol. 5., pp. 233-249.

6. Burton Bigelow, "Should Business Decentralize Its Counter-Propaganda," Public Opinion Quarterly, April, 1938, Vol. 2, pp. 321-324.

7. W. R. Brown, "State Regulation of Union Political Action," Labor Law Journal, November 1955, Vol. 6, pp. 769-776.

8. Bureau of National Affairs, Daily Labor Report, May 5, 1961.

9. _______. June 19, 1961.

10. Fay Calkins, The CIO and the Democratic Party (Chicago: The University of Chicago, 1952).

11. Angus Campbell, P. E. Converse, W. E. Miller, and D. E. Stokes, The American Voter (New York: Wiley and Sons, 1960).

12. Angus Campbell and H. C. Cooper, Group Differences in Attitudes and Votes (Ann Arbor: University of Michigan, 1956).

13. Angus Campbell, Gerald Guin, and W. E. Miller, The Voter Decides (Evanston: Row, Peterson, 1954).

14. Alfred S. Cleveland, "NAM: Spokesman for Industry?" Harvard Business Review, May 1948, Vol. 26, pp. 353-371.

15. Congressional Quarterly, Almanac, 1957, Vol. XIII.

16. _______. Almanac, 1960, Vol. XVI.

17. _______. Almanac, 1961, Vol. XVII.

18. _______. Weekly Report, 1959, Vol. XVII.

19. Congressional Record, August 13, 1959.

20. "Corporate Political Affairs Programs," Yale Law Journal, June 1961, Vol. 70, pp. 821-862.

21. Robert N. Denham, "Labor's Growing Political Power," in American Management Association Spotlighting the Labor-Management Scene (New York, 1952).

22. William H. Form, "Labor's Place in the Community Power Structure," Industrial and Labor Relations Review, July 1959, Vol. 12, pp. 526-539.

23. H. E. Freeman and M. Showel, "Differential Political Influence of Voluntary Associations," Public Opinion Quarterly, Winter 1951-52, Vol. 15, pp. 703-714.

24. Joseph Gaer, The First Round (New York: Duell, Sloan, and Pearce, 1944).

25. S. H. Greenberg, G. C. Thompson, "The Company, the Employee, and Political Affairs," Management Record, February 1962, Vol. XXIV, pp. 24-27.

26. Alexander Heard, The Costs of Democracy (Chapel Hill: University of North Carolina, 1960).

27. _______. Money and Politics (New York: Public Affairs Committee, Inc., 1956).

28. Ruth A. Hudson and Hjalmar Rosen, "Union Political Action: The Member Speaks," Industrial and Labor Relations Review, April 1954, Vol. 7, pp. 404-418.

29. Max M. Kampelman, "Labor in Politics," Interpreting the Labor Movement (Madison: Industrial Relations Research Association, 1952).

30. Arthur Kornhauser, H. L. Sheppard, and A. J. Mayer, When Labor Votes--A Study of Auto Workers (New York: University Books, 1956).

31. H. J. Lahne, "The Failure of PAC in 1946" in Joseph Shister (ed) Readings in Labor Economics and Industrial Relations (New York: Lipincott, 1951).

32. John F. Lane, "Analysis of the Federal Law Governing Political Expenditures by Labor Unions," Labor Law Journal, October 1958, Vol. 9, pp. 725-744.

33. Paul F. Lazarsfeld, Bernard Berelson, and Hazel Gaudet, The People's Choice (New York: Duell, Sloan, and Pearce, 1944).

34. Sar A. Levitan, "Union Lobbyist's Contributions to Tough Labor Legislation," Labor Law Journal, October 1959, Vol. 10, pp. 675-682.

35. Theodore Levitt, "Business Should Stay Out of Politics," Business Horizons, Summer 1960, Vol. 3, pp. 45-51.

36. Seymour M. Lipset, Political Man (Garden City: Doubleday, 1959).

37. Duncan Mac Rae, Jr., "Occupations and the Congressional Vote, 1940-1950," American Sociological Review, June 1955, Vol. 20, pp. 332-340.

38. Nicholas A. Masters, "The Politics of Union Endorsement of Candidates in the Detroit Area," Midwest Journal of Political Science, August 1957, pp. 136-150.

39. S. M. Mathes and G. C. Thompson, "Business and the Political Process," Business Record, September 1959, Vol. XVI, pp. 424 ff.

40. William R. McIntyre, "Corporations and Politics," Editorial Research Reports, October 8, 1958.

41. Willard V. Merrihue, "The Business Leader's Role in Politics," Business Horizons, Summer 1960, Vol. 3, pp. 38-44.

42. National Association of Manufacturers, The Battle of Ideas (New York, 1955).

43. ________. "What Organized Labor Expects of Management," by George Meany. "What Management Expects of Organized Labor," by Charles R. Sligh, Jr. (New York, 1956).

44. Richard L. Neuberger, "What Labor Unions Forget," Nation, December 23, 1950, Vol. 171, No. 26, pp. 674-676.

45. New York Times, August 16, 1959, Section IV.

46. ________. May 30, 1947.

47. Bernard D. Nossiter, "Management's Cracked Voice," Harvard Business Review, September-October 1959, Vol. 37, pp. 127-133.

48. John W. O'Leary, "The 'What Helps Business...' Campaign," Public Opinion Quarterly, October 1938, Vol. 2, pp. 645-650.

49. Orme W. Phelps, "Community Recognition of Union Leaders," Industrial and Labor Relations Review, April 1954, Vol. 7 , pp. 419-433.

50. Michael D. Reagan, "Seven Fallacies of Business in Politics," Harvard Business Review, March-April 1960, pp. 60-68.

51. Walter P. Reuther, "Practical Aims and Purposes of American Labor," Annals of the American Academy of Political and Social Science, March 1951, Vol. 274, pp. 71-72.

52. Arnold M. Rose, Union Solidarity (Minneapolis: University of Minnesota, 1952).

53. Frederick Rudolph, "The American Liberty League, 1934-1940," American Historical Review, October 1950, Vol. 56, pp. 19-33.

54. Frederick R. Shedd and George S. Odiorne, Political Content of Labor Union Periodicals (Ann Arbor: University of Michigan, 1960).

55. Richard L. Strout, "The Next Election is Already Rigged," Harper's Magazine, November 1959, Vol. 219, pp. 35-40.

56. Charles P. Taft, "Should Business Go in for Politics?," New York Times Magazine, August 30, 1959, pp. 10 ff.

57. Joseph Tanenhaus, "Organized Labor's Political Spending: The Law and Its Consequences," Journal of Politics, August 1954, Vol. 16, pp. 441-471.

58. Leo Troy, Distribution of Union Membership Among the States, 1939 and 1953 (New York: National Bureau of Economic Research, 1957).

59. David B. Truman, The Governmental Process (New York: Knopf, 1955).

60. Gus Tyler, "The Labor Vote," in James M. Cannon (ed) Politics USA (Garden City: Doubleday, 1960).

61. United Automobile, Aircraft and Agricultural Implement Workers of America, Proposal to Limit Campaign Contributions (Detroit, 1956).

62. U.S. Senate Subcommittee on Privileges and Elections, Hearings (Washington: Govt. Printing Office, 1956).

63. William H. Whyte, Jr., Is Anybody Listening? (New York: Simon and Schuster, 1952).

64. Harold L. Wilensky, "The Labor Vote: A Local Union's Impact on the Political Conduct of Its Members," Social Forces, December 1956, Vol. 35, pp. 111-120.

65. Edwin E. Witte, "The New Federation and Political Action," Industrial and Labor Relations Review, April 1956, Vol. 9, pp. 406-418.

CHAPTER VI

SUMMARY AND CONCLUSIONS ON THE NATIONAL SCENE

This part of the thesis has attempted to use published data on the national scene to determine whether or not the political dimension of labor-management relations has been expanding in recent years, and, if so, what some of the implications of this movement might be for our country's industrial relations system.

We have defined the political dimension of labor-management relations as that dimension which involves either labor or management making recourse to any of the institutions of government as an aid in the industrial rule making process, or when the government itself intervenes in the struggle for authority to establish the "web of rule" which relates our workforce to our industrial society. Chapter II noted that today the federal government touches the industrial rule making process in many ways and with different degrees of effectiveness. As our economy has become more industrialized and more complex over time, there does seem to have been a general expansion in the role of government in the industrial rule making process—both with regard to labor-management relations legislation and with regard to protective labor legislation. Historically, however, this expansion has been uneven in its development over time. The substansive content of government policy has also been modified considerably, and the means of effectuating government controls have shifted within branches of government and between levels of government, but the present legal framework is still highly diversified with regard to both procedure and substance.

It is difficult to explain all of the historic changes in the role of government in the industrial rule-making process simply in terms of the activities of organized interest groups on the labor-management political scene, but there is no doubt that at the present time there are strong and articulate political organizations representing both management and labor on most major governmental issues. These organizations in turn have evolved in response to the pressures of a changing industrial and social environment.

After nearly a century of oscillation, dichotomy, and experimentation, the American Federation of Labor evolved a basic philosophy of "voluntarism" which sought little from government but the removal of certain restrictions on trade union activities and generally opposed a full-blown program of social reform legislation on the grounds that it would weaken the need for trade unionism except in special cases such as women, children, seamen and government employees. In support of its rather limited legislative program, the AFL established a Washington lobby, but its technique of rewarding friends and punishing enemies, in practice, amounted to little more than the circulation of the voting records of incumbent Congressmen.

The failure of unionism to expand during the 1920's and the economic catastrophe of the 1930's, however, resulted in a gradual reshaping and revitalizing of much of organized labor's approach to things political as union membership began to increase rapidly under the stimulation of worker discontent, government legislation, and

AFL-CIO rivalry. The adjustment did not occur without considerable reservation within the labor movement itself, however, and one of the ironies of history is that organized labor itself had a relatively small influence in enacting the most sweeping and most favorable labor legislation in American history.

Regardless of labor's influence in its enactment, however, the labor legislation of the New Deal gave organized labor a new stake in politics. Indeed, much of their subsequent political activity can be explained in terms of: (1) trying to protect the labor policies of this unusual period in American history in an increasingly hostile environment, and (2) trying to expand and enlarge the basic provisions of the protective legislation of this period in a society that has come in general to accept a larger role for government in the economic life of the whole nation, including the labor movement.

The 1936 elections marked somewhat of a watershed in American history as far as economic matters in presidential elections were concerned. The bitterness of the clash between the "New Dealers" and the "Economic Royalists" severely modified the previous attempts of both major parties to appeal to all economic classes, and for the first time really substantial sums of money were contributed to the National Democratic Committee by strong independent national unions. The subsequently overwhelming support that the Smith-Connally Act, the Taft-Hartley Act, and the Landrum-Griffin Act received from Republicans also made it increasingly difficult for the politically conscious segment of the labor movement to identify itself with the GOP at the national level. Each of these legislative landmarks, furthermore, triggered off an increased political response within the labor movement. The CIO-PAC was established after Smith-Connally; the AFL-LLPE was created after Taft-Hartley; and the hitherto inactive Teamster's Union organized its own political arm, DRIVE, following the enactment of the Landrum-Griffin Act.

Like organized labor, American management also has a long history of participation in the political process, but there is considerably less information available on the details of management's political activity than is the case with the labor movement. One reason for this is probably the fact that businessmen for the most part have traditionally relied on tactics that shy away from the more visible electioneering aspects of politics and have relied primarily on campaign contributions and institutional advertising in addition to formal lobbying by individual companies and business organizations.

With regard to labor matters, the most visible business or employer groups have been the National Association of Manufacturers and the Chamber of Commerce of the United States. In its early years the NAM was much more predisposed toward direct participation in specific election campaigns than it has been in more recent times, but the Association toned down many of its political activities following the "exposé" of its efforts during the Underwood Tariff Debates of 1913. Despite changes in the size and composition of its membership over the years, the main thrust of the NAM's communications and public relations efforts have been strongly opposed to some of the most basic labor union activities and programs since it turned its attention to these matters in 1903.

The Chamber of Commerce of the United States was organized in part by the NAM and other groups in 1912. Although the NAM and the Chamber reached a parting of the ways in 1922, both organizations opposed section 7-a of the NIRA. They also opposed the Wagner Act vigorously. Following the Jones and Laughlin decision in 1937, however, the Chamber began a campaigh for "equalizing" amendments whereas the NAM argued for outright repeal until 1946, on the grounds that the government should not intervene in labor-management relations. This latter argument was also used by both organizations in opposing the protective labor legislation of the 1930's. With the apparent shift in the public attitude toward unionism,in the immediate post-World War II period, however, both organizations accepted the principle of more government regulation to control union power. Each group was influential in the enactment of the Taft-Hartley Act, and since 1947 both organizations have emphasized the need for further controls, even going beyond those incorporated in the Landrum-Griffin Act.

In addition to the NAM and the Chamber, of course, there are other national business organizations which from time to time become concerned with the political aspects of labor-management issues, and many individual corporations and businessmen are known to have their own independent apparatus for political influence.

In general the postwar legislative scene has been marked by management groups pressing for more government regulation of union activities, and by organized labor opposing any expansion of government regulation in the area of labor-management relations. On the other hand, much of organized labor seems to have come to a relatively modern view which sees the trade union movement not as a rival to the government in dispensing benefits to workers, but more as an instrument through which greater pressure might be exerted on government to secure benefits not only for union members but for all workers regardless of their affiliation. In this connection, a situation exactly the opposite of the one in labor-management relations has prevailed in the area of protective legislation and other welfare measures. Here it is organized labor which has been pushing for more government action, and management has generally opposed any expansion of the role of government in these areas. Despite a general broadening of organized labor's legislative outlook, however, it is still true that it gives more emphasis to and fight harder on those aspects of public policy which have the most immediate connection with collective bargaining and trade unions as bargaining institutions.

With this information as background, we can turn to the basic question posed in Chapter I, namely: "Has the political dimension of labor-management relations been expanding in recent years?" It has just been noted that in one sense the conception of what is a labor-management issue appears to have broadened considerably, even within the postwar period. A. H. Raskin, for example, has stated:

> Fifteen years ago organized labor's legislative program could be summed up in the single slogan: "Repeal the Taft-Hartley Slave Labor Act." Today labor is urging the 88th Congress to enact legislation it believes will spur national economic growth, improve public education, safeguard civil rights and otherwise expand the role of government in promoting the general welfare. [21, p. 12]

It was also noted above, however, that despite its more comprehensive legislative program, organized labor still tends to show more cohesion and militancy on union-oriented issues than it does on such matters as rent controls, public housing, federal aid to education, or fair employment practices legislation, for example. The fact that the NAM and the Chamber have lined up on opposite sides of organized labor on these issues, as well as such items as expansion of the Social Security Act, minimum wage legislation, and aid to depressed areas, has made it somewhat difficult to interpret the postwar legislative experience. The issues of housing, education, depressed areas, and civil rights, for example, involve many interests and forces beyond the labor and management lobbies involved, and the fact that these issues have become major areas of contention does not mean that these groups have been the prime movers or even the most influential interests in determining their disposition by Congress. This is less true for the areas of social security and minimum wages, and things are much more clear-cut on the basic measures of the Taft-Hartley and Landrum-Griffin bills, which were clearly basic labor-management struggles.

Going beyond the legislative arena, Chapter V's detailed analysis of the entire postwar labor-management political scene offers some mixed evidence that there has been a general expansion of labor-management political activity, but with no clear signs of any marked acceleration in recent years. Further analysis seems to indicate that much of the apparent concern aroused about this problem during the late 1950's was the result of an undue amount of publicity being given to two events—one on the labor side and the other on the management side of the political fence. With regard to organized labor, it seems clear that the AFL-CIO merger was surrounded by a tremendous amount of publicity, speculation, and conjecture concerning the political "potential" of a "unified" labor movement, which in retrospect simply hasn't been justified by subsequent events. Also on the management side, the upsurge in publicity surrounding the announcement of new political affairs programs by several major corporations in 1958 and 1959 may or may not prove to be justified by subsequent events. There is less evidence on this point than on the AFL-CIO merger, but there has been enough of a hiatus in the publicity being given to these programs to raise a legitimate question concerning the long-run significance of these activities.

Whether one decides that the political dimension of labor-management relations has actually been expanding in recent years or not, however, one cannot ignore the fact that the present political dimension of labor-management relations certainly is expanded compared to earlier times. Today the government is more deeply embroiled in all aspects of the industrial rule making process than ever before, and there do not appear to be any forces on the scene likely to result in a diminishing of its present influence. Indeed, the most likely directions for further change seem to point to more, not less, of a role for the various institutions of government.

To keep things in perspective, however, it is also true that the vast bulk of the industrial rule making power continues to remain in the private dimension of labor-management relations. Indeed, it seems fair to say that most of the postwar changes in labor legislation have had only a marginal impact on the large majority of established employer and employee relationships. The provisions of

Taft-Hartley and Landrum-Griffin have probably had their greatest impact not where employers and their employees have already established working relationships, but at the more hotly contested fringes of labor-management relations where unions have tried to expand into previously unorganized territory or where employees have tried to sharply modify existing arrangements. While the postwar changes in the Social Security Act have affected a majority of our workforce, the number of employees directly affected by the changes in the prevailing wage laws and the minimum wage laws has been only a small fraction of the total number. Yet, it seems that cases and actions on the frontiers tend to draw a disproportionate amount of our attention---particularly when changes in these areas are often loudly contested in the political arena by articulate and well organized labor and management groups.

As was pointed out in Chapter V, it is extremely difficult to get objective and accurate data in the area of labor-management political struggles; and if we look at public pronouncements alone it is all too easy to assume a greater degree of cohesion and unity within the contending camps than actually exists, and it is also very easy to mistake noise and publicity for influence in both the legislative and the electoral process---particularly as far as organized labor is concerned.

Aside from several scholarly, and primarily historical, studies of trade union political activity, most of the contemporary information available at any given time on a labor or management political issue usually comes from the parties at interest themselves. Their statements in the heat of an immediate encounter naturally tend to be the most newsworthy; but, on _a priori_ grounds, one should be at least a little wary of relying completely on AFL-CIO convention resolutions or pronouncements of the NAM board of directors for information in this area. Much of this activity is in reality propaganda aimed at influencing the existing situation rather than an attempt to report or describe actual conditions, and thus both labor's friends and foes are prone to at least some exaggeration.

The union staff men in charge of political activities naturally have a vested interest in making their actions appear effective, and likewise those who have no hope of labor support run little risk in predicting dire consequences for American democracy as a result of a labor political machine-- a machine, incidentially, which is nearly always discussed in terms of its potential rather than its actual performance. For example, both sides in discussing COPE are more prone to refer to the formal paper structure of the organization (which shows a national COPE for the AFL-CIO, a COPE for each national union and for each of their locals and intermediate bodies, a COPE for every state federation and city council, and, if not already covered, a COPE in every state and national legislative district) rather than the actual structure which does not even approach this degree of organization at election time--let alone on the continuing basis envisioned in many AFL-CIO and NAM pronouncements.

Another instance of confusing formal appearances with actual practice often surrounds the appeals of labor leaders for voluntary political contributions. As usually reported in the headlines, these appeals can be very misleading. For example COPE has a goal of a $1 contribution from every member of an AFL-CIO affiliated union. This, however, does not mean that COPE actually collects upwards of $13 million a year. Rather, experience has shown that in election years an average of about one of every eight or nine members actually makes a contribution--a far cry from the "potential" results often bandied about in partisan discussions.

Perhaps the best illustration of this point is the number of extravagant statements from both labor and management sources at the time of the AFL-CIO merger concerning the political power (really the political potential) of a "unified" labor movement. Much of this furor was reminicent of the controversy surrounding the formation of the CIO-PAC thirteen years earlier, and like most of the earlier "predictions", subsequent experience has proven that most of the assertions were unfounded.[1]

Shortly after the merger, Edwin Witte, noted:

> In the speculation as to effects of the AFL-CIO merger, the repercussions of the new federation in the political sphere have more and more become the major aspect discussed in the general press. . .
>
> Speeches and resolutions presented at the first convention of the AFL-CIO in December 1955 clearly evidenced the interest of the merged labor organization in political action.
>
> In the early stages of the attempts at merger, however, political action as a motive was not emphasized or even acknowledged. Emphasis was placed, instead, upon strengthening the economic position of unions,

---

1 Many of the earlier attacks on the PAC are discussed from the labor point of view in Gaer, [9], Maguire [16], and Fuller [8].

The second of these articles quotes the New York Mirror's September 29, 1944 denunciation of the PAC as "The Hillman-Browder Communist conspiracy to take over the U.S. through the machinery of the alleged Democratic Party". [16, p. 588]

Much of the communist angle was missing by 1955 due to the CIO purge of the communist-dominated unions in 1949 and 1950, but Witte observed "In many articles, editorials, and speeches, the merger has been represented as an attempt by labor to dominate American politics". [27, p.406]

> furthering union organization, and eliminating union raiding. What accounts, then, for the recent emphasis upon the new federation as a vehicle for political activity? Two factors in particular may be responsible. The first is the apparent difficulty of resolving interunion disputes as successfully as initially was hoped; the second may be increasing concern of labor leaders over efforts by union opponets to weaken unions through restrictive legislation and limitations on labor's political activities. [27, pp. 406-07]

Obviously not oblivious of some of the aforementioned resolutions at the merger convention, the National Association of Manufacturers, which was holding its Congress of American Industry meeting in New York at the same time, invited George Meany, the newly elected president of the AFL-CIO, to address them. Then, in a companion speech, Charles R. Sligh, Jr., then chairman of the Board of NAM, stated:

> This week, organized labor formed itself into one gigantic federation, with our guest, Mr. Meany, at its head. A careful reading of the constitution of this new body-- and the publicly expressed views as to its aims and objectives--has caused considerable misgivings.
>
> Is it the primary purpose of this organization to seize political control of the country? Mr. Meany disavows any intention of setting up a "labor party". He also disclaims any desire to seize control of either of our two existing political parties. But the question is not answered by such disavowals.
>
> A proclaimed purpose of the organization is vastly stepped up activity in the political field. The men who control the new federation will have vast funds and manpower and means of communication at their disposal. This sheer weight of concentrated power may enable them to exercise effective control over either or both political parties. . . .
>
> Will this new organization become in effect a "ghost government"? Will a handful of men, not elected, not authorized by the American people pull strings behind the scenes to direct the destinies of the nation? It is the potentials of this situation which worry industry--and many other thoughtful citizens as well. [17, p. 17]

Irritated at what he considered shabby treatment to an invited guest, and prodded by reporter's questions at an impromptu meeting with Mr. Sligh following the speeches, Mr. Meany let fly with a widely quoted and equally unrealistic threat to form a labor party. He stated:

> If the N.A.M. philosophy to disenfranchise unions is to prevail, then the answer is clear. If we can't act as unions to defend our rights, then there is no answer but to start a labor party. [18, p. 1]

In analyzing the whole incident, A. H. Raskin of the New York Times observed:

> It all proved once again that labor and management do most of their fighting and most of their hating over abstract issues, even when experience has shown that they can live peacefully and prosperously together.
>
> Charles R. Sligh, Jr., Chairman of the N.A.M. board, with whom Mr. Meany had his impromptu debate, has never had a strike in any of his four midwest furniture plants. Most of the association's high command has had an equally harmonious record of labor-management relations.
>
> Its incoming president, Cola G. Parker, reported that the Kimberly-Clark Corporation had had labor pains only once in the forty-five years of his association with the giant paper company. And that was a three day wildcat stoppage, disowned by the union.
>
> Mr. Meany made it clear in his luncheon talk that he was no hand for using labor's economic strength to shut down the country. In fact, he revealed that he had become the head of the merged labor federation without ever having been on strike in his life. What's more, he said, he never ordered anyone else to go on strike or organized a picket line. [22, p. 14]

Following the Meany-Sligh confrontation, however, the NAM continued to voice its fear of union dominance in the political process at its 61st Congress of American Industry held the following year, as witnessed by the following exerpt from a speech given on that occasion.

> There is no doubt that many union labor bosses are in this political picture more so than they are in the bona fide business of representing dues-paying members in labor-management relations. These leaders intend to stay in the political arena and build as much power and control over as many elected officeholders as they possibly can. This is not a partisan problem. It affects the Democratic Party as much as it does the Republican Party. In fact, it affects the Democratic Party more because the labor bosses intend to gain

> control of the Democratic Party. If this march toward power continues, one day the term "Democratic Party" will be a misnomer, for it will actually be the labor party. I mean a party controlled by labor bosses. [10, pp. 12-13]

Suffice it to say that while all this may make good polemic, there is very little evidence in Chapter V's detailed analysis of organized labor's postwar political activities to indicate that any of these charges have any relation to the realities of today's political process. Chapter III discussed in some detail the reasons why a viable labor party has never been formed in this country, and any ideas of a monolithic labor movement "capturing" one of the existing parties seems equally fanciful.

The figures on the number of union organizations reporting lobbying expenditures or continuious campaign contributions included only a small number of all the unions in the United States, and until the Teamsters became active as a result of the Landrum-Griffin bill, they did not include the largest union in the country. Most of the larger unions do have political programs, however, and ignoring the unaffiliated unions for a moment, the AFL-CIO does collect money from and attempt to speak for all of its affiliated members. By its own admission, however, only 61 of its member unions participated in its registration drive of 1956, which constitutes the most widely accepted aspect of their campaign program.

Samuel Gomper's old principle of autonomy for affiliated national unions has long prevented the national labor federations from dominating the bargaining activities of their members, and it is unlikely that these bodies will surrender their independence in the realm of political action although several have evidenced a willingness to cooperate in many situations. The degree of this cooperation, however, should not be overemphasized. The lingering and intractable jurisdictional disputes among some of the affiliated unions often prevents wholehearted unity in other areas as well, and several of the member internationals having formal political committees are not affiliated with COPE. Even those unions having an active political program are not able to excite all of their local officers or member in the same manner as the Hudson and Rosen study of the Machinists union pointed out. Despite the great amount of publicity generated at higher levels, the basic unit of organization as far as the actual contacts of the vast majority of union members are concerned is the local union. This only multiplies the opportunities for diversity and inconsistency in the effectiveness of national political programs. But, as was also mentioned in Chapter V, not all of the diversity is confined to the local level. The Teamsters and a few other unions failed to support Kennedy in 1960, and Wittee reported that several prominent leaders within the AFL-CIO supported Eisenhower in 1956.

Speaking at Cornell University in the fall of 1946, Harvard University's eminent labor economist Sumner H. Slichter observed that:

> The trade union movement has not yet adjusted itself to the increasingly important role which the government is playing in determining conditions of employment. . . . it has not yet worked out an accepted policy for political operations. [24, pp. 17-18]

While no one would deny that the American labor movement has made great strides toward working out a political policy since Slichter spoke, the relative ineffectiveness of labor's lobbying efforts in handling the Landrum-Griffin bill described above indicates that there is still a long way to go. Furthermore, the lack of organizational dicipline and the absence of party cohesion in this country make it almost impossible for any interest group with a well defined though relatively limited program to capture either party, for in the strictest sense of the word there are no parties to capture.

David Truman has stated:

> Serious difficulty is encountered in an effort to analyze the relations between parties and interest groups because the term "political party" has so many different meanings in this country. . . .
>
> It usually means in election campaigns something very different from what it means when applied to activities in a legislature. . . .
>
> the relationships that produce the vote for a president in a State or locality may be quite different from those that elect senators and congressmen, to say nothing of governors. . . . the effective constituencies of the two sets of officials are different and even conflicting. The political interest groups supporting them are correspondingly different. . . .
>
> variations in party structure must be accompanied by similar variations in the relations between parties and interest groups. [26, pp. 272-75]

Confirming himself to the national political arena, James M. Burns has stated:

> We can understand our party system best if we see each major party divided into presidential and congressional wings that are virtually separate parties in themselves. They are separate parties in that each has its own ideology, organization, and leadership. . . . But the main difference between the presidential and congressional parties is over policy; both presidential parties are more liberal and internationalist than both congressional parties. [5, p. 65]

Later in this article, Professor Burns goes on to elaborate why the presidential parties are liberal and the congressional parties are conservative in these words:

> In a sense, every presidential contest turns more than the last one on issues of liberalism, if only because of the steady flow of voters into urban areas, and hence the ever-increasing need for expanded government. The impetus toward liberal emphasis in presidential contests is also intensified by the mechanics of the electoral college. We hear much about congressional districts being gerrymandered to overrepresent conservatives - which they are, of course; sometimes we forget that our presidential electoral system is gerrymandered in the opposite direction, toward liberalism. For, under that system, with its winner-take-all device, each candidate fights desperately for the large urban states, where the balance of power is supposedly held by organized blocs - labor, Negroes, and so forth - who tend to vote liberal.
> . . .
> Why will conservatives win control of Congress. . .? One reason, of course, is that Congress overrepresents rural and conservative voters because of gerrymandering. Another is that most leaders of the congressional parties - notably the committee chiefs in House and Senate - are sure to hold their seats no matter what happens in national politics, for they represent one-party areas, as in the South and in rural sectors of the North and West, where there is no real competition from the opposition party and precious little within the dominant. And even if any of these leaders did lose, their places in Congress would be taken in most cases by equally conservative men who had sat their way up the seniority ladder.
>
> Conservatives will win Congress next fall also because of the coalition system in House and Senate. No matter which party gains majorities on Capitol Hill, power gravitates toward the Old Guard leaders in each party, who get along better, ideologically at least, with their counterparts across the aisle than they do with the liberals in their own party. No matter which party wins the presidency this fall, the new President will have to negotiate with - which means making concessions to - the men who run the committees. [5, pp. 66-67]

With the electoral system thus gerrymandered in such a way that the urban areas tend to control the national presidential conventions, labor's influence within a political party is therefore most likely to be exerted in this most publicized of all political arenas. Its political influence at this level can not be extrapolated downward in all cases, and it is difficult to say what its real influence at this level is. Since the national Democratic party in particular seems to be a coalition of several minority groups, this implies that any one of them (including labor) may have a veto power over any particular candidate even if it can' always get its first choice accepted by the other members of the ever changing coalition. The necessity of labor's having to accept Lyndon Johnson for vice-president in 1960, may imply that even their veto power has declined within the Democratic Party since the days of 1944, when the need to "clear it with Sidney" at least enabled the CIO to block the vice presidential bid of James F. Byrnes even though they couldn't get their champion Henry Wallace renominated. Going from the presidential level to the congressional level, the task of "capture" becomes even more difficult if not impossible because even though not all congressional districts are the personal property of a conservative incumbent, "Congressional leaders whether conservative or liberal, hold office on different assumptions, different mandates, different expectations from the President's".[6,p.65]

Moving from these general observations to the specifics of the present situation, the New York Times' Joseph Loftus asserted:

> It has been said that labor has already captured the Democratic party. That's a lot of nonsense. Judging by the batting averages of labor in recent congresses, it might be just as accurate to say that the Democratic party has been captured by the Republicans, with the consent of the south. [15, p. 5] 1

---

1 Loftus also has an antedote on the possibility of a labor party. He reported:

> George Meany, Secretary-Treasurer of the AFL, said, "no", when asked on a television program if there was any possibility of a labor party. Asked why not, he told of a (continued on following page)

While thus emphasizing that much of the propaganda surrounding organized labors alleged political power may not be well-founded, it would nevertheless be a serious mistake to go to the other extreme and argue that labor is powerless. Furthermore, the records of Chapter V clearly indicate that much of its present influence is, indeed, exercised within the Democratic party. Even this fact, however, may tend to put a limit on the amount of influence that organized labor can bring to bear on the political process. It would seem likely that the continued support of the unions for the Democratic candidates in the vast majority of the cases in the political arena, (even though this choice is of necessity and based "on the records") is bound to blunt the effectiveness of any labor threat to transfer its support should it decide its "friends" are no longer so friendly. First, much of the member support labor has for its political program is the result of a long period of cultivation which might not be able to survive many sharp switches from one party label to another. Second, if labor wants to shift its support it must have some place to go. The irony of this situation is reflected in labor's predicament following the passage of the Landrum-Griffin Bill.

With regard to this situation, A. H. Raskin reported:

> A somewhat groggy labor movement took stock this week of the acid fruits of its political "victory" last November and wondered whether it could survive another such triumph. . . .

---

short encounter in Europe with a British labor leader who said to him: "When are you fellows going to wake up over there? When are you going to form a labor party?" Meany must have jolted his British friend a bit with the reply, "When our economic status gets as low as the British". [15, p. 3]

> Even when allowance was made for the federation's own tactical blunders and internal differences in mobilizing its lobbying resources, union chiefs were left with a feeling that they had been "sold down the river" on the issue that meant more to them than any other in this session of Congress.
>
> Their sense of frustration was not lessened by a realistic recognition that there is not much they can do within the present structure of either the Democratic or Republican parties to ward off a similar disappointment in future elections.
>
> There has been no wavering in the conviction of most top unionists that the national councils of the Republican party are dominated by big business and that its policies are directed at undermining or destroying union strength. Labor is equally aware that the center of Democratic power in Congress is with the Southern bloc, which it regards as no less reactionary than the most hide-bound Republican.
>
> In its convention report, the A.F.L.-C.I.O. executive council has called for a massive political effort to upset the established order in Southern politics. But the threat of a political counterpart of "operation Dixie", labor's ill-starred attempt to unionize Southern workers, is not taken seriously even by the men who signed the report.
>
> We've got as much chance of making over the Dixiecrats in our image as we have of organizing a closed shop in the National Association of Manufacturers", one federation vice-president declared. . . .
>
> This is especially so because the federation itself is far from united. Its two principal leaders, George Meany and Walter P. Reuther, are at war on almost every question of union or political tactics. . . . It is hardly likely under these circumstances to make over the country's political face. [23, p. 10]

Despite organized labor's continuing problems in the political arena, however, some reasonable factor must be allowed for improvement with continued practice. Joseph Loftus has stated:

> The union member who is apathetic about politics because he doesn't see the connection between it and spendable income is having this connection explained to him. . . . Sooner or later that sort of thing is going to be effective. [15, pp. 7-8]

How effective it will be depends largely on the extent to which unions can overcome the other loyalties of their membership in the political process and persuade them that their best interest lies in supporting organized labor's official legislative program. Ignoring the problems of a relatively stagnant membership base in our growing population and the geographical imbalance of union membership, past experience has revealed that these are some definite limits on the extent to which a union can command its members loyalties and active participation in the political process. Historically they seem to have been most successful in times of economic adversity or when the institutions of the trade union movement appear to be under attack.

While such refined distinctions do not make good campaign rhetoric, the actual impact and future potential of organized labor in the American political process does not appear to justify any fear of labor dominance in the foreseeable future. Nevertheless, the American labor movement is today, as never before, a full participant in the political process of our society, and there is no evidence that their present influence is likely to recede greatly. Indeed, the writer feels that labor's efforts to win support for their legislative goals are more likely to increase than diminish in the future--particularly if they feel that their present position in the institutional life of our country is threatened.

Going below the heat of public discussion to the available evidence, which is not as adequate as one would like, the reported figures on federal lobby spending by organized labor groups do indicate that there has been a substantial increase in both the number of labor groups reporting lobby expenditures and the amount of such expenditures reported, although the amount of this labor total reported by the AFL-CIO national headquarters has declined in both absolute and percentage terms since the merger in 1955. The figures on labor-reported campaign contributions in federal elections are less clear. The number of labor committees reporting such contributions has shown a fairly steady increase from 13 in 1948 to 43 in 1956. There was a drop to 32 labor committees reporting in 1958, and a sharp increase to 60 in 1960, with 16 new committees being associated with the Teamster's formation of DRIVE.

Despite the changes in the number of labor committees reporting however, over 76% of the total funds reported in 1960 were accounted for by a dozen committees with a continuous record of contributions going back to the 1948 elections. Within this "hard core" of continuous contributors, the amounts reported by the AFL-CIO-COPE have tended to be somewhat less than the totals reported separately by the AFL-LLPE and the CIO-PAC in the years preceeding the merger. The total amount of labor reported campaign contributions have shown less clear-cut trends than the changes in the number of committees reporting, but the amounts reported in presidential election years have averaged about $530,000 more than those reported in non-presidential years, with the $2,450,944 reported in 1960 being almost double the $1,291,343 reported in 1948.

Thus, with regard to organized labor's participation in the political process, it seems fair to conclude that there has been a substantial increase during the entire postwar period, but with no clear signs of any marked acceleration in this activity following the AFL-CIO merger in 1955.

Despite this increased activity, however, organized labor's legislative batting average has not been as good as that of the business community on the major bills before Congress during the postwar period, and it has shown a tendency to decline since the merger. Of course, no one knows what their batting average might have been had they not made these efforts, and the fact that the business community's batting average has been improving does not mean that it is satisfied with the results. Although they supported the Taft-Hartley and the Landrum-Griffin bills, both the NAM and the Chamber continue to demand further restrictions on union activities, and they have not been successful in defeating such programs as federal aid to housing, increasing minimum wages and depressed areas legislation although they did help to delay the eventual enactment of several of these measures which were strongly supported by organized labor.

The lobby spending figures reported by the Chamber and the NAM are too inadequate to determine if they have been increasing in recent years, and there are no time series data on the indirect political advertising or individual campaign expenditures of businessmen to compare with the labor figures cited above. A detailed examination of individual campaign contributions in only one year, however, did indicate that in 1956 the top executives of 199 of America's largest firms alone contributed $131,365 more than that of all the labor groups combined in that year, and the contributions of only 12 of America's wealthiest families equalled 64% of the labor total of $1,805,482 reported in federal elections.

The initiation of practical politics courses for executives

and other employees and the increased vocalness of several of America's largest firms on certain political issues in 1958 and 1959, no doubt added to the publicity surrounding managements political efforts in those years, but whether they will lead to any permanent increase in business' political activity can't be determined until more data are available on how many persons take these courses and how they apply them to the political process. The questions of individual corporations (and unions) spending general funds to finance statements on political issues to the public at large also highlights some of the unresolved questions in our present federal political statutes.

We will return to the question of the general adequacy of our present federal laws regulating the political dimension of labor-management relations later. For the present we can summarize this lengthy answer to our first question by saying that while many 1958 elections were more clearly contested on labor-management issues than is usually the case, subsequent events don't seem to indicate any pronounced acceleration in the political dimension of labor-management relations. The general arena for labor-management political struggles, however, does seem broader today than it was 10 or 15 years ago; and, in terms of results, management seems to have wielded the upper hand on purely union-management issues while gradually being forced to yield in a holding action on broader welfare matters.

Given this rather fuzzy answer to the main question posed in Chapter I, we can turn to an examination of the subsidiary questions raised in that chapter about some of the possible implications of an expanded political dimension of labor-management relations.

With regard to basic structural or internal changes within the contending parties, no dramatic changes appear to have yet materialized. The initiation of more active corporate political programs does not yet appear to be a threat to the traditional positions of the NAM and the Chamber as "spokesmen for industry". Indeed, both the Chamber and the NAM have supported the new "business in politics" movement by providing specially designed and organized material for the individual companies wishing to initiate the new "practical politics" courses for their employees. The separate corporate statements on public issues seem designed to supplement rather than substitute for the NAM and Chamber publicity on similar issues---although it is not known if the companies now financing their own statements continue to contribute to the national organizations at their "pre-awakening" level or not. (Indeed it is not even known if the companies now speaking out on their own are even contributors to the Chamber or the NAM, but it seems very likely that they are). The establishment of the Effective Citizens Organization and the Americans for Constitutional Action to stimulate political activity by businessmen also seem designed more to supplement rather than replace the NAM and the Chamber by the nature of the fact that these groups seem more concerned with the election rather than the lobbying aspects of politics.

All of these activities can be seen as rivals only in the sense that the money devoted to one of these programs or activities is not available for the other. Unless there is some sort of fixed "political fund" doctrine operation in American industry, however, a general increase in the amount of money made available for all political activities can go a long way to reduce whatever competitive element may exist. As noted, it is not possible to say if this has in fact happened but there are grounds for some supposition that this may be the case.

On the other possibility of structural change within the business community as a result of an increased interest in politics to increase the importance of geographically based employers associations relative to that of individual firms, evidence is simply not available from published sources. The studies of employer associations which have been published recently, have tended to focus on bargaining or "negotiatory" associations rather than on "legislative" or political associations,[1] but more will be said on this point in the subsequent parts of this thesis based on the Massachusetts experience.

Turning again to the organized labor movement, there seems to be mixed evidence concerning the type of structural changes one might expect if the unions were really serious about expanding its political activities on a major scale. At the very top of the labor movement, for example, the fact that the AFL-CIO continues to hold its bi-annual conventions in odd numbered years rather than in the even numbered years during which federal elections are held indicates that it is passing up an opportunity to convene the single largest aggregation of the American labor movement at a time that might have the maximum impact in terms of stimulating the delegates and in turn their unions on the importance of political affairs.

---

1 See the papers by McCaffree, Wortman, and Munson in [13] and the article by Frank Pierson [20].

Going beneath the national federation level, Chapter I pointed out that geographical boundaries rather than industrial product market lines played a larger part in politics than in collective bargaining, yet recent years have not seen any significant increase in the influence of politically-oriented geographical federations relative to the bargaining-oriented national union structure within the labor movement, although there is some evidence of an awareness of this problem which the hypothesis of Chapter I might lead us to expect.

In the spring of 1959, the AFL-CIO, for the first time, created the position of Coordinator of State and Local Central Bodies, and Stanton E. Smith, the former President of the Tennessee State AFL-CIO, was appointed to this position. There is some evidence that the motivation behind this move was largely to strengthen organized labor's political efforts. In the American Federationist in 1961 Mr. Smith stated:

> Frustration of legislative efforts and spasmodic political results have caused the AFL-CIO and many of its affiliated national and international unions to realize that maximum results in these fields and in the related activities of community relations will be greatly advanced by strengthening the state and local central labor councils so they, in turn, can give effective support to these essential programs. Coordination of legislative and political activities is just as essential at the state and local as at the national level.
>
> Currently, the AFL-CIO has two major projects under way to strengthen the state and local central bodies: a national campaign to secure maximum affiliation of local unions with these branches of the AFL-CIO and the institution of a system of annual reports covering the basic kinds of information needed to secure a comprehensive picture of the existing situation and practices in the various central bodies. In the course of time, there will follow projects which will contribute to improving the programs and effectiveness of the councils. [25, p. 8]

The report to the AFL-CIO's bi-annual Convention later in

1961 indicated that the affiliation and reporting programs were having moderate success in these words:

> The initial check by the state federations shows that only 48.5 percent of 33,327 locals were affiliated with their respective state federations. However, the total affiliated membership as reported by the state federations is 8,281,800. . . .
>
> The annual reports from state and local central bodies filed during the first half of 1961, while the affiliation campaign was in its early stages, shows that 1,362 local unions have affiliated with state federations and 505 local unions have affiliated with local central bodies as a result of the affiliation campaign. The figure for local central bodies is based on reports from approximately half of the 820 local councils. These affiliations represent only a small fraction of the potential. [4, pp. 52-53]

Aside from this campaign to strengthen state and local central bodies however, it is still true that at the present time these bodies do not wield a great deal of influence within the labor movement. A resolution to increase the representation of state labor organizations at the bi-annual AFL-CIO conventions from 1 delegate to 2 delegates at the 1957 convention in Atlantic City was not concurred in by the resolutions committee of the convention and was not adopted. [1, p. 442] A similar resolution was also defeated in 1959. [2, p.404] An attempt to "adopt a resolution calling on international unions to revise their constitutions to make affiliation mandatory with state and local central bodies" was also defeated at the AFL-CIO convention in 1961, but a substitute motion to emphasize "the need for all national, international and local unions to fully cooperate and do what they can to bring about full affiliation" was adopted. [3, pp. 653-668] The following sections' description of the Massachusetts labor scene will yield some further insights into the problems of the relations between national unions and state and city central federations.

One other hypothesis, mentioned in Chapter I, concerns the possible relation between increased union political activity and internal democracy as it reflects membership interest and participation in union affairs. In discussing the problems of the UAW in the early postwar period, for example, Howe and Widdick stated:

> The union, we think, can involve large layers of the membership in its work only if it offers them a new source of interest; a compelling program of political activity sustained by a large social motivation. On this rests the future of the UAW. [11, p. 266]

The fact that the UAW has remained one of the most politically vocal and one of the most democratic of American unions lends at least surface plausibility to this contention. Most of the published data reviewed in Chapter V, however, indicates that there may not be a simple cause and effect relationship between these facts. Indeed, these studies indicated that rank and file inertia and apathy on political matters was one of the strongest limitations on union political programs, and that a strong socially conscious political program not directly related to job centered needs might actually cut rather than increase participation in union affairs. In commenting on the broadening of the AFL-CIO's political goals, for example, A. H. Raskin has commented:

> The unanswered question is whether union members will give a labor movement dedicated to such broad goals of long-term social improvement the kind of support they proffered when unions were on the march for more meat and potatoes and for the emancipation of the worker from the menacing shadow of the "boss". [21, p. 15]

The Hudson and Rosen survey of Machinists' attitudes indicated that only 31% of the rank and file and 46% of the officers and stewards felt that politics should "always or usually" be discussed at local union meetings, [12] and Kornhauser, Sheppard, and Mayers' study of Detroit autoworkers concluded: "In view of the union's active political campaigning the autoworkers' degree of political interest and personal involvement in political action can be considered only moderate." [14, pp. 262-63]

While most union members appear to be willing to go along with most union political programs, there is little evidence that political activities, as such, are a strong source of attraction and interest for most members. Rather, most of the evidence indicates that the people who are active in the union's other activities also seem to be willing to take on political work if they see it tied in with their interest in the union. Indeed, it was among just such "actives" that the programs reviewed in Chapter V seemed to have their greatest effect. On the other hand if a person with only moderate or ordinary union attachments really wanted to do something about civil rights or medical care for the aged, there is no reason to believe that he would necessarily turn to his union as a vehicle for these interests. There are usually other groups devoted to these issues *per se*, which might be more attractive to him. COPE activities at the local level also seem to be performed by the existing officers or stewards rather than by attracting otherwise inactive members to this "new" area of union work, but the following chapters' more detailed analysis of the Massachusetts experience will also throw more light on this question.

Finally, Chapter I also raised the question of whether or

not there might be some relation between what appeared to be a new "business in politics" movement and the recent "hardening" of management attitudes in collective bargaining noted by several observers of the American labor-management scene. The *a priori* reasoning underlying this hypothesis was that a firm entering the more polarized atmosphere of the stringent and often unrealistic discourse of the political arena might, through its new involvement, also be more inclined to become increasingly adamant in its private bargaining relations with unions. The fact that the General Electric Company was prominently associated with both the "business in politics" and the "tough line" movements also helped to form this initial speculation. Subsequent analysis, however, indicates that, as in the case of the UAW's political activities and its internal democracy, there is no apparent simple cause and effect relationship between these two phenomena.

With regard to the General Electric Company, it seems clear that they evolved their "new look" in collective bargaining several years before President Cordiner announced the company's political "awakening" in 1958. With regard to other companies, Herbert Northrup has offered some evidence that much of the increasing firmness in management's approach to collective bargaining in recent years is "the result of some ugly economic facts of life which management has all too belatedly recognized" [19, p.9], rather than from forces stemming from the political arena. It is also true that in most of the large companies "speaking out" on public issues in recent years, their political and public affairs programs are under separate direction from their industrial relations programs at the operating level, although the top management of these companies is of course responsible for the conduct of both activities. A further look at the principle labor and management organizations operating in the political arena also makes clear that these activities are still handled largely at the federation level by the AFL-CIO, the Chamber of Commerce of the U.S. and the NAM, which are organizationally and operationally considerably removed from the centers of power that negotiate the labor-management agreements that govern much of the private sector of our industrial relations system.

While it would thus be difficult to say that the political battles of recent years have had any direct influence on the conduct of most labor-management negotiations, it is probably also fair to state that the acrimony of recent labor-management political debates has done little to facilitate more cooperative approaches to the negotiation of labor-management differences. Indeed, as has been pointed out above, much of the fighting in the political arena is over issues that have already been resolved, or at least accommodated by the pressures of necessity in the bargaining arena.

To summarize briefly the conclusions to this point, there is considerable evidence that the political dimension of labor-management relations today is expanded compared to earlier times, but only mixed evidence that it has been expanding in recent years; and only a few of the possible implications of an expanding political dimension posited in Chapter I appear to be materializing. Talk of a labor party or organized labor capturing one of the existing parties seems ill-founded, and there does not appear to be any evidence of political programs stimulating either a significant increase in membership participation in union affairs or a widespread membership opposition to existing union political activities. There is some evidence, however, that the labor movement is attempting to strengthen its geographically based state and local central bodies in an attempt to strengthen its political posture. Within the management camp, much of the publicity surrounding the "business in politics" movement of 1958-59 appears to have subsided, and there does not appear to be any direct relation between this series of events and the "tougher" approach management has been taking to collective bargaining problems in recent years.

Each of these tentative conclusions will be examined in further detail in light of the Massachusetts experience presented in the remainder of this thesis. Before turning to these considerations, however, one or two other conclusions appear to stand out from this review of the national labor-management political scene.

John T. Dunlop has noted the lack of "consensus" that dominates our national labor policy, [7] and Chapter V's review indicates that this situation extends beyond issues of labor-management relations to many other issues concerning the appropriate role of government and social welfare in our industrial society. Yet, current labor and management political activities are not aimed at any form of consensus building that can serve as the foundation for a more stable long run labor policy. Rather, each side seems bent on forcing its intractable position on the other in a highly partisan and polarized atmosphere that is far removed from the practical problems of the day to day work level of our industrial society.

As mentioned in Chapter II, the political dimension of labor-management relations is somewhat unique in the political arena in that there are highly organized adversaries on each side of practically every issue. The adversaries are fairly evenly matched in such a way that it is difficult to get any change in policy until an abnormal combination of circumstances or a temporary "crisis" shifts the balance of power momentarily to one side or the other. Such a "crisis" atmosphere, when it does arise, is not conducive to the kind of sober reflection or judicious consideration that should serve as the basis for sound long run policy. Under these circumstances of persistent deadlock in a highly partisan and polarized atmosphere which brooks no compromise and results in action only when one side or the other can take advantage of monentary shifts in the public attitude or surrounding circumstances to force its will in a way that is almost guaranteed to set up counter forces to immediately modify whatever new policy is hastily or expidently agreed on, the public and our legislators tend to be exposed only to the most extreme views of labor and management spokesmen. The trend to increasingly detailed regulation noted in Chapter II seems to be the inevitable result of such a situation, and barring a major modification it seems unlikely that this trend can be easily reversed. At present, there are no strong or effective channels through which "moderates" in either labor or management affairs can easily make their views known on a continuing basis. President Kennedy's establishment of a tri-partite, 21-member Advisory Committee on Labor Management Policy, however, may be a step in this direction.

In the interim, the tremendous amount of acrimony continuously generated at the political level by such perennial issues as union security is disconcerting in view of some of the other problems presently facing our industrial relations system. By its very nature union security is an issue that almost defies solution at the political level which would attempt to make a legislated policy applicable to many diverse employer and employee relationships. This seems to be one issue that can never be solved once and for all for everybody everywhere. Yet the pressures of the private bargaining process are such that the issue can be accommodated to suit the different needs of different relationships in a way that parties can at least live together without continuous attempts to force their accommodation on others or have their existing agreement disrupted by outside forces.

Indeed, the complex problems of policy in all areas of labor-management relations must always balance two considerations: the consideration that private arrangements do not adversely affect those not party to the agreement; and the consideration that those without a direct knowledge of or interest in a private arrangement do not make basic decisions which adversely affect the parties that are directly involved. Regardless of where one thinks the balance should be drawn on these two considerations with regard to union security, it seems clear that the disproportionate amount of attention shown to this issue in the political arena in recent years has prevented or at least militated against the serious consideration of some other problems which seem to be more clearly beyond the power of individual bargaining relationships to deal with effectively. The whole area of technological change which disrupts existing product market and labor market patterns, for example, poses problems that are often beyond the ability of individual employers or unions to combat efficiently. The cost of retraining, transfer, and encouraging mobility from obsolete plants can quickly become prohibitive for any single employer or union, and seem much more amenable to political policies at a broader level. Yet the parties at the broader levels to date seem to have been too preoccupied with old battles to rise to the challenges of new opportunities for more constructive efforts. One can only speculate as to what might have been accomplished had all of the funds, talent, and effort expended on the futile right to work battles in 1958 been turned to the problem of accommodating to the present pace of technological change.

This latter speculation brings us to the final observation of this review of the national labor-management political scene. Namely, that it is presently almost impossible to estimate how much is spent by labor and management groups on political activities. Our present reporting laws are grossly inadequate with respect to both lobby spending and federal campaign contributions.

It is clear that both labor and management groups have vital interests and large stakes in the political process and few would deny their right to participate effectively in these areas. Certain limitations, however, also seem proper, and a full and complete accounting of all efforts made would seem to be a reasonable responsibility to accompany the right of effective political participation. With regard to lobbying expenditures, more clearly defined reporting requirements and standard reporting forms with appropriate sub divisions and clearly spelled out penalties for filing fradulant or inaccurate returns seem appropriate for all groups attempting to influence the course of federal legislation, including labor and management groups.

The problems of legitimate political participation becomes more complex as one moves from legislative lobbying to the election of the legislators themselves. The links between particular issues and particular candidates is often strong, but it is also true that once elected candidates influence a variety of other issues not necessarily germane to those decisive in the campaign, and the directness of the relations between certain issues such as medical care for the aged under social security and the immediate interests of unions or corporations also becomes a grey area.

At present both corporations and unions are prohibited from making direct campaign contributions to federal candidates, but such candidates can be endorsed in internal communications directed to union members or corporate employees or stockholders, and public statements on specific issues are permitted. Outright endorsements directed to the public at large are presently outlawed except in certain special circumstances, however, but the constitutionality of this prohibition is questioned by many as long as the endorsement is made in the name of the corporation or the union, and it is sometimes difficult to separate a public statement on an "issue" such as "right to work" from the endorsement of candidates closely identified with these issues.

The present prohibitions on the direct contribution of union dues money or corporate funds to particular candidates or party committees seem reasonable in view of the other political channels open to union and management groups, and there seems no reason why this prohibition should not be extended to state as well as federal elections. A case can also be made for a more complete reporting of the now permissible contributions by individual corporate executives and by union political committees collecting voluntary political funds. These reports should cover both state and federal elections, and primary as well as general elections.

The use of corporate funds and union dues money for internal and external statements on candidates and issues raises somewhat more difficult questions of the direct interests of the union and corporate institutions, since in some sense practically every issue from world peace on down has some relation to these institutions. It also raises questions of the interests of union members and corporate stockholders as separate from the interests of the institution themselves. The Supreme Court ruling in the Georgia Case of Machinists vs Street seems to offer greater protection to union members than the present law offers to stockholders since the SEC ruling that the General Electric management did not have to reveal the costs of its political programs to stockholders unless it wanted to, which it did not.

It might be argued that as a practical matter it is easier for a stockholder to sell his stock than it is for a union man to join another union or get another job if he disagrees with certain political pronouncements. But the basic philosophy of the case is weaker than its practical manifestations. And in any case it seems reasonable to require that both unions and corporations make a full accounting of the cost of both their internal and external political pronouncements on both candidates and issues. Then if a union man under a union shop contract objects to this use of his dues money he may be able to get a proportionate refund of his dues money under the Machinists vs Street ruling. Union members not under a union shop and stockholders receiving this information could then decide to go elsewhere, stay and work for change in the existing organization, do nothing, or press for further legal protection of their interests relative to those of their union or company. Whether or not further legal protection is needed or not is not possible to say at this time, but should become much clearer if the reports described above do in fact become required.

Turning from desirability to feasibility, how likely is it that the reforms suggested will be adopted? First, if they are proposed in a way that pertains only to unions and corporations their chances are better than if they require a complete amending of the Federal Regulation of Lobbying Act and the Federal corrupt Practices Act as they now apply to all groups. Past experiences with attempting to amend these latter statutes are not encouraging, but given the possibility of some major influence scandal causing a widespread demand for Congressional reform, this alternative, which is preferable, is not inconceivable but still not very likely. If one were willing to settle for a change applying only to labor and management groups as a starter, the possibilities are greater. A rather modest change in the present reporting laws required under the Landrum-Griffin Act might do the job as far as unions are concerned, and the same route might be used for corporations and such organizations as the NAM and the Chamber of Commerce of the U.S. Or, special SEC or tax rulings might furnish the data for corporations and possibly other employer groups as well.

REFERENCES - CHAPTER VI

1. American Federation of Labor-Congress of Industrial Organizations, Proceedings of the AFL-CIO 2nd Constitutional Convention, 1957, Vol. I.

2. _______. Proceedings of the AFL-CIO 3rd Constitutional Convention, 1959, Vol. I.

3. _______. Proceedings of the AFL-CIO 4th Constitutional Convention, 1961, Vol. I.

4. _______. Proceedings of the AFL-CIO 4th Constitutional Convention, 1961, Vol. II.

5. James M. Burns, "White House vs. Congress," The Atlantic, March 1960, Vol. 205, pp. 65-69.

6. _______. "Memo To The Next President," The Atlantic, April 1960, Vol. 205, pp. 64-68.

7. John T. Dunlop, "Consensus and National Labor Policy," Industrial Relations Research Association, Proceedings of the 13th Annual Meeting (Madison, 1961).

8. Helen Fuller, "Smearing the PAC," New Republic, July 22, 1946, Vol. 1 pp. 68-70.

9. Joseph Gaer, The First Round (New York: Duell, Sloan, and Pearce, 1944).

10. George F. Hinkle, "Implication of Labor's Political Activities," in Some Major Problems Looming Ahead in 1957 (New York: National Association of Manufacturers, 1957).

11. Irving Howe and B. J. Widick, The UAW and Walter Reuther (New York: Random House, 1949).

12. Ruth A. Hudson and Hjalmar Rosen, "Union Political Action: The Membe Speaks," Industrial and Labor Relations Review, April 1954, Vol. 7, pp. 404-418.

13. Industrial Relations Research Association, Proceedings of the 15th Annual Meeting (Madison, 1963).

14. Arthur Kornhauser, H. L. Sheppard, and A. J. Mayer, When Labor Votes-A Study of Auto Workers (New York: University Books, 1956).

15. Joseph Loftus, "Organized Labor and Politics: A Reporter's View" in American Management Association, *Spotlighting the Labor-Management Scene* (New York, 1952).

16. Fred Maguire, "The Press Gang-Up on the PAC," *New Republic*, October 30, 1944, Vol. 111, pp. 558-563.

17. National Association of Manufacturers, *"What Organized Labor Expects of Management," by George Meany. "What Management Expects of Organized Labor," by Charles R. Sligh, Jr.* (New York, 1956).

18. *New York Times*, December 10, 1955.

19. Herbert R. Northrup, "Management's 'New Look' in Labor Relations," *Industrial Relations*, October 1961, Vol. 1, pp. 9-24.

20. Frank C. Pierson, "Recent Employer Alliances in Perspective," *Industrial Relations*, October 1961, Vol. 1, pp. 39-56.

21. A. H. Raskin, "Labor's Legislative Goals," *Challenge Magazine*, January 1963, pp. 12-15.

22. ________. "Labor and N.A.M. Speak," *New York Times*, December 10, 1955.

23. ________. "Labor Leaders Taking New Look at Politics," *New York Times*, September 20, 1959, Section IV.

24. Sumner H. Slichter, *The Challenge of Industrial Relations* (Ithaca: Cornell University, 1947).

25. Stanton E. Smith, "The Challenge Facing Central Labor Bodies," *The American Federationist*, May 1961, Vol. 68, pp. 7-9.

26. David B. Truman, *The Governmental Process* (New York: Knopf, 1955).

27. Edwin E. Witte, "The New Federation and Political Action," *Industrial and Labor Relations Review*, April 1956, Vol. 9, No. 3, pp. 406-418.

PART II

THE CURRENT SETTING AND HISTORICAL BACKGROUND OF LABOR-MANAGEMENT POLITICAL STRUGGLES IN MASSACHUSETTS

CHAPTER VII

AN INTRODUCTION TO THE DYNAMICS AND STRUCTURE OF MASSACHUSETTS GOVERNMENT

This chapter will attempt to sketch in the historical background necessary for a minimum comprehension of the contemporary economic and political forces operating within the Massachusetts governmental structure. In launching this endeavor, it is probably best to begin with the Commonwealth's most basic resource--the people who have populated the state and given human vitality to its economic and political institutions. Secondly, the changing economic composition of the state will be examined as a prelude to a discussion of the shifting political tides in Massachusetts as they have reflected themselves in the formation and activities of Bay State political parties. Finally, the actual governmental machinery of the Commonwealth will be examined as a prelude to the more detailed discussion of labor legislation and its advocacy and opposition by particular interest groups, which follows in succeeding chapters.

The Population of Massachusetts: Assimilation and Change

The early Puritan settlers of Massachusetts were men of substance, determination, and education. They had experience in both business affairs and self-government, and they arrived on these shores determined to establish and maintain a religious Commonwealth. Even after the power of the Puritan theocracy wanned, the colony's immigration policy afforded a scant welcome to newcomers--particularly if they were of different economic circumstances or possessed different social or religious views.

Economic and political ferment in Europe at the end of the eighteenth century, however, began a slowly increasing tide of immigration to the United States. Massachusetts shared in this influx; but the increase was gradual, and the process of assimilation of the newcomers was relatively successful. This picture changed with stunning suddeness during the 1840's.

Between 1846 and 1856, 214,573 foreign born immigrants entered Boston by sea. Most of the immigrants were Irish Catholics, with 129,387 coming directly from Ireland, and many of the 38,049 from Canada and the 22,777 from England also being Irish victims of the potato famine.[2, p. 249] Boston was ill prepared to receive them. The sheer physical impact of this flood of immigration would have been enormous--even had there been no complicating factors, of which there were many.

In the early 1840's Boston was a slowly growing, well-to-do community of about 120,000 people. Though it was densely settled, filling operations in the flats around the city had created new land, and the comparative wealth of Boston meant that city improvements and sanitation had reached a high level. Interest in the arts, letters, and social problems flourished, and Bostonians were proud of their city--perhaps to the point of smugness.

In such a community, a few distressed souls might have found welcome and help, but the realities of the problems raised by the arrival of thousands upon thousands of hopeless, homeless, penniless immigrants were overwhelming. Along with the physical problems presented by these multitudes of newcomers, their Catholicism awoke all the old suspicion, distrust, and bigotry of Puritan days. Proper Boston, in the main, was horrified, suspicious, and dismayed.

Forced into the worst-paid occupations, huddled into housing worse than slums, the Irish had to concentrate on the pressing problems of bare subsistance. They had neither the time nor the encouragement to share old Boston's concern with the social issues of slavery or temperance.[1] But their first bitter years in America taught the immigrants that political freedom and political power were their only means to social and economic betterment. Consequently, increasing numbers of naturalized Irish voters came to the polls.

In response, the Know-nothing Party was formed largely to oppose the entrance of the Irish immigrants into politics. This party, which swept the state in the 1854 elections, united both the high-minded reformer and the bigot by attracting the southern slave power and the foreign Pope as equally un-American. Although the anti-foreign, anti-Catholic supporters of the Know-nothings were not conspicuously successful in limiting the political rights of the newcomers, the identification of "Irish" with "Catholic" was intensified and harassment of the immigrant community continued for some years.

---

1 Although the Catholic Church never supported the institution of slavery as such, it did not share in the anti-slavery agitation of most Protestant denominations; and Catholic newspapers urged their readers to support the law and the country's established institutions.

Much of the most bitter conflict was resolved during the Civil War, when the immigrant's loyalty to the government, once manifested in opposition to the abolitionists, then showed itself in adherence to the union. The political repercussions of the Know-nothing era have died hard, however, and, as will be seen later, they are still reflected in present party alignments in the Bay State.

While the Irish immigration certainly produced the major shift in the composition of the population of Massachusetts, immigration from northern Europe and Canada continued high during the second half of the nineteenth century. By the beginning of the twentieth century, however, a large majority of the immigrants were coming from southern and eastern Europe. This trend continued until the quota systems of the Federal immigration laws passed in the 1920's sharply curtailed this latter immigration.

As a result of over 170 years of immigration, Massachusetts, once the most homogenous of the 13 original states, has become second in the union in the proportion of foreign born to native population. Table 27 compares the proportions of ethnic minorities in Massachusetts and in the United States in 1920, 1950, and 1960.

Perhaps less startling than the Bay State's population change but equally significant has been the shift in the industrial composition of Massachusetts.

TABLE 27 - Proportions of Ethnic Minorities in Massachusetts and the United States - 1920, 1950 and 1960

	Percent of population foreign born			Percent of population born of foreign or mixed parentage		
	1920	1950	1960	1920	1950	1960
United States	14.5%	7.5%	5.4%	23.9%	17.5%	13.6%
Massachusetts	28.3	15.3	11.2	39.3	33.4	28.8

Source: 1920 and 1950 figures adapted from [9 , p. 306]
1960 figures from [11, p. 251]

The Changing Industrial Composition of the Bay State

At the close of the Revolutionary war, Massachusetts was a sparcely settled community, predominantly agricultural and maritime in occupation. Commerce dominated the life of the Commonwealth from 1790 to 1820. Though the embargo and the War of 1812 seriously interfered with Massachusetts trade, they also provided impetus for the growth of manufactures. By 1820, the predominantly agricultural and commercial economic pattern in Massachusetts had permanently shifted to industrial pursuits.

The accessibility of water power in Massachusetts had already permitted early craft industries to expand into factories. Capital for new industries came from the fortunes built in trade. Labor was first supplied by New England farm girls and later through natural population growth and immigration. Although hats, leather goods, and woolens were successfully manufactured in the state, textiles soon became the outstanding product.

Following the Civil War, the industrial development of

Massachusetts continued at a rapid pace; and by the middle of the 1880's Massachusetts was the nation's unchallenged industrial leader. She was the largest manufacturer of textiles and boots and shoes, and also produced fine paper, machines, and other diversified industrial products. During the early years of rail development, however, Massachusetts still had a strong maritime economy, and was never very agressive in developing rail transport. This, when combined with the subsequent development of electric power in other parts of the country, proved to be a serious handicap.

Massachusetts' supremacy in the manufacture of fine textiles, worsted, woolens, boots, shoes, and high-grade paper remained unchallenged in the early years of the twentieth century; and newer industrial developments included rubber, confectioneries, and hand tools. With the development of electrical power elsewhere, and the increasing importance of transportation cost as the nation continued its rapid expansion, however, Massachusetts lost her previous advantage in textile production; and she has since been struggling hard to compete industrially with other parts of the nation.

This situation has recently been summed up quite eloquently by the Massachusetts historian, Henry F. Howe:

> Massachusetts has fought for two generations a delaying action, a Dunkirk, a battling withdrawal, in the attempt to find substitutes for production of cotton textiles and manufacture of shoes, the two industries in which she held pre-eminent leadership in the nineteenth century, both of which have been reluctantly moving south and west. Cotton and hides once came by sea, and Massachusetts cloth and shoes were shipped by sea. When rail replaced shipping, and markets moved west, the attrition began. No tariff could protect any industry from the free competition of the other states

> of the Republic. The result, with bulk products like cotton and hides, was certain. As soon as adequate labor could be found to man factories nearer the centers of population, these New England industries were gradually forced out of their markets. For a while Yankee ingenuity, more efficient production techniques, and a pool of trained labor could stem the tide, and did. But when the flow of overseas immigration slowed down in the 1920's, when westward migrants, no longer needed on mechanized farms, turned to factory employment, and when enterprising midwestern and southern investors acquired sufficient capital, electric power, and efficient management to build the plants, the process of competition operated inexorably to reduce the Yankee supremacy. [3 , pp. 248-49]

Recent figures show that Massachusetts is still predominantly an industrial state, but the growth of new industry in other parts of the nation has hurt Massachusetts' relative competitive position. Despite the serious setbacks in the textile and shoe industries, however, there has been an increasing effort to introduce a new industry into the Bay State, such as electronics and other electrical machinery. Indeed, Howe states, "Research now has become, quite seriously, Massachusetts' most valuable asset."[3 , p. 254] There has also been an effort to develop non-manufacturing or service industries in the Commonwealth, such as tourism and, particularly, insurance.

We will return to the Massachusetts' economy as it effects, and is affected by, the Bay States' political process later. Now, however, we will turn to an examination of the structure and history of Massachusetts' government and its political parties.

The Formal Structure of Massachusetts Government

The Massachusetts constitution, ratified in 1780, is the

oldest state constitution still in existence. It bears a direct relationship to the Declaration of Independence, which preceded it by four years, and to the Constitution of the United States, which was adopted nine years later. The Massachusetts Constitution established a frame of government providing for the now familiar separation of powers between the legislative, judicial, and executive branches.[1]

The Massachusetts legislature is officially known as the General Court. Its two branches are the Senate with 40 members and the House of Representatives, whose 240 members make it one of the nation's largest lower houses. The General Court meets annually, and its members are elected bi-annually. The only exceptions to the legislature's exclusive power to make and repeal laws are the provisions for initiative and referendum, which give the people the power to initiate constitutional amendments or laws and to approve

---

[1] The original Massachusetts Constitution had no provisions for amendment, but when Maine was separated from Massachusetts to become a separate state in 1820, a constitutional convention was called. In addition to passing some amendments, the 1820 convention provided that after a proposed amendment had passed in two successive sessions of the General Court it would be submitted to a popular vote for final passage. A 1918 Constitutional Convention provided that amendments could also be introduced by initiative petition. The amendment procedure was again changed in 1950 to provide that either branch of the legislature may propose a joint session or a Constitutional Convention for the purpose of considering amendments to the Constitution.

There have been three constitutional conventions and over 80 amendments to the Massachusetts Constitution, but the League of Women Voters note: "Of all the amendments to date, only three may be said to belong more properly to the field of detailed legislation. They are: Amendment Forty-four, prohibiting the graduated income tax, Amendment Fifty, regulating advertising in public places, and Amendment Severty-eight, requiring that revenue from the use of motor vehicles be used for highway purposes only." [7, p. 38]

or reject laws passed by the legislature. Bills passed by the General Court must be approved by the governor, or repassed over his veto by a two-thirds vote of both branches.

The Massachusetts legislature uses a joint committee system which works best when the same party controls both houses. Committee work loads tend to be very heavy since Massachusetts has a system of "free petition", which means that any citizen can file a bill by merely obtaining the counter signature of any member of the legislature. Massachusetts also requires a public hearing on all bills, and no bill can be killed in committee. They must be reported out to the full body of the Senate or the House where they all are debated and acted upon. In recent years, however, more and more bills seem to be referred to post-prorogation study sessions rather than being passed or killed outright.

The turnover of members in the General Court is small--about one-fourth each term--and most legislators have some business or profession apart from their legislative work. The Massachusetts League of Women Voters reports:

> A survey of the 1955-56 legislature shows that the legal profession was the most highly represented; eleven of the forty senators and sixty-two of the 240 House members were lawyers. The insurance business supplied four senators and twenty-four representatives. Except for these two areas, the legislature appears to represent a cross-section of occupations, with almost every trade or profession represented. [7 , p. 46]

Massachusetts provides justice to its citizens through a system of courts that includes the Supreme Judicial Court, the Superior Courts, the Probate Courts, the Land Courts, and the District Courts. The legislature is responsible for the establishment of the courts. All judges are appointed for life by the governor, and all the procedures and administration of the courts are supervised by the Supreme Judicial Court, which gives the system an over-all unity.

Since the Massachusetts Constitution gave little power to the governor, his role was originally very limited. The Constitutional Convention of 1917-19 reorganized the executive branch, however, and more power and responsibility were granted to the governor. This Convention also established a two year term for all elected state officials, and it provided that: "executive and administrative work of the Commonwealth shall be organized in not more than twenty departments, in one of which every executive and administrative office, board, and commission, except those offices serving directly under the governor or the council shall be placed." [7 , p. 64]

In Massachusetts, a major share of the governor's actions must be approved by an executive council, which is composed of the lieutenant governor and eight councilors elected from special councilor districts. This institution is a vestige from colonial days when the council was established as a check on the governor, who was then appointed by the King of England. Although it still supposedly acts as adviser to the governor on executive policy, its role in administration is negligible. Since the council does have the power to approve appointments, however, it does get involved in patronage; and this is certainly the point of its most significant influence.

Since the governor is required to submit an executive budget outlining all proposed revenues and expenditures of the Commonwealth, his legislative program serves as the base point for all major legislative operations in Massachusetts. As a result of the 1917-19 Constitutional Convention, the legislature can not include in the regular budget any new item which the governor has not requested, but it can alter the amounts allotted to the various specific programs. If any new programs are to be submitted, they must come through separate proposals with separately provided financing. This, obviously, serves as a strong deterent to independent programs. Also intergal to the executive budget is the governor's power to veto or reduce any item of the budget as passed by the legislature. This "item veto" makes it easier for the governor to secure a budget in line with his original requests.

Legislative vetoes are not very frequent in Massachusetts. The governor has one opportunity to return any legislative measure presented to him to the General Court with his recommendations for change. If he does finally veto a bill, a two-third vote of the legislative is required to override his action.

The expansion of the administrative organization of the state did not stop with the 1919 reorganization. The constitutional limitation of 20 administrative departments, however, has made it impossible to create additional departments to administer state responsibilities assumed since 1919. Nevertheless, the legislature still has the power to reorganize the existing departments to make room for a new one when such a move seems necessary or desirable. One such example occurred in 1953 when the legislature first abolished the Board of Industrial Accidents, a separate department; then created a new Division of Industrial Accidents, having the same functions, as an independent agency in the Department of Labor and Industries; and thereby made it possible to create the new Department of Commerce.

Using such awkward arrangements, there are now over fifty agencies not subject to department control--in addition to over twenty agencies operating directly under the governor and council, and a large number of independent agencies that do not fall within any division of the executive branch. Nevertheless, the state administration remains fitted into the duly authorized twenty departments.

The scope of this thesis justifies particular mention of only two of these Departments and one commission under the governor and council--the Department of Labor and Industries, the Department of Commerce, and the Massachusetts Commission Against Discrimination.

Department of Labor and Industries

Today, the Department of Labor and Industries administers approximately 1,500 statutory laws--the most important of which will be reviewed historically in the following chapters. As now constituted, the Department is administered by a Commissioner; an Assistant Commissioner, who must be a woman; and three Associate Commissioners, one of whom shall be a representative of labor and one a representative of employers. The third, though not so specified in the law, is generally chosen to represent the public. All of the above are appointed by the governor and council for three-year terms, and it has become increasingly customary to appoint a labor man as Commissioner to administer the overall activities of the department.

There are three divisions within the department which are headed by commissioners. Six other divisions have directors appointed by the commissioners with the approval of the governor and council. And, finally, there are three autonomous divisions not subject to departmental control. We will briefly examine the divisions in each of these three categories.

Divisions Headed by Commissioners--The three divisions within the Department of Labor and Industries which are headed by commissioners are the Board of Conciliation and Arbitration, the Division of Minimum Wage, and the Division of Employment of Older Workers.

The three associate commissioners of the Department of Labor and Industries constitute the Board of Conciliation and Arbitration. This Board dates back to 1886, and was placed in the Department of Labor and Industries in 1919. Table 28 shows the number of arbitration and mediation cases handled by the Board from 1920 through fiscal 1961 (July 1, 1960 to June 30, 1961), the last year for which complete details are available.[1]

In fiscal 1961, the Board received a total of 662 cases, and serviced another 21 cases pending from the previous year. Three hundred and ninety-three cases were closed by conciliation and another 27 conciliation cases were withdrawn or settled prior to conference. Two hundred and seventeen arbitration cases were closed by Board award, and another 45 arbitration cases were withdrawn or settled. Sixty-three of the 662 cases serviced by the Board in 1961 were

---

1 The early history of the Board and a comparison of the mediation and arbitration efforts of Massachusetts and New York from 1886 to 1900 are [6, pp. 23-26]. A more recent discussion, from which the 1920-1940 figures in Table 28 are taken is [5, pp. 187-192].

work-stoppage cases directly involving 17,998 employees.

TABLE 28 - Arbitration and Mediation Cases of the Massachusetts State Board of Conciliation and Arbitration, 1920-1961*

Year	Arb. Cases	Med. Cases	Year	Arb. Cases	Med. Cases
1920	333	31	1941	360	468
1921	573	70	1942	319	470
1922	592	48	1-43 to 7-43	156	171
1923	568	52	1944	283	282
1924	394	37	1945	379	198
1925	316	Less than 70	1946	329	268
1926	269	Less than 70	1947	405	308
1927	194	Less than 70	1948	464	427
1928	118	Less than 70	1949	414	455
1929	48	Less than 40	1950	475	420
1930	72	-	1951	246	431
1931	375	-	1952	224	378
1932	121	-	1953	224	421
1933	111	-	1954	224	421
1934	75	-	1955	259	434
1935	89	-	1956	254	487
1936	120	More than 105	1957	253	462
1937	271	Approx. 250	1958	253	468
1938	326	311	1959	262	374
1939	314	336	1960	252	349
1940	325	380	1961	262	420

*Calendar Year 1920-1943. Fiscal Year (7-1 to 6-30) 1944-1961.

Source: Annual Reports of the Board on file at Room 473 State House, Boston, Massachusetts.

Over the years Massachusetts has had one of the best records of industrial peace among the industrial states of the nation. Table 29 gives the state and the national figures for work stoppages due to labor-management disputes from 1945 through 1960.

The female assistant commissioner of the Department of Labor and Industries has particular responsibility for all matters relating specifically to women and minors and for the Division of Minimum Wage.

TABLE 29 – Work Stoppages Due to Labor-Management Disputes in Massachusetts and in United States--1945-1960

Year	No. of Stoppages Beginning in Year		No. of Workers Involved (In Thousands)		No. of Man-Days Idle As % of Estimated Working Time	
	Mass.	U.S.	Mass.	U.S.	Mass.	U.S.
1945	239	4,750	60.7	3,467		.47
1946	266	4,985	111.0	4,600		1.43
1947	177	3,693	56.4	2,170		.41
1948	130	3,419	29.8	1,960		.37
1949	113	3,606	24.6	3,030		.59
1950	193	4,843	58.4	2,410		.44
1951	151	4,737	60.0	2,220		.23
1952	143	5,117	39.9	3,540	.21	.57
1953	176	5,091	46.1	2,400	.15	.26
1954	113	3,468	23.4	1,530	.08	.21
1955	142	4,320	64.8	2,650	.31	.26
1956	170	3,825	55.0	1,900	.20	.29
1957	144	3,673	56.6	1,390	.14	.14
1958	164	3,694	49.0	2,060	.13	.22
1959	134	3,708	43.0	1,800	.21	.61
1960	120	3,333	48.5	1,320	.40	.17

Source: U.S. Department of Labor, Work Stoppages: Fifty States and the District of Columbia 1927-62, BLS Report No. 256 (Washington: U.S. Government Printing Office, 1963)

This Division can authorize inspections of wage and hour records and hold hearings if violations of the state minimum wage law are changed. Under Massachusetts law it is also possible to authorize rates below the state statutory minimum in particular circumstances or in certain industries. In 1962, the statutory minimum wage in Massachusetts was raised to $1.15 per hour, but wage board orders in certain industries permit minimums as low as $.75 per hour where employees customarily receive tips.

The Division of Employment of Older Workers was established in 1954, and is also administered by the assistant commissioner with the help of a ten-member advisory council appointed to study and bring in recommendations concerning problems of the aging.

Divisions Headed by Appointed Directors--In addition to the three divisions, which are headed by commissioners, there are six other divisions whose directors are appointed by the commissioners with the approval of the governor and council. These divisions are: Industrial Safety, Occupational Hygiene, Standards, Necessaries of Life, Statistics, and Apprenticeship Training.

The Division of Industrial Safety investigates accidents to employees, and complaints of employees, supervises the distribution of home workers' certificates, and supervises compliance with state labor laws. In fiscal 1961, the division made a total of 63,606 inspections and visits. During the year some 17,578 orders were issued, 12,037 of which were verbal orders that were complied with at the time of issuance, and 5,541 of which were written orders requiring subsequent compliance.

The Division of Occupational Hygiene tries to prevent industrial diseases, and its functions are closely related to the Division of Industrial Safety and the state Department of Public Health. The Division of Standards enforces the laws regulating weights and measuring devises, and serves as the central licensing authority for "hawkers, peddlers, and transient vendors". The Division of Necessaries of Life compiles a state cost-of-living index and administers the motor fuel sales law. The Division of Stastics collects and supplies statistics on labor and manufacturing, and it publishes monthly surveys of employment and earnings in Massachusetts. The Division of Apprentice Training provides for an apprenticeship council of eight members--three representing employers, three representing union members, and two others. Industries and plants are encouraged to establish apprentice training programs for the development of skilled workmen, and the Director of Apprentice training may set up committees and establish standards for training in cooperation with the Department of Education. As of June 30, 1961, there were 1,895 programs involving 4,971 companies training 3,348 apprentices that were registered with this division.

Autonomous Divisions--The three autonomous divisions within the Department of Labor and Industries are the Division of Industrial Accidents, the Division of Employment Security, and the Labor Relations Commission. These divisions, in reality, are of departmental status, but have not been so designated because of the constitutional limit.

The Division of Industrial Accidents is headed by a nine

member Industrial Accident Board, whose members are appointed for five years. This division is chiefly responsible for administering the Massachusetts Workmen Compensation Act. The Division of Employment Security administers the Massachusetts Unemployment Compensation law and supervises the state employment offices which are located throughout the Commonwealth. This division is headed by a single director, with an advisory council of six members.

The Labor Relations Commission was established by the Massachusetts State Labor Relations Act in 1937, and it is the smallest of the three independent agencies in the Department of Labor and Industries. The three-man commission is appointed by the governor and Council for five-year terms. Table 30 shows the number and types of cases received by the Massachusetts Labor Relations Commission from the time of its establishment through fiscal 1961, the last year for which complete figures are available.

This brief review of the structure of the Department of Labor and Industries indicates that there is considerable overlapping and in some cases near duplication of functions. Yet, when Massachusetts created a Special Commission on the Structure of State Government (the so-called "Baby Hoover" Commission) in 1948, which lasted through 1954, its recommendations concerning the Department of Labor and Industry were opposed by the Bay State labor movement and largely ignored by the General Court.

Department of Commerce

The Department of Commerce was created by the General Court in 1953 to meet the threatened deterioration of economic morale in

Massachusetts which accompanied the shift of some industries--largely textiles--to other states. The department has no regulatory or police functions, but rather establishes a single agency to which businesses and communities may go for information and assistance in order to "to promote and develop the industrial, agricultural, commercial, and recreational resources of the Commonwealth."

TABLE 30 - Cases Received by the Massachusetts Labor Relations Commission 1937-1961

Year	Total Cases	Unfair Labor Practice Cases	Representation Cases
8-26 to 11-30, 1937	83	73	10
1938	340	216	124
1939	361	156	205
1940	283	174	109
1941	265	133	132
1942	207	82	125
12-1-42 to 6-30-43	57	26	31
7-1-43 to 6-30-44	99	45	54
1945	81	27	54
1946	201	64	137
1947	429	66	363
1948	256	76	180
1949	186	44	142
1950	N.A.	N.A.	N.A.
1951	223	72	151
1952	176	55	121
1953	116	46	70
1954	97	48	49
1955	146	40	106
1956	166	57	109
1957	118	32	86
1958	107	25	82
1959	110	52	58
1960	116	52	64
1961	137	80	57

Source: Annual Reports of the Board on file at Room 473 State House, Boston, Massachusetts.

The Department of Commerce is headed by a commission appointed by the governor and council, and two deputy commissioners appointed by the commissioner with the approval of the governor and council. The department has three main divisions, each under a director appointed by the commissioner.

The Division of Research is authorized to compile information on all economic variables useful to industrial and commercial development. The Division of Development seeks to attract new business to the commonwealth by promoting existing industries and by finding favorable locations for new business. The Division of Planning is charged with the preparation of a master plan for the physical development of the Commonwealth.

Massachusetts Commission Against Discrimination

The Massachusetts Commission Against Discrimination is an independent, three-member agency serving directly under the governor and council. Established as the Massachusetts Fair Employment Practices Commission in 1946, the commission's name was changed in 1950, when its responsibilities were broadened to include discrimination in places of public accommodation and public housing as well as employment. Thus, the commission now enforces the laws prohibiting discrimination in these three areas because of age, race, color, religious creed, or national origin, and it also carries on an educational program with the aid of specially appointed councils of unpaid, civic-minded persons.

Underlying this formal governmental apparatus and giving life to the political process in Massachusetts are the political parties and their related interests in the state.

Party Politics in the Bay State

The first American political party was the Federalist party. Its leaders included most of the men who had taken part in framing the United States' Constitution, with Alexander Hamilton perhaps the foremost among them. They had the support of the merchants, the lawyers, and the property owners--all of whom stood to profit by sound money and the promotion of commerce and industry. Popular approval of the Constitution and the proposed federal government was sufficient not only to secure ratification, but also sufficient to insure a Federalist majority in the new Congress.

In 1800 the Jeffersonian party charged that the Alien and Sedition Laws, passed by the Federalist Congress in 1798, were an attempt to consolidate the power of the few by taking away the liberties of the many; and they were successful in driving the Federalist from power on this issue. Massachusetts, however, continued to vote Federalist in national politics until 1804, By that time Federalism appeared on the wane in Massachusetts as elsewhere, but Jefferson's embargo Act of 1807 severely hurt Massachusetts commerce. Bay State Federalists led the successful pressure for repeal; but, in the prosperity which followed, the Jeffersonian, Elbridge Gerry, was elected Governor of Massachusetts in 1810.[1]

---

1 Gerry's name, of course, survives as part of the political vocabulary of the country. Under him, the Jeffersonians, hoping to sustain themselves in power, redistricted the state--a devise as old as politics, but not always accomplished so flagrantly. A cartoonist, looking at a map of the South Essex District (now the 7th Congressional) as the Jeffersonians had drawn it, was struck by its likeness to a salamander, and christened it the "Gerrymander".

The War of 1812 brought such economic crisis to Massachusetts that the Federalists began to discuss seriously the possibility of secession. Before their plans matured, however, the war ended; and their party was nationally discredited as treasonable. Nevertheless, the Massachusetts Federalists kept control of the Bay State for another ten years after their party disappeared from the national scene.

After Andrew Jackson formed the modern Democratic party, which won the national election in 1828, they were opposed nationally by a new coalition party calling itself by the popular old name of Whig. In Massachusetts, the Whigs were supported by the manufacturing and commercial interests, which had supported John Quincy Adams in his battle with Jackson. This party dominated the state, with brief exceptions, until 1850. In Massachusetts, the minority of opposing Democrats included such diverse elements as radical agrarians and the shipowners of Essex County who opposed the protective tariff.

Two minor parties arose in Massachusetts in the 1830's: the Antimasons, and the Workingmen. The Antimasons enjoyed a brief success in coalition with the Whigs, after which many of them went into the Whig party. The Workingmen, unsuccessful as a party, mostly took refuge with the slowly fading Democrats.

By 1850, the Free-soil party, which opposed both the extension of slavery and the reaffirmation of the Fugitive Slave Law, had superseded the Democrats in second place in state elections. Through a coalition with the Democrats, the Free-soilers ousted the Whigs from all state offices and replaced Daniel Webster in the United States Senate. This coalition faded entirely, however, when they promoted a constitutional convention in 1853, only to have the results rejected by the people at the polls.

By 1854, both the Whigs and the Democrats were split by the slavery question, and at this juncture the Know-nothing party rose to sweep the state in its first election. While openly opposed to the entry of the Irish immigrants into politics, and while emphasizing the unwillingness of the Irish to align themselves against slavery at that time, the Know-nothing party was also consciously used by many of its supporters to disrupt the Whigs' and the Democrats in the hope that a new party antagonistic to slavery would evolve. After two years such a party--the Republicans--did develop.

In Massachusetts, the Republicans supplanted the Whigs, the Free-soilers and the Know-nothings. They were in complete control of the state by 1857; and, with the beginning of the Civil War, the period of experimental political parties may be said to have ended in Massachusetts despite a few schisms and some rather persistent but rather minor parties. The Republican and Democratic parties of today are still recognizable as they were in 1860; but in Massachusetts, it is only recently that the Democrats have been able to emerge from a long period of Republican dominance. Indeed, one writer has observed that "the story of Massachusetts Republicanism is one of graceful retreat on many fronts." [9, p. 136] This rise of the Democratic party from defeat and exclusion to a position of vigorous competition with the Republicans is inextricably connected with the settlement of Irish, French-Canadian, Italian, and Polish ethnic groups in the Bay State.[1]

[1] It may be noted in passing that these nationalities which have (continued on following page)

The League of Women Voters in Massachusetts notes:

> The Republican and Democratic parties in Massachusetts are strikingly different both in the people they represent and in the way their organizations function. Historically, the Democrats have represented the urban population, the Republican the rural. In the popular view, the Democrats have represented labor and the Republicans management; the "Yankees" have tended to be Republican and the "Irish" Democratic; but other facts are making this distinction less valid. Perhaps no party leader is entirely happy about the homogeneity of his state party. Pleas for a "balanced ticket" seem to indicate as much. But the combination of historical, economic and social factors which underlie our current political situation may make this an intricate problem to solve. [7,pp. 331][2]

Since the Whigs, the Know-nothings, and the Republicans, who derived largely from the remnants of these earlier parties, were largely anti-Catholic and anti-immigrant, it was natural that the Irish as the first commers turned to the Democratic party. The Democrats made a special appeal to the Irish in these early days, and it paid off handsomely. When later immigrants from Catholic countries came into Massachusetts the Democrats had at least somewhat of a head start on the Republicans, who, if not outrightly antagonistic to the newcomers, at least had a record of antagonism to live down.

(Footnote 1 continued from preceding page)

settled in Massachusetts are all primarily from the Catholic parts of the world. This fact may be of greater long run significance than ethnic factors per se, since ethnic distinctions and attachments are much more likely to be worn away over time than are religious differences.

[2] The same statement also observes that "The Republican party appears to be a relatively tight organization.... The Democratic party is more of a loose confederation of locally popular leaders, who are strong when they unite, but who have been reluctant to subordinate their own influence to that of any central group....Republican financing seems to be mainly a joint party effort, while Democratic candidates collect and disburse their own funds." [7, p. 331]

Leaving religion aside for a moment, however, entry of the new ethnic groups into the Democratic party was far from automatic. As the Democratic party became more and more urban, the leadership element began to reflect the rise of Irish political leadership in the cities. This dominance of the Democratic party by the Irish was no warm welcome to the Italians and French-Canadians. Yet, Massachusetts was rapidly industrializing during these waves of immigration, and Boston employers used the abundance of labor to keep wages low.[1] The Democrats were again the beneficiaries and its opponets the loosers as a result of the antagonisms aroused by these industrial conditions. For, in the long run, the element of economic status in political choice tended to favor the Democratic party as far as these new groups were concerned. The vast majority of the immigrant population occupied the lowest rungs of the economic and social ladder, and once the Democratic party had taken its trend toward a more liberal position it could make a successful appeal to the working-class ethnic minorities.

While the extent of industrialization and the heavy waves of immigration seem to have predestined the rise of the Democratic party in Massachusetts, however, the emergence of the Democrats was a slow process.

Localized Democratic victories began back in the nineteenth century, but it was not until 1928 that the fullest impact of

---

[1] Handlin [2, pp. 54-87] describes in vivid detail the difficulties of economic adjustment for the immigrants facing a constant labor surplus.

immigration and industrialization began to appear in Massachusetts election returns. The candidacy of Al Smith hit home with the Catholic-worker elements of the state; and, with the exception of the two Eisenhower majorities in 1952 and 1956, the Democrats have carried the presidential elections in Massachusetts ever since. A different picture emerges in the races for the governorship, however, where the Democrats have won only 10 of the last 18 bi-annual elections. The Republicans were even more successful in retaining control of the state legislature, where they held on to the Senate until 1958, even though the Democrats began to carry the House a decade earlier. These differences between state and national party successes in Massachusetts, however, tend to be explained by a closer examination of the nature of the state parties in Massachusetts.

The Massachusetts Republican Party

The traditional Brahmin first-family influence, which has contributed so much to the goverance of Massachusetts, has given the Republican party in the state a natural conservative bent. Both internal and external forces have gradually forced the leadership to adapt the party credo and performance to the changing spirit of the times, however, and as a result, the moderate conservatism of such national figures as Leverett Saltonstall, Henry Cabot Lodge, Jr., and Christian Herter is typical of Republicanism in Massachusetts today.[1]

---

[1] An example of the moderate nature of Massachusetts conservatism can be found in the fact that the 1952 presidential preference primaries found most of the big names of the party in the state in the Eisenhower camp, and in the election returns the Taft forces were completely routed by a margin of about 7 to 3.

Although the state party organization has slipped from its one time position of phenomenal power, the Republican organization in Massachusetts is far stronger than its Democratic counterpart. The Republican party tends to collect money centrally and pass it down to the town committees for their use. In the Democratic party whatever is spent locally is usually collected locally, too. The Republicans have also been much more successful than the Democrats in withstanding the winds of divisiveness that seem to blow from primary elections and nuisance challenges.[1] Nevertheless, the enactment of a pre-primary convention law in 1954 was very important to the Republicans, since they have been very desirous of getting a better ethnic balance to their state wide tickets,[2] and Lockard has noted:

> Whether for reasons of social climbing, acquisition of wealth leading to conservative views, or disgust with occasional Democratic dishonesty, many of the foreign-stock groups in recent years have abdanoned their usual association with the Democratic party.

---

1 Democratic primaries in Massachusetts are notorous for the success of outsiders whose only qualifications are good Irish names.

2 As a result of their party organization and pre-primary conventions, the Republicans now have balanced tickets, but how much effect these balanced tickets have had on state elections is hard to say. In 1960, for example there was much criticism of their "United Nations" ticket of Volpe (Italian) for Governor, Means (Yankee) for Lt. Governor, Brooke (Negro) for Sec. of State, Tribulski (Polish) for State Treasurer, and Wardwell (Yankee) for State Auditor. Only Volpe was elected.

> In addition, zealous efforts to attract such voters with balanced tickets and appointments of minority group leaders to patronage positions have put new faces and new names into the ranks of Republican leadership. For the most part the newcomers have not moved into the inner circle of leadership, but entry into even the outer circle was an exception to a long-established rule. [9, p. 146]

The nomination and election of an Italian-Businessman-John A. Volpe by the Republicans in 1960 may mark a significant shift in Bay State politics. How significant remains to be seen; but it is extremely crucial for the Republicans in Massachusetts, since the prestige, influence, and financial interest of the first families can only go so far in offsetting the political force of sheer numbers. For, indeed, the forte of the Democratic party in Massachusetts is precisely numbers.

Yet the character and quality of the Democratic party and its leadership at the state level in Massachusetts has much to do with the fact that the fullest possibilities of the Democratic vote have not been realized in state elections.

The Massachusetts Democratic Party

Although it might seem that the heavy "foreign-stock" population and the heavy industrialization of the state would assure a relatively liberal Democratic party in Massachusetts, the fact is that the party takes its liberalism in moderation. Lockard notes: "This is presumably associated with the strength of the Republican party, the merits and prestige of the candidates it offers, and the outlander's dislike of big-city politicians. . . ." [9, pp.134-135] To this might be added a strong Catholic distaste for anything which might be labeled "left-wing" or "pinkish" in nature, and just plain deviseness within the party.[1]

Intra-party divisions tend to reflect basic facts of geography and social composition as well as personality conflicts, and the Democratics have seldom been able to present the united front their Republican opponents do. As a result, Democratic party leadership has in general less prestige and less authority than the Republican leadership. The questionable behavior of some Democratic officials, grave enough to involve several jail sentenses for Congressmen, ex-governors, mayors and others, has not enhanced the party's chances.[2]

---

1 John H. Fenton, also, offers the following explanation:

"The reasons for the relatively conservative cast of the Massachusetts Democratic party are several. One factor is the popular primary in Massachusetts, which tends to reduce the effectiveness of the party organization in presenting a slate of candidates who fairly represent the party. . . .

The heterogeneous composition of the Democratic party in Massachusetts is, perhaps its most important moderating feature. . . . the Massachusetts Democratic party is a coalition of various competing ethnic groups, labor unions, and liberals. The Irish and Italian groups associate themselves with the Democratic party primarily as a means of social mobility. . . .

The labor unions in Massachusetts are many and varied in their interests. They are primarily "bread and butter" unions narrowly concerned with the protection of the interests of the unions and their members. . . . Thus their impact on the Democratic party is not a particularly liberalizing one.

The liberal element in the Democratic party is more strident than potent. In fact, Democrat such as Furcolo get political mileage out of attacking the ADA." [1, p. 60]

2 Lockard notes:

"The incarceration of former Governor, Congressman, and Mayor James M. Curley is a well known story. Others like Congressman Thomas J. Lane have hardly been as asset to the party. Lane won renomination for Congress in 1956 two weeks after being released from the Danbury Federal prison, having been there after conviction for tax evasion." [9, p. 123]

More recently, shady dealing in Massachusetts politics, largely under Democratic influence, but with some hints of Republican compliance if not involvement, have received increasing national attention. One recent book, for example, contains a 9-page listing of scandals that have beset the Bay State with increasing frequency in the past 40 years. See [8, pp. 54-68]

Geographically, there tends to be a Boston-versus-the-rest of the state dichotomy within the Democratic party. Boston and its immediate environs contain the largest single concentration of Democrats in the state, and there is a definite trend toward a greater and greater proportion of the Democratic nominees for statewide office to be from the Boston area. Since most Democratic candidates count on losing heavily in the rural towns and many suburban areas, however, the votes in western cities are vitally important. Nevertheless, in all the battles to provide a pre-primary convention to recommend statewide slates, the Democratic leadership was anti-convention.

Ethnic competition in the Democratic party is normally between the Irish and the more recent comers, such as the Italians, the Polish, and the French-Canadians. It is always the Irish who have to be ousted in these battles, since they were well fixed in the Democratic party before the others came. And in many areas where the Irish now comprise a minority of the population, they continue to control positions of party leadership.

In addition to these geographic, ethnic, and morality factors, there is also a great deal of just plain personality conflict within the Massachusetts Democratic party, which has tended to greatly weaken the party organization. Lockard notes:

> The Democratic organization in fact seems at times to be nothing at all. . . . Personal organizations are numerous and various strong men often go their own way without regard for other candidates in a campaign. . . . In some smaller urban centers where there are Democratic majorities, the party organization may practically give way to labor groups who do most of the work of campaigning. [9, p. 125]

Legislative Policy and Affiliated Interest Groups

Although there is always some question as to how important "issues" are in state politics, the class distinctions implicit in the party alignments in Massachusetts tend to make for class politics of a sort in the legislature. Therefore, on the "issues" concerning labor, taxation, appropriations, economic regulation, and public welfare there is some evidence that the parties do significantly affect legislative policy making in Massachusetts.[1] And, since the party organizations do sit astride the channels through which all controversial legislation must flow, the interest groups in Massachusetts have adapted to this fact by becoming what might be called "built-in" pressure groups. These "built-in" interests, of course, expect some return for services rendered, and they are often disappointed in the end. Nevertheless, Lockard notes:

> Their clientele are so aligned with one party or the other, and their interests so dominantly represented by the general position of one of the parties, that they come to be almost a constituent part of one party. . . . the ties are much closer than between the pressure organizations and the national political parties in the United States. Farm groups on the national level have not aligned themselves with either party, but in Massachusetts they are with the Republicans. Labor nationally is more sympathetic to the Democratic party and is much more helpful to it, but it maintains cordial relations with many Republicans and does not move into the inner councils of the Democratic party to the extent that it does in Massachusetts. In some areas the Democratic party in Massachusetts will leave to labor almost the whole job of campaigning for

[1] Malcom E. Jewell examined the 1947 legislative session of the Massachusetts General Court in his comparison of the party legislative cohesion in eight two party states, and he ranked Massachusetts high in this respect. See [4]

> state candidates, and in many campaigns the money labor gives is a very crucial factor in the Democratic effort. [9, p. 163]

Turning from the farmers and organized labor, other significant interest groups and their affiliations include: the Americans for Democratic Action (ADA) and the Commonwealth Organization of Democrats (COD) with the Democrats; and the public-utility, real-estate, and insurance companies with the Republicans, along with the Associated Industries of Massachusetts, the Greater Boston Chambers of Commerce, and the Massachusetts Federation of Taxpayer's Associations.[1]

There are also several relatively powerful interest groups which do not align themselves strictly with either party. These include the state employees, the race tracks, the liquor interests, and veteran's groups--to name a few. All told, in an average session, some 300 to 400 lobbyists register and subsequently report their expenses. The League of Women voters have stated: "Lobbying in Massachusetts has been regulated for more than fifty years. . . . the largest expenditures are made by the utility companies, with insurance companies, labor groups, banks, and racing interests following in that order." [7, p. 56]

Chapter 3 Section 48 of the General Law of Massachusetts states:

> Within thirty days after the progoration of the general court, every person whose name appears upon the

---

[1] William V. Shannon [10, pp. 44-54] gives some rather dated character sketches of the leading personalities associated with the different interest groups in Massachusetts during the late 1940's.

TABLE 31 - Reported Lobby Expenditures by Selected Massachusetts Interest Groups, 1954-1961

	Amount Reported in							
Group Reporting	1961	1960	1959	1958	1957	1956	1955	1954
Associated Industries of Mass.	$ 7,500	$ 10,000	$10,000	$ 10,000	$10,000	$6,500	$ 6,500	$ 6,500
Greater Boston Chamber of Commerce	6,000	5,000	6,000	6,000	5,000	5,000	7,000	14,000
Mass. Fed. of Taxpayers Association	3,200	3,200	3,200	4,300	4,500	6,000	6,000	6,000
Mass. State Chamber of Commerce	-	-	-	500	500	600	-	500
Mass. State Labor Council, AFL-CIO	16,000	8,500	18,704	-	-	-	-	-
Mass. State Fed. of Labor, AFL	-	-	-	4,500	6,000	N.A.	5,150	4,500
Mass. State Industrial Union Council, CIO	-	-	-	4,875	4,875	4,875	4,875	4,000
Total Reported By All Groups Included in Sec. of State's Report	$275,058	$317,232	N.A.	$307,886	N.A.	N.A.	$330,787	N.A.

Source: Reports on file in the Archives Division of the Commonwealth of Massachusetts

> dockets so closed as the employer of any legislative counsel or agent shall render to the state secretary a complete and detailed statement, on oath, of all expenses incurred or paid in connection with the employment of legislative counsel or agents or with promoting or opposing legislation. . . .

The Annual Report of the Secretary of the Commonwealth then is supposed to publish the total nember of registrants and the total expenditure reported. In practice, however, the Secretary doesn't issue an annual report every year; and when he does the total figures are not very helpful in determining the relative expenditures of different groups such as business, labor, race tracks, etc. A detailed examination of the reports in the Archives at the State House soon reveals that the names of some of the groups are so deceptive that no easy classification is possible, or even fruitful since only a varying proportion of direct legislative agent's salaries are reported; and the percentage of these salaries reported is subject to the discretion of the reporting groups.

Nevertheless, Table 31 represents the information the writer was able to dig up (literally) on the total expenditures reported and the expenditures reported by the groups known to be interested in labor legislation for the years 1954 through 1961.

We will now turn to a closer look at these groups in the next chapter.

REFERENCES - CHAPTER VII

1. John H. Fenton, "Party Politics and Political Responsibility" in Robbins (ed) State Government and Public Responsibility, 1960 (Medford: Tufts University, 1960).

2. Oscar Handlin, Boston's Immigrants (Cambridge: Belknap Press, 1959).

3. Henry F. Howe, Massachusetts: There She Is - Behold Her (New York: Harper, 1960).

4. Malcom E. Jewell, "Party Voting in American State Legislatures", American Political Science Review, September, 1955, Vol. 49,pp.773-791.

5. Harold S. Kaltenborn, (Governmental Adjustment of Labor Disputes (Chicago: Foundation Press, 1943).

6. Ting Tsz Ko, Governmental Methods of Adjusting Labor Disputes (New York: Columbia University, 1926).

7. The League of Women Voters of Massachusetts, Massachusetts State Government (Cambridge: Harvard University, 1956).

8. Murray B. Levin and G. B. Blackwood, The Compleat Politician: Political Strategy in Massachusetts (Indianapolis: Bobbs-Merrill, 1960).

9. Duane Lockard, New England State Politics (Princeton: Princeton University, 1959).

10. William V. Shannon, "Massachusetts: Prisoner of the Past" in Robert S. Allen (ed) Our Soverign State (New York: Vanguard, 1949).

11. U.S. Department of Commerce, Bureau of the Census, U.S. Census of Population 1960, U.S. Summary, General Social and Economic Characteristics (Washington: U.S. Government Printing Office, 1962).

CHAPTER VIII

A CLOSER LOOK AT THE MAJOR GROUPS ATTEMPTING TO INFLUENCE CONTEMPORARY LABOR LEGISLATION IN THE COMMONWEALTH OF MASSACHUSETTS

Since Massachusetts was one of the first states in the nation to industrialize, it was also one of the first to experience labor problems arising out of the industrialization process. In response, the Bay State quickly assumed a leading position among the states in enacting protective labor legislation to deal with these problems. The early record shows that the Massachusetts General Court enacted:

The first state law concerning child labor	1836
The first law providing factory inspection by state officials	1866
The first law establishing a bureau of labor statistics	1869
The first law limiting the day's work for women and minors	1874
The first law setting up a state board of conciliation	1886
The first child labor educational provision, requiring all children to attend school at least 3 months of the year until they come to the age of 15	1886
The first employer liability law relating to accidents	1887
The first minimum wage law.	1912

[4, 9-18-49]

Though many of these measures seem commonplace by modern standards, they were sweeping innovations in their day. Massachusetts has continued to remain one of the most active states in the area of labor legislation and it still ranks among the "leaders" in many areas, but it can no longer claim the position of almost unique supremacy it once held. As will be seen in the following chapters, which trace the history of labor legislation in Massachusetts, many of the groups instrumental in proposing and opposing much of this early legislation are no longer in existence. There seems to be, however, a greater continuity in the formal structure of the labor movement in Massachusetts than in the formal structure of the employer groups now actively interested in labor legislation in the Bay State.

Before turning to a more detailed examination of the evolution of Massachusetts labor legislation, however, it is probably best to identify in a little more detail the labor and employer groups now most interested in labor legislation at the state level in Massachusetts.

The Organized Labor Movement In Massachusetts

What is available of the early history of the Massachusetts labor movement can be found in any of the standard works of labor history mentioned in Part I of this thesis, since the early American labor movement was largely confined to Massachusetts, New York, Pennsylvania, and a few other industrial states. Beginning in 1908 Massachusetts began publishing official statistics on trade union membership in the Commonwealth, and Table 32 lists the number of local unions and the number of union members in Massachusetts for each year from 1908 through 1961.

TABLE 32 – Number of Local Unions and Trade Union Membership in Massachusetts, 1908-1961*

Year	No. of Locals	No. of Members	Year	No. of Locals	No. of Members
1908	1,160	161,887	1935	1,220	216,141
1909	1,185	168,037	1936	1,230	231,710
1910	1,250	187,310	1937	1,423	297,038
1911	1,282	191,038	1938	1,423	297,038
1912	1,361	236,768	1939	1,434	295,866
1913	1,403	241,726	1940	1,473	319,674
1914	1,392	234,266	1941	1,503	358,674
1915	1,425	243,535	1942	1,695	463,015
1916	1,416	257,007	1943	1,782	525,104
1917	1,460	277,720	1944	1,782	504,461
1918	1,485	313,099	1945	1,799	515,370
1919	1,554	368,486	1946	1,801	505,731
1920	1,628	346,653	1947	2,005	591,269
1921	1,512	294,852	1948	2,037	598,840
1922	1,423	271,938	1949	2,036	576,358
1923	1,392	265,969	1950	2,005	566,389
1924	1,302	251,446	1951	2,033	605,220
1925	1,280	228,142	1952	2,120	606,297
1926	1,253	226,841	1953	2,086	614,385
1927	1,213	206,701	1954	2,069	592,884
1928	1,182	204,295	1955	2,082	564,938
1929	1,142	191,528	1956	2,069	574,098
1930	1,118	176,507	1957	2,068	579,532
1931	1,097	167,611	1958	2,063	559,446
1932	1,040	155,342	1959	2,077	565,147
1933	1,228	236,591	1960	2,052	558,600
1934	1,241	246,411	1961	2,013	547,261

* In the years prior to 1939, figures are related to December 31 of the preceding year. From 1939 on, figures are related to January 15 of the year shown.

Source: Massachusetts Department of Labor and Industries, Annual Report on the Statistics of Labor, various years.

The membership figures in this table reflect the overall pattern of total trade union membership in the United States during the years covered. Thus, the number of union members in Massachusetts fell from a post World War I peak of 368,486 in 1919 to a 1932 trough of 155,342. After 1932, membership began to increase rapidly despite reported setbacks in 1935 and 1938. During World War II membership went and remained above 500,000 for the first time, and the all-time peak of trade union membership in Massachusetts occurred in 1953, when the State Department of Labor and Industries reported 614,385 members in Massachusetts trade unions. Since 1953 union membership in the Bay State has declined to a reported 547,261 in 1961.

Although the union membership figures compiled by the Massachusetts Department of Labor and Industries are not broken down by official international union affiliation, they are classified by "Industries, Trades, and Groups". These classifications give some indication of the international unions which may be the strongest in the Bay State, and over time they also provide some insights into the changing internal composition of the state labor movement. Table 33 shows a breakdown of Massachusetts trade union membership by industries, trades, and groups at five-year intervals for the post World War II period, and it also shows the changes in each category during the postwar period. The number of local unions in each trade or industry is also shown for these years.

TABLE 33 - Number of Local Unions and Trade Union Membership in Massachusetts by Industries, Trades, and Groups, 1946, 1951, 1956, and 1961

Industry Trade or Group	1946		1951		1956		1961		
	No. of Locals	No. of Members	No. of Locals	No. of Members	No. of Locals	No. of Members	No. of Locals	No. of Members	% Change From 1946
Boot and Shoe Industry	50	24,494	57	25,839	52	25,024	53	23,890	-2.47
Building Trades	287	34,445	277	53,446	279	51,735	284	55,973	+62.50
Clerks, Wholesale and Retail	36	14,563	43	21,914	42	19,012	35	25,062	+73.09
Clothing and Garment Trades	70	28,154	66	34,345	60	36,752	52	40,327	+43.24
Gas and Electric Workers	-	-	51	10,037	51	12,298	54	12,417	-
Hotel and Restaurant Workers	-	-	29	9,998	26	9,880	23	9,342	-
Metal and Machinery Trades	185	109,887	245	120,592	256	118,718	273	113,940	+3.69
Municipal and State Employees	99	14,683	139	34,830	169	39,436	182	44,318	+201.83
Paper and Allied Industries	50	11,774	65	12,465	76	13,753	84	14,921	+26.73
Printing and Allied Trades	76	10,552	79	14,348	74	15,416	75	15,298	+44.98
Rubber Workers	19	15,667	22	16,827	23	18,385	27	14,754	-5.83
Teaming and Trucking	24	24,031	38	29,098	39	36,654	34	33,784	+40.59
Telephone Operators - Workers	100	13,890	117	16,010	117	19,505	99	15,262	+9.88
Textile Industries	142	69,912	157	77,918	148	35,178	105	19,837	-71.63
Railroads	197	26,447	185	21,699	176	20,665	158	13,420	-49.31
Street Railway and Passenger Bus Cos.	40	11,729	45	13,673	41	8,807	27	8,091	-31.02
All Other Industries, trades and Groups	426	95,473	418	92,181	440	92,880	448	86,625	-
Totals	1,801	505,731	2,033	605,220	2,069	574,098	2,013	547,261	+8.21%

Source: See table 32.

In 1961, 288,342, or about 53% of the total 547,261 trade union members in Massachusetts, were employed in the metal and machinery trades, the building trades, the clothing and garment trades, teaming and trucking, or in municipal or state positions. Each of these industries has seen an increase in the number of union members during the postwar period, and in 1946 only about 42% of the Massachusetts labor movement was employed in these five industries. The largest percentage increase in union membership has been in the area of municipal and state employment where membership has increased over 200% from 14,683 in 1946 to 44,318 in 1961. Membership among wholesale and retail clerks has also increased substantially since 1946. In addition, union membership has also increased in the paper, printing, and telephone industries.

On the other side of the ledger, textile union membership has fallen the most, declining by over 70% from 69,912 in 1946 to 19,387 in 1961. Railroad union membership in Massachusetts has also fallen about 50% from 26,477 to 13,420 during the past 15 years. Other areas experiencing a decline in union membership are the streetcar and passenger bus companies, the rubber workers, and the boot and shoe industry.

Geographically, trade union membership in Massachusetts is concentrated in the eastern part of the state with the Boston-Cambridge area alone accounting for over 37% of the state's trade union membership in 1961. Table 34 shows the number and membership of local labor

TABLE 34 - Number and Membership of Local Labor Organizations in the Massachusetts Cities With The Largest Trade Union Memberships, 1946, 1951, 1956, 1961

City	1946		1951		1956		1961		% Change
	Locals	Members	Locals	Members	Locals	Members	Locals	Members	From 1946
Boston	426	160,512	462	196,560	477	194,969	459	195,177	+21.60%
Brockton	50	13,285	49	13,020	55	13,915	52	11,695	-11.97
Cambridge	33	10,552	41	11,069	41	12,023	37	8,244	-21.87
Chicopee	-	-	17	10,077	17	7,942	20	7,921	-
Fall River	45	24,583	48	29,814	69	25,436	64	22,817	- 7.18
Haverhill	-	-	32	8,713	29	9,935	30	9,742	-
Holyoke	41	7,534	50	8,631	47	7,382	47	6,572	-12.77
Lawrence	61	23,819	73	31,225	72	13,362	65	11,219	-52.90
Lowell	63	11,551	73	12,366	63	10,544	53	8,243	-28.64
Lynn	43	33,436	50	25,292	51	21,927	44	19,192	-42.60
New Bedford	71	26,676	70	25,182	68	19,611	60	21,000	-21.28
Pittsfield	34	9,604	34	11,168	38	9,287	38	8,016	-16.53
Quincy	-	-	28	10,367	29	8,245	27	14,067	-
Springfield	121	31,384	128	32,291	132	36,632	129	30,866	- 1.65
Waltham	-	-	23	9,980	26	15,021	29	19,279	-
Worcester	81	15,596	94	28,323	101	27,531	106	25,340	+62.48
All Other Municipalities	732	137,199	761	141,142	754	140,336	753	127,871	
Total	1,801	505,731	2,033	605,220	2,069	574,098	2,013	547,261	+ 8.21%

Source: See Table 32.

organizations in each of the 16 Massachusetts cities with the largest trade union membership in 1946, 1951, 1956, and 1961. The 16 leading cities have not changed during this period, but the union membership in some of the individual cities has changed markedly during the post-war years. Indeed, of the 12 cities leading in union membership in 1946 only Boston and Worcester have shown an increase. The other 10 cities have all experienced a decline in union membership with Lawrence showing the biggest loss of almost 53%. Three of the four cities added to the basic 12 in 1951, however, have shown an increase in the last 15 years with Waltham almost doubling in the number of union members. These shifts reflect the basic industrial changes in the Bay State's economy. Many of the losses are in former textile cities, and much of Waltham's increase is due to the location of Raytheon there.

In 1961 there were 19 local labor councils in Massachusetts most of which are located in the trade union centers listed in Table 34 All of these labor councils are affiliated with the Massachusetts State Labor Council, AFL-CIO, which was formed in 1958 through a merger of the previously existing Massachusetts Federation of Labor (AFL) and the Massachusetts State Industrial Union Council (CIO). The merger at the state level occurred only after lengthy negotiations between the state AFL and CIO bodies, and the national AFL-CIO had to intervene before the merger was completed. There is still some evidence that the merger has not yet been completely digested by all segments of the Massachusetts labor movement, but the State Labor Council does carry on unified legislative and political activities for the affiliated local unions. At present, approximately 1,250 locals from about 100 national unions are affiliated with the State Labor Council. The Teamsters, District 50 of the United Mine Workers, the railroad brotherhoods, and the independent telephone workers union are the main elements in the Massachusetts labor movement not affiliated with the State Labor Council.

A brief highlighting of the history of each of the state labor federations, a description of the eventual merger, and some discussion of the activities of organized labor in Massachusetts since the merger may be helpful at this point before turning to a description of the employer organizations attempting to influence legislation at the state level in Massachusetts. A more detailed insight into the activities of the state labor movement is included in the analysis of the historical evolution of Massachusetts labor legislation in the following chapters.

The Massachusetts Federation Of Labor, AFL, 1887-1958

The Massachusetts State Branch of the American Federation of Labor was organized in August 1887. This group soon developed a legislative interest which gradually became one of the main characteristics of the organization. The practice of printing records of legislative roll calls on labor measures was adopted for the first time in 1904 when a pamphlet entitled "Seven Labor Measures" was issued.

The pamphlet described and gave labor's arguments in favor of an anti-injunction bill, a bill to permit peaceful picketing, a bill for an effective 8-hour day for public employees, a bill for a 54-hour week for women and minors in the textile industry, a workmen's compensation act, a bill providing for the initiative and referendum, and a bill permitting unions to fine their members.

The State Branch made the office of Secretary-Treasurer a permanent, salaried position in 1913, and a permanent headquarters was established for the organization in the following year. In 1925 the duties of Legislative Agent were also assigned to the Secretary-Treasurer, and the power of leadership gradually centered in this office rather than in that of the unpaid President. Depending upon the incumbent, the office of President in the State Branch was more or less honorary in its significance, and there was a much greater turnover in this office than in that of the more influential office of Secretary-Treasurer-Legislative Agent.

Martin T. Joyce of the Electrical Worker's Local 103, Boston, was elected to the post of Secretary-Treasurer when the office was created in 1913. He served continuously until his death in 1931, assuming the additional duties of Legislative Agent in 1925. Robert J. Watt of the Central Labor Union in Lawrence was elected to replace Joyce, and he served as Secretary-Treasurer-Legislative Agent until 1936, when he resigned to take a position on the State Unemployment Compensation Commission and later became a member of the national staff of the AFL. Kenneth I. Taylor of the Springfield Typographical Union replaced Watt and, except for a leave of absence during World War II, he served until 1946, when he resigned to take an industrial relations position with a mid-west business firm. During the war Thomas E. Wilkinson served as Acting Legislative Agent, and in 1946 Kenneth J. Kelly of the Quincy Central Labor Union and a former meatcutter with a Boston College degree replaced Taylor as the Secretary-Treasurer-Legislative Agent of the Massachusetts State Federation of Labor.

The Massachusetts State Branch of the AFL officially changed its name to the Massachusetts State Federation of Labor in 1928, and in 1948 the name was officially shortened to the Massachusetts Federation of Labor. In 1948 a state arm of the LLPE was established in Massachusetts when Earnest A. Johnson of the Building and Construction trades was elected to be the Director of the Massachusetts Citizen's League for Political Education. After the 1948 elections, the executive boards of the Federation merged the functions of the Massachusetts Citizen's League for Political Education and the functions of the previously existing Education Committee under one "Director of Political and Other Education." Ex-teamster Francis E. Lavigne was elected to this post at the 1949 convention. In January 1954, the Federation created a Legislative Advisory Council to act as the lobbying "arm" of the AFL just as the Committee on Political and Other Education acted as the electing "arm".

Massachusetts State Industrial Union Council, CIO, 1937-1958

The CIO unions were officially purged from the State Federation of Labor in 1937, and the Massachusetts State Industrial Union Council was chartered in November, 1938, following an earlier convention in November, 1937, at which time Michael F. Widman, Jr., of the United Mine Workers was elected interim president of the CIO in Massachusetts. Later, Joseph A. Salerno of the Amalgamated Clothing Workers was elected President of the State Industrial Union Council and J. William Belanger of the Textile Workers Union was elected Secretary-Treasurer. Unlike the State Federation (AFL) the President was the most powerful officer in the State Industrial Union Council (CIO).

In 1947, Albert J. Clifton, was appointed as the Legislative Agent for the Industrial Union Council, and Joseph Cass was appointed director of the state CIO's Political Action Committee.

Late in 1948 Salerno resigned as President of the Massachusetts State Industrial Union Council, pleading compulsion to do so under an added burden of responsibility as a national vice president of his own international union. Belanger was then elected to replace Salerno as President, and Salvatore Camelio of the Rubber Workers was elected to Belanger's old post as Secretary-Treasurer.

The CIO Industrial Union Council in Massachusetts was one of the nation's pioneers in curtailing communist influence in the American labor movement. Starting years before the national CIO acted on the issue, the State Industrial Union Council took decisive steps to curtail communist penetration of the Massachusetts labor movement in 1942 by purging the Boston Industrial Union Council of the left-wing elements which originally dominated it. The most decisive move against communism in Massachusetts, however, came in 1946 when the State Industrial Union Council amended its Constitution to ban communists from holding office and reduced the number of Council officers from 37 to 15.

The Amalgamated Clothing Workers and the Textile Workers Union led in this anti-communist drive, and the Fur and Leather Workers, the United Packinghouse Workers, and the United Electrical Workers were the unions most affected in Massachusetts. Since Albert J. Fitzgerald, the international president of the U.E., was a former member and officer of the local in Lynn, Massachusetts, he persuaded this local and several other U.E. unions in the state to disaffiliate from the State Industrial Union Council following the 1946 purge. This influential local, the largest in New England, parted company with their former officer and national leader over the candidacy of Henry Wallace and the Progressive Party in 1948, however, and in the following year they voted to bring Fitzgerald to trial for violating the policy of the union as defined by a referendum. [4, 9-28-49]

Efforts Toward Merger

Prior to the 1958 merger of the Massachusetts Federation of Labor and the Massachusetts State Industrial Union Council there were significant differences in the size, composition, and character of the two organizations. When the national AFL-CIO merger was consummated late in 1955, state labor bodies were given two years to unite. At that time a reporter for the Christian Science Monitor reported that the AFL outnumbered the CIO in Massachusetts by about 350,000 members to 200,000 [4, 10-10-55]. Most of the AFL members were located in the Boston-Cambridge area, and the Teamsters were probably the largest single AFL union in the state with over half of its approximately 35,000 members located in this area. Other large AFL unions with a Boston concentration were the Carpenters, the ILGWU, and the State, County, and Municipal Workers, and the Streetcarmen.

The CIO unions, on the other hand, were more dispersed geographically. Although the large and influential Amalgamated Clothing Workers was centered in Boston, the CIO in Massachusetts had more of a "mill town" flavor than did the Boston-centered AFL. Their largest numbers outside Boston were located in Springfield, Worcester, Lynn, Fall River, and Pittsfield. The IUE which replaced the old UE in many Massachusetts locals and the TWU were the largest constituents unions, but the latter was losing members as a result of the exodus of the textile industry to the South. In addition to the Amalgamated Clothing Workers, the Rubber workers and the Steelworkers also had a significant number of members in Massachusetts, although most of the Steelworkers' strength was confined to Worcester.

Despite its greater geographic dispersion, the CIO tended to be more centralized in its operation than the AFL in Massachusetts. Thus the resolutions presented to the December Convention of the CIO Industrial Union Council were usually pre-screened by the executive Committee and debate at the Convention tended to be quite limited with more time being devoted to speeches by various dignitaries and guests. The August Conventions of the AFL Federation of Labor, however, were more prone to be wide open affairs, and considerable time was spent in discussing resolutions. The Central Labor Unions in the AFL seem to have exercised more influence than the local Industrial Union Councils in the CIO, and the AFL locals generally tended to be more autonomous in their actions than their CIO counterparts.

The Industrial Union Council put more emphasis on international union affiliation in electing its executive board members than did the Federation of Labor, and the CIO appointed more of its staff officers than did the Federation. Thus the state AFL organization in Massachusetts emphasized geographical districts in electing 14 vice presidents from 7 geographical districts. In addition, the Federation of Labor elected 2 vice presidents at large, and the President, Secretary-Treasurer-Legislative Agent, and the Director of Political and Other Education were also elected "state wide" without respect to geographical considerations. The State Industrial Union Council, on the other hand, elected all of its Executive Board Members, including the President, Secretary-Treasurer, and three vice presidents from the state at large, but with the provision that no international union could have more than 4 members on the state executive board. The executive board then appointed the council's legislative agent, PAC director, and other staff officials.

The Constitution of the Industrial Union Council was a rather general 15-page document which left a good bit of discretion to the state executive board, whereas local autonomy for affiliated unions tended to be more pronounced in the Federation of Labor, whose 34-page constitution spelled things out in more detail.

The State Federation also kept a detailed record of its convention proceedings, and a verbatim transcript was published annually along with the official officers' reports to the conventions. Published information by the industrial union council, however, was much less frequent, and most of the writer's information about this group was gleaned from the yearbooks that were issued periodically by the CIO organization or from newspaper sources.

Despite these differences, however, there was some precedent for cooperation between the state labor bodies in Massachusetts prior to the two-year merger deadline handed down by the national AFL-CIO in 1955. Indeed, in 1948, Massachusetts witnessed the first formal cooperation between the AFL and the CIO in the country following the national schism in 1937, when the labor forces in the state joined with the state chapter of the Americans for Democratic Action to form a United Labor Committee to oppose three "anti-labor" referenda on the ballot in the 1948 Massachusetts elections. These elections witnessed the first important "right to work" campaign under section 14(b) of the Taft Hartley Act, and the United Labor Committee was successful in having this proposal and two other proposals regulating union elections defeated at the polls.

The ULC was not organized for general political action, but for the specific purpose of defeating the 1948 referenda. As an *ad hoc* coalition the ULC gradually lost its cohesion and disintegrated once a common threat to all unions subsided and the more divisive problems of working out a positive program and supporting particular candidates came to the fore. Both labor federations in Massachusetts followed the policy of endorsing only statewide candidates with labor records to offer as credentials for consideration, and in both organizations the central labor unions or local industrial union councils were responsible for endorsing candidates for the state legislature and local offices. As might be expected, there is a record of some locals in the state endorsing their own candidates regardless of state or city central policy, but since the state CIO did all of its endorsing in a special two day state wide economic and political action endorsing conference, there was less independent, cross-purpose endorsing of candidates in this group than in the AFL where endorsements were either made at the annual convention or at special meetings of the Committee on Political and Other Education.

Given the initial cooperation on the United Labor Committee, the essential similarity of the functions performed by state labor federations, and the two-year deadline handed down by the national AFL-CIO, at least one commentator on the Massachusetts labor scene felt that most of the differences outlined above could be ironed out without too much difficulty. He stated "merging the state AFL and CIO groups in Massachusetts is not expected to prove a difficult task ... observers believe that most of their difficulty will be in finding satisfactory positions in the merged organization for the strong personalities on both sides". [10] Events proved that the second part of this statement was much more accurate than the first.

No less than 33 separate merger meetings were held in Massachusetts between May 4, 1956 and December 6, 1958, when the Massachusetts State Labor Council AFL-CIO was finally formed at a joint merger convention in Boston. Before a final agreement was reached, the national AFL-CIO had to send official representatives into Massachusetts to aid the negotiations, and as in the national AFL-CIO merger, concluded three years previously, a path of "organic unity" rather than "functional cooperation" was decided upon. Thus, even as the merger was being concluded, it was recognized that several unresolved problems remained to be decided within the Massachusetts labor movement.

The Merger Consummated

The two main issues at least partially resolved prior to the merger convention were the number and nature of the offices to be created in the merged organization, and the duration, representation, and voting procedures governing the annual conventions.

Since the Federation of Labor traditionally met for a week in August, and the Industrial Union Council met for a shorter period of time in December, it was finally decided that the merged organization would meet annually for a three day convention beginning the first Wednesday in October. Prior to the merger, both the state AFL and CIO in Massachusetts allowed one convention delegate for each 200 per capita paying members or majority fraction of 200 from each local, but the CIO allowed one delegate from a local to vote the full representation of his local (one vote for each per capita paying member) whereas the AFL simply counted the number of delegates voting on any issue at the convention. It was finally decided that delegates from central bodies (limited to two from each central) would be entitled to one convention vote each, individual delegates from large locals would be limited to 600 votes each, and delegates from locals having less than 200 membership could vote their actual memberships (one vote per member) at the annual convention.

With regard to officers, thirty-five executive council positions were created in the merged organization, including four executive officers and 31 Vice Presidents. The office of Secretary-Treasurer was made a full time paid position, and the other unpaid executive offices were President and two Executive Vice Presidents.

The pre-merger negotiations concluded that the office of Secretary-Treasurer in the merged organization would go to an AFL man, and Kenneth J. Kelley was elected to fill this post. J. William Belanger, the former president of the State Industrial Union Council, was elected to the position of President in the merged organization. The other two executive council positions were split between the AFL and the CIO when William Calahan, former president of the State Federation, and Salvatore Camelio, former Secretary-Treasurer of the State Industrial Union Council, were elected Executive Vice Presidents in the newly formed Massachusetts State Labor Council, AFL-CIO.

The 31 vice presidents in the merged organization were split 17 for the former AFL and 14 for the former CIO. Following its customary practice, the final convention of the State Federation elected its vice presidents on a regional basis. Fifteen were elected from specific geographical districts, and two were elected from the state at large with the requirement that one of the at-large vice presidents had to be a woman.

The final convention of the State Industrial Union Council also continued its past practice by electing its 14 vice presidents in the new organization at large with a stipulation limiting the number of offices that could be held by members of the same international union.

The initial Constitution of the merged organization was deliberately vague on how the vice presidents were to be subsequently elected, but at the second annual convention of the Massachusetts State Labor Council the following Constitutional Amendment was adopted regarding the election of vice presidents:

> Of the 31 Vice Presidents, 15 including one woman shall be nominated and elected at large; 16 shall be nominated and elected as resident candidates from the districts they are to represent. The eight districts shall be arranged in the following order...
>
> No more than one (1) Vice President from each district shall be a member of the same International Union or directly affiliated organizations. No more than three (3) Vice Presidents shall be members of the same International Union or directly affiliated organizations. [11, p. 25]

These 31 vice presidents along with the 4 executive council offices have subsequently been elected annually at the October convention of the State Labor Council.

In addition to the 35 elective offices mentioned above, the 1958 merger Convention also created four staff departments to offer services to affiliated organizations in the areas of Education and Research, Legislation, Political Education, and Publication and Public Relations. The directors and members of each of these four departments are appointed by the Executive Council, and all of the original appointees have continued in office since the merger in 1958. Francis Lavigne, formerly of the State Federation, has served as the Director of the Education and Research Department. James A. Broyer of the AFL was made the Legislative Director, and Albert G. Clifton of the CIO has acted as the Legislative Agent for the State Labor Council. Joseph Cass and Gerald Kable of the CIO continue to operate as directors of political education and public relations respectively.

In addition to these four staff departments, the merger

constitution also created eight standing committees of 11 members each in the areas of Education and Research, Organization and Affiliation, Taxation, Workmen's Compensation, Social Security, Housing, Community Services, and Civil Rights.

A Legislative Advisory Committee consisting of the members of the Executive Council, together with the Chairmen of the aforementioned eight standing committees, was also established by the State Labor Council's constitution.

Adjustments Since Merger

Although Joseph Cass was appointed the staff director of Massachusetts COPE in 1958, the formal structure and policy making apparatus of the merged Labor Council's Committee on Political Education was not completely established until a year later when an official set of COPE by-laws was adopted at the 1959 annual convention.

These by-laws were finally approved only after considerable discussion within the labor movement over the respective roles of the State Labor Council and the affiliated local labor councils in the endorsement of candidates for the state legislature. When the new endorsement policy represented by the proposed COPE by-laws was originally announced by the State Labor Council in July, 1959, the *Christian Science Monitor* stated:

> Under the new endorsement policy local labor groups and not the state organization will decide which candidates merit the union's support for local offices.

The statement explicitly spells out that endorsements of candidates for municipal or town offices "shall not be made by the state council." This is considered the exclusive function of the respective city central labor groups.

At the same time, the new policy makes it very clear that the State Council shall have the sole power to make endorsements concerning candidates for the Congress of the U.S., statewide constitutional offices, and both branches of the Massachusetts Legislature.

It spells out, however, that recommendations for these offices may be sent by local unions, or central labor groups, to the state council for consideration.

Perhaps equally important, the new policy tackles the controversial subject of labor appointments.

Local central labor councils have for some time criticized the practice of the state organization making the endorsements for appointments to statewide offices and positions or to state agencies.

Now, the new "endorsement policy" confers this function exclusively on the state labor council. Recommendations may be made by subordinate labor groups.

But, endorsements for appointees to city offices and positions are left entirely to the local central labor organization.

Both Hugh Thompson, regional director of the AFL-CIO and James L. McDevitt, national COPE director, have approved the new endorsement policy. [4, 7-9-59]

Later in the same month, however, the Monitor also noted:

J. William Belanger, president of the Massachusetts State Labor Council, AFL-CIO, had announced that the 21 central labor bodies in the state had accepted a plan by which the state group would make the recommendations for endorsements.

Stephen S. McCloskey, executive secretary of the Boston Council, the largest member, asserted this was not so, that the Boston group, included in the announced 21, had voted just the opposite at a meeting last Thursday.

"We unanimously opposed such a policy of complete regimentation" declared McCloskey. He quoted a letter from George F. Meany, president of the AFL-CIO, in which he stressed a state council had no authority or jurisdiction over a local central council.

Belanger explained that the purpose only was to guarantee "unity of action" and to make certain "the AFL-CIO label will not be misused for personal profit or promotion." Also he pointed out that the local central bodies were affiliated

> with the state council and joined in the decisions. [4, 7-31-59]

This dispute was not the first time that Mr. McCloskey had been at odds with the leaders of the state labor movement in Massachusetts, and in part this dispute also reflected a deeper division within the Bay State labor movement between the State, County and Municipal Workers Union and the leaders of the State Labor Council. The State Labor Council and both of its AFL and CIO predecessors had a long standing opposition to a sales tax in Massachusetts, but the government employees felt that a sales tax was the only way enough revenue could be raised to assure them adequate pay scales. Since the government employees tended to dominate the Boston Labor Council, therefore, this dispute was probably involved in McCloskey's objection to the proposed endorsement policy.

After considerable discussion, a revised set of COPE by-laws was adopted at the October, 1959, annual convention of the State Labor Council. These by-laws, which are still in effect, did not technically outlaw conflicting endorsements by labor groups affiliated with the State Labor Council, but they clearly stated:

> No COPE officer, executive board, committee member or delegate to the endorsing conference shall act in any official capacity whatsoever, on behalf of any political candidate in opposition to the endorsement of state COPE. In the event that any officer, executive board, committee member or delegate takes a position on any candidate in opposition to the endorsement of State COPE, he shall automatically be disqualified from acting or serving as an officer, executive board, committee member or delegate until the conclusion of the campaign involved. [11, p. 83]

As adopted, the by-laws provide for a State Committee on Political Education consisting of approximately 150 persons including the Executive Council of the State Labor Council, a representative from each AFL-CIO Trade and Industrial Department or Council, a representative from each affiliated international union in the state not already represented in one of the above categories, a representative from each County, City or Congressional District COPE within the state, the AFL-CIO Regional Director, and "such additional representation as the Executive Council of the State AFL-CIO may decide". The entire committee is required to meet once a year, and the Executive Board of the Massachusetts COPE, consisting of "the Officers and Executive Council members of the Massachusetts State Labor Council, AFL-CIO, together with at least fifteen (15) members-at-large appointed by the President in consultation with the Executive Officers and approved by the Executive Council", is required to meet quarterly.

With regard to endorsement policy, the Massachusetts COPE by-laws provide:

> In the making of endorsements, the past record of the individual shall be employed as criteria for endorsement. The record of candiates which shall be used for endorsement shall be the roll call record on issues supplied by the National and State AFL-CIO.
>
> Any AFL-CIO member has the same right as any other American citizen to seek public office. However, any AFL-CIO member seeking public office who desires COPE endorsement should, before filing his nomination, meet with the proper Committee of State COPE and discuss his candidacy and any other matters connected with his campaign. [11, p. 83]

And, with regard to financing, they state:

1. Each AFL-CIO member shall be asked to contribute voluntarily at least $1.00 per year to COPE. Of this dollar, $.50 shall be for the use of National COPE in critical Federal campaigns, and $.50 shall be available for use by the State COPE. These monies allocated by National COPE to the State COPE shall be used only in campaigns of candidates for U.S. President, U.S. Vice President, U.S. Senate, and U.S. House of Representatives, but the apportionment among the several federal campaigns shall be made at the discretion of the State COPE.

2. The State COPE and its sub-divisions are authorized to raise additional finances for their work by any legal means, as long as such activity does not interfere with the National COPE drive for individual contributions. [11, p. 84]

According to the financial report to the 1961 annual convention, the Massachusetts State COPE spent $29,000 during the 1960 elections.[1]

With regard to official COPE endorsements since the AFL-CIO merger in Massachusetts, the debates surrounding the adoption of the by-laws referred to above indicated that there might be some difficulty in securing unanimous labor endorsements (or at least unified labor action) in all cases. Indeed, such has proven to be the case.

The standing prohibition on any officer, representative, or affiliate of the State Labor Council taking "an official" position independent of the political stand of the Council's COPE organization can easily be circumvented on the technical basis that most Bay State labor officials and their organizations wear at least two hats. An official or affiliated organization can make an endorsement or take a

---

1 The corresponding figure for the 1962 election is $32,635.

position as a representative of their local or international and not use their State Labor Council title. For example, a local union president, who is also an officer of the state labor organization, can say "as president of local X, I feel thus and such", and he may or may not mentioned that he is not speaking in his capacity as an "official" state labor representative. Local unions in a particular town can also act in concert or independently as locals of their international unions rather than as affiliates of the local labor council.

In practice, however, not even this technical subterfuge need be resorted to. For example, in the 1962 Democratic primaries one local labor council endorsed a candidate who was related to a powerful local union officer independent of the State COPE's official endorsement policy. The "penalty" of such "independents" being denied "official" status for the duration of the campaign involved has obviously not always served as a powerful deterent.

The 1960 gubernatorial elections, which saw the Republicans nominate an Italian-American candidate who has earned a reputation as a "good" employer in his construction business with the relatively conservative building trades, also put strains on the official COPE endorsement of his Democratic opponent. The problems of political unity, however, have not been the only problems confronting the labor movement in Massachusetts since the shotgun wedding which created the AFL-CIO State Labor Council in 1958.

The method of voting at conventions, which was adopted as part of the merger agreement in 1958, was closer to the CIO suggestion in this area than to the AFL position. Thus, when the counting of the ballots for the election of officers at the 1959 convention consumed an inordinate amount of time, Secretary-Treasurer Kelley stated:

> May I say that it is a shame that it took from 1:00 p.m. when the polls closed until 10:20 p.m. to count 1,190 ballots. In my opinion this per capita method of voting is cumbersome, confusing and a frankenstein monstrosity. If we do not do something about it by the next Convention then we will be severely criticized and derelict in our duties as trade union leaders. [11, p. 93]

These remarks then brought the following retort from Council Vice President Anthony Accardi:

> I don't want to be fresh but I think the last remarks by the Secretary-Treasurer were uncalled for. Locals are entitled to per capita representation and to send anyone they properly can to this Convention to cast the number of votes their locals are entitled to. I think every local should have representation on the number of members that they pay per capita tax on. I hope that as long as I am a member of the Council and even if I am not all locals should be given per capita representation. [11, p. 93]

At the third annual convention of the State Labor Council in 1960 a constitutional amendment was introduced to change the convention voting procedure to give each delegate only one vote, but the convention simply referred the amendment to the incoming executive council. An amendment to require at least two rather than one woman on the Executive Council was defeated in 1960, but an amendment to lengthen the annual convention of the State Labor Council from three to four days was adopted at the third annual convention and modified at the fourth convention in 1961 to read:

> The regular convention of the Council shall be held annually commencing on the first (1st) Tuesday of October and shall remain in session four (4) days until the business before the convention is completed; at a time and place designated by the Executive Council. In cases of extreme emergency, the Executive Council, by a three-fourths (3/4) vote, may change the date of the Convention. [12, p. 54]

Beneath these surface adjustments in the merger agreement, there has been persistent talk of lingering personality differences between some of the old AFL and old CIO members on the State Labor Council, with each group trying to increase its influence in the merged organization. Not all of the clashes have been along former AFL-CIO lines, however, and the differences between Secretary-Treasurer Kenneth Kelley and James Broyer, the former AFL man who took over part of Kelley's old duties as Director of the Legislative Department in the merged organization, were a poorly kept "secret".

The possibility that at least some of these personality differences might be alleviated presented itself in January 1962, when Kelley resigned his post as Secretary-Treasurer of the State Labor Council to accept a job in Washington, D.C., as the Director of Labor Affairs for the Agency for International Development (A.I.D.). Kelley's resignation left a big gap at the top of the Massachusetts labor movement, and it is still too early to determine all of the eventual consequences of this move. Immediately after Kelley's resignation the Executive Council of the state labor body elected an incumbent Vice President, James P. Loughlin of the Hotel, Restaurant and Bartenders Union, to serve as Secretary-Treasurer until the fifth annual Convention. The Council's Newsletter atated:

> Vice President James P. Loughlin of Worcester was elected by a unanimous vote at a special meeting of the Massachusetts State Labor Council on February 1st to succeed Kenneth J. Kelley as Secretary-Treasurer. The motion to make the vote unanimous was made by Martin E. Pierce of the Boston Firefighters, the only other mentioned candidate for the office. [8, p. 1]

Since there were more former AFL members than former CIO members on the Executive Council it seems likely that an old AFL man would be elected to replace Kelley. Loughlin is not considered to be as forceful a personality as was Kelley, however, and it is felt that the former CIO members will have more room to maneuver in the state labor movement with Loughlin in control than if a more dominant person had been elected.

As the above exerpt from the Newsletter indicated, however, there was more than one candidate mentioned to succeed Kelley, and there were rumors of the possibility of a contested election for the post of Secretary-Treasurer at the October 1962 convention of the State Labor Council. There were also rumors that there might be a proposal to make the position of President of the State Labor Council a full time paid position in addition to the Secretary-Treasurer's post. Neither of these moves occurred, however, but there remains the feeling that Massachusetts labor movement is still in a state of flux and that not all of the adjustment problems in the Bay State have yet been resolved.

A more detailed analysis of the political activities of the Massachusetts labor movement will be incorporated in the following chapters. We will now turn to a closer examination of the main employer organizations operating on the Bay State political scene.

Employer Organizations In Massachusetts Politics

The Greater Boston Chamber of Commerce

The Greater Boston Chamber of Commerce has the longest history of any of the employer organizations now operating in Massachusetts. Although its antecedents can be traced back to Colonial days, there have been many changes in the membership, leadership, title and scope of the activities of this organization. The present organization received its charter in 1909, but after many changes it began to develop its present state legislative program in about 1949 with Mr. E. J. Brelant in charge of the Chamber's legislative activities.

The most recent change of major significance in the Chamber's operation came in 1954, when the name of the organization was changed from the Boston Chamber of Commerce to the Greater Boston Chamber of Commerce, and William J. Bird became the managing director of the organization's activities. This 1954 change in title signified not only an expansion of the Chamber's geographical base but also an expansion in the scope of its activities under Mr. Bird's leadership.

The Greater Boston Chamber began publishing a weekly, and later bi-weekly, Greater Boston Report in January 1956, and most of the writer's knowledge of this organization has been gleaned from this source or from interviews with present staff personnel. In 1957 William J. Bird's title was changed from managing director to executive vice president, and in 1958 James G. Roberts was named general manager of the Greater Boston Chamber to assist Mr. Bird with the executive duties of the organization.

When Mr. Bird resigned his chamber post in 1959 to become Western vice president of the John Hancock Mutual Life Insurance Company, Mr. Roberts was named the executive vice president of the organization. Later, in 1960, Walter E. Knight was named general manager of the Greater Boston Chamber and Thomas J. Moccia was appointed administrative assistant to executive vice president Roberts. This three man team currently heads a staff of approximately 45 professional and secretarial personnel divided into seven functional divisions or "service areas" for carrying out the Chamber's program of work.

The Greater Boston Chamber's seven service areas are: (1) Membership and Member Relations; (2) News and Publications; (3) Research and Development; (4) Urban Renewal; (5) Transportation and Foreign Trade; (6) Governmental Affairs; and (7) a Convention and Tourist Bureau, which is the largest of these functional divisions. Superimposed on this administrative or staff organization is the formal policy making organization of the Chamber responsible to the membership which elects it.

In the summer of 1961 the Chamber could boast a membership of approximately 3,400 members representing about 2,600 companies. The Chamber's membership is broadly representative of the diversified Boston economy. Some of the larger membership components are: manufacturers, about 18%; financial institutions, about 12%; retail, insurance, transportation companies, and hotel and restaurants, about

10% each.

With this membership base, the Greater Boston Chamber of Commerce is by far the largest chamber organization in the state of Massachusetts. While it enjoys good relations with the national chamber, the Boston organization is a thriving and prosperous unit in its own right and it is completely free to act independently on any issue. The Greater Boston Chamber of Commerce has no connection at all with the Massachusetts State Chamber of Commerce. This latter group is not large and is not representative of local chambers in the state.

The Greater Boston Chamber of Commerce enjoys informal relations with the other local Chambers in the state through the Massachusetts Association of Chamber of Commerce Executives. This group meets about four times a year, and is composed of the professional staffs of the local Chambers throughout the state. The Greater Boston Chamber, as the largest member, does some staff work for this group which prepares legislative bulletins for its members. The executives' association merely serves as an informal communications device, however, and the Greater Boston Chamber has no authority or dominance over the constituent groups, which are autonomous units.

"Any individual, or any firm, association, corporation, or other business organization interested in the development of Greater Boston and New England" is eligible for election as an active member of the Greater Boston Chamber of Commerce according to the organization's by-laws, so long as such election is "in accordance with the rules and regulations adopted by the Board from time to time".

The organization's by-laws also provide that "The government of the affairs of the Chamber, the direction of its work, and the control of its property shall be vested in a Board of Directors". The Board of Directors consists of 24 members elected by the Chamber's membership in addition to the other elected officers of the Chamber, which are "a President, a Chairman of the Board, a Chairman of the Executive Committee, two or more Vice-Presidents, one or more Honorary Vice-Presidents, a Secretary, and a Treasurer."

The President is the chief elective officer of the Chamber and he acts as their official spokesman. Each President is limited to a one-year term of office as president, but upon retiring from the presidency he usually moves to the position of Chairman of the Board of Directors for one year, then to the position of Chairman of the Executive Committee for one year, and then he is usually made an honorary vice president of the Chamber.

The executive committee is responsible for the routine transaction of Chamber business between meetings of the Board. According to the by-laws, "The Executive Committee shall be composed of the President, the Chairman of the Board, the Chairman of the Executive Committee, the Secretary, and the Treasurer, ex-officers, and six other Directors appointed annually by the Board".

The Board has the power to appoint, change the membership of, or terminate the existence of any committees it may deem advisable or necessary to advance the interest of the Chamber or carry on its work. No finding or recommendation of any committee can be reported or published as the action of the Chamber, however, until it has been approved by the Board or a meeting of the members of the Chamber.

Committees of Chamber members are usually appointed to study proposals and make policy recommendations in the areas of administrative staff concern outlined above, i.e., Membership and Member Relations, Urban Renewal, Research and Development, etc. For example, the staff of the Governmental Affairs Department works with membership committees on State Affairs, National Affairs, and Labor-Management Relations. These three main committees are also subdivided into areas of more specific concern. Thus, the Chamber's State Affairs Committee is concerned largely with matters of taxation and government organization. The National Affairs Committee contains sub committees on federal-local relations and labor legislation-social security. The Labor-Management Relations committee has five sub committees on employment security, workmen's compensation, business regulation, labor relations, and automation.

These membership committees serve as policy recommending units and a communication devices with the Chamber's professional staff in these areas. Eric H. Hanson replaced E. J. Brehaut as the manager of the Chamber's Governmental Affairs Department late in 1959, when Mr. Brehaut retired after 40 years of service to the Chamber. At this writing Mr. Hanson is assisted by John J. Leahy, Jr., Director of Legislative Services; William F. Malloy, Legislative Counsel, and Dale G. Stoodley, Research Assistant. The January, 1961, <u>Program of Work</u> of the Greater Boston Chamber of Commerce stated:

> The staff activities of this Department cover eight principal areas. These are: (1) definitive research on the potential effects of pending national, state, and local legislation which would affect the legitimate interests of the business community, (2) development of policy on these matters through the appropriate committee and the Board of Directors, (3) reporting on pending legislation to the membership and allied organizations by means of publications or direct communication, (4) full-time representation by legislative counsel at the State House, (5) information and advisory services, (6) development of opportunities for membership participation, (7) representation at Boston City Council and other municipal meetings, and (8) participation in the Labor Council of the Chamber of Commerce of the United States. [5, p. 5]

In addition to these activities John J. Leahy, the Director of Legislative Services, now also oversees the administration of the national Chamber's Practical Politics Action Course.

The U.S. Chamber's Action Course in Practical Politics consists of nine two-hour workshops. The following topics are covered in a non-partisan manner: the individual in politics, political party organization, the political precinct, the political campaign, political clubs, the political leader's problems, political meetings, businessmen in politics, the politicians speak. Any group can sponsor the action course, and the national chamber makes available all the necessary work materials at $8 a set for participant's pamphlets, and $12 a set for discussion leader's manuals.

Despite Mr. Leahy's duties in this area, the course sessions are usually taught by another person, and the Practical Politics Action Course is not an integral part of the program of the Chamber's Government Affairs Department. The department's operations are in no way dependent upon the participants in the program, and a staff member of the chamber has indicated that member interest in the practical politics course has been only moderate. Indeed, many non members "who would be of no help to us", have taken the course and it has been estimated that in Boston more Democrats than Republicans have graduated from this course.

In May, 1960, the Chamber of Commerce of the United States announced "About 4,500 Action Courses for more than 67,000 citizens in 1,063 communities have been held, are now underway or are definitely planned by business firms, chambers of commerce, trade and professional associations and other community organizations." [3, p. 1] This listing showed a total of 79 courses in Massachusetts, of which seven were in Boston. This number of seven was exceeded in Massachusetts by only one city, Worcester with 22, which ranked it among the leading cities in the country of any size. Boston's figure of seven, however, put it near the bottom of large cities listed in the Chamber Report which showed Wichita, Kansas, with 61, Pittsburgh, Pennsylvania and Columbus, Ohio, with 57, St. Louis with 56, Niagara Falls, New York with 55, Chicago 54, Hartford, Connecticut 48, New York City 44, Indianapolis 34, and Minneapolis 30, etc.

These figures don't say how many persons were in each course or who the sponsoring organization was in each case, but one reason for Boston's apparently low participation may be the fact that the Greater Boston Chamber had a few years earlier launched a fairly intensive "Business Climate" campaign and thus many of its members may have already been politically aroused before the Practical Politics

Course became available.

Perhaps a better index of member interest in the Greater Boston Chamber's Political activities is the fact that about 1,700 of the organization's 3,500 members subscribe to the organization's Legislative Bulletin in addition to the distribution of this report through MACE channels.

A March 3, 1961 copy of the Chamber's Greater Boston Report stated "The highly successful course in practical politics has graduated more than 150 interested students since its beginning eighteen months ago". And it continued "James G. Roberts, Chamber Executive Vice President, said that 'because of the continued interest in the Practical Politics Action Course, two additional courses are being offered by the Chamber: The courses will be held at the Chamber's headquarters on eight successive Tuesdays beginning March 14." [6, p. 4]

To briefly sum up, the Greater Boston Chamber of Commerce is vitally concerned with the matters of state labor legislation in Massachusetts. Its policies in this area are formulated by membership and staff committees subject to approval by the Board of Directors. Once these policies have been formulated, they are implemented by the professional staff of the Governmental Affairs Department. Most recently the Chamber's main legislative concerns in the area of Massachusetts labor legislation have been in the areas of strengthening state picketing laws and opposing the expansion of state minimum wage legislation. It has also taken vigorous stands on a host of other issues, however, as subsequent chapters will clearly indicate. Although the Greater Boston

Chamber sponsors periodic sessions of the United States Chamber of Commerce's Practical Politics Course, it is not dependent on this source to implement its political or legislative program at the state level in Massachusetts.

The Associated Industries of Massachusetts

The Associated Industries of Massachusetts was chartered in 1915 with the primary purpose of protecting the legislative interests of the manufacturing enterprises in the state.[1] It sought to pattern its legislative activities after those successfully pursued by the railroad industry at that time. Membership in the Association grew until the Great Depression of the 1930's; and then it fell off sharply, reaching a low point in 1935. At that time Roy F. Williams took over as the Association's Executive Vice President and Chief administrative officer and virtually rebuilt the Association from scratch. In 1958 Mr. Williams was made an honorary officer and Robert A. Chadborne was made the Executive Vice President of AIM.

Although it maintains close cooperation with the National Industrial Council and the conference of State Manufacturers'

---

1 In an interview on July 23, 1962, the Association's Assistant Vice President and Secretary to the Board, Mr. Clifford I. Fahlstrom, said that the primary purpose of the organization at the time of its founding was to "protect industry from what was then deemed to be unwise legislation", and he cited the Massachusetts Workmen's Compensation Act and the national threats of governmental take over of the railroad industry as examples.

Associations, the A.I.M. has remained essentially a state manufacturers' association, and today it represents over 2,000 firms. While this number is less than 25% of the 9,058 manufacturing firms operating in the Bay State in 1959, Massachusetts is predominantly a small employer state. Only about 90 firms employ over 1,000 persons, and all of these firms are members of A.I.M. This helps to explain the fact that, while some 75% of the A.I.M. members employ fewer than 100 employees, the Association's membership nevertheless represents "the vast majority of the industrial payrolls in the Commonwealth." [1, p. 2][2]

While the A.I.M. states:

> Basically, the association provides the Massachusetts manufacturer with four kinds of service in exchange for his dues—professional talent; training; tools; and information which will enable him to operate his business more profitably in the Commonwealth of Massachusetts. [1, p. 3]

The organization has remained very close to its original concern with state legislation. Recent years have seen a conscious effort to modify and improve its approach to legislative problems, however, and the Association's Public Affairs Action Program, initiated in 1958, has attracted a large amount of publicity in its attempt to improve the Massachusetts "business climate".

The policy of the organization is officially formed by a 13-man Executive Committee working with the assistance of 6 sub committees

---

2 In an interview on December 29, 1960, Mr. John Hamilton, then the AIM's Director of Public Relations, estimated that the AIM's members accounted for 80% of the state's industrial payroll.

in the areas of workmen's compensation, unemployment compensation, taxation, transportation, industrial relations, and legislative priorities. These sub committees are composed of interested members firms and staff personnel, and all policy proposals must be approved by the A.I.M.'s 75-man Board of Directors. Once the policy is formulated, it is implemented and put into effect by the Executive-Vice President and his professional staff. The Legislative Department is the largest single staff specialty, and, as indicated above, it has recently been supplemented by a special Association interest in a Public Affairs Action Program.

Jarvis Hunt, a former Republican President of the Massachusetts Senate, became the Legislative Counsel of the Associated Industries at the end of World War II and served in this capacity until 1958. When Mr. Chadbourne replaced Mr. Williams as the A.I.M.'s Executive Vice President in 1958, Mr. Hunt was made the Association's General Counsel. Walter Meuther was appointed as Legislative Counsel, and Mr. Meuther is currently assisted by Mr. William McCarthy who is the Association's Associate Legislative Counsel. Backing up and supplementing the A.I.M.'s legislative program is the Public Affairs Action Program aimed at helping Massachusetts businessmen improve the states "business climate".

An Association publication states:

> The sustained decrease in manufacturing jobs available which has contined almost without interruption since 1943---lies at the base of the Association's Public Affairs Program aimed at improving the business climate...

...Obviously, there are a number of natural disadvantages to industry which cannot be changed--such as the state's distance from the markets and lack of raw materials.

But, compounding the Massachusetts problem are man-made obstacles to economic growth which can be changed. Together, these man-made factors comprise the business climate. Virtually all of these competitive handicaps have been created and can be changed through the political process.

To this end, the Associated Industries of Massachusetts is dedicated--by providing its members with the training, tools, and information which will equip business managers to cope with the effect of political forces on business. [1, pp. 4-5]

The A.I.M.'s Public Affairs Action Program was inaugurated in 1958 under the direction of Mr. John Hamilton, a former employee of the General Electric Company, and it immediately attracted considerable attention both in Massachusetts and elsewhere.

The program won the George Washington Medal of the Freedom Foundation at Valley Forge, Pennsylvania, and has been described in a national magazine in the following words:

The AIM program urges its members to deal as businessmen with voters and public officials.

The organization's attack is planned around state senatorial districts. To get a program rolling, a cooperative company president is induced into sponsorship of the AIM education series. He signs all invitations to the first AIM-prepared workshop and he makes the keynote address. There are three of these workshops, led by the local industrialists themselves. After the third meeting the group's set free in the political arena to champion the cause of management.

...

AIM leaves it up to each company to decide if it wants to encourage actual employee participation in the political process. [9, p.

The political activities of some of the Association's larger members, such as the General Electric Company, the Bethlehem Steel

Company, and the Raytheon Manufacturing Company are generally well known. Some of the General Electric communication techniques with employees and the general public mentioned in the earlier chapter on national employer activities have been used in Massachusetts. The top management of the Bethlehem Steel Company's Fore River Shipyard has also occasionally publicized "open letters" to its employees, and Raytheon's president, Charles Francis Adams, has made a few well publicized speeches on the Massachusetts "business climate". The appearance of General Electric and Raytheon legal counsel at legislative hearings before the General Court also increased appreciably after the 1958 elections in Massachusetts.

In order to find out more about how the Associated Industries' Public Affairs Program operates for some of the smaller or less well known member firms, however, the writer conducted several interviews with Mr. John Hamilton at the time he was the Director of Public Relations for the A.I.M. Mr. Hamilton also arranged some interviews with member firms for the writer to examine their individual public affairs programs in more detail.

Mr. Hamilton began by emphasizing that there are essentially two types of business political programs which deal with the four main areas of political activity. He said that the four areas of political activity are: Money, Organization, Candidates, and Issues. The first three areas he felt are partisan and thus corporations cannot legally participate as entities. Therefore, he said, some organizations such as the Chamber of Commerce and others encourage executives and employees to participate on an individual basis as part of a citizenship program. While the AIM's public affairs program "plays ball" with these efforts it does not promote them. Rather it focuses on the fourth area of politics-issues-and encourages Bay State employers to take a stand on certain vital economic issues on a bi-partisan basis.

The philosophy behind the AIM's Public Affairs Program is that legal political activity on issues is a responsibility to stockholders just like any other corporate responsibility, and that it should be a 9 to 5 job for the businessman going beyond the old "leave it to George" attitude of leaving lobbying activities to employer associations only.

In its public affairs program, the AIM encourages its member corporations to do three things: meet the state legislators from the district in which the firm is located, explain key issues to their employees by relating the state's business climate to their job security, and encourage other firms to become active on selected issues by forming an area committee of businessmen in each of the 40 Massachusetts state senatorial districts. Although the AIM depends on its member firms to carry the ball, it provides the "training, tools, and information" to aid them in doing an effective job in the political arena.

In the area of "training, tools, and information", the AIM, in addition to its regular publications, lists the following services: A Basic Public Affairs Action Kit, which is described as a series of "practical, 'how-to-do-it' booklets designed to assist the smaller company in implementing its public affairs program"; Communications

Tools, described as "inexpensive materials designed to help the smaller company to tell the business climate story to employee and other groups"; Information Tools, which are "specialized source materials which provide the foundation for effective action"; an A.I.M. Speakers Bureau; and three different Training Programs described as:

1. The Basic Public Affairs Workshop - a do-it-yourself program for multi-employer groups, designed to acquaint companies with the fundamentals of effective action in the field of public affairs.

2. The In-plant Public Affairs Workshop - a program designed for single company use, for developing a company public affairs program and for training its supervisors and foremen in this new management field.

3. Regional Workshops on the Key Business Climate Issues - a series of seminars in functional subject matter such as workmen's compensation, unemployment compensation, taxation, and labor relations, designed to explore in depth the business problems created by political action. [2]

To get a better flavor of how this whole program actually works in practice, the writer visited two of the A.I.M.'s member companies that have formally participated in the Public Affairs Program. One large textile firm (1900 employees) began its participation late in 1960 with a program designed to encourage its middle management personnel to become acquainted with their state legislative representatives. After a "kickoff dinner" at which the president of the company gave his complete approval of the program, a workshop session of some 50 middle management personnel was scheduled. The first workshop was built around the AIM booklet "How to Influence Your Legislators", and the participants prepared a list of recommendations for further action by the company.

Top management later approved these recommendations. As a result, the company has held a series of seminars with AIM staff personnel explaining various issues and various aspects of the political process, a series of trips to the state capital have been made by middle management executives to talk to their representatives, a typewriting service has been established for persons wishing to write their legislators, periodic bulletins are issued to supervisory personnel on various legislative issues, and a company vice president has assumed the chairmanship of the business climate committee in the State Senatorial district in which the plant is located. To date, this company's public affairs program has been confined to supervisory personnel, and largely aimed at influencing existing legislators. The possibility of extending the program to include non-management personnel in their role as voters, however, is being considered for future action. So far the company feels that the program has been a success, and they feel that a group of their supervisors actually changed four votes on the graduated income tax amendment during their visit to the General Court on March 29, 1961.

Another smaller AIM member firm (200 employees) has taken a more employee-voter oriented approach to its public affairs activities. It officially began its program on November 29, 1959, when a letter was sent to each employee's home. After encouraging the employees to become good citizens by taking an active part in community and state affairs as a voter and, if possible, as an office holder, the letter then stated:

"A meeting of approximately 40 employees was held on Thursday, November 12, to outline a new program which we hope to institute in the company. A plan was set forth at this meeting which can be described very simply as a citizen action group to "arouse and inform" every member of the Company regarding issues of government which affect them.

It should be stated at the outset that this activity will be non-partisan in its efforts. There is no intention to convert Democrats to Republicans or Republicans to Democrats. The slogan of the United Church group perhaps best fits the theory behind this program, "We do not care which party you vote for (or which office you may hold) as long as you do vote." This program, also is not intended to take the place of any other political action group but is meant to augment their activities in order to bring greater emphasis to the need for active participation in our political life.

In addition to our efforts to get every employee registered to vote, and through them to get every employee's family and friends to vote, we will attempt to keep you informed on legislative and governmental issues which will directly affect your citizenship."

Although there had been previous mailings to employees homes on public affairs issues, this letter was regarded by the company as "the opening shot in a fairly sustained program to educate and influence our employees in order to obtain a better business climate in Massachusetts." There have been subsequent mailings at a rate of one about every four or five weeks. These mailings have encouraged employees to register and vote in primary as well as general elections, and several have included AIM enclosures.

For example each employee was sent a copy of the award winning booklet "How Politics and Government Work in Massachusetts", and a detailed compilation of Massachusetts Legislators, which included a map showing the Senatorial Districts of Massachusetts. Use has also been made of the AIM's "Massachusetts Economic Service", which provides regular articles on business-related public issues for direct distribution in pamphlet form. For example, the letter dated May 11, 1961 enclosed the pamphlet "Somebody is Looking for Your Job", and stated "the cost of doing business in Massachusetts is higher than it is for our competition in other states. This puts us at a disadvantage."

One of these direct mailings was partisan in nature, however, and this led to an evening debate on the company premises between the company president and a spokesman from the international union that represents the company's employees. These events occurred just before the 1960 elections when the president departed from the usual non-partisan nature of company's public affairs communications and sent, from his home, a newspaper editorial citing "Labor Bossism" as an issue in the election. The president's accompanying letter said this editorial emphasized one of the reasons why he was not voting for John F. Kennedy in the November election.

Following the mailing of this letter, the local union president contacted the company's personnel director and inquired if the company president would be willing to debate this issue with a union representative in front of the employees. In response, an evening meeting was arranged. The company provided dessert, and the employees were encouraged to bring their families.

Approximately 200 persons attended the debate. According to the company president, a good time was had by all, although he feels that he drew a few more boos and catcalls than his labor opponent.

In addition to its direct mailing activities to its employees, this company's public affairs program has included the following activities:

1. Prior to the 1960 elections, about one dozen candiates from both parties were invited to the plant cafeteris for lunch, and an opportunity to speak and answer employee's questions.

2. The company has made known its willingness to encourage any employee interested in running for office, regardless of party, by agreeing to make facilitating arrangements on an ad hoc basis. To date nobody has taken advantage of this opportunity.

3. Two AIM films on the how and why of unemployment compensation and on "What Makes Massachusetts Tick" were shown to approximately 25 supervisory personnel in the company cafeteria, and there have occasionally been other meetings of management personnel to discuss public affairs problems on company time.

4. Plans are being made to conduct a more formal public affairs course for supervisory personnel, and, "if possible, following with all others interested on a voluntary basis from within the company."

5. The company personnel director is a member of the AIM's senatorial district business climate committee, which, in this case, consists of about 20 persons who meet monthly for a luncheon discussion of public affairs matters. This committee serves as a communications devise for contacting legislators, and its individual members are trying to screen the area for good candidates to back for election.

6. The company personnel director has appeared before state legislative committees to testify on several pending measures which, if enacted would affect the company's cost of doing business.

The activities of these two companies just described are probably slightly more vigorous than those of the "typical" firm participating in the AIM's Public Affairs Action program, but they are representative of the types of activity that the Association would like to encourage among its members. At the time these interviews were conducted (Summer 1961), about 100 Massachusetts firms were actively participating in the AIM's public affairs program, and business climate committees existed on paper at least for all but five of the state's senatorial districts. Since this time, there have been some disagreements among member firms on certain issues before the General Court, and John Hamilton, who supplied the program with unified and vigorously enthusiastic leadership, has left the AIM to become the assistant to the president of a member firm. Therefore, it is not possible to say with any certainty at the present time whether this program is gaining or losing momentum in Massachusetts, but the AIM feels that the program is very successful and they can point to some specific legislative accomplishments as evidence.

More will be said on these points after taking a much briefer look at the third major employer group actively operating on the Bay State Political Scene.

The Massachusetts Federation Of Taxpayers' Associations

The youngest of the three major employer organizations concerned with statewide legislation in the broad area of labor-management relations in Massachusetts is the Massachusetts Federation of Taxpayers' Associations. The organization was founded in 1932 "for the purpose of promoting greater efficiency and economy in government local, state, and federal". In 1961 the Federation stated that its "major objectives" are:

"1. To curb waste and extravagance in government.

2. To improve the business climate of Massachusetts.

3. To secure better legislation and legislative procedures.

4. To assist in the establishment of sound governmental policies and practices.

5. To contribute to the information and education of the citizens of Massachusetts in the affairs of their government." [7, p. 1]

The organization of the Taxpayers' Federation in 1932 reflected a general concern with problems of state and local taxation during the depression. In 1937 the Massachusetts Foundation was established as a voluntary trust to finance the Massachusetts Federation of Taxpayers' Associations through funds received from individuals and corporations. With the onset of recovery and the influx of defense contracts into Massachusetts some of the local interest began to fade and the number of local taxpayer organizations in Massachusetts is now 45 compared to a peak of 87 during the 1930's. The State Taxpayers' Federation is now generally recognized as a spokesman for the business community with a special competence in research and tax matters. It is organized along lines similar to the Greater Boston Chamber of Commerce and the Associated Industries of Massachusetts, and there is occasionally some overlapping of individual's membership on the boards of these organizations.

An executive committee, a legislative committee, and an organization committee along with the elected president, vice presidents, secretary, and treasurer, work with the 25-man board of directors in formulating federation policy. Frank J. Zeo is the Executive Director and chief administrative officer of the Federation. Until his untimely death late in 1961, W. Rea Long had served as the Federation's Assistant Executive Director, and Mr. Long had a reputation as a strong management protagonist in the areas of employment security and workmen's compensation.

The Federation's administrative staff is presently organized into the functional areas of public relations and public information, legislative services, research and statistics, municipal services, state services and business climate, and field operations with the 45 local associations.

In its Beacon Hill activities in the area of labor legislation, the Federation has most often been identified with the problems of financing and administering the workmen's compensation act and the employment security act, and with the relations between state and municipal employees and their governmental employers. Indeed, this brings us to the point that while the main employer groups in Massachusetts often have similar legislative interests and frequently cooperate on selected issues, they also are to some extent competitors for membership contributions. Each has developed some special areas of emphasis, reflecting in part differences in the composition of their membership, and reflecting in part the need for each of the groups to solicit some of the same large employers in the state. This had led to conflicting independent actions in some cases and also posed problems of which group should receive the major portion of the credit when a program favored by all of the groups is adopted.

More will be said on both the problems of employer and organized labor political unity, after examining the history of Massachusetts labor legislation in the subsequent chapters of this thesis.

REFERENCES - CHAPTER VIII

1. Associated Industries of Massachusetts, Your Stake in A.I.M. (Boston, 1962).

2. A.I.M.'s Public Affairs Tools for the Small Businessman (Boston, Undated Pamplet of the Associated Industries of Massachusetts).

3. Chamber of Commerce of the United States, Action Course in Practical Politics (Washington, May 1960).

4. Christian Science Monitor.

5. Greater Boston Chamber of Commerce Program of Work (Boston, January 1961).

6. Greater Boston Report, March 3, 1961, Vol. VI.

7. Massachusetts Federation of Taxpayers' Associations, Legislators Digest of Financial Facts (Boston, 1961).

8. Massachusetts State Labor Council, AFL-CIO, Newsletter, January-February, 1962, Vol. 3.

9. Lawrence F. Mihlon, "Should You Play the Game of Politics?", Factory, June 1960, Vol. 118, pp. 89-97.

10. Everett G. Martin, "State AFL-CIO Links Seen Partly Forged," Christian Science Monitor, October 10, 1955.

11. Massachusetts State Labor Council, AFL-CIO, Proceedings of the Second Annual Convention (Boston, October 7-9, 1959).

12. ______. Proceedings of the Fourth Annual Convention (Boston, September 27-30, 1961).

CHAPTER IX

EARLY (PRE 1930) MASSACHUSETTS LABOR LEGISLATION

Massachusetts' early ascendency in the field of protective labor legislation was briefly alluded to at the beginning of the preceding chapter. This chapter will trace in more detail the evolution of much of this legislation. It should be recognized from the outset, however, that in Massachusetts, as elsewhere, effective enforcement often lagged behind legislative enactment in this area. Indeed two early researchers concluded:

> Not only in her laws regulating conditions of labor, but in laws requiring their enforcement, does Massachusetts seem to stand toward the top in the United States. But she has fallen far behind our other states in providing the machinery for enforcing these laws. [21, p. 264]

This chapter's analysis of early Massachusetts labor legislation will be divided into two chronological periods: (1) legislation prior to 1900; and (2) legislation from 1900 to 1930. Legislation from 1930 to the end of World War II will be covered in Chapter X, and the post World War II legislative struggle in the area of labor legislation will be discussed in Part III of this thesis. Topically it might be best to discuss the legislation during each period covered in this chapter under the headings of child labor legislation, legislation regulating the hours of work, safety and sanitation legislation, workmen's compensation legislation, and legislation on wages, labor disputes, injunctions, unemployment compensation, and other matters of more recent concern. Due to the evolution of history, however, the topics of child labor, hours of work, and safety and sanitation will naturally receive the bulk of the attention in the earlier years, while the other subjects become more important as we begin to approach the contemporary scene.

In each period the forces working for and against the various pieces of legislation will be discussed, and comparisons between periods will be made. In addition to providing a background for a better understanding of the contemporary situation, this discussion of early Massachusetts labor legislation may help to make some now obscure and difficult to locate historical materials known and more easily accessible to present day readers.

Legislation Prior to 1900

As in England, child labor was the first type of labor problem to receive legislative attention in the United States. Following Pennsylvania's example, the Massachusetts' Senate investigated the question of child labor in 1825. Charles E. Persons has stated that "the investigation was largely inspired by anxiety lest the factories, through the constant employment of children, should foster the formation of an uneducated class." [20, p. 6] Although the investigating committee did not recommend legislation, agitation continued; and the movement for child labor laws became a part of a broader concern with the hours of labor in general.

Although the first child labor law was enacted in 1836, there were four more or less distinct waves of agitation before the 10 hour law for women and minors was secured in 1874. Short-lived labor organizations of various sorts were active throughout much of this period, but most of them suffered from loose organization and an inability to focus on any one single, well-defined measure at a time. As a result, much of the early labor legislation in Massachusetts owed its enactment to various humanitarian and reform elements, rather than to organized trade unions as such.

The Nature of Early Agitation for Legislation: The Ten-Hour Movement in Massachusetts

The Massachusetts branch of the Workingmen's Party, the New England Association of Farmers, Mechanics and other Workmen, and the Boston Trades Union all contributed to the first wave of agitation in the early 1830's.[1] These organizations did not attract

---

[1] The Workingmen's Party in Massachusetts touched both the question of child labor and that of shorter hours. A branch of the previously mentioned Workingmen's Party which originated in Philadelphia in 1827 was active in Massachusetts from 1830 to 1833. Persons states: "The General Court is said to have contained seven workingmen. The available information is meagre, but it seems evident that the party achieved no extensive or stable organization in Massachusetts." [20, p. 11] The title of this organization might also be deceptive as far as Massachusetts is concerned. John R. Commons observed: "Outside Philadelphia and New York the Workingmen's Party included small employers. In Boston its platform appealed to 'laboring men, mechanics, tradesmen, farmers, and others standing on the same level'... The class division of employer and employee was as yet limited to a few localities. Labor politics was a part of the general protest of the times raised by the 'productive classes' against 'aristocracy'.... Here were the beginnings not only of the general organization of labor, but also of humanitarian and reform movements." [4, pp. 327-29].

The New England Association of Farmers, Mechanics, and other Workingmen seems to have been an organization of a distinctly different

the support of the more influential members of the community, however, and Persons notes: "The regular press was deaf to their arguments and almost without exception joined in a conspiracy of silence so far as publishing accounts of their doings was concerned." [20, p. 17]

When the first child labor law was enacted in 1836, it was considered primarily as an educational matter. Its enactment was largely the result of the work of James G. Carter, who had written widely on the need for widespread education and ardently advocated the expansion of the public school system. Carter served as the chairman of the legislative committee on education in 1836, and is believed to have authored the bill which prohibited the employment of children under 15 years of age who had not attended school at least 3 months during the preceding year. There was no mention of the hours of labor, and there were no provisions for enforcement.

The child labor law was amended five times before 1867, when the whole matter was recodified and supposedly strengthened. In 1842 school committees were given the duty of prosecuting violations, and the first provisions for hours of labor were made when these 1842 amendments said children under 12 could not work more than 10 hours a day. These and other amendments had little effect, however, and Sarah Whittelsey states: "They were simply dead letters upon the statute books and stood at best for the ineffectual recognition of a social need, a cold statement of prevailing social sentiment". [23, p.10]

Footnote 1 continued from preceding page

type. It met annually from 1831 through 1834 and supported a periodical, The New England Artisan, which was probably the first labor paper in Massachusetts. This group sought shorter hours through economic as well as political means, and was soon confronted by an association of Boston merchants to oppose their demands.

The Boston Trades Union, formed in March 1934, also contributed to the agitation of the day, but not much more can be said about this group.

Nevertheless, the point can be made that at least some precedent had been set for the principle of legislative interference in the industrial rule making process. Following the enactment of child labor legislation in 1836, the issue of restricting a day's work to 10 hours became the primary target of various reform groups.

James Leiby has stated:

> "The ten-hour movement drew its strength from the mill workers and its leadership from philanthropists and politicians; it was quite distinct from the Eight-Hour Grand League, led by Ira Steward and George McNeill. The Eight-Hour League spoke for the organized trades, especially the smiths and machinists; it was strongest in the towns around Boston and found a voice in Boston's only labor newspaper." [10, pp. 44-45] [1]

The first direct pressure on the legislature for a 10-hour day through the medium of petitions addressed to the General Court came in 1842.[2] Most of the signatures on these petitions were presumably those of workers, and the issue began to assume party dimensions. Persons notes:

---

1 The 10-hour movement of this period received especially strong support in the Massachusetts cities of Lawrence, Lowell, and Fall River--all of which were predominantly textile towns.

2 Persons states:

> "It is noteworthy that these earliest petitions came from the towns in the southeastern section of the state where the foreign element was largest and where it had at first appeared. Here the effects of English example and the experience gained in English Agitations might be expected to show results before it was evident elsewhere." [20, p. 24]

> Seemingly, the Democrats had espoused the cause of the operatives. Most of those in authority in the Lowell mills were Whigs. In consequence there were numerous charges advanced on the one hand of undue corporate influence in state politics; and, on the other hand, of undue interference in the management of the mills suggested by political considerations. [20, p. 24]

Legislative petitions were submitted annually after 1842, and a new organization arose among the working men to give support to the 10-hour movement. The New England Association of Workmen was founded in 1844, and its organizational structure, as well as its name, resembled the old New England Workingmen's Association of 1831-34. Although the organization suffered from loose organization and a hetrogeneous membership, it sustained two publications, the Lynn Awl and the Voice of Industry, during its brief existence; and one of its constituent elements, the Female Labor Reform Association, composed initially of the "Lowell factory girls" under the leadership of Sarah G. Bagley, attracted widespread attention. The organization initially had great difficult focusing on any one issue due to the divisive influence of a Brook Farm contingent which advocated the abstract, utopia ideas of the Forrier movement. After shedding the more radical Socialistic influences, however, the group changed its name in 1846 to the New England Labor Reform League, and attracted the support of men like Francis Amasa Walker and Edward Tyrrel Channing.[1]

---

[1] Francis Amasa Walker was the Chairman of the Economics Department at M.I.T. He directed the U.S. Cencus of 1870, and was the long-time President of the American Statistical Association. He also served as President of the American Economics Association, and was perhaps the most respected economist in the nation at this time.

Edward Tyrrel Channing was the Professor of Rhetoric and Oratory at Harvard University, and he trained many of America's major writers of this period including Emerson, Thoreau, Holmes, and Edward Everett Hale.

The importuning of the petitioners resulted in legislative consideration of 10-hour legislation in 1845 and 1846, when a committee of the House and a committee of the Senate reported in respective years. Both committees refused to recommend action, however, and their reports were thoroughly impregnated with the laissez faire doctrine, that dominated the social thought of the times. Nevertheless, they reviewed both sides of the case; and since much the same arguments lie at the foundations of subsequent labor legislation, they may be worth a short review.

The petitioners largely based their case on two grounds, the effect of excessive hours on: (1) the health of the operatives, and (2) lack of time for "mental and moral culture". Both committees rejected these contentions and went on to advance their own arguments in opposition. They contended the existing conditions did not injure health, degrade morals, or result in the formation of an ignorant factory class. They found most of the factory operatives were farm girls who worked in the mills for a few years, saved a few hundred dollars, and then returned to their home to marry and rear families. They contended that these farmer's daughters inherited strong constitutions and possessed good health as a result of an early life spent in country districts. They came from homes where the strictest morals prevailed, and their education had been attended to before they entered the mills.

The report also argued that industrious Massachusetts workers, unlike the illiterate masses covered by English law, were quite capable of making their own bargains, and there was no ground for legislative interferences. It was also contended that such legislation would make competition with outside mills impossible, and would surely result in a reduction in wages and eventually lead to a complete collapse of the Massachusetts economy.

Following these adverse reports, the New England Labor Reform League faded; and it was not in existence when agitation for the 10-hour law was resumed in 1850. In the interim between 1846 and 1850, significant changes had taken place in the composition of the factory workers, due to a sharp recession in the cotton industry and increased immigration into Massachusetts.

In the years of distress, the New England women in the Massachusetts mills had returned to their homes by thousands; and they never returned in full numbers. Instead, their places were filled with Irish immigrants. The Irish were also used as permanent strike-breakers during the depression, since they exhibited a greater willingness to accept lower wages and to accede to the demands of their employer than did their native counterparts in the labor force.

This change in the composition of the workforce naturally weakened the laissez faire arguments against 10 hour legislation. The law's advocates took full advantage of this circumstance; and one committee, led by the poet John Greenleaf Whittier, circulated an open letter stating:

> The effect of the continuance of the existing system (of hours) must be to drive from our manufacturing villages the best portion of the native population and to fill their places with a vagrant, dependent and irresponsible class. [20, p. 56]

The years of legislative indifference to 10-hour petitions were now past. The forces of advocacy also were of a different nature during this third period of agitation. Many of the older elements of the 1840's remained active, but there was no comparable female element. For the first time, a limited, single purpose organization was established to enact a 10-hour law in Massachusetts. Leadership was assumed by a member of the Massachusetts General Court, James M. Stone. Stone was assisted by two other members of the legislature in the persons of Benjamin F. Butler, and William S. Robison, whose paper the Lowell American was devoted to the advocacy of the principles of the Free Soil Party.

Under this leadership the "workingmen" of Massachusetts were urged to meet and elect delegates to a Ten Hour State Convention. At this convention, a five man executive committee was set up to give the movement more direction and coordination than the preceding 10-hour movements. Named the Ten Hour State Central Committee, this executive group arranged three statewide conventions, sponsored meetings in all the industrial cities of the state, secured petitions for the General Court, and tried to place "10-hour men" in the legislature. The organization functioned from 1850 to 1856, and the agitation reached its heights in 1852 and 1853.[1]

---

[1] During the early 1850's, elections in the mill towns often turned on the 10-hour issue. Feeling ran exceptionally high at Lowell in 1851, when it was ruled that the winning Coalition (Democrat and Free Soil) ticket did not receive a majority of the votes cast and a second runoff election would have to be held between the Coalitionists and the Whigs. Persons notes: "It soon became noised abroad that the Booth Corporation through its agent, the Honorable Linus Child, had threatened

In the legislature, there were majority reports against and minority reports in favor of 10-hour petitions in 1850, 1852, and 1853. In 1855, the House committee reported unanimously in favor of a 10-hour measure. In 1856, a majority of the Senate committee did likewise. The 1850 minority report was accompanied by a carefully drawn 10-hour bill, which came to a vote in the House where it was defeated. The bill was also defeated in the House in 1852. In 1853 the bill passed the House with a majority of 42 votes (107 Coalitionists and 30 Whigs in favor, and 6 Coalitionists and 89 Whigs opposed). The Senate, however, amended the bill to make "ten hours a day's labor for all

---

Footnote 1 continued from preceding page

to discharge any man voting the Coalition ticket in the second election." [20, p. 71]

Although the Coalitionists also carried the second election, a legislative investigation was demanded in 1852, and Persons notes:

> "The majority of the committee reported a bill which proposed to make any interference, by threats, bribes or menance, with the right of suffrage of an employee a misdemeanor, punishable by a $100 fine or one year's imprisonment. With this the controversy was allowed to rest." [20, p. 74]

Although there is no evidence that an employers' association was formally organized to oppose the State Ten Hour Central Committee, there is evidence of united employer effort. In September 1852, just a month prior to elections, there was a simultaneous reduction of hours to 11 in the machine shops of Lowell, Lawrence, Manchester, Biddeford, and Holyoke where a male labor force predominated. In the factories where the women did not have the vote, however, the hours remained as before.

classes unless otherwise provided by contract. The House refused to concur in this emasculation, and the bill was lost.[1]

After this narrow defeat, however the 10-hour movement began to lose strength. The corporations simultaneously extended their

---

[1] As this result indicates the opponents of 10-hour legislation, which were always stronger in the Senate than in the House, developed new tactics during this period of increased agitation. In addition to continuing their laissez faire arguments and their predictions of adverse economic consequences, they began to concede support of legislation of "general application" with provisions for "special contracts".

Persons states:

> "The idea that the law should be of general application, together with the mischievous suggestion that the law should provide only for the legal length of a day's labor in the absence of contract ... was throughout the contest the favorite method of attack adopted by opponents of the measure. On the one score they appealed confidently to the agricultural interest for support in defeating the proposed legislation; on the other, pretended friends and weak-kneed opponents preferred innocuous acts as a sop to public opinion, which they knew would be absolutely destitute of effect." [20, p. 49]

The proponents of effective 10-hour legislation opposed special contracts on the grounds that there could be no real bargaining between an individual laborer and a large corporation or factory; and they sought only to regulate hours in the factories, where they felt the worse abuses existed. In response to the arguments for general application, they claimed that more limited legislation would not be discriminatory, since in most trades outside the factories the old tradition of working from sun to sun had already given way to the 10-hour system.

By this time the 10-hour advocates could also cite experience to refute the claim that shorter hours would lead to wage cuts and loss of business for Massachusetts' industry. The English experience was said to support the contention that factories could cut hours and still remain competetive. It was also claimed that some Massachusetts industries outside the factories had already cut their hours with no wage reductions or loss of business. Despite these arguments, the opponents continued to prevail by an increasingly smaller margin.

concessions to the female operatives in the mills, and 11 hours became the general rule in September 1853. Perhaps as a result of these concessions, the entire Whig ticket was elected in Lowell in 1854, and Robison's Lowell American was driven from the city. Probably more significant, however, was the fact that the Civil War was approaching. This brought new problems and new tasks to the members of the Free Soil Party, and the 10-hour reform was temporarily disregarded after 1856.

Due to the wartime labor shortage, many women and children were pressed into factory employment. The number of foreign laborers in the Massachusetts mills also increased rapidly, and to the Irish were now added large numbers of French from Canada. Often these groups were recruited as whole families and employed in the mills as a unit. Such conditions attracted much humanitarian sentiment, and the spirit of the times made for a sympathetic attitude toward shorter hour legislation. Some leaders from the anti-slavery crusade enlisted directly in the movement--the most notable example being Wendell Phillips, who frequently spoke and wrote urging shorter hours during the late 1860's.

Due to the more spectacular demands of Ira Steward's 8-hour proposals, however, the 10-hour movement in Massachusetts was not resumed immediately after the war. Steward succeeded in revising The Labor Reform Association, with himself as Secretary, and he later formed the Eight Hour Grand League to capture the enthusiasm of most of the labor organizations in New England. The agitation of these groups, however, was as short lived as it was strenuous.

A commission was appointed in 1865 and 1866 to investigate prevailing employment practices regarding the hours of work, but they reported against a shorter hour measure of any sort--let alone an eight-hour day. As a concession to the demands for reform, however, the child labor laws were ineffectively revised in 1867; and in 1869, the Massachusetts Bureau of Statistics of Labor was established "to investigate the relation which the reduction of hours of labor bears to the industrial, commercial and social interests of the State." Attaining no real results, therefore, the Grand Eight Hour League lost its effectiveness; and the field was soon cleared for the revival of the more moderate 10-hour movement. In this respect, Persons notes:

> The character of the movement was somewhat modified - partly because of the progressive change in the character of the mill population; partly because of the coming of new leaders to the support of the old and tried organizers of the movement; but most of all because of the change in the nation's leadership and ruling ideals - due to the spirit aroused in the war. There is less insistence on actual injury to the health of operatives; more on his right to share, through enlarged leisure, in the higher things of life. There is an absence of socialistic or communistic ideas; a pervading and all-including spirit of humanitarianism. One hears less often that labor is the sole source of value; very frequently that all deserve a fair share in that which all have created. [20, p. 102]

After being elected Speaker of the Massachusetts House in 1866 and 1867, James M. Stone resumed his position as the leader of the 10-hour forces. Although there were various forms of labor organization in existence at the time, Stone's 10-hour men do not seem to have been directly connected to any of them. While they appealed directly to workingmen for the bulk of their support, their organization was quite distinct. Assuming the title Short Time Amalgamated Association, the organization resorted to the methods employed earlier in calling Ten-Hour State Conventions and in establishing Short Time Committees in the industrial cities.

Before the return of the soldiers from the war had removed the temporary advantage of labor scarcity, there had been some successful 10-hour strikes; but these victories were later nullified when the mills unilaterally returned to an 11-hour day. The first real break in the ranks of the employers came in 1868, when the Atlantic Cotton Mills at Lawrence installed a ten-hour system in advance of legislation, not forced by threat of strikes, and with the full approval and support of the Agent, William Gray. Mr. Gray became an enthusiastic supporter of the ten-hour reform, and was instrumental in the final legislative victory.

Although the arguments of both sides were well known by this time, the right of the legislature to regulate the hours of men was still disputed. The advocates decided they could get more humanitarian support by limiting the act to women and minors, and they also felt any such law's practical application would inevitably affect the men employed in the factories. The old attempt to limit the law's application to incorporated companies was also given over, since the 10-hour system was now widespread outside the factories, and the contention that such legislation was "partial" or "discriminatory" no longer held. Therefore, the bill reported by the General Court's Joint Labor Committee in 1871 provided that:

> No minor under the age of eighteen, and no female over that age, shall be employed in laboring by any person, firm or coproration in this Commonwealth in the manufacture of cotton, woolen, jute or silk fabrics more than ten hours in any one day, or sixty hours in any one week; except when it is necessary to make repairs to prevent the stoppage or interruption of the ordinary running of the mill or machinery. [20, p. 123]

This measure was passed by the House in 1871, 1872, and 1873, only to be defeated in the Senate. In 1874, however, the bill carried both houses; and it was passed with Governor Washburn's active support. Although the penalty clause of the 1874 laws was rendered ineffective by amending it to apply only to "willful" violations, this provision was strengthened in 1879, when an attempt to repeal the law was turned back and the act was strengthened.

A considerable amount of time and space has been devoted to this discussion of the first legislative limitation on the hours of work in Massachusetts. Although the law was not rigorously enforced for many years after its initial enactment, its real significance lies beyond its immediate impact. Its mere passage was an index of the changing political sentiment of the times, and its subsequent importance as a precedent merits the rather detailed attention which has been given to the long period of agitation proceding its final passage. This study also gives an insight into the complexities of agitation and parliamentary tactics often necessary to enact a measure into law, and it is interesting to note that the drive for a 10-hour law resulted in some concessions in other areas, such as the child labor amendments and the creation of the Massachusetts Bureau of Statistics of Labor in 1869. Since many of the arguments and techniques used during the 10-hour battles were later applied to other types of legislation, we can now spare ourselves the necessity of repetition.

This rather lengthly discussion was also necessary since the different forces supporting the 10-hour cause during this period were somewhat complex and amorphous. Although the driving forces behind most labor legislation in Massachusetts becomes easier to analyze following the creation of the Massachusetts State Branch of the American Federation of Labor in 1887, this is so because this body published the proceedings of its annual convention, not because it became the prime mover in the field of protective labor legislation. It is important to understand that there was a substantial body of "reform" sentiment and an increasing number of poorly-treated immigrant voters outside the ranks of organized labor. Even after permanent labor unions were formed in Massachusetts, the majority of them catered for a long time only to a skilled and limited minority of the working class; and they often had to obtain a broader base of support to obtain the legislative enactments they desired.

This tends to reflect the general situation with regard to organized labor's political activities throughout the country at this time. The Knights of Labor were active advocates of child labor laws as well as certain other types of labor legislation, but there is no record of their particular influence in Massachusetts. Elizabeth Brandeis has noted:

> "Many of labor's political objectives in the earlier years were not labor legislation--as that term in used today. Statistics providing for universal suffrage, free public schools, and free homesteads were labor only in the sense that organized labor sought their passage. As for labor legislation proper, the amount secured and even the amount sought by the labor movement was small." [3, p. 399]

Once the principle of legislative interference was established by the limited 10-hour legislation of 1874, however, it later proved easier to secure other types of labor legislation. But it proved to be much easier to amend and improve existing legislation than to create new areas of legislative enactment. Between 1874 and 1887 primary attention was devoted to expanding and improving the existing child labor laws and the limited 10-hour law for women and minors to make them enforceable. After 1887, increasing attention was devoted to the safety hazards of industrial employment, sanitation in industry, and industrial homework. There was also some other miscellaneous labor legislation passed between 1874 and 1900 dealing with the methods and frequency of wage payments, the problem of industrial disputes, union labels and union organization. Each of these areas will be summarized briefly.

Late Nineteenth Century Labor Legislation

Child Labor — There were as many as 15 amendments or new child labor laws enacted in Massachusetts between the first recodification in 1867 and the year 1892. These measures dealt with various occupational coverage and enforcement procedures, and the whole body of child labor legislation was recodified for the second time in 1894. A statute of 1898 raised the age limit to 14 and barred children under that age from employment in "factory, workshop and mercantile establishments." It also imposed somewhat stricter conditions concerning certificates of birth, age, and schooling. A law completely prohibiting the employment of minors in brewing and other beer bottling establishments was passed in 1899.

Hours of Work -- Amendments to reduce evasion of the 10-hour law for women and minors were added after 1879, and coverage was extended to mechanical and mercantile establishments as well as textile factories. Provisions for meal hours were added, and night work was prohibited by women and minors from 10 pm to 6 am. In 1892 the hours for women and minors in manufacturing were limited to 58 per week and this reduction was subsequently extended to non-manufacturing occupations.[1]

Some special hours legislation regarding particular occupational groups regardless of age or sex was also enacted during this period. In 1896, a 9 hour day was enacted for employees of the Commonwealth. This was extended to counties and municipalities in 1891, and in 1893 to all manual labor on state government contracts. A later statute of 1899, curtailing hours to 8 per day, was made optional, depending upon acceptance by the voters of the cities and towns. In 1893 another special restriction reduced the hours for street car conductors, motormen, and drivers to a daily service of 10 within 12 consecutive hours, and required that extra time receive extra compensation.

---

1 The legislative struggles and enforcement problems leading to these amendments and expansions of coverage in the child labor and hours laws are discussed in some detail in Clara M. Beyer. [2, pp. 20-31]

Safety Legislation and Early Employer's Liability Laws -- The first Massachusetts enactment involving safety conditions in places of employment came in 1877. This act followed an 1874 investigation of the Bureau of Statistics of Labor, which resulted in the decision that industrial safety conditions constituted an appropriate field of legislative activity. The law of 1877 was primarily concerned with guarding dangerous machinery, regulating the storage of explosives, and providing fire escapes and exits in case of emergency. Gradually, more explicit and more stringent inspection procedures and building certificates were required.

The drive which eventually resulted in the Massachusetts Workmen's Compensation Act was also initiated during this period, but it did not achieve success until after the turn of the century. An act of 1877 declared void all special contracts which enabled an employer to exempt himself from all responsibility in industrial accidents involving his employees, but the employer's common law defenses were left intact. In 1882 the Bureau of Labor investigated the question of employer's liability in industrial accidents and issued a report in favor of enacting legislation similar to the then existing English laws. No action was taken on this report, but a law requiring the reporting of fatal and serious injuries was passed in 1886.

The first steps toward an employer's liability law came in an act of 1887. This statute was not considered satisfactory, however, since the common law defenses were only slightly changed and the maximum damages allowed were $4,000 except in special cases of death, which included injury. In these cases the maximum claim allowed varied from $500 to $5,000 depending on the culpability of the employer and the amount he contributed to the total of an employee's benefit fund. This law was amended slightly in 1888 and in 1906, before it was eventually made obsolete by the Workmen's Compensation Act of 1911.

Sanitation and Industrial Homework -- Special laws concerning general sanitation, cleanliness, and ventilation of factories and workshops were enacted in 1887 and 1888. At first, these laws concerned only manufacturing establishments; but later they were extended to mercantile establishments and other industries.

In addition to the ordinary requirements of the general sanitary laws concerning tenements, two acts were passed in 1891 and 1892 to regulate the "sweating system" of homework on clothing and wearing apparel. The law provided for the registration of tenement workshops, and required that tenement-made goods be clearly labeled. Subsequent amendments made definitions clearer and required workers to obtain licenses from the police department before receiving employment. These requirements were further clarified in an act of 1898.

Miscellaneous Labor Legislation -- In addition to some early Massachusetts lein laws designed to guarantee that workers received wages they had already earned, there was also some agitation for wage laws regulating the method of payment. The first law of this type was passed in 1875 and provided that where a worker was required to give notice before leaving under penalty of forfeiting any part of his wages earned, a similar penalty should be enforceable against the employer discharging without notice, except for incapacity or misconduct.

Although certain Fall River unions began agitation for weekly payment of wages after this concession was refused by employers in 1875, the first weekly payment law was not passed until 1879; and then it applied only to city laborers. In 1886, however, it was extended to certain corporations, and subsequent amendment after subsequent amendment steadily widened its scope. The use of special contracts by employers to exempt themselves from the obligation of weekly payments was finally forbidden in 1896.

The regulation of fines levied upon workers began with regard to weavers in 1887, and such fines were entirely forbidden in 1891. This law was declared unconstitutional in 1892, however, but subsequent acts prohibited the "grading" of weavers wages, except for imperfections pointed out to the weaver, and by amounts agreed to by both parties.

In 1894 provisions were made for more complete information for piece workers, and penalties for time lost during machine stoppages were enjoined in 1898.

Massachusetts attempted to meet the problem of labor disputes by establishing boards of arbitration. Before 1886 there was a system of local boards open to the voluntary recourse of disputants. In 1886 a permanent 3-man State Board of Conciliation and

Arbitration was installed as a sort of court of appeal from decisions of the local boards. Since the local boards had little to do, however, the state board had even less; and in 1887 the board was given the power of initiative in tendering its services. It was also given the ordinary court powers of subpoena. The powers of initiative and subpoena made the Massachusetts Board much more powerful than a similar board in New York, but there is no evidence that the Board being a major force in Bay State labor-management relations in the nineteenth century.[1]

It was made illegal to counterfeit trade union labels in 1892, and there were also some rather innocuous laws relating to the legal aspects of union organization during this period. In 1875 a law was passed forbidding unionists to interfere with the employment of nonmembers. This was supposedly balanced in 1892 when employers were prohibited from intimidating their workers in order to prevent them from joining unions. In 1888 a general law was passed allowing labor unions to acquire the legal rights of an incorporated body, but no unions acted under its provisions. Following a ruling of the state law department that union benefit payments made them subject to the laws regulating beneficiary organizations, a law was passed in 1899 specifically exempting unions from the general insurance laws.

---

[1] For comparisons of the Massachusetts Board and the New York Board, see [8, pp. 187-88] and [9, pp. 25-26].

Just how influential organized labor was in securing much of this latter legislation is difficult to say. As can be seen from the above summary there was a substantial increase in the amount of labor legislation after 1887, which was the year that the Massachusetts State Branch of the American Federation of Labor was created. Since there were several sporadic citizens groups active in various reform causes during this period, however, this coincidence may be more indicative of public opinion favoring labor organization than labor unions influencing public opinion. A brief review of the early history of the State Branch tends to support this view, since the organization did not grow very rapidly at first and it apparently became interested in politics only gradually.

Formation of the Massachusetts State Branch of the AFL

The Massachusetts State Branch of the American Federation of Labor, which later became the Massachusetts State Federation of Labor in 1928, was organized in August 1887 at a convention called by the Cigarmaker's Local No. 97 of Boston. The call to convention outlined the object of the proposed state branch as follows:

> to encourage the formation of local trades and labor unions; for advancing the interests of the working classes, both in organization and in legislation; and for adopting a plan of general assistance in case of strikes, lockouts and other difficulties. [5, p. 12]

At the organization meeting held in Boston's Pythian Hall, opposition to the Knights of Labor was voiced, and the presence of

Samuel Gompers himself assured that this new state organization would be definitely affiliated with the newly formed and growing AFL. G. G. Wilkins, of the Boston Typographical Union No. 13, was elected President, and Frank K. Foster of the same union, who became the driving force of the organization in its early years, was elected Treasurer. Despite the mention of legislative action in the call to convention, however, Heintz and Whitney state "It is to be noted that little sentiment was expressed at this first convention as to definite legislative action, and the theory of having a legislative agent was not brought up." [5, p. 17]

At a second state convention held in October, 1887, however, a legislative committee was created under the leadership of Frank Foster. It was resolved to continue agitation for the 8-hour day and to demand the strict enforcement of child labor laws. The desirability of endorsing candidates for the state legislature was also discussed, and the precedent was set at this time that such endorsements should not be given. There was some socialistic third-party sentiment in the Massachusetts labor movement at this time, however, and the question of political activity again came to the foreground in the 1891 convention. Although the third-party forces were defeated, a resolution was passed urging that an effort be made to have the State Branch recognized by all political parties; and Heintz and Whitney report:

> At the convention in 1891, the legislative committee formulated the first definite legislative program to be adopted in regular convention by the Federation; this

> marked the beginning of the emphasis on legislation that eventually was to become one of the principal characteristics of the State Branch. The recommendations of this report, as adopted, were: Fifty-eight hours for factory women and children, eight-hour law for public employees, and raising the school age to sixteen. [5, p. 23]

After 1892, legislative questions began to receive more emphasis, but the State Branch still failed to attain any great prominence before the turn of the century. In 1893, Frank Foster initiated a campaign within the Federation to encourage direct legislation through the initiative and referendum. He felt this would give labor more influence over legislation than any attempt to unite with a political party, and a bid to cooperate with the Socialists-Labor Party was rejected in 1894. The State Board of Conciliation Arbitration was subject to strong criticism at the 1895 convention. The amount of child labor remaining in thetextile industry was also deplored, and a resolution in favor of the income tax was passed. The most dramatic political step taken by the State Branch during the nineteenth century, however, came at the convention of 1896. In that year a resolution was adopted pledging the opposition of the organization to the candidacy of William Murray Crane for the Lt. Governorship on the grounds that he had an interest in the North Adams Transcript, which had experienced trouble with organized labor. Crane was nominated on the Republican ticket nonetheless, and riding this party's "escalator" he later served as the Governor of Massachusetts from 1900 to 1903.

Given these rather modest beginnings late in the nineteenth century, it is rather obvious that much of the legislation previously discussed cannot be attributed solely to the efforts of the organized labor movement in Massachusetts, or at least not to the efforts of the State Branch of the AFL.

In her 1929 analysis of the History of Labor Legislation for Women in Three States (Massachusetts, New York, and California) Clara M. Beyer of the Women's Bureau of the U.S. Department of Labor discussed the support for women's labor legislation under nine headings: organized labor; state labor officials; bureaus of labor statistics; special legislative committees or commissions; governors; pioneering employers; social, civic, philanthropic, and church groups; factual studies; and "the spirit of the time". The role of these various forces in early child labor legislation and the 10 hour law of 1874 has already been traced in some detail. Much the same story apparently holds true for most of the other legislation mentioned in this chapter up to this point. Although organized labor, as such, did not play a dominant role in the earliest legislation its influence increased in later years and more will be said on this shortly.

With regard to state labor officials, Mrs. Beyer states:

> During the eighties and nineties the factory inspectors of Massachusetts, through their director, the chief of the district police, were instrumental in securing amendments to the existing labor laws making evasion less easy. But they never took the initiative as did the New York inspectors. [2, p. 3]

Although the Massachusetts Bureau of the Statistics of Labor advocated and supported the early hours law for women and children, over the long run Mrs. Beyer indicated "The information furnished by the

Massachusetts Bureau of Statistics of Labor was as often used against the legislative proposals of labor as for them. The tendency of the bureau was to hold back legislation rather than to promote it". [2, p. 6] With regard to special legislative committees or commissions she stated they "have played no part in the history of labor legislation for women in California, have had a minor influence in Massachusetts, and have been one of the largest determining factors in the labor legislative history of New York." [2, p. 6]

The influence of Governor Washburn and the Atlantic Cotton Mill's Agent, William Gray, on the 60 hour law of 1874 has already been noted, and similar elements were at work in securing later legislation--particularly in the battle to reduce the legal workweek from 60 to 58 for women in textile mills in 1892. Mrs. Beyer has stated: "The support given the movement for shorter hours by Governor Russel in his message of 1891 and again in 1892 was a deciding factor in breaking down the senate opposition." [2, p. 30]

Organizations which might best be classified under the broad heading of "social, civic, philanthropic, and church groups," also played a major role in the legislation enacted prior to 1900. With specific regard to Massachusetts labor legislation before the turn of the century, Mrs. Beyer later indicated that various civic-minded reform groups played a key role in extending the women's hours laws from the textile industry to other non-manufacturing mercantile establishments. She said:

> The source of the support for mercantile legislation in the earlier days is indicated by the persons appearing at the hearing in 1888. Among the speakers in favor were two doctors, a college professor, a representative of the Knights of Labor, and Harriet Robinson, a former mill worker who had become a writer of some prominence. . . .
>
> Later an organization known as the Federal Labor Union, made up largely of women friendly to the labor movement and a few labor leaders, became the active supporter of hours legislation for the mercantile industry . . ..
>
> Almost immediately upon its organization in 1898, the Consumers' League of Massachusetts took the lead in the campaign for legislation governing the work of women in stores. . . .
>
> Feeling that the facts of extremely long hours justified legislation, the consumers' league began to secure the necessary public support. Women's clubs were enlisted in the ranks of supporters, among them the civic department of the Twentieth Century Club, the Massachusetts Association of Working Women's Clubs, and the Women's Educational and Industrial Union. These organizations all backed the 58-hour bill for women in mercantile establishments introduced by the Federal Labor Union in 1899. The measure failed to pass. The following year the consumers' league, in cooperation with the civic division of the Twentieth Century Club and the Union for Industrial Progress - formerly the Federal Labor Union - had a bill for the extension of the 58-hour week to the mercantile industry drawn up and introduced in the legislature. The hearing was well planned and widely attended. The legislature was duly impressed and the bill, amended to allow an exemption for the month of December, was passed and signed by the governor. [2, pp. 44-46]

Factual studies have been a part of practically all of the legislation considered in this chapter, but it is difficult to isolate their influence. Much of the data has been gathered by state officials, special legislative commissions, or independent civic groups already mentioned. The "spirit of the time", however, remains as perhaps the most nebulous of the nine factors mentioned by Mrs. Beyer. Yet it also looms as one of the most significant--particularly if one takes a long view and compares the general acceptance of modern labor legislation with the long drawn out struggles previously mentioned as necessary to secure anything as basic as an enforceable 10 hours a day, 6 days a week law for women and minors in factory occupations. The reformist spirit aroused in Massachusetts by the passions surrounding the Civil War no doubt aided the cause for labor reform legislation at that time, and the reforming zeal which swept the country at the turn of the century also aided in the passage of labor legislation in the next period we are about to examine.

Since a special reforming "spirit of the time" was necessary to get much early labor legislation passed, this meant that the general "spirit of the time" obviously was not overly receptive to this type of legislation over most of the period discussed to date. This point has to deal with the phenomenon of "unorganized interests" mentioned in Chapter II of this thesis. Massachusetts employers did not formally organize in opposition to much of the early Massachusetts labor legislation, although they did sometimes act in concert as has been pointed out. The *laissez faire* spirit of the nineteenth century and the division of powers between branches of government provided strong institutional obstacles to new labor legislation and are much more responsible for the long delays in obtaining early labor legislation than the organized opposition of employers as such. The employers were forced to organize only when the general "rules of the game" or unorganized interests of

Massachusetts society no longer served as an adequate safeguard for their own interest.

For a long time the opposition to reforms in labor legislation could rely on the inertia of the status quo and the strong element of individual freedom in the American ethos to present obstacles that were extremely difficult to overcome without considerable efforts on the part of proponents, which explains why these groups were the first to organize and tended to attract the most publicity. As the proponents continued to hammer away at their cause and arouse the elements of humanitarianism and sympathy for the underdog in the American ethos, however, the underlying consensus of the unorganized interests began to shift from general opposition to at least neutrality, and towards the end of the century the employers in the textile industry formally organized for political purposes. There are also signs that organized labor in Massachusetts was becoming more effective as such in supporting "humanitarian" legislation late in the century despite the avowedly narrow purposes of the AFL, which was the dominant element in the Massachusetts labor movement after 1887.

Clara M. Beyer has stated:

> Ostensibly, the organized workmen supported labor legislation for women on grounds of humanitarianism, but in reality self-protection was the dominant motive. In the first place, by securing shorter hours for women through legislation they hoped to obtain the same shorter hours for themselves; and, in the second place, they wanted to prop up by legislation and make standard the shorter hours that the more strongly organized trades had secured by bargaining. [2, p. 2]

Thus by the time that the opponents and proponents lined up for the struggle that reduced the legal work week for women and minors in textiles from 60 to 58 in 1892, Mrs. Beyer could state:

> Both parties to the controversy were fairly well organized by 1890. The textile manufacturers had formed the Arkwright Club and had a paid legislative agent to plead their cause and to organize their defense. Labor, on the other hand, could marshal the State Branch of the American Federation of Labor, the city central bodies, the Amalgamated Building Trades Union, the State Alliance of the Knights of Labor, and nearly every international and State organization, besides the local craft unions. The textile unions and central labor bodies had a joint legislative committee with an agent at the capitol. The State Branch of the American Federation of Labor also had a legislative agent to look afters its interests. [2, p. 29]

The total strength of the labor movement in Massachusetts before the turn of the century does not appear to have reached 100,000 however, so that it was by no means a dominant influence in Massachusetts politics at this time as the previously mentioned failure to unseat Murry Crane in 1896 pointed out.

All of these forces helping to explain the course of Massachusetts labor legislation prior to 1900 will now be examined during the period from 1900-1930.

Legislative Advance and Stagnation: 1900-1930

Following the prosperity in Massachusetts and in the nation as a whole at the turn of the century, the fortunes of the Massachusetts State Branch of the American Federation of Labor improved considerably from their nineteenth century beginnings. This period initiated an age of reform throughout the country, and

Massachusetts gradually became the acknowledged leader in enacting the popular reforms of the day. The anti-trust and reform sentiment of the times also aided union growth to some extent, and in Massachusetts more local unions began to participate actively in the State Branch of the AFL. The number of local unions and central bodies represented at the annual conventions of the state branch jumped from 44 in 1899 to 70 in 1900. This number increased to 82 in 1901 and 97 in 1902.

Changing Strength of the Massachusetts Labor Movement

Table 35 shows the number of local and central labor bodies represented at the annual convention from the founding of the state

TABLE 35 - Number of Local and Central Bodies Represented at the Annual Convention of the Massachusetts State Branch, AFL, 1887-1935

Year	Number	Year	Number
1887	125	1916	197
----	---N.A.	1917	195
1897	42	1918	203
1898	40	1919	143
1899	44	1920	172
1900	70	1921	172
1901	82	1922	133
1902	97	1923	121
1903	103	1924	114
1904	95	1925	131
1905	89	1926	129
1906	99	1927	146
1907	115	1928	142
1908	102	1929	150
1909	95	1930	149
1910	123	1931	143
1911	128	1932	152
1912	135	1933	148
1913	168	1934	143
1914	201	1935	204
1915	179		

Source: Heintz and Whitney, [5, pp. 115-16].

branch in 1887 to 1935, except for the years 1888-1896 which are not available. Although these figures represent only a small fraction of the total number of local unions in Massachusetts reported by the Department of Labor and Industries during these years, it should be recognized that not all of the affiliated organizations sent delegates to the annual conventions. For example, in 1930 the auditors report to the convention listed 230 locals and 17 central labor unions affiliated with the State Branch in 1929. Yet only 150, or about half, sent delegates to the convention in that year. Similar detailed auditor's reports are not available for the other years covered in Table 35, but the 230 local unions affiliated in 1929 were paying, or owed, dues on a reported membership of 52,428. Since dues were involved, this figure was not likely to be exaggerated, and these 52,428 members in the 230 locals represented 27.4% of the total of 191,528 members reported by 1,142 local unions to the State Department of Labor and Industries in 1929. This would seem to indicate that the larger and presumably the more influential unions in the state tended to affiliate with the State Branch of the AFL, since the average size of affiliated locals (228) was a good bit (36%) larger than the average local in the state (168).

Coming as it did in 1930 after a long period of decline in union membership during the 1920's, this report may have understated the average number of affiliates and overstated the average size of affiliated unions, since many small locals may have disaffiliated with the State Branch during the 1920's for economy reasons.

Nationally, the upsurge of union membership, which jumped from 440,000 in 1897 to 2,067,000 in 1904, caused a reaction by the employers of the country and the NAM launched a vigorous open shop campaign. There is also evidence of increasing employer opposition to trade unions in Massachusetts after 1904, and from 1908 to the outbreak of the First World War the State Branch devoted its economic efforts largely to consolidating its previous gains. The office of Secretary-Treasurer was made a permanent salaried position in 1913. This allowed a full time official to devote much more time to the business of securing affiliations, and the results are reflected in Table 35 by the net increase of 66 affiliates attending the convention of 1914 compared to the convention of 1912. A permanent headquarters for the State Branch was established in 1914 which may also have served to increase the effectiveness of the organization. Since the Secretary-Treasurer was the only full-time paid position in the organization, the power of leadership gradually moved to this office rather than to that of the Presidency, which slowly became more or less honorary in meaning depending upon the incumbent. Dennis D. Driscoll of the Horseshoers Local No. 5 in Boston served as the Secretary-Treasurer from 1899-1911, and he was succeeded by Martin T. Joyce of the Boston Electrical Workers 103. Joyce then served as Secretary-Treasurer until his death in 1931.

During the doldrums of the 1920's, the duties of Legislative Agent were added to those of the Secretary-Treasurer as an economy move in 1925; and these duties remained combined until the merger with the CIO industrial union council in 1958.

The Massachusetts picture with respect to labor legislation from 1900 to 1930 roughly follows the trend of union membership in the state during these years, but these trends are only indirectly related.

During the first decade and a half of the twentieth century, organized labor formed a constituent element of a highly successful reform coalition which succeeded in enacting legislation dealing with the political machinery, business regulation, and educational system of Massachusetts, as well as labor legislation. Following the state constitutional convention during and after the First World War, however, the coalition disintegrated; and during the 1920's labor leaders in Massachusetts were forced to spend most of their time repelling attacks on the gains they had made in earlier, friendlier years. A brief topical review of the labor legislation enacted between 1900 and 1930 will be followed by a more or less chronological review of the role played by the State Federation and other organizations in securing its enactment.

Early Twentieth Century Labor Legislation

Child Labor -- There were laws passed to improve upon the existing body of child labor legislation in 1906 and 1911. Then, in an effort to keep Massachusetts in the forefront of child labor legislation, the Uniform Child Labor Law was adopted in 1913. This statute excluded minors from many objectionable occupations and reduced the workday to 8 hours for children between 14 and 16 years of age. There is also some evidence that the enforcement of these laws improved during this period. Thus, a Boston University professor writes in 1909:

> The present provision for the enforcement of the age and educational restrictions upon the employment of minors are as effective as could well be devised. The enforcement is entrusted primarily to the factory inspectors, of whom there are now 14, acting under the direction of the chief of the district police of the state. . .. All the available evidence goes to show that the enforcement of these laws is exceptionally thorough and that cases of violation or evasion are extremely rare. [1, p. 287]

The operation, cleaning, or repair of freight elevators was added to the prohibited occupations for minors in 1920.

<u>Hours of Labor</u> — A weak 8-hour bill for all public employees was passed in 1906 and strengthened in 1911. Nineteen eleven also saw the hours for women and minors in certain industries shortened to 54 hours a week, and a further reduction was obtained in the 48 hour week bill passed in 1919. A 1921 amendment extended the coverage of this act to women and children who had been excluded previously. In the textile industry, the Overtime Bill of 1907 prohibited certain overtime work for women and minors after 6 P.M.

The street-carmen gained another point in 1912 with a law providing that a day's work for all conductors, motormen, and trainmen should be arranged by the employer upon the basis of nine hour's work. The following year their hours were restricted to nine in eleven.

Workmen's Compensation -- The 1911 enactment of the Massachusetts Workmen's Compensation Law was one of the really significant break-throughs of the "progressive era" in Massachusetts politics. As we will note later, the law did not pass in a form entirely suitable to organized labor; but the employer's old common law defenses in damage suits were voided, and only those employees injured by reason of their own serious and willful misconduct were excluded from compensation.

The provisions of the act regarding the extent of coverage, the amount of compensation, the length of waiting period, special funds for certain injuries, etc., were gradually liberalized. Some of the major benchmarks being: the increase of benefits from 50% to 66 2/3% of the wage in 1914; the reduction of the waiting period to 10 days in 1916, and 7 days in 1923, the maximum payment increase from $10 to $14 a week in 1919; the minimum payment increase from $4 to $5 in 1918; the increases in total compensation to $6,400, and the increase in the amount of the burial allowance from $100 to $150 in 1922.

Wages -- Two very limited minimum wage bills for certain public employees, and a law requiring payment of wages during regular working hours were passed in 1911. In the following year Massachusetts really established herself as the pioneer in minimum wage legislation when an act of 1912 authorized a commission to investigate wages paid women in any branch of industry and recommend wages considered adequate to provide a proper living standard. The commission was authorized to publish the names of firms that refused to accept its recommendations. Thus, while the commission was not mandatory, and while it depended upon publicity for its results, it nevertheless attracted national attention to this type of legislation.

Other specific laws dealing with wages befo e 1930 included a 1914 Prevailing Wage Law for mechanics on public works, 1917 extension of this law to include Teamsters, a 1918 law forbidding excessive fines for employee tardiness, and a 1918 law prohibiting employers from taking the "tips" of employees who checked clothes.

Miscellaneous Labor Legislation -- A Department of Labor was created in 1912, and agitation for anti-injunction legislation finally resulted in two acts defining the rights of workers on strike and restricting the use of injunctions in labor disputes in 1913. However, a stronger anti-injunction act of 1914 was later declared unconstitutional in 1916. There were also some other minor bills enacted, which will be mentioned in the chronological description which follows. Meanwhile it is interesting to note that the early years of the "progressive era" witnessed a concern not only with the worker's on-the-job experience, but also with the broader aspects of economic opportunity and economic security in general. Along these lines the most notable additions to the labor code were the establishment of public employment bureaus in 1906, an attempt to extend industrial education by the creation of a five man commission to further vocational training in 1905, and the creation of a low cost system of savings bank life insurance which went into effect in 1907. These measures were of an "uplift" nature, and they were only briefly mentioned in the reports of the legislative committee to the annual convention of the State Branch, again indicating that support for workingmen's causes must have existed outside the ranks of organized labor during this period. Also, as a part of the reform coalition, organized labor supported some measures which were not directly related to their immediate self interests. Proposals for the initiative and referendum were introduced directly by the State Branch for several years, but in 1911 it was decided to let the bill be handled by the Initiative and Referendum League and to give it labor support. The State Branch also endorsed the equal female suffrage proposal in 1910, and in 1911 the Equal Suffrage Bill was introduced into the General Court by labor for the first time. Although not part of their formal legislative program, organized labor also favored direct primary elections and popular election of United States Senators, both of which were eventually enacted into law in Massachusetts.

Labor's political activities and legislative program were not always the subject of complete agreement during these years, however, and there is considerable evidence of a lack of cohesion within the State Branch in several instances. There were numerous pleas from the leadership requesting more support for the legislative program, and it was frequently urged that the Federation limit its program to a small number of "basic" bills and allow individual labor groups to introduce more limited and more specific proposals with the Federations support. There was also a long struggle between the Legislative Committee and the Executive Council of the Federation over which group was to assume primacy in legislative matters.[1] During the 1920's, perhaps the most controversial matter that entered into the proceedings of the State Federation — aside from the disputes surrounding financial difficulties — concerned the type of insurance fund to be supported with regard to workmen's compensation payments.

Political Action by the Massachusetts Labor Movement

Although the State Branch sought to adhere to the official non-partisan policy of the AFL in the strictist sense, it pursued this policy with varying degrees of enthusiasm at different times, and third party sentiment emerged periodically in the Bay State between 1900 and 1930. The State Branch approved the action of the AFL in endorsing Robert M. LaFollette for President in 1924 and created a campaign committee to work in his support. In the following year it likewise endorsed the AFL's opposition to a labor party. The following account traces the vicissitudes of the State Branch's political activity, and its influence on labor legislation between 1900 and 1930.

---

1 In this continuing dispute, the officers of the State Branch favored having a single Legislative Agent directly responsible to the Executive Committee. Although the number of members on the Legislative Committee was reduced from 5 to 3 in 1912, the annual conventions continued to vote to retain the committee until 1918. In this year a Legislative Agent was appointed to report to the executive board. In 1925 the office of the Legislative Agent was combined with that of Secretary-Treasurer. This step came after labor's political influence had waned, and it was an economy move to save money during a period of financial adversity for the Federation.

Following their unsuccessful attempt to prevent Crane's election as Lt. Governor in 1896, the State Branch's next significant foray into politics was more vigorous and more successful. In 1903 an active campaign against child labor was instituted; and two members of the Executive Committee gave the matter much publicity by touring the state and investigating existing conditions. Then, in 1904, the practice of printing records of legislative roll calls on labor measures was used. Governor John L. Bates' veto of the "Overtime Bill" in 1904 particularly aroused labor's wrath, and Michael Hennessy notes: "Labor leaders organized 'Flying Wedges' and went after the Governor's political scalp with vengeance." [6, p.83]. How much credit organized labor should be given for Governor Bates' defeat remains problematical, however, since some of his appointments had already turned strong elements of his own party against him, and the Overtime Bill was again defeated in the next session of the legislature — although there was a very close battle before it was voted down in the Senate.

After this second defeat of the Overtime Bill, a protest rally was called at Faneuil Hall on April 24, 1906. At this meeting it was voted to organize wage earners' clubs to assist friends and defeat enemies, but there is no record of any real success along this line, and a real controversy developed when some of the wage earners' clubs found themselves supporting Republican candidates, which were being opposed by the Executive Committee of the State Branch.

The President's Report in 1907 noted:

> During the last campaign a number of our wage earners' clubs were engulfed in the vortex of a political party which posed as the Messiah of the working classes. . . Bills were presented by individuals marked labor, but were a direct obstruction to measures presented by our legislative agent, notably, the Picketing Bill, Injunction Bill and Employers Liability Bill. Not wishing a repetition of such use of our Wage Earners Clubs, we call your attention to maintain the integrity and the literal meaning and use of your clubs. [12, p.15].

Despite this apparent division within organized labor's ranks, an 8-hour bill for public employees was passed in 1906; but the bill's effectiveness was greatly weakened by amendments attached to secure its passage. A few public employment offices were also established in 1906, when a limited budget was approved for the Chief of the Bureau of Labor Statistics to open offices in such cities as might be selected by him. The Overtime Bill was finally passed in 1907, and the 8-hour bill was amended slightly; but labor remained unsatisfied with this legislation, and continued to press for further revision. It is worth noting, however, that employer opposition began to organize at this time. In reporting on the 1906 defeat of a labor-sponsored anti-injunction bill, the Legislative Committee observed:

> This bill, which was defeated in the Senate, met with far bitterer opposition than ever before, the hearing of the remonstrants drawing out large numbers of eminent attorneys, summoned by the Citizens' Alliance, manufacturers and other associations of employers. [11, p.28].

In 1907, references are made to "The pernicious efforts of the Employers' Association of Massachusetts in endeavoring to tear down organized labor", [12, p.13], and the President's Report stated:

> I desire to call the attention of the Convention to the following fact, thatatall hearings at the State House (1907) all proposed labor legislation was strongly, bitterly and maliciously opposed by the representatives of the Employers' and Master Builders' Association. [12, p. 15].

In 1907, a Recess Commission was appointed to study several labor measures and report to the 1908 session of the legislature. The most significant recommendation of this Recess Commission dealt with the issuance of injunctions in labor disputes. The recommendation which later became known as the Turtle Peaceful Persuasion Bill, prevented the issuance of injunctions against peaceful picketing. The fate of this bill in the 1908 legislature is disclosed in the following account from the Legislative Committee Report.

> This Bill passed the House of Representatives with very little opposition, the Bill being ordered to a third reading by a vote of 112-69 and went to the Senate, better known this year as the Slaughter House for all labor Legislation, and the most surprising feature of the senators who served on the Recess Committee and signed the report recommending the Bill, and when the vote was taken did a handspring and voted against it. [13, p.19].

This episode illustrates the difficulty the State Branch sometimes had in finding reliable "friends" or identifying real "enemies." Following this narrow defeat of labor's most sought after measure, another protest meeting was held in Faneuil Hall on June 30, 1908, but little was accomplished by it. In fact, labor's greatest legislative successes of the year were the defeat of three anti-labor measures, whose introduction into the legislature was not unrelated to the previously mentioned formation of several employer's associations. The three measures defeated dealt with forbidding the solicitation of members for trade unions, legalization of the blacklist, and the prohibition of a union to have a death benefit without the consent of the insurance commission.[1]

In 1909, Governor Draper vetoed labor's attempt to strengthen the 1906 8-hour law for public employees. The Executive Board called a special convention of the State Branch to consider what action should be taken. On August 11, 1909 the convention condemned the action of Draper and recommended that an effort be made to defeat him. They adopted the slogan "Remember the Eight Hour Bill", and a campaign committee was selected and financed by contributions for a campaign fund. In spite of these efforts there were still signs of political division in the ranks of organized labor, and Governor Draper was re-elected and he vetoed the bill when it was presented again.

This is more or less typical of 1908 and 1909, when very little in the way of labor legislation was passed. The Senate was much less favorable to labor legislation than the House during these years, and the Upper House becomes known as the "Graveyard" and "Slaughter House" among labor men. Some of this lack of success was also of labor's own doing. The convention proceedings of these years devote

---

[1] The labor movement regarded this latter measure as an attempt by employers to use insurance reports to gain information on the strength and financial position of unions.

much time to the fact that many unions were "pulling their own oar" to the detriment of labor unity and there were complaints of too many bills being filed.[1] The 1908 convention, therefore, decided to introduce only four bills the next year in contrast to the 23 previously submitted. Actually, however, five bills were officially introduced by the State Branch, and it was agreed to strongly support three others. The five bills which constituted the heart of organized labor's program during these years were: (1) an anti-injunction bill; (2) a bill to permit peaceful picketing; (3) a bill to make the 8-hour law for public employees effective; (4) a bill to strengthen the Employers Liability Act; and (5) a bill providing for the initiative and referendum. The other three receiving support were a seamen's bill, a 54-hour bill for textile workers, and a bill permitting unions to fine their members. All of these measures were lost in 1909--most of them being killed in the Senate--but roll calls of the votes were printed and distributed to the members.

In 1910, the Legislative Committee for the first time attempted to appeal to the general public outside the labor movement. A pamphlet entitled "Seven Labor Measures" was issued. Each bill was described, and labors supporting arguments for each measure were presented. The seven bills involved were similar to the eight measures supported in 1909 except the seamens bill was dropped and a workmen's compensation act was favored instead of an employer's liability law.

---

[1] In particular see the Presidents comments to the 1908 convention of the State Branch. [13, p. 13]

Five of these bills received favorable committee reports; but, despite several close votes, only the 8-hour bill was passed by the General Court, and this was vetoed by Governor Draper.[1] Some concessions, however, were gained. A compulsory arbitration bill was defeated. A law requiring employers to mention an existing labor dispute in labor advertisements was passed, and a Recess Commission was appointed to consider the Workmen's Compensation Bill again.

After these results in 1910, the General Court of 1911 was the most favorable to labor of any in years. One reason for this may be found in the gubernatorial election of 1910, in which the Democratic candidate, Eugene N. Foss, defeated labor's old enemy, the incumbent Governor Draper. Foss, who had previously run for Congress on the Republican ticket, was a wealthy businessman who just barely won the Democratic nomination in a bitter fight with Charles S. Hamlin and the former Democratic gubernatorial candidate James H. Vahey. Foss' labor record was a question mark during both the nominating and election battles, and Hennessy describes each as follows:

---

1 Senate President Treadway's vote caused a tie defeating the 54 hour bill. The initiative and referendum bill received a 112-102 favorable vote in the House; but, since a constitutional amendment was involved, a 2/3 majority was required for passage. The anti-injunction bill lost by 6 votes in the House, and the picketing bill failed in the Senate despite a favorable committee report. In a reversal of the usual pattern, the bill permitting the fining of strikebreaking union members passed the Senate, but was defeated in the House after a bitter fight requiring three roll calls.

> During the pre-Convention fight the Vahey adherents attacked Foss' labor record and quoted Samuel Gompers, head of the American Federation of Labor, against him. Mr. Gompers didn't like Mr. Foss' labor record in Congress, but in E. Gerry Brown, one of his new political lieutenants, prominent in labor circles, Mr. Foss found a ready champion who claimed that Mr. Foss' labor record was satisfactory to organized labor.
>
> In the last week of the campaign the labor men, who supported Foss, got a letter from Samuel Gompers in which the latter said that if Foss would be true to labor he ought to be supported and Draper ought to be defeated. To prove that Mr. Foss did urge Governor Draper to veto the Eight Hour Bill, the Republicans produced Foss' letter signed, "B. F. Sturtevant Company, E. N. Foss, Treasurer." But labor didn't care. They were out to get the scalp of Draper. [6, p. 143]

Foss later proved to be a rather unreliable ally, but the election of a Democratic Governor in Massachusetts was enough in itself to create a stir and there were other signs of a rising progressive spirit in the state. Thus, labor fared well in 1911. The Eight Hour Bill, and the bill permitting unions to fine their members were passed in modified form. Two minimum wage laws for public employees were passed, and trial by jury was required in contempt cases. Governor Foss signed the 54 hour bill under pressure, but he vetoed labor's "Peaceful Persuasion Bill", which was a milder form of their picketing bill. The picketing bill itself was killed by a tie vote in the Senate, and a bill reducing the hours of street carmen was also defeated.

Since loopholes were subsequently found in the Eight Hour Law and the 54 Hour Law, the Workmen's Compensation Act was undoubtedly the most important of the measures which were enacted. Organized labor alone was not responsible for its passage, and it did not pass in a form entirely satisfactory to their desires. They had hoped for a compulsory state fund to finance the workmen's compensation benefits, but the Act passed was voluntary in nature and it permitted private insurance companies to do business under the law. Labor was successful in preventing a "self-insurance" amendment from being attached, since they felt any employer insuring himself under the law would force his employees to contribute the accident fund; and they exhibited a willingness to compromise on the "insurance company" amendment. Although they felt the profits of the insurance company "middlemen" would increase cost and decrease benefits compared to a state-administered fund, the Legislative Committee felt "a more direct fight could be made against the insurance amendment if the bill itself was passed than if we should begin all over again before the next legislature." [14, p. 42][1]

Things were much tougher in the 1912 Legislature, however, and the Legislative Committee of the State Branch reports " a considerable number of the members declared that organized labor had secured more than it had any right to expect in a generation, and

---

1 While this slight degree of flexibility probably indicates an increasing degree of political sophistication on the part of the State Branch, it also served to illuminate the increasing tension between the Executive Committee and the Legislative Committee over who should control legislation. The dispute had become acute two years previously when the State Branch's President Durin was attacked as causing the defeat of the Textile Worker's 54 hour bill. This particular hassle arose because the Textile Workers were willing to accept a compromise as to the date when the act would become effective, but Durin felt he was bound to support the bill presented to him by the previous annual convention.

that it should be content to wait some time before any further advance was made." [15, p. 39] They also stated:

> It was openly charged on the floor of the House that between $150,000 and $200,000 had been spent in the effort to prevent us from taking the liability insurance companies out of the Workmen's Compensation Act. Nobody denied it, and indeed, the long list of eminent attorneys, the tremendous amount of literature distributed and the pressure brought to bear through the insurance brokers, agents and others, who were filled with alarm about the loss of income, indicated a large expenditure. . . . The result was a defeat for the workers by a vote of 77 to 131. [15, p. 40]

The Peaceful Persuasion Bill was again vetoed by Governor Foss, and labor also had a stiff battle in defeating an amendment to the Workmen's Compensation Act which would have allowed large corporations to carry their own insurance. Nevertheless, several gains were made. The voluntary Minimum Wage Board for women was established. A bill requiring street car schedules to be made on a 9-hour basis was passed. Provisions were made for the State Board of Health to make rules regarding the employment of women in core rooms. Prison made goods were not allowed to compete with goods produced by free labor, and a State Board of Labor and Industry was created to take over work that had been scattered among several departments. Again, labor was not alone in securing this legislation; and, with regard to the so called "Labor Department Bill", the Legislative Committee notes "a number of other forces were energetic in their assistance, among them being the Massachusetts Association of Labor Legislation, the Industrial Relations Committee of the Boston Chamber of Commerce and the Massachusetts Child Labor Committee." [15, p. 40]

Nineteen-thirteen again proved to be a year of substantial gains mixed with some losses and more trouble with Governor Foss. Among the most important bills passed were the Uniform Child Labor Law, a law extending the coverage of the 54-hour law to women in most industries and occupations, and a law defining the rights of workers on strike and the use of injunctions in strikes. Another version of the 8-hour day for public employees was passed, but it was still necessary for any city or town to adopt by referendum vote the provisions of this act for it to be effective.

The Governor vetoed a barber's licensing bill, and a 9 in 11 hour bill for the trolleymen. The latter was pased over his veto in a weakened form, but the Governor also aroused the wrath of the State Branch when he tried to eliminate the Bureau of Labor and Industries, which had just been created the year before, by consolidating it with the Industrial Accident Board set up under the Workmen's Compensation Act. The main bone of contention between the State Branch and Foss, however, arose when the 1,500 employees of the Sturtevant Blower Works went on strike for higher wages. The Sturtevant Company was controlled by the Governor, but, despite his stand in favor of arbitration in other cases, Foss refused to submit the dispute to arbitration. He dismissed the strike as an attempt to embarrass his political aspirations, and, after a long drawn out effort, the strikers returned empty handed.

Organized labor, however, was not the only group put out by the "Old Boy", as Foss was known; and Hennessy notes "By the time the Legislature adjourned, practically every Democrat, high and low, was lambasting Governor Foss". [6, p. 194] As the breach widened between the Governor and most of the leading Democrats, David I. Walsh, the Roman Catholic Lt. Governor announced his gubernatorial candidacy. Foss then tried for the Republican nomination. He was refused; and the 1913 elections saw Walsh win the Governorship with Charles Summer Bird the Bull Moose Progressive Candidate besting the Republican Augustus P. Gardner for second place.

The progressive movement in Massachusetts politics reached its pinnacle during the administration of David I. Walsh. Legislation was enacted regarding public health services, primary elections, regulation of public service corporations, conservation of natural resources, and many other "reform" measures. Labor was also in a position to benefit from this favorable milieu. During his first term Walsh signed every labor measure presented to him. Lt. Governor Edward P. Barry was a former union member, and State Treasurer Frederick W. Mansfield had previously appeared at legislative hearings in support of organized labor and had drawn up several bills for the State Branch. Although the Republicans got enough support from the Bull Moose Progressives to return Grafton Cushing as Speaker of the House, there was still great pressure for more reform, and there were supposed to be about 25 men in the 1914 Legislature who carried union cards. Among these, Senator John F. Sheehan of Holyoke and Representative P. Joseph McManus of Boston led the fight for an anti-injunction bill, and in 1914, Massachusetts became the first state to write a strong anti-injunction bill into law. This law was short-lived, however, for the Supreme Judicial Court of Massachusetts declared the act unconstitutional in 1916. The State Branch then renewed their demands for the popular election of judges and for provisions allowing the recall of judicial decisions.

Other labor legislation secured during the Walsh administration met a better fate, since it merely consisted of consolidating previous gains rather than breaking into new areas. There were improvements in the Workmen's Compensation law, a law for better sanitary conditions and greater safety in industry, a more effective minimum wage law for women and minors, and some reductions of hours for public employees through a half-holiday on Saturday. Governor Walsh also removed the members of the Board of Labor and Industry named by Governor Foss, who failed to appoint a bona fide trade unionist on it. Mr. John Golden, President of the United Textile Workers, was named to represent labor on the Walsh-constituted Board.

Despite these successes, however, there is still evidence of disunity in the ranks of the State Branch, and all of the elements of the progressive coalition did not always stick together. For instance, although the State Branch continued to support the initiative and referendum and the female suffrage amendments, they remained non commital on Governor Walsh's call for a state constitutional convention, since they were not certain what forces would control such a convention. The Legislature finally refused the

Governor's request, but such a convention was later called in 1916 after Samuel W. McCall reunited the Republicans and Bull Moose Progressives to defeat Walsh in the 1915 elections.

With regard to the continuing division within the Massachusetts labor movement on political affairs, the President's Report to the 1915 convention of the State Branch of the AFL contains these remarks:

> Pursuant to the instructions of the Boston Convention your president went to New Bedford about a week before the last state election and carried on a campaign to bring about the defeat of Senator Andrew P. Doyle. ... As Senator Doyle was opposed to the passage of the bill submitting the question of woman's suffrage to the referendum of the people I thought it wise to secure speakers from the leagues interested in the passage of the bill. I made a request of the Massachusetts Woman's Suffrage Association and the Political Equality Union that they provide speakers for the entire campaign... .
>
> One of the most contemptible and disgusting phases of this campaign and one which merits the severest censure of this convention, was the action of some of the local unions in New Bedford, and the inaction of others. Several unions, although affiliated with the State Branch and the New Bedford Central Labor Union, came out in the public print as condemning myself and the action of the Boston convention for condemning Senator Doyle and individuals, officers and others, came out in support of him. [17, pp. 13-16]

Despite these continuing signs of division within the Bay State labor movement, the question of a labor party in Massachusetts was also debated during these years. In 1911 and 1912 there was some feeling that the trade unionists should contact various farmer's organizations, and resolutions advocating the formation of a labor party were defeated in 1910 and 1912. The leadership continued to staunchly advocate non partisanship, and the

1913 Presidential address to the annual convention contains these comments:

> At various conventions of the State Branch resolutions have been presented urging the advisability of forming a so-called labor party. That proposition has always been voted down by an overwhelming vote....
> I earnestly hope the delegates to this convention will not seriously consider any such proposition. This State Branch is not a political organization. Our mission is to bring relief to those who toil. Our efforts are purely along industrial lines, except that we inform political candidates of our desires for legislation and favor or oppose them according to their attitude. [16, p. 22]

In 1915, however, the annual convention adopted a resolution to instruct the Executive Council to devise ways and means to launch a labor party in the State of Massachusetts before 1916. On April 29, 1916, a meeting was held in Boston to decide on the formation of the labor party and to which every affiliated union was requested to send representatives. Grant Hamilton, American Federation of Labor representative, addressed the gathering and declared that the Federation thought the move unwise. It was decided to take a referendum vote on the question. Returns were obtains from 1739 members in 60 unions. The vote on forming a labor party was: in favor, 438; opposed, 1301; as to whether the unions were willing to pay their share of the cost of forming such a party, 10 voted "yes", 34 voted "no", and 16 did not state.

Following Samuel W. McCall's defeat of Governor Walsh in 1915, the fate of the progressive movement in Massachusetts was unclear. Prior to his election, McCall insisted on making the Republican platform more attractive to the reluctant progressives.

A weak statement on "reasonable hours of labor" was adopted. The Old Guard declared for the constitutional convention demanded by the progressives, and Hennesy notes "The Progressives flocked back to the Republican party, paying little attention to Clark, their own party candidate for Governor." [6, p.221].

In his inaugural address, Governor McCall proved unusually progressive for a Republican Governor of these times. Three times he advocated a compulsory social and health insurance plan based on the "German model", but nothing ever came of these requests and they were lost in the shuffle surrounding the First World War. The Governor's call for a constitutional convention was heeded in 1916, however, and the Legislature authorized a special non partisan election for 320 delegates. The actual convention stretched out over a three year period, and the last recommendations were made in 1919. For all practical purposes, this convention marked the end of the progressive era in Massachusetts politics, and following the aftermath of World War I the conservatives within the Republican party regained ascendency in the state, until the election of David I. Walsh to the U.S. Senate in 1926 proved a harbinger of the Al Smith revolution in 1928.

The elections for convention delegates were held on May 17, 1917. The State Branch of the AFL called a special labor convention in Worcester in January of that year to consider the proposed revisions to be presented at the convention, and a committee of 10 was appointed to combat the agitation of a newly formed employers association.[1]

At the Constitutional Convention, organized labor supported the initiative and referendum proposal, but they were disappointed when its final passage stipulated that these devises could not be used in any matters relating to judges. The proposal for biannual instead of annual elections also passed despite the fact that labor was opposed to this measure on the grounds that the Legislature would become less responsive to the will of the people. Although Massachusetts later ratified the Federal equal suffrage amendment, this convention marked the end of the progressive era in Massachusetts politics. Indeed, the "sectarian" amendment which was passed at this convention clearly indicated one of the lines along which the progressive coalition would eventually break up.[2]

---

1 The delegates at the Special Convention expressed concern over a resolution which had been sent to all the manufacturers and large employers in the state by the American Employers Association. The resolution announced that the formation of the "Organization of American Employers' Association, Incorporated". One year previous, on November 4, 1915, the Associated Industries of Massachusetts was officially organized, and its constitution stated: "The purpose of this Association shall be to improve the manufacturing conditions of the industries of Massachusetts in the public interest; to advocate fair and equitable legislation affecting the interests of its members and their employees; to inculcate just and equitable principles among its members, and between its members and their employees; to acquire, possess, and disseminate useful information for its members; and generally to promote the welfare of its members and their employees and the prosperity of the Commonwealth of Massachusetts and its industries."

2 The "sectarian" amendment was aimed primarily at the parochial school system and was the result of a fear of rising Roman Catholic influence in the state. This subject had aroused religious feeling in the Massachusetts General Court for years, and as passed by the convention and ratified at the regualr 1917 elections, the amendment provided that no public funds or credit could be used "for the purpose

There are probably many reasons for the progressive era ending after World War I in Massachusetts. Most of the popular progressive measures had been enacted, and the sustained activity necessary to compile that record probably "tired out" many Bay State crusaders. The disillusion of the postwar period also played havoc with the constitutional elements of the progressive coalition.

In terms of the voting elements involved, Joseph Huthmacher contends that the success of the liberal movement in the Bay State was based on a cooperation between old stock believers in the "social gospel", who had been willing to launch the state on social experiments since they felt the time had come to regulate the "interests" more strictly while giving the "common people" a helping hand through humanitarian legislation, and reform minded Newer Americans, organized labor, and some "advanced liberal" intellectuals.

Footnote 2 continued from preceding page

of founding, maintaining or aiding any school, college or other educational institution, any church or religious denomination or religious society or infirmary, hospital or undertaking which is not a public institution or undertaking which is not a public institution or under the order and superintendence of public officers." [6, p. 257]

During the convention debates, the "Minute Men" and other patriotic organizations vigorously supported the amendment, while Cardinal O'Connell attacked the measure as "an insult to Catholics". Only 9 of the 94 Catholic delegates to the convention voted against the amendment, however, and it was approved by the people of Massachusetts at the polls on November 6, 1917. The animosity aroused by this fight surrounding the "sectarian" amendment was indicative of things to come, however, since during most of the 1920's the cultural tensions embodied in such "issues" as Prohibition, Ku Kluxism, and immigration restriction occupied much of the country's attention.

The Great Red Scare of 1920, a rash of strikes in the post-war years, including the Boston Police Strike in 1919, and what was believed to be increasing "paternalistic" attitude of government following the increased federal controls during the war, however, tended to engender increasing fears among the traditionally conservative elements of the progressive coalition. Muckraking and the social gospel rapidly became things of the past, and fears of Bolshevism "big labor", and paternalism gained sway over the middle class Republican inhabitants of the farms, the small towns, and suburban cities of Massachusetts and the Back Bay.

Before analyzing the breakup of the progressive coalition in greater detail, however, the writer would like to briefly identify the main elements of the coalition primarialy interested in labor legislation.

Political Action by Various Reform Groups, and Dissolution of the "Reform Coalition"

Throughout the nation one of the primary concerns of the reform movement of the early twentieth century was the problem of child labor, which we have seen had long been a matter of legislative concern in Massachusetts. Although membership in the National Child Labor Committee, which was founded in 1904, was by individuals rather than by organizations, Elizabeth S. Johnson has noted:

> A number of national organizations such as the National Consumers' League, the General Federation of Women's Clubs, and the American Federation of Labor co-operated in the work of the National Child Labor Committee. [3, p.408]

Mrs. Johnson continued:

> One of the first steps taken by the new Child labor movement was to formulate some definite standards for legislation. A model bill was issued in 1904 based on the best features of the Massachusetts, New York, and Illinois laws. In 1911 this bill, in slightly revised form, was published as a proposed "Uniform Child Labor Law" and was recommended to the states by the National Conference on Uniform State Laws. It called for a minimum age of 14 years for employment in manufacturing and 16 years for employment in mining; a maximum work day of eight hours; prohibition of night work from seven p.m. to six a.m.; and documentary proof of age. In 1904 there was no state with a law measuring up to all five standards. [3, pp.408-409].

As we have seen, Massachusetts adopted the Uniform Child Labor Law in 1913 with the State Branch of AFL, the Women's Trade Union League, the Consumers League, the Women's Educational and Industrial Union, and other groups supporting the Massachusetts Child Labor Committee. Since the Massachusetts Law of 1913 was the first 8-hour law passed in an important textile state, it was nationally recognized as a great victory for the advocates of child labor legislation.

During these years there was also strong sentiment for improving the enforcement of all the state's labor laws, and Clara M. Beyer states:

> There was continuous talk among interested groups of transferring enforcement to the health department. A bill for that purpose was introduced in 1907. At the hearing the following organizations appeared in support: Massachusetts Medical Society, Women's Educational and Industrial Union, State Federation of Women's Clubs, Massachusetts Civic League, Massachusetts Consumers' League, Women's Trade Union League, Women's Labor League, Associated Charities of Boston, and various settlement houses.

> Enforcement of the labor laws dealing with lighting, sanitation, and ventilation was turned over to the State board of health in that year. Probably the protest of this representative group of organizations was responsible, at least in part, for this transfer. [2, p.25].

Although the reform coalition was not always as unified as the preceeding quotation indicates it nevertheless remained effective prior to World War I. And, Mrs. Beyer's comments on the night work bill are illuminating in this regard. She notes that in 1906 the legislation was defeated in the following manner:

> There was very little real debate. The opposition to the bill, content with having the votes, refused to be drawn into a discussion. When the advocates of the bill found that it was likely to be defeated they tried to leave the chambor and break the quorum, but the doors were locked against them. Then came appeals and motions and the defeat after a tedious parliamentary battle of the opposing sides. [2, p.52].

After the vigorous labor campaign on the "Overtime Bill" in 1906, however, the law prohibiting the work of women and minors after six p.m. in the textile industry was passed and signed by the governor in 1907. Mrs. Beyer stated:

> One powerful organ of the textile interests, after having opposed the bill for years, came out early in the session with the statement that the bill was of "little importance". . .
> After the passage of the bill this same journal commented editorially that it was passed "more out of fear of political death thanfor any merit" it contained. In a later number it blamed the "reformers" for making the weavers-the chief malcontents among the textile workers - so "irrational as to put through legislation such as the overtime law." It traced "the secondary cause at least for the unrest of the women weavers" to this body of "wealthy women particularly, but, sad to say, many men of prominence." "From the published doings of these reformers they [the weavers] really believe that they are being abused and underpaid, and that they are altogether too good to work at their occupation." [2, p.53].

In addition to improving and expanding the coverage and enforcement of hours legislation, two of the significant breakthroughs achieved by the reform coalition in Massachusetts were in the areas of minimum wage legislation and workmens compensation. Organized labor was a much more active element in the coalition in the latter battle than in the former.

With regard to the pressures leading to minimum wage legislation in Massachusetts, Elizabeth Brandeis has stated:

> The creation of the Massachusetts investigating Commission was secured by a committee organized in December 1910 representing the state branches of the Women's Trade Union League, the National Consumers League, the American Association for Labor Legislation and certain local organizations of like character. the president of the United Textile Workers was the only labor leader active in behalf of minimum wage, either in this preliminary stage or later. The rest of the organized labor movement in Massachusetts (aside from the Women's Trade Union League) gave purely nominal support. [3, p. 508] [1]

As the preceding chronology of the activities of the State Branch indicated, organized labor took a much greater interest in the Workmen's Compensation Act of 1913—particularly with the way the benefits were to be financed. In 1917 the U.S. Supreme Court in a series of three decisions upheld the three types of compensation laws then prevailing within the various states. New York Central Rail Co. v. White, upheld a compulsory law; Mountain Timber Co. v. State of Washington, upheld an elective law; and Hawkins v. Bleakly, upheld a compulsory law with an exclusive state fund. It was this latter type of law which the State unsuccessfully tried to secure.

---

1 A detailed description of the campaign for the Massachusetts' Minimum Wage Law is in [2, pp. 55-61]. After over 25 years of operation, Clara M. Beyer estimated that in 1929 the Law applied to approximately 75,000 women and girls, "or about one-fifth of all the female wage earners in the state to whom it is practicable to apply the minimum-wage law." [2, p.61]

During World War I a special War Emergency Industrial Commission was given the power to temporadily suspend some of the Bay States labor provisions, but this Commission had no long run effect on labor standards in Massachusetts. Following the War, however, a reaction to government "paternalism", the "Red Scare", and the Boston Police Strike of 1919 tended to split the old reform coalition along economic lines, and many rural and middle class progressives returned to the conservative fold.

In addition to the dissolution of the coalition along economic lines, the divisiveness created by the sectarian amendment at the Bay State Constitutional Convention also contributed to a division along ethnic lines. Here, Huthmacker contends that there was a basic difference in the underlying motives and ideology of the old stock and the new American elements which provided much of the mass support for the progressive coalition. He states:

> The Irish and New Immigrant masses supported labor and humanitarian reforms as means of guarding against the insecurities of the industrial, urban civilization in which they lived. They supported political machinery reforms as a way of making their demands more effectively heard. Hence to these Newer Americans, Progressivism was a movement toward economic, social, and political self-improvement. On the other hand, to many old stock inhabitants of Boston's Back Bay andthe farms, small towns, and suburban cities of Massachusetts, the Progressive movement was largely aimed at uplifting other. It was a crusade to uplift the "inferior" cultural traditions of the Irish and New Immigrant masses, andpreserve "American" ways of living. Alleviating the economic plight of the newer arrivals was one means to that end, and thus wage and hour laws merited support. [7, pp.64-64].

This underlying difference quickly became accentuated after 1920, when the term "reform" dropped its primarily economic connotation and began to point more directly to cultural matters as such. The time and effort formerly spent by the Protestant "church lobby" and women's organizations on behalf of labor and welfare measures were now largely devoted to legislation forbidding Sunday movies, to warding off attempts to legalize professional boxing in the state, and to pressuring the General Court for an act to make the Massachusetts liquor laws conform with the national Prohibition code. These attempts to "Americanize" those traits of the Newer Americans which ran contrary to the norms of the old settlers were as essential to Progressivism as workmen's compensation as far as the old stock was concerned. To the Irish and the New Immigrants they were not.

The old stock's emphasis on using the government to forcibly alter the Newer Americans "inferior" standards made the latter increasingly suspicious of reformers and reform measures in general. They even began to join their former conservative opponents in opposing centralization and government "meddling". For example, to the Irish and New Immigrants, Prohibition was the most glaring example of unwarranted interference with their way of life. Since many of the traditionally conservative elements of the business community, though of old stock lineage, also distrusted Prohibition as an example of that extension of government control which might one day threaten their own economic interests, this issue not only forced a wedge in the ranks of the Progressive coalition, but it also served to drive the New American element of that coalition into a tentative alliance with the conservative men who had contributed least of all to the reform movement of the previous decade.

The "school issue" had the same effect when reformers saw the parochial schools as a block to its effort to uplift cultural standards. Like Prohibition, "Americanization" reforms in the realm of education heightened the New Americans suspicious of reform in general.

The reform coalition did not completely dissolve immediately after the "sectarian amendment" at the Constitutional Convention, however, and the battle for the 48-hour week bill for women and minors in the textile industry in 1919 was apparently fought more along the economic lines of the battles of the preceding decade rather than along the ethnic or religious lines which became dominant during the 1920's. The coverage of the 1919 law was expanded to include other industries in 1921. Clara M. Beyer gives the following account of these battles:

> All the labor forces throughout the State were marshalled in support of the measure. Civic and social organizations were lined up in its favor. Chief of these were the Consumers' League of Massachusetts, the Women's Clubs, and the Massachusetts Association of Women Workers. . . .
>
> The Arkwright Club and the Associated Industries carried on a vigorous campaign to defeat the 48-hour bills. At the hearings they relied upon the arguments that the industries of the State could not stand a further reduction in hours and compete with other States and that a decrease in hours would mean a decrease in wages and work hardship upon the very ones it was designed to protect. [2, pp. 38-47]

Despite this success in 1919, and the extension of coverage in 1921, however, the crowning blow in the developing schism between the old stock and the Newer American elements in the reform coalition came in 1924, when Massachusetts, long the pioneer in child labor legislation, refused to ratify the Federal Child Labor Amendment at the polls.

Within the state, the Massachusetts Federation of Labor and the Massachusetts League of Women Voters worked for the amendment's passage. It was opposed by the Associated Industries of Massachusetts, but the most decisive factor in the election was probably Cardinal O'Connell's scathing indictment of the pending amendment as a threat to the private school system and a further interference with the rights of parents in an already overcentralized state. The effect of his words on wary Irish and New Immigrant Catholic voters showed with telling results in the overwhelming defeat at the Massachusetts referendum on ratification in 1924. The real effect was even more widespread, however, since the amendment's opponents in other states pointed to the Massachusetts example; and the Massachusetts Legislature, although not bound by the vote, continued to use it as the justification for taking no further action on the measure.

In addition to this ethnic dissolution of the progressive movement, organized labor itself must share some of the responsibility for its lack of legislative progress during the 1920's. During the progressive era union spokesmen had strongly backed measures which seemed to confer many benefits and impose few restraints on the workingman. But the growth of government bureaucracy during the war, and the assumption of control over that bureaucracy by elements traditionally hostile to labor after 1920, brought a national reassertation of the more conservative labor leader's old philosophy of reliance on private bargaining and hostility to government intervention in their affairs. Thus when legislation for unemployment insurance was first introduced into the Massachusetts General Court during the 1922 depression, prominent labor spokesmen testified against it. Pressure from the annual conventions eventually altered this stand in Massachusetts, however, and the leaders of the State Federation did espouse some reform proposals—particularly injunction relief—which did not seem conducive to excessive government "spying and prying."

During the 1920's Democrats at the State House and those Republicans who represented mill districts continued to support most of the labor and other welfare reform proposals as in the past, but they no longer won the support of the middle class Republican representatives from the rural and suburban constituencies, and this support had been essential to the success of the progressive coalition.[1] Huthmacher notes "Year after year the A. F. of L's legislative agent lobbied in vain. . . The same frustration greeted the welfare organizations that sponsored even more advanced social measures, like unemployment insurance." [7, p. 70]

During the war the Massachusetts State Branch of the AFL had reached a peak in terms of affiliations and members, but the war's end started a chain of events that reacted seriously against organized

1 See [22].

labor in Massachusetts, as elsewhere. The postwar depression seriously affected union workmen. The financial position of the State Branch steadily weakened, and the Boston Police strike alienated much support from labor's former progressive allies.[1] Not one major reform measure appeared on the Massachusetts statute books during the 1920's. In a message to the Massachusetts General Court in 1920, Governor Calvin Coolidge set the tone for the state, and, indeed, for the nation during this decade with the following remarks:

> In general, it is a time to conserve, to retrench rather than to reform, a time to stablize the administration of the present laws rather than to seek new legislation. . . . The greatest benefit you can confer is the speedy making of necessary appropriations, adjustment of some details, and adjournment. You can display no greater wisdom than by resisting proposals for needless legislation. [7, p. 58]

Reaction to "Reform" in the Bay State and Attempts to Reorganize the "Reform Coalition"

Much of labor's legislative effort during the 1920's was devoted to repelling attacks on the gains they had previously secured. In this they were generally successful. Defeated rather handily in the General Court were measures which would have repealed all the labor laws of the state, authorized investigations of labor unions, limited the right to strike and picket, and establish compulsory arbitration of labor disputes. More serious were the more or less

---

[1] The annual convention of the State Branch was being held at the time of this famous dispute. The convention sent a communication to Governor Calvin Coolidge, who had addressed them on the opening day, requesting him either to remove Police Commissioner Curtis or to reinstate the policemen. He did neither, and was catapulted into the national limelight as a result of his handling of this dispute.

annual attempts to repeal or weaken the workmen's compensation act, the 48-hour law, the law forbidding nightwork for women and children in textile mills, and the noncompulsory minimum wage law for women; but these too were withstood. Nevertheless some measures did pass over labor's opposition. The State Branch opposed the prohibition bills in the General Court, but their major defeat came in 1921 when a state police force was established. Labor opposed this act as a strikebreaking measure, but the act passed and the force was expanded in 1923.

One of the hottest legislative struggles of the early twenties was the fight on the "Sue Bill" or Voluntary Associations Act, which would have permitted unions to sue or be sued in their own name. Defeated by labor in 1921, the act was passed by the legislature in the following year. The State Branch decided to make use of the initiative and referendum measure for the first time in an effort to save the organization from the deletorious effects of the bill. The Executive Council was successful in securing the necessary 15,000 signatures to a petition to place the bill on the ballot. A vigorous fight was waged with a continuous speaking campaign. Although the first count of the votes in the 1922 election indicated that the bill had been sustained by about 500, a recount showed its defeat by nearly one thousand votes. Labor leaders stated that this victory demonstrated the great worth of the referendum, but they were later forced to reconsider its effectiveness when they were unable to get a provision for a compulsory state workmen's compensation fund on the ballot in 1928.

The whole matter of what type of insurance fund should be used to finance workmen's compensation payments was a matter of controversy both inside and outside the State Branch during most of the 1920's. As we have seen, the State Branch disapproved of the provisions in the Massachusetts act which provided for insurance to be written by private companies. Therefore, in 1921 the Legislative Agent and the Executive Council conducted an investigation of all the state workmen's compensation acts in the country. Their report favored an exclusive compulsory state fund, but it also stated that if a choice had to be made between insurance with private companies and an exclusive state fund that also permitted self-insurance by individual concerns, they favored the private company insurance because of the better service even though at a higher cost.

Several state conventions endorsed this stand in favor of eliminating private insurance companies, but not at the cost of permitting self-insurance. This soon brought the State Branch in open conflict with the American Federation of Labor, which favored the universal adoption of the Ohio plan's compulsory state fund with self-insurance permitted. At the 1923 session of the Massachusetts Legislature another labor group formed an association to support the Ohio plan in opposition to the State Branch's proposed "Massachusetts Plan". When both bills were refused consideration by the Legislature, a member of the State Branch accused the Legislative Agent of causing the defeat of a labor measure, and William Green addressed the annual convention of the State Branch in 1923 uring them to support the national

AFL policy. Nevertheless, on a roll call vote, the Massachusetts Plan was upheld by the convention, 130 to 19. This did not end the controversy, but the officers of the State Branch continued to hold sway. Some amendments to the act were obtained; but in 1927, it was finally decided that the legislature was not going to pass the bill desired. An attempt was then made to secure an initiative and referendum on the question.

The bill was submitted to the Attorney General for his certification in 1928, but was rejected on the grounds that it was too loosely drawn. Several redrafts were prepared, but these were rejected on the charge that the bill related to the powers of the courts and as such was not a matter for the initiative and referendum. If such an interpretation were to be allowed, the state labor leaders felt that no labor matters could be handled by the initiative, so they protested strongly against the decision of the Attorney-General. A firm of lawyers tried to change the bill to make it acceptable, and the Attorney-General was requested to allow the courts to decide on the legality of the question, but to no avail. There was nothing left to do but reintroduce the bill into the legislature, where it was defeated again in 1929.

This same futility accompanied labor's other efforts to secure legislation during the 1920's. There was a continued fight to gain relief from injunctions in labor disputes, to make the states minimum wage law for women mandatory, and to eliminate the yellow dog contract. During the latter part of the period, non-contributory old-age pensions, unemployment insurance, and the 5-day week also became principal objectives.[1] Following the defeat of the Federal Child Labor Amendment at the polls in 1924, the Executive Board of the State Branch developed a scheme of regional conferences to meet throughout the state and discuss legislation affecting labor, but there is no evidence of any effective results coming from these meetings.

Meanwhile, the failure of Massachusetts to share adequately in the national benefits of "Coolidge prosperity" was working against organized labor's short run advantage at this time; but it was also beginning to draw attention to economic matters which eventually were to reunite many elements of the former progressive coalition. Until 1925 the ups and downs of the business cycle in Massachusetts roughly paralleled national trends, but thereafter the Bay State lagged far behind. New England's shoe and textile industries were being outstripped by other parts of the country, and firms began to migrate from Massachusetts leaving unemployment and economic distress in their wake.

This undermining of Massachusetts' former industrial primacy was ascribed to various causes. High tax rates were cited. Some claimed that nearness to raw materials favored competitors.

---

[1] Perhaps the single most definitive statement of the State Branches legislative program during the late twenties came at the 1928 convention, when the name of the organization was changed to the Massachusetts State Federation of Labor. A special committee of 15 members was appointed to draft planks to be sent to the political parties with a request to have them included in their platforms for the 1928 elections. See [19, p. 81]

Others charged that discriminatory freight rates unduly burdened Massachusetts industries. The widely accepted argument most detrimental to organized labor's interests during this period, however, claimed that the Commonwealth's progressive labor laws limiting the hours of work for women and children and forbidding night work, gave her rivals an advantage--as did their relative freedom from the influence of labor unions.[1] Other profound reasons were also cited. Some claimed that the old Yankee ingenuity and the spirit

---

1 The earliest and one of the most scholarly attempts to assess the impact of Massachusetts labor legislation on the state's economy and its working class came at the turn of the century. Thus, with regard to economic effects, Sharah Whittelsey concluded: "A real and appreciable tax has been put upon the industry of Massachusetts. This has been a goal, increasing the ordinary incentive of competition to urge the use of better machinery and more careful management. . . Whereas statistics of manufacture show Massachusetts to be growing at a normal rate, and with no evidence of injury from her labor laws; one industry of importance is in an unmistakably critical situation. There is reason to believe that the heavy-grade cotton mill is leaving the state. In this case natural conditions weighed already against Massachusetts, and legislative restrictions have been a tax tending to hasten the departure of the industry to the more favored South" [23, pp. 67-68]

With respect to the non-economic effects she stated: "The legal sanitary requirements of cleanliness, light, ventilation, etc., in the factory act to improve the health and spirits of the workers, and tend to induce the same conditions in their homes. . . Weekly wage payments appear to have encouraged household economy rather than to have fostered dissolute living. Restrictions upon labor have brought increased social and educational opportunities within reach of the operatives; have advanced the interests of good citizenship among them; have tended to raise their standards of living, with important economic consequences in broadening the home market." [23, pp. 77-78]

of risk-taking had vanished from the Bay State, and that the Commonwealth industry had been allowed to lag behind modern developments. Huthmacker, for example, states:

> The complaint was that earlier New England industrialists, meeting with success and prosperity, had grown stale - too intent on security and sure dividends. Lacking faith in their son's ability to manage the industrial empires they amassed, the fathers bequeathed their properties in the form of trusts. Their sons became coupon clippers, and their properties passed under the control of absentee managers - conservative trustees with little industrial interest or know how. [7, p. 218]

This observation is supported by the following excerpt from the contemporary American Wool and Cotton Reporter:

> It isn't Southern competition. . . . [but] superannuated equipment, poor management, poor merchandising, poor styling . . . not knowing what is going on in the world . . . that is to blame for the failure or liquidation or abandonment of the Seaconnet Mills, the Hebronville, Dodgeville, Thorndike, Whitin, Shetucket and scores of other similar concerns. The tide just went out and left them on the beach. [24, p. 142]

The remedies proposed for the state's economic plight were as numerous as the alleged causes, but there were several indications that the Massachusetts electorate was becoming increasingly dissatisfied with the existing order of things. The magic of Republican economic doctrine began to fade when the administration could not emulate the national prosperity in President Coolidge's home state, and the old progressive coalition began to regroup with in increasing number of Irish and New Immigrants voters flocking to the Democratic fold as that party gradually became "wetter" and began to establish itself as the party of cultural liberalism. They were joined by labor leaders, intellectual liberals, and some old stock Republicans who were dissatisfied with their party's strong prohibition posture. David I. Walsh was the first to mobilize the power of the new coalition when he defeated the Republican National Chairman William M. Butler in the statewide race for the U.S. Senate in 1926. Butler was a Massachusetts textile manufacturer and Calvin Coolidge's former campaign manager. His corporate connections made a good target for organized labor to shoot at, and they rallied behind Walsh. Hennessy notes: "Organized labor was opposed to Butler who had, as a member of the Legislature andthe United States Senate and as President of the Arkwright Club, an organization of cotton manufacturers, opposed measures for the benefit of labor." [6, pp.358-359].

Walsh's victory was a harbinger of Al Smith's triumph in Massachusetts in 1928, and four years later the new coalition helped Massachusetts join the rest of the nation in ushering in the New Deal to cope with the worst depression in the nation's history.

Before turning to this next period of concern, however, it might be helpful to note that the factors accounting for much of the labor legislation in Massachusetts prior to 1900 were also influential in the period from 1900 to 1930 - although, as has been indicated, most of the activity during this latter period ended shortly after World War I. During these years organized labor played a more prominent role in the political process, and several employer associations, including the AIM which survives to this day, appeared to oppose the trust of the reform coalition. Returning to the nine factors mentioned by Mrs. Beyer in her 1929 survey of women's labor legislation in three states, she notes that organized labor was more prominent in the move for women's labor legislation in Massachusetts than in most other states. She said:

> The role played by organized labor in securing legislation for women was more prominent in Massachusetts than in New York. This was due to a number of factors. In the first place, the dominant industry in Massachusetts is the manufacture of textiles. The leaders among the workers in this industry, particularly in the early days, had an English background and naturally employed the method used by the textile workers of England to better their conditions-- namely, legislation. Secondly, the concentration of the industry in certain cities gave the textile workers a political strength out of proportion of their numbers. Thirdly the low standards obtaining in the textile industry during the early years of the agitation for hours laws were a constant menace to the labor movement of the State as a whole, and the organized workers hoped by legislation at least to approximate for textiles the conditions existing in other industries. [2, pp.2-3].

With regard to state labor officials during the period from 1900 to 1930 she said:

> The State Board of Labor and Industries of Massachusetts, created by law in 1912, took over the functions of inspection formerly exercised by the district police. Reorganizations and changes in personnel have prevented the board from being a noteworthy factor in the promotion of labor legislation. It has recommended minor statutes but its general policy has been to keep out of legislative controversies. [2, p.5].

Nothing much can be added to the comments made on State Bureau's of Labor Statistics or Special Legislative Committees at the end of the preceeding section, but the key role of Governor David I. Walsh in securing much of the reform legislation during the "progressive" era in Massachusetts as well as the earlier vetoes of Governor Bates and Foss and the later inaction of Coolidge and others reinforce the emphasis on the role of the Chief Executives in the timing and content of labor legislation in Massachusetts. With regard to the role of pioneering employers during the period 1900-1930, Mrs. Beyer states:

> The fact that some employers were able to pay a living wage to their employees and yet prosper as much as, if not more than, their competitors with a much lower wage scale was one of the leading arguments in support of the minimum-wage law of Massachusetts. [2, p.9].

The role of social, civic, philanthropic, and church groups has also been emphasized as necessary elements of the reform coalition. Mrs. Beyer states:

> At times more than 20 organizations have been pushing jointly a given piece of legislation affecting women's work. Most of these societies have been interested primarily in questions other than industrial, such as suffrage, politics, prohibition, civic reform.
>
> Of the three organizations whose chief function has been the improvement of working conditions, one - the American Association for Labor Legislation - has devoted itself largely to the promotion of workmen's compensation laws, but in addition it has played a real part in familiarizing the public with the need for safeguarding the work of women and the progress being made in that direction.
>
> The other two organizations - the Consumers' League and the Women's Trade Union League - National, State, and local - have confined their activities to the improvement of the working conditions of women and children. [2, p.10].

Factual studies as presented by these reform groups and others played a role, and with regard to the "spirit of the time". Mrs. Beyer added:

> Leaders and organizations have left their stamp upon specific pieces of legislation, but behind these leaders and organizations are discernible always the social forces pushing on toward a better economic order. The overpowering urge toward social justice accounted for the flood of industrial legislation during the years 1911 to 1914. More important legislation affecting women's work was put on the statute books of each of the three States in that 3-year period than in any other period of corresponding length. Massachusetts shortened hours for almost all groups of women workers andpassed the first minimum-wage law in the United States. [2, p.12].

The changing spirit of the time after World War I, which removed much of the reforming impetus of the previous years, has also been detailed in the preceeding discussion of the dissolution of the reform coalition along economic and religious lines during the 1920's. This period showed signs of coming to an end on the legislative front in Massachusetts in 1930, when the General Court passed a law providing pensions for aged dependents.

Most of the state pension laws passed before 1929 were greatly weakened by the fact that they were made optional with the counties (the unit of government most responsible for the indigent aged) and the counties had to provide the funds. Elizabeth Brandeis, however, has noted:

> The year 1929 marks the turning point in the history of old age pension legislation. For the first time the American Federation of Labor openly supported this legislation. Partly due to this addition to the ranks of its supporters, California, Minnesota, Utah, and Wyoming were added to the six pension states.
>
> In the following year, 1930, two thickly populated and highly industrialized states, Massachusetts and New York, provided pensions for aged dependents.
>
> Both laws were mandatory on all counties and provided for state contributions to costs. [3, p.614].

Summary and Conclusions

In an attempt to pull together this rather lengthy story of Massachusetts labor legislation up to 1930, it might be best to begin by emphasizing that since Massachusetts was one of the first states in the nation to develop an industrial economy it was also one of the first to experience the labor problems associated with the industrialization process. In responding to these problems the Bay State quickly established itself as a pioneer in the area of labor legislation. Although many of the early laws were weak in nature and innocuous in their enforcement, the General Court gradually increased the effectiveness and expanded the scope of Massachusetts labor legislation.

The earliest agitation for legislation in the area of working conditions was led by a host of rather amorphous humanitarian groups which tended to emphasize the need for legislation regulating child labor and long hours of work along with various other reform proposals. They based their arguments largely on reasons of health and the need for more leisure to cultivate "mental and moral culture". The first child labor law enacted in 1836 was more concerned with the education of the children than with their conditions of employment, but the law was successively amended and expanded throughout the nineteenth century. Beginning in the early 1850's single purpose organizations aimed at shorter hours legislation, led by middle class reform elements and with substantial labor followings in the industrial towns, began to emerge and replace most of the broader gauged and ephemeral of the early reform groups.

The changing composition of the labor force and the sentiments aroused by the civil war added impetus to the cause of factory reform in Massachusetts during the late 1860's, and an emphasis on a share in the increasing wealth of an expanding economy was added to the earlier arguments on the need for education and health. Broader support from the established political parties and some "enlightened" employers was added to the agitation for hours legilation, and a weak 10 hour day, six days a week, law for women and minors in the textile industry was enacted in 1874. The drive for this legilation also resulted in some amendments to the Bay State's child labor statutes and the creation of a Massachusetts Bureau of Statistics of Labor in 1869.

Although it proved to be relatively easier to amend existing legislation than to create new areas of legislative enactment, attention gradually expanded beyond the concerns of child labor and hours for women to include the areas of hours legislation for men in certain occupations, sanitation and safety legislation, and regulation of industrial homework. During the latter part of the century legislative attention also turned to methods of wage payment andto the settlement of industrial disputes after organized labor unions began to become more or less permanently established in the Bay State.

Although the Massachusetts State Branch of the American Federation of Labor was organized as a state federation of local unions in 1887, there is little evidence that it was much of a political force during the nineteenth century. On the other side of the fence there is evidence that Massachusetts employers, particularly in the textile industry, often acted in concert, but they apparently did not organize into formal groups in opposition to much of the early Massachusetts labor legislation. This situation changed, however, during the struggle surrounding the enactment of the 1892 legislation lowering the hours of work for women and minors in the textile industry from 60 to 58 a week.

The *laissez faire* spirit of the nineteenth century andthe separation of power between branches of government provided strong barriers to new labor legislation. The inertia of the *status quo* and the strong element of individual freedom in the American ethos presented obstacles that were extremely difficult to overcome without considerable effort on the part of the proponets of labor legislation. The employers were forced to organize only when the "rules of the game" or unorganized interests in Massachusetts no longer served as an adequate expression of their own interests. Thus, with the humanitarian sentiment aroused by the Civil War in Massachusetts and the increasing nation-wide hostility being built up against certain "Robber Barons" during the latter part of the nineteenth century, the textile manufacturers of Massachusetts finally organized the Arkwright Club and hired a paid legislative agent to plead their case and organize their defense in 1892.

Given the relative limitations of the organized labor movement in Massachusetts before the turn of the century, the bulk of the agitation for early Massachusetts labor legislation fell to various humanitarian, social, civic, and philanthropic reform groups. Although the earliest organizations, such as the New England Labor Reform League, the Ten Hour State Central Committee, and the Short Time Amalgamated Association, did not survive as permanent organizations other groups rose to take their place. Indeed, at the turn of the century there were at least four different women's organizations on the scene: The Twentieth Century Club, the Massachusetts Association of Working Women's Club, the Women's Educational and Industrial Union, and the Union for Industrial Progress. In addition, the Consumers League of Massachusetts was formed in 1898 to lead the battles for much subsequent legislation.

The strength of the organized labor movement in Massachusetts increased significantly between the turn of the century and the end of the First World War; but there is evidence that, despite substantial agreement, the Massachusetts State Branch of the AFL was sometimes divided over both the scope and the means of implementing its legislative program during these years. There is also evidence that Bay State labor leaders sometimes split on theparties and the candidates that they supported during certain key elections. Although there was some sentiment fora labor political party in Massachusetts during this period, such proposals were constantly opposed by the State Branch of the AFL and in 1916 such a proposal was defeated by almost a 3-1 margin in a statewide referendum conducted by the Bay State labor federation. Despite these internal problems, however, the strenghtened labor movement in Massachusetts formed a constituent element of a highly successful reform coalition that during the second decade of the twentieth century succeeded in enacting legislation dealing with the political machinery, business regulation, and educational system of Massachusetts as well as labor legislation.

In the area of labor legislation some of the most significant landmarks achieved during this period were the Workmen's Compensation Act in 1911, the first state Minimum Wage Law for women in the United States and the establishment of the State Department of Labor and Industries in 1912, the Uniform Child Labor Law in 1913, and the short lived Anti-Injunction Law of 1914. There were also substantial improvements in the state's hours laws during these years, including a prohibition on overtime work for women and minors in the textile industry after 6 P.M., and culminating in 48 hour week law for women and minors in the textile industry in 1919.

The Massachusetts labor movement was not the only organized group supporting these bills, and they did not support all of these measures with the same degree of enthusiasm. There were also several labor proposals that were not adopted; but, on balance, the reform coalition of social minded, middle class, civic and philanthropic groups, certain intellectual elements, and the organized labor movement in Massachusetts combined with the increased voting strength of the immigrant population to enact basic changes in the economic and political fabric of the Bay State during the second decade of the Twentieth Century.

Thus, the American Association for Labor Legislation, which had been founded by Professor John R. Commons of the University of Wisconsin and others, primarily to promote the adoption of workmen's compensation laws throughout the country, rendered considerable assistance to the State Branch of the AFL in advocating the 1911 Workmen's Compensation Law in Massachusetts through its state affiliate known as the Massachusetts Association for Labor Legislation. The

Industrial Relations Committee of the Boston Chamber of Commerce joined the State Branch, the Massachusetts Association for Labor Legislation, the Massachusetts Child Labor Committee, and a host of other groups in securing the establishment of the State Department of Labor and Industries in 1912. Organized labor, however, played a much more modest role in the minimum wage legislation of the same year, which secured passage largely through the efforts of a formal coalition of the Massachusetts Branches of the Women's Trade Union League, the National Consumers League, and the American Association for Labor Legislation.

The State Branch strongly supported the passage of the Uniform Child Labor Law in Massachusetts in 1913, and the Consumers League, the Women's Trade Union League, andthe Women's Educational and Industrial Union also lent strong support to the main thrust of the Massachusett's Child Labor Committee. There were also other groups supporting the expansion and enforcement of the existing sanitation and hours legislation during these years, including the Massachusetts Medical Society, the State Federation of Women Clubs, the Massachusetts Civic League, the Women's Labor League, and the Associated Charities of Boston.

Following the dissension created by the "sectarian amendment" at the 1916-1919 constitutional convention, the fears surrounding the Boston Police Strike in 1919, the "Red Scare" and the general reaction that followed the First World War, the progressive coalition in Massachusetts' politics began to break up along both economic and ethnic lines. Many old stock, rural andmiddle class progressives returned to the conservative fold, and many New Americans became disenchanted with reform when it shifted from economic areas such as workmen's compensation and hours of work to cultural areas such as prohibition and out-lawing Sunday movies. The overwhelming defeat of the National Child Labor Amendment in 1924 in the same state that had enthusiastically adopted the Uniform Child Labor Law only 11 years previously, clearly indicated the extent to which the reform coalition had dissolved in Massachusetts.

One significant feature of the progressive era in Massachusetts politics is the extent to which employers in the state organized to withstand the assault on their general laissez faire principles. Given the pervasiveness of "muckraking" and the social gospel at the turn of the century, the conservative elements in the community found that they could no longer safely rely on the unorganized interest or "rules of the game" according to which their contemporary society was being conducted. Thus, other employer associations and their representatives began to join the counsel of the Arkwright Club in opposing labor legislation in Massachusetts; and the proponents of labor legislation found that they now had to overcome strongly organized proponents of laissez faire, whereas previously they had only to combat the unorganized interests and inertia of the status quo that tended to protect the principle of non intervention in the industrial rule making process.

The nationwide "satellite" groups established by the National Association of Manufacturers apparently operated in the Bay State, and records are available indicating the opposition of the Employer's Association of America to various labor proposals early in the twentieth century. The Associated Industries of

Massachusetts was founded on November 24, 1915, and the Organization of American Employer's Association solicited members in the Bay State just prior to the outbreak of the First World War.

As a result of this organized opposition, the weakened labor movement in Massachusetts spent most of its time during the 1920's trying to stave off proposals to repeal or modify much of the legislation enacted from the preceeding decade. In this case, the inertia of the _status quo_ favored the proponets of strong labor legislation, andthe attempts to repeal or modify the existing statutes were not successful. No significant new labor legislation was enacted, however, and this included a very strong employer attempt to make union liable for legal suits in their own name as well as other measures favored by the State Branch of the AFL, particularly anti-injunction legislation and an attempt to establish a state fund for financing workmen's compensation in Massachusetts.

The failure of the Massachusetts economy to share in the nationwide prosperity after 1925 caused sufficient economic distress in the Bay State to indicate that perhaps the elements of the old reform coalition could overcome the cultural antagonisms of the early 20's and regroup under the Democratic banner in Massachusetts. The election of former Governor David I. Walsh to the United States Senate in 1926 and the Massachusetts votes in favor of Al Smith in 1928 and in favor of F.D.R. in 1932, after the entire nation had fallen into the depression that had gripped Massachusetts earlier, indicated that this was a distinct possibility. To understand why this possibility was not fully realized, Chapter X will now turn to an examination of labor and management activities during the Great Depression and the World War II period in Massachusetts politics.

REFERENCES - CHAPTER IX

1. F. Spencer Baldwin, "Recent Massachusetts Labor Legislation," Annals of the American Academy of Political and Social Science, March, 1909, Vol. 33, pp. 287-300.

2. Clara M. Beyer, History of Labor Legislation for Women in Three States, Bulletin of the Women's Bureau, No. 66 (Washington: U.S. Department of Labor, 1929).

3. John R. Commons and Associates, History of Labor in the United States (New York: Macmillan, 1935) Vol. III.

4. John R. Commons, "Labor Organizations and Labor Politics, 1827-37," Quarterly Journal of Economics, February 1907, Vol. 21, pp. 323-329.

5. A. M. Heintz and J. R. Whitney, History of the Massachusetts State Federation of Labor, 1887-1935 (Worcester, Massachusetts: The Labor News Printers, 1935).

6. Michael E. Hennessy, Four Decades of Massachusetts Politics: 1890-1935 (Norwood, Massachusetts: The Norwood Press, 1935).

7. J. Joseph Huthmacher, Massachusetts People and Politics, 1919-1933 (Cambridge: Belknap Press, 1959).

8. Howard S. Kaltenborn, Government Adjustment of Labor Disputes (Chicago: Foundation Press, 1943).

9. Ting Tsz Ko, Governmental Methods of Adjusting Labor Disputes (New York: Columbia University, 1926).

10. James Leiby, Carroll Wright and Labor Reform (Cambridge: Harvard University, 1960).

11. Massachusetts State Branch, AFL, Proceedings of the Twenty-First Annual Convention (Lawrence, October 8-11, 1906).

12. _______. Proceedings of the Twenty-Second Annual Convention (Milford, October 14-17, 1907).

13. _______. Proceedings of the Twenty-Third Annual Convention (Lowell, October 12-15, 1908).

14. _______. Proceedings of the Twenty-Sixth Annual Convention (Haverhill, September 18-21, 1911).

15. _______. Proceedings of the Twenty-Seventh Annual Convention (Fitchburg, September 16-19, 1912).

16. ______. Proceedings of the Twenty-Eighth Annual Convention (Fall River, September 15-18, 1913).

17. ______. Proceedings of the Thirtieth Annual Convention (New Bedford, September 20-24, 1915).

18. ______. Proceedings of Special Convention (Worcester, January 22-24, 1917).

19. Massachusetts State Federation of Labor, Proceedings of the Forty-Third Annual Convention (Salem, August 6-10, 1928).

20. Charles E. Persons, "The Early History of Factory Legislation in Massachusetts," in Susan M. Kingsbury (ed.) Labor Laws and Their Enforcement (New York: Longmans, Green, and Co., 1911).

21. Edith Reeves and Caroline Manning, "The Standing of Massachusetts in The Administration of Labor Legislation," in Susan M. Kingsbury (ed.) Labor Laws and Their Enforcement (New York, Longmans, Green, and Co., 1911).

22. David I. Walsh, "Labor in Politics: Its Political Influence in New England," Forum, August, 1919, Vol. LXII, pp. 215-218.

23. Sarah S. Whittelsey, Massachusetts Labor Legislation (New Haven: Yale University, 1901).

24. Dan Yorke, "Bad Business in New England," American Mercury, October 1926, Vol. 9, pp. 139-144.

BIBLIOGRAPHY

Books

Bailey, Steven K. Congress Makes A Law. New York: Columbia Univsity, 1950.

Berelson, Bernard R., Lazarsfeld, P. F., and McPhee, W. N. Voting. Chicago: The University of Chicago, 1954.

Beyer, Clara M. History of Labor Legislation for Women in Three States. Bulletin of the Women's Bureau, No. 66, Washington: U.S. Department of Labor, 1929.

Bonnett, Clarence E. Employer's Association in the United States. New York: Macmillan, 1922.

Calkins, Fay. The CIO and the Democratic Party. Chicago: The University of Chicago, 1952.

Campbell, Angus, Converse, P.E., Miller, W. E., and Stokes, D. E. The American Voter. New York: Wiley and Sons, 1960.

Campbell, Angus, and H.C. Cooper. Group Differences in Attitudes and Votes. Ann Arbor: University of Michigan, 1956.

Campbell, Angus, Guin, Gerals, and Miller, W. E. The Voter Decides Evanston: Row, Peterson, 1954.

Childs, Harwood. Labor and Capital in National Politics. Columbus: Ohio State University, 1930.

Commons, John R., and Andrews, J.B. Principles of Labor Legislation. New York: Harper, 1936.

Commons, John R., and Associates. History of Labor in the United States. New York: Macmillan, 1936.

Corwin, Edward S. Office and Powers, 1787-1957. New York: New York University, 1957.

Council of Economic Advisers, Committee on the New England Economy. The New England Economy. Washington: U.S. Government Printing Office, July, 1951.

Derber, Milton, and Young, Edwin. Labor and the New Deal. Madison: University of Wisconsin, 1957.

Employers Labor Relations Information Committee, Management's Political Activities: An Annotated Bibliography. New York: 1959.

Farr, Grant N. Origins of Recent Labor Policy. Boulder: University of Colorado, 1959.

Fine, Nathan. Labor and Farmer Parties in the United States 1828–1928. New York: Russell and Russell, 1961.

Gaer, Joseph. The First Round: The Story of the CIO Political Action Committee. New York: Duell, Sloan and Pearce, 1944.

Goldberg, Arthur J. AFL-CIO: Labor United. New York: McGraw-Hill, 1956.

Goldberg, Lewis. Organized Labor and Politics as a Factor in the 1936 Election. New York: ILCWU, 1937.

Gregory, Charles O. Labor and The Law. New York: Norton, 1958.

Hacker, Andrew. Politics and the Corporation. New York: The Fund For the Republic, 1958.

Handlin, Oscar. Boston's Immigrants. Cambridge: Belknap Press, 1959.

Harriss, Seymour E. The Economics of New England. Cambridge: Harvard University, 1952.

Heard, Alexander. The Cost of Democracy. Chapel Hill: University of North Carolina, 1960.

_______. Money and Politics. New York: Public Affairs Committee, Inc., 1956.

Heintz, A. M., and Whitney, J. R. History of the Massachusetts State Federation of Labor, 1887–1935. Worcester, Massachusetts: The Labor News Printers, 1935.

Hennessy, Michael E. Four Decades of Massachusetts Politics: 1890–1935. Norwood, Massachusetts: The Norwood Press, 1935.

Herring, E. Pendleton. Group Representation Before Congress. Baltimore: John Hopkins, 1929.

Howe, Henry F. Massachusetts: There She Is - Behold Her. New York: Harper, 1960.

Howe, Irving, and Widick, B.J. The UAW and Walter Reuther. New York: Random House, 1949.

Hutmacher, Joseph, J. Massachusetts People and Politics, 1919-1933. Cambridge: Belknap Press, 1959.

Kaltenborn, Harold S. Governmental Adjustment of Labor Disputes. Chicago: Foundation Press, 1943.

Karson, Marc. American Labor Unions and Politics. Carbondale: Southern Illinois University, 1958.

Key, V. O. Jr. Southern Politics in State and Nation. New York: Knopf, 1949.

Ko, Ting Tsz. Governmental Methods of Adjusting Labor Disputes. New York: Columbia University, 1926.

Kornhauser, Arthur, and Mayer, A. J. When Labor Votes--A Study of Auto Workers. New York: University Books, 1956.

Lazarsfeld, Paul, Berelson, Bernard, and Gaudet, Hazel. The People's Choice. New York: Duell, Sloan, and Pearce, 1944.

Leiby, James. Carroll Wright and Labor Reform. Cambridge: Harvard University, 1960.

Lester, Richard A. The Economics of Unemployment Compensation. Princeton: Industrial Relations Section, Princeton University, 1962.

Levin, Murray B., Blackwood, G. B. The Compleat Politician: Political Strategy in Massachusetts. Indianapolis: Bobbs-Merrill, 1960.

Lipset, Seymour M. Political Man. Garden City: Doubleday, 1959.

Lockard, Duane. New England State Politics. Princeton: Princeton University, 1959.

Massachusetts League of Women Voters. Massachusetts State Government. Cambridge: Harvard University, 1956.

McKean, Eugene C. Unemployment Insurance Cost of the ABC Corporation in Michigan and Nearby States. Kalamazoo: Upjohn Institute, 1962.

Miller, Glen W. American Labor and the Government. New York: Printice Hall, 1948.

Millis, H. A., and Brown, E. C. From the Wagner Act to Taft Hartley. Chicago: The University of Chicago, 1950.

Morris, Richard B. Government and Labor in Early America. New York: Columbia University, 1946.

National Planning Association. The Economic State of New England. New Haven: Yale University, 1954.

Perlman, Selig. *A History of Trade Unionism in the United States*. New York: Macmillan, 1922.

Perlman, Selig. *A Theory of the Labor Movement*. New York: Macmillan, 1928.

The Public Interest in National Labor Policy. New York: Committee for Economic Development, 1961.

Rayback, Joseph G. *A History of American Labor*. New York: Macmillan, 1959.

Rose, Arnold M. *Union Solidarity*. Minneapolis: University of Minnesota, 1952.

Schriftgiesser, Karl. *Business Comes of Age*. New York: Harper, 1960.

Shaw, D. A., and Kearns, L. M. *Labor Relations Guide for Massachusetts*. Boston: Little Brown, 1950.

_______. *Labor Relations Guide for Massachusetts--1953 Supplement*. Boston: Little Brown, 1953.

Shedd, Frederick R., and Odiorne, George S. *Political Content of Labor Union Periodicals*. Ann Arbor: University of Michigan, 1960.

Slichter, Sumner H. *The Challenge of Industrial Relations*. Ithica: Cornell University, 1947.

The Social Sciences in Historical Study. New York: Social Science Research Council, 1954.

Taylor, Albion G. *Labor Policies of the National Association of Manufacturers*. Urbana: University of Illinois, 1928.

Troy, Leo. *Distribution of Union Membership Among the States, 1939 and 1953*. New York: National Bureau of Economic Research, 1957.

Truman, David B. *The Governmental Process*. New York: Knopf, 1955.

U. S. Department of Labor. *Growth of Labor Law in the United States*. Washington: U.S. Government Printing Office, 1962.

Whittelsey, Sarah S. *Massachusetts Labor Legislation*. New Haven: Yale University, 1901.

Whyte, William H., Jr. *Is Anybody Listening?* New York: Simon and Schuster, 1952.

Zimand, Savel. *The Open Shop Drive*. New York: Bureau of Industrial Research, 1921.

Signed Articles

Baldwin, F. Spencer. "Recent Massachusetts Labor Legislation," Annals of the American Academy of Political and Social Science, March, 1909, Vol. 33, pp. 287-300.

Barbash, Jack. "Unions, Government, and Politics," Industrial and Labor Relations Review, October 1947, Vol. 1, pp. 66-79.

Bernstein, Irving. "John L. Lewis and the Voting Behavior of the C.I.O.," Public Opinion Quarterly, June, 1941, Vol. 5., pp. 233-249.

Bigelow, Burton. "Should Business Decentralize Its Counter-Propaganda," Public Opinion Quarterly, April, 1938, Vol. 2, pp. 321-324.

Blum, Albert A. "The Political Alternatives of Labor," Labor Law Journal, September 1959, Vol. 10, pp. 623-631.

Bonnett, Clarence E. "Employer's Association," Encyclopaedia of the Social Sciences, Vol. V, pp. 509-514.

_______. "The Evolution of Business Groupings," The Annals of the American Academy of Political and Social Science, May, 1935, Vol. 179, pp. 1-8.

Boulware, Lemuel R. "Politics - The Businessman's Biggest Job in 1958," Labor Law Journal, August 1958, Vol. 9, pp. 587-594.

Brown, D. V. and Myers, C. A. "The Changing Industrial Relations Philosophy of American Management," Industrial Relations Research Association, Proceedings of the Ninth Annual Meeting (Madison, 1957).

_______. "Historical Evolution" in Shister (et. al.) editors, Public Policy and Collective Bargaining (New York: Harper and Row, 1962).

Brown, W. R. "State Regulation of Union Political Action," Labor Law Journal, November 1955, Vol. 6, pp. 769-776.

Burns, James M. "White House vs. Congress," The Atlantic, March 1960, Vol. 205, pp. 65-69.

_______. "Memo To The Next President," The Atlantic, April 1960, Vol. 205, pp. 64-68.

Cantwell, Frank. "Public Opinion And The Legislative Process," American Political Science Review, October 1946, Vol. XL, pp. 924-935.

Cleveland, Alfred S. "NAM: Spokesman For Industry?" Harvard Business Review, May 1948, Vol. 26, pp. 353-371.

Commons, John R. "Labor Organizations and Labor Politics, 1827-37," Quarterly Journal of Economics, February 1907, Vol. 21, pp. 323-329.

Dahl, Robert A. "Business and Politics: A Critical Appraisal of Political Science" in Social Science Research on Business: Product and Potential (New York: Columbia University, 1959).

David, Henry. "One Hundred Years of Labor in Politics" in Hardman and Neufeld (eds.) The House of Labor (New York: Prentice-Hall, 1951).

Denham, Robert N. "Labor's Growing Political Power," in American Management Association Spotlighting the Labor-Management Scene (New York, 1952).

Dunlop, John T. "Consensus and National Labor Policy," Industrial Relations Research Association, Proceedings of the 13th Annual Meeting (Madison, 1961).

Edelman, Murray. "Government and Labor-Management Relations," The American Journal of Economics and Sociology, October 1950, Vol. 10, pp. 51-60.

Fenn, Dan H. Jr. "Problems in Review: Business and Politics," Harvard Business Review, May-June, 1959, Vol. 37, pp. 6ff.

Fenton, John H. "Party Politics and Political Responsibility" in Robbins (ed) State Government and Public Responsibility, 1960 (Medford: Tufts University, 1960).

Form, William H. "Labor's Place in the Community Power Structure," Industrial and Labor Relations Review, July 1959, Vol. 12, pp. 526-539.

Freeman, H. E., and Showel, M. "Differantial Political Influence of Voluntary Associations," Public Opinion Quarterly, Winter 1951-52, Vol. 15, pp. 703-714.

Fuller, Helen. "Smearing the PAC," New Republic, July 22, 1946, Vol. 115, pp. 68-70

Gable, Richard W. "NAM: Influential Lobby or Kiss of Death?", Journal of Politics, May 1953, Vol. 15, pp. 254-273.

Greenberg, S. H, and Thompson, G. C. "The Company, the Employee, and Political Affairs," Management Record, February 1962, Vol. XXIV, pp. 24-27.

Hinkle, George F. "Implication of Labor's Political Activities," in Some Major Problems Looming Ahead in 1957 (New York: National Association of Manufacturers, 1957).

Hudson, Ruth A., and Rosen, Hjalmar. "Union Political Action: The Member Speaks," Industrial and Labor Relations Review, April 1954, Vol. 7, pp. 404-418.

Jewell, Malcom E. "Party Voting in American State Legislatures," American Political Science Review, September 1955, Vol. 49, pp. 773-791.

Kampelman, Max M. "Labor in Politics," Interpreting the Labor Movement (Madison: Industrial Relations Research Association, 1952).

Kerr, Clark, and Siegel, Abraham. "The Structuring of the Labor Force in Industrial Society: New Dimensions and New Questions," Industrial and Labor Relations Review, January 1955, Vol. 8, pp. 151-168.

________. "Reply" [To a communication by Milton Derber]. Industrial and Labor Relations Review, October 1955, Vol. 9, pp. 118-121.

Lahne, Herbert J. "The Failure of the PAC in 1946," in Joseph Shister (ed.) Readings in Labor Economics (New York: Lippincott, 1951).

Lane, John F. "Analysis of the Federal Law Governing Political Expenditures by Labor Unions," Labor Law Journal, October 1958, Vol. 9, pp. 725-744.

Lenhart, R. F., and Schriftgiesser, Karl. "Management in Politics," Annals of the American Academy of Political and Social Science, September, 1958, Vol. 319, pp. 32-40.

Levitan, Sar A. "Union Lobbyist's Contributions to Tough Labor Legislation," Labor Law Journal, October 1959, Vol. 10, pp. 675-682.

Levitt, Theodore. "Dilemmas and Dangers in an American Labor Party," Labor Law Journal, September 1955, Vol. 6, pp. 613 ff.

________. "Business Should Stay Out of Politics," Business Horizons, Summer 1960, Vol. 3, pp. 45-51.

Lipset, Seymour M. "Trade Unions and Social Structure," Industrial Relations, October 1956, Vol. 1, pp. 75-89.

Loftus, Joseph. "Organized Labor and Politics: A Reporter's View" in American Management Association, Spotlighting the Labor-Management Scene (New York, 1952).

Macarthur, W. "Political Action and Trade Unionism," The Annals of the American Academy of Political and Social Science, September 1904, Vol. 24, pp. 316-330.

Mac Rae, Duncan, Jr. "Occupations and the Congressional Vote, 1940-1950," American Sociological Review, June 1955, Vol. 20, pp. 332-340.

Maguire, Fred. "The Press Gang-Up on the PAC," *New Republic*, October 30, 1944, Vol. III, pp. 558-563.

Marsh, John. "Some Impressions of Industrial America," *Industrial Welfare*, May-June, 1959, Vol. XLI, pp. 119 ff.

Martin, Everett G. "State AFL-CIO Links Seen Partly Forged," *Christian Science Monitor*, October 10, 1955.

Masters, Nicholas A. "The Politics of Union Endorsement of Candidates in the Detroit Area," *Midwest Journal of Political Science*, August 1957, pp. 136-150.

Mathes, S. M., and Thompson, G. C. "Business and the Political Process," *Business Record*, September 1959, Vol. XVI, pp. 424 ff.

McIntyre, William R. "Corporations and Politics", *Editorial Research* Reports, October 8, 1958.

Merrihue, Willard V. "The Business Leader's Role in Politics," *Business Horizons*, Summer 1960, Vol. 3, pp. 38-44.

Mihlon, Lawrence F. "Should You Play the Game of Politics?", *Factory*, June 1960, Vol. 118, pp. 89-97.

Mills, Edgar M. "Bay State GOP Reverses Traditional Stand on Labor in Hope of Luring Union Support From Curley," *Christian Science Monitor*, October 5, 1938.

Neuberger, Richard L. "What Labor Unions Forget," *Nation*, December 23, 1950, Vol. 171, No. 26, pp. 674-676.

Northrup, Herbert R. "Management's 'New Look' in Labor Relations," *Industrial Relations*, October 1961, Vol. [illegible], pp. 9-24.

Norton-Taylor, Duncan. "How to Give Money to Politicians," *Fortune*, May, 1956, Vol. 53, pp. 113 ff.

Nossiter, Bernard D. "Management's Cracked Voice," *Harvard Business Review*, September-October 1959, Vol. 37, pp. 127-133.

O'Leary, John W. "The 'What Helps Business...' Campaign," *Public Opinion Quarterly*, October 1938, Vol. 2, pp. 645-650.

Overacker, Louise. "Labor's Political Contributions," *Political Science Quarterly*, March 1939, Vol. 54, pp. 56-58.

Persons, Charles E. "The Early History of Factory Legislation in Massachusetts," in Susan M. Kingsbury (ed.) *Labor Laws and Their Enforcement* (New York: Longmans, Green, and Co., 1911).

Phelps, Orme W. "Community Recognition of Union Leaders," Industrial and Labor Relations Review, April 1954, Vol. 7, pp. 419-433.

Pierson, Frank C. "Recent Employer Alliances in Perspective," Industrial Relations, October 1961, Vol. 1, pp. 39-56.

Raskin, A. H. "Labor's Legislative Goals," Challenge Magazine, January 1963, pp. 12-15.

_______. "Labor and N.A.M. Speak," New York Times, December 10, 1955.

_______. "Labor Leaders Taking New Look at Politics," New York Times, September 20, 1959, Section IV.

Reagan, Michael D. "Seven Fallacies of Business in Politics," Harvard Business Review, March-April 1960, pp. 60-68.

Reeves, Edith, and Manning, Caroline. "The Standing of Massachusetts in The Administration of Labor Legislation," in Susan M. Kingsbury (ed.) Labor Laws and Their Enforcement (New York, Longmans, Green, and Co., 1911).

Reuther, Walter, P. "Practical Aims and Purposes of American Labor," Annals of the American Academy of Political and Social Science, March 1951, Vol. 274, pp. 71-72.

Reid, T. R. "Management Programs to Encourage Political Participation," Industrial Relations Research Association, Papers Presented at the 1960 Spring Meeting, (Madison, 1960).

Rudolph, Frederick. "The American Liberty League, 1934-1940," American Historical Review, October 1950, Vol. 56, pp. 19-33.

Schultz, George P. "The Massachusetts Choice-of-Procedures Approach to Emergency Disputes," Industrial and Labor Relations Review, April 1957, Vol. 10, pp. 359-374.

Shannon, William V. "Massachusetts: Prisoner of the Past" in Robert S. Allen (ed) Our Soverign States (New York: Vanguard, 1949).

Sheldon, Horace E. "Business Must Get Into Politics," Harvard Business Review, March-April, 1959, Vol. 37, pp. 37-47.

Smith, Stanton E. "The Challenge Facing Central Labor Bodies," The American Federationist, May 1961, Vol. 68, pp. 7-9.

Stanley, Marjorie Thines. "The Amalgamation of Collective Bargaining and Political Activity by the U.A.W.," Industrial and Labor Relations Review, October 1956, Vol. 10, pp. 40-47.

Strout, Richard L. "The Next Election is Already Rigged," Harper's Magazine, November 1959, Vol. 219, pp. 35-40.

Studenski, Paul. "Chambers of Commerce," Encyclopaedia of the Social Sciences (New York: Macmillan, 1930) Vol. III, pp. 325-328.

Taft, Charles P. "Should Business Go in for Politics?" New York Times Magazine, August 30, 1959, pp. 10 ff.

Taft, Philip. "Labor's Changing Political Line," Journal of Political Economy, October 1937, Vol. XLV, pp. 634-650.

Tanenhaus, Joseph. "Organized Labor's Political Spending: The Law and Its Consequences," Journal of Politics, August 1954, Vol. 16, pp. 441-471.

Tyler, Gus. "The Labor Vote," in James M. Cannon (ed) Politics USA (Garden City: Doubleday, 1960).

Vose, Clemet E. "Litigation as a Form of Pressure Group Activity," Annals of the American Academy of Political and Social Science, September 1959, Vol. 319, pp. 20-31.

Walsh, David I. "Labor in Politics: Its Political Influence in New England," Forum, August, 1919, Vol. LXII, pp. 215-218.

Wilensky, Harold L. "The Labor Vote: A Local Union's Impact on the Political Conduct of Its Members," Social Forces, December 1956, Vol. 35, pp. 111-120.

Williams, G. Mennen. "Can Businessmen be Democrats?", Harvard Business Review, March-April, 1958, Vol. 36, pp. 102-106.

Witte, Edwin E. "The New Federation and Political Action," Industrial and Labor Relations Review, April 1956, Vol. 9, pp. 406-418.

Wright, Chester M. "Labor in American Politics," Current History, August 1924, Vol. 20, pp. 741-747.

Yorke, Dan. "Bad Business in New England," American Mercury October 1926, Vol. 9, pp. 139-144.

Zeller, Belle. "The Federal Regulation of Lobbying Act," American Political Science Review, April 1948, Vol. 42, pp. 239-271.

_______. "Regulation of Pressure Groups and Lobbyists," The Annals of the American Academy of Political and Social Science, September 1958, Vol. 319, pp. 94-103.

Unsigned Articles and Pamphlet Material

Associated Industries of Massachusetts. Annual Legislative Reports, by Jarvis Hunt, 1946-1961.

_______. Your Stake in A.I.M. Boston, 1962.

_______. A.I.M.'s Public Affairs Tools for the Small Businessman. Boston, Undated.

Bennett, Wallace F. The Very Human History of "NAM". New York: The Newcomen Society of England, American Branch, 1949.

"Beyond the War of Words," Merchants National Bank of Boston, Monthly Business Letter, May, 1960.

"Businessmen Getting into Practical Politics," Congressional Quarterly Weekly Report, April 3, 1959.

Chamber of Commerce of the United States. Action Course in Practical Politics. Washington, May 1960.

_______. American Management-Labor-Relations and Management Attitudes. Washington, 1946.

_______. Federal Regulation of Labor Relations. Washington, 1937.

_______. Labor Law in the Public Interest. Washington, 1953.

_______. Labor Relations Letter, January, 1959.

"Corporate Political Affairs Program," Yale Law Journal, June 1961, Vol. 70, pp. 821-862.

Greater Boston Chamber of Commerce Program of Work. Boston, January, 1961.

Industrial Relations Research Association. Proceedings of the 15th Annual Meeting. Madison, 1963.

Kelley, Kenneth J., Belanger, J. William, and Segal, Robert M. The Massachusetts Story. Boston: United Labor Committee of Massachusetts, 1948.

Massachusetts Federation of Taxpayers' Associations. Legislators Digest of Financial Facts. Boston, 1961.

The Massachusetts State CIO Council: 20 Years of Progress. Boston, December 1958.

"The Misuse of Organization," Guntons Magazine, June, 1903, Vol. 4, p. 475.

National Association of Manufacturers. The Battle of Ideas. New York, 1955.

______. "What Organized Labor Expects of Management," by George Meany. "What Management Expects of Organized Labor," by Charles R. Sligh, Jr. New York, 1956.

______. Labor Law Reform: The Faults in the Kennedy-Ives Bill: What is Needed to Protect Working People and the Public. New York, 1958.

"Political Action: Training Pays Off," Nations Business, November 1961, Vol. 49, pp. 62-63.

Shreve, Earl O. The Chamber of Commerce of the United States of America. New York: The Newcomen Society in North America, 1949.

"Union Political Activity Spans 230 Years of U.S. History," American Federationist, May 1960, Vol. 67, pp. 6-11.

United Automobile, Aircraft and Agricultural Implement Workers of America. Proposal to Limit Campaign Contributions. Detroit, 1956.

Public Documents and Government Publications

Commonwealth of Massachusetts. House Document No. 1875. Report of the Governor's Labor-Management Committee. March, 1947.

______. House Document No. 2432. Governor's Veto of House Bill 1742. June, 1948.

U. S. Bureau of the Census. U.S. Census of Population 1960. Summary, General Social and Economic Characteristics.

U. S. Congressional Record. 1959. Vol. 106.

U. S. Department of Commerce. Survey of Current Business. April, 1962. Vol. 42.

U. S. Department of Labor. Employment and Earnings Statistics for the United States, 1909-62. BLS Bulletin 1312-1. 1963.

U. S. Department of Labor. Employment and Earnings Statistics for States and Areas, 1939-62. BLS Bulletin 1370. 1963.

_______. State Workmen's Compensation Laws. Bulletin No. 212. 1964.

_______. Unemployment Insurance: State Laws and Experience. BES No. U-198. 1961.

_______. Unemployment Insurance: State Laws and Experience. BES No. U-198 Revised. 1963.

_______. Work Stoppages: Fifty States and the District of Columbia, 1927-62. BLS Report No. 256. 1963.

U.S. House Select Committee on Lobbying Activities. Expenditures by Corporations to Influence Legislation. House Report 3137, 81st Congress 2nd Session, 1950.

U.S. Senate Subcommittee on Privileges and Elections. Hearings Relative to Senate Resolution 205. 84th Congress, 2nd Session, 1956.

Newspaper and Periodic Publications
(Specific Issues Cited in the Reference Sections at the End of Each Chapter)

American Federation of Labor, Report of the Proceedings of Annual Conventions 1895-1936.

American Federation of Labor-Congress of Industrial Organizations, Proceedings of Bi-annual Constitutional Conventions, 1957-1961.

Boston Globe.

Boston Herald.

Bureau of National Affairs, Daily Labor Report.

Christian Science Monitor.

Congressional Quarterly Almanac, 1946-1961.

Congressional Quarterly Weekly Report, 1959.

Greater Boston Report (Bi-weekly paper of the Greater Boston Chamber of Commerce).

Industry (Monthly publication of the Associated Industries of Massachusetts).

Massachusetts State Branch, AFL, Proceedings of the Annual Convention, 1906-1927.

Massachusetts State Federation of Labor, AFL, Proceedings of the Annual Conventions, 1928-1947.

Massachusetts Federation of Labor, AFL, Proceedings of the Annual Conventions, 1948-1958.

Massachusetts State CIO Industrial Union Council, Year Book for Annual Conventions 1953-1957.

Massachusetts State Labor Council, AFL-CIO, Proceedings of the Annual Conventions, 1959-1960.

New York Times.

Scammon, Richard M. America Votes. Pittsburgh, Government Affairs Institute. 1956-1961.

Unpublished Material

Ricker, William. "The CIO in Politics, 1936-1946" (Unpublished Ph.D. Thesis, Harvard University, 1948).

Steinberg, Joseph L. Labor in Massachusetts Politics: The Internal Organization of the CIO and the AFL for Political Action, 1948-1955 (Unpublished Senior Thesis, Harvard University, 1956).

Thompson, Charles A. The Barnes Bill--An Analysis of Labor Legislation Regarding Financial Reports (Unpublished Bachelor Thesis, Massachusetts Institute of Technology, 1947).

www.ingramcontent.com/pod-product-compliance
Lightning Source LLC
LaVergne TN
LVHW020645110826
845149LV00012B/1921
9781138352414